this book
is for
january
kuan yin
sig
keith QC
lynn druid
ruth and julian
living astrologers
the oak dragon family
rangjung rigpe dorje's new incarnation
beggars and thieves of the court of miracles
renatodix and the twelve
cerridwen
and
you

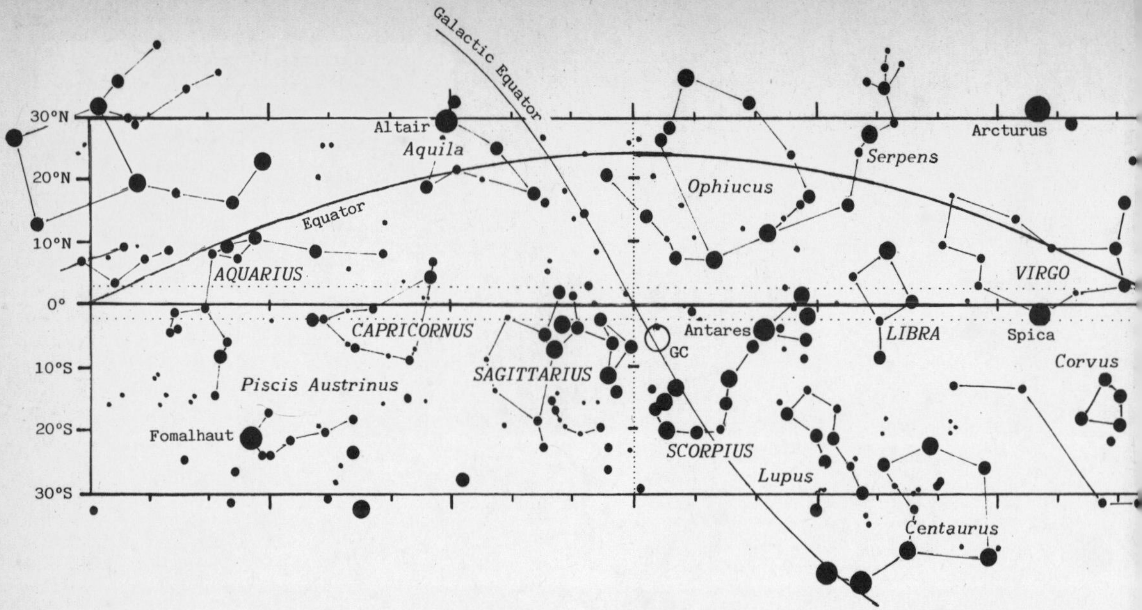

LIVING IN TIME

Palden Jenkins

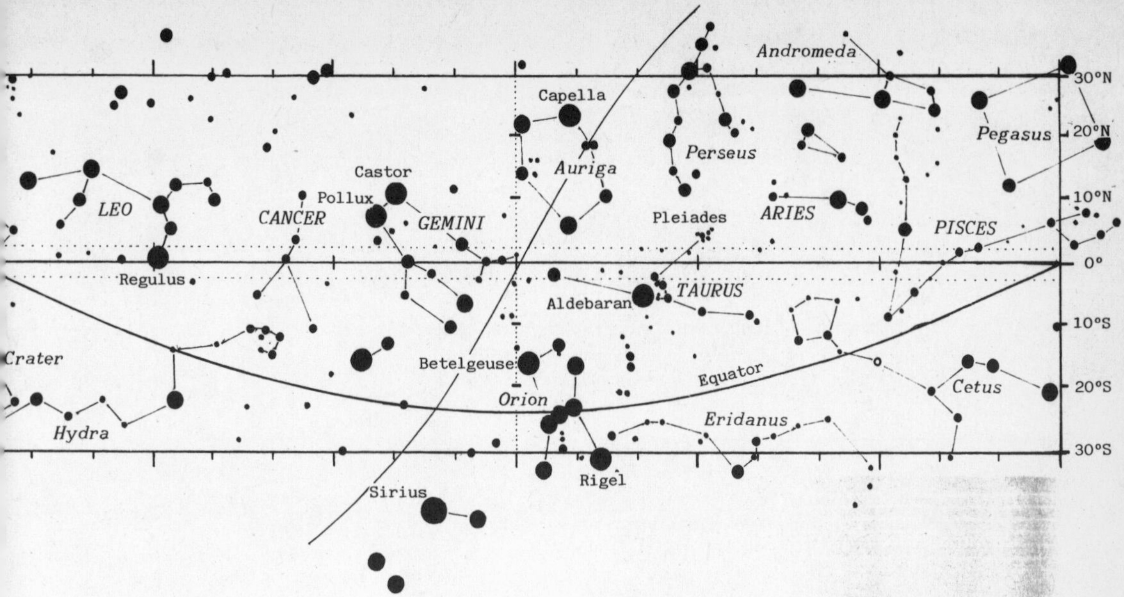

The constellations on the ecliptic in relation to the signs of the zodiac. The ecliptic – the sun's path as seen from earth – is shown as a time in the middle of the map. Although the constellations and zodiac signs unfortunately bear the same names we use the zodiac signs in astrology: the constellations and signs are very different things.

Learning to Experience Astrology in your Life

Foreword by Charles Harvey

Gateway Books, Bath

First published in 1987
by GATEWAY BOOKS
19 Circus Place, Bath, BA1 2PW

Distributed in the U.S.A. by
SLAWSON COMMUNICATIONS
3719 Sixth Avenue,
San Diego, CA 92183

Diagrams by the author; pictures by Jan Graves

Set in Monotype Palatino by
Wordsmiths Typesetters, London
Printed by W.B.C.Print, Bristol

British Library Cataloguing in Publication Data:
Jenkins, Palden
Living in time: learning to experience astrology in your life.
1. Astrology
I. Title
133.5 BF1708.1

ISBN 0.946551.21.9

Acknowledgments

Thanks to Foulsham & Co and Neil Michelson for permission to reproduce parts of the Raphael's and American Ephemerides.

To Alick Bartholomew for being the kind of publisher I gave up looking for, and to January Jane for bearing with me in my addiction to the green screen: even though most authors acknowledge their mates, it's not just a formality, but a real expression of recognition for being an alchemical part of the process!

To the people of alternative Glastonbury, for being a multifaceted, kaleidoscopic, swirling lot, full of energy, inspiration and healthy chaos, and to the people of the Living Astrology gatherings and camps for encouragement, for being the people I was writing for.

To the spirits, waterfalls and the red kite of Cwm Pennant, the nadir of my soul in this life, and to HH Gyalwa Karmapa for bringing me back to earth. To Renatodix and the Twelve, for empowering me to work in the way I do in astrology, and to Jan and Tom Graves, for pictures and words.

Contents

This book doesn't have to be read from beginning to end. You can do what you like with it. The chapters are presented in an order which you might enjoy following if you are starting off in astrology. If you want to pick around, however, give each chapter a good scan, for this book offers an approach which sees things in wholes, and you'll miss the point if you simply seek bits.

Rules for being human

★ **You will receive a body.** You may like it or hate it but it will be yours for this time around.

★ **You will learn lessons.** You are enrolled in a full-time informal school called *life*. Each day in this school you will have the opportunity to learn lessons. You may like the lessons or think them irrelevant of stupid.

★ **There are no mistakes, only lessons.** Growth is a process of trial and error: experimentation. The failed experiments are as much a part of the process as the experiment that lands up working.

★ **A lesson is repeated until learned.** A lesson will be presented to you in various forms until you have learned it. When you have learned it you can then go on to the next lesson.

★ **Learning lessons does not end.** There is no part of life that does not contain lessons. If you are alive, there are lessons to be learned.

★ **'There' is no better than 'here'.** When your 'there' has become 'here' you will simply obtain another 'there' that will again look better than 'here'.

★ **Others are merely mirrors of you.** You cannot love or hate something about another person unless it reflects to you something you love or hate about yourself.

★ **What you make of life is up to you.** You have all the tools and resources you need — what you do with them is up to you. The choice is yours.

★ **The answers lie inside you.** All you need to do is look, listen and trust.

★ **You will forget all this!**

I wish I myself had written this. I was told it was copyright-free, but if there is someone with a proprietary claim to it, please write, and we'll acknowledge you!

Foreword

A knowledge of Astrology can open us to the Music of the Spheres, awakening us to the ever sounding symphony of creation which Time and the planets unfolds. Yet all too often the astrologer slices up the Music of Time so that we hear but one bar, the one beat of the individual birth chart, disconnected from the larger harmony. In this refreshing book Palden Jenkins, of Glastonbury Camp fame, brings us his long experience in helping people attune themselves in an immediate and practical way to both the smaller and larger themes of the time. Firmly relegating personal birth charts to the end of the book, Palden quite rightly insists that much of the real mystery and magic of astrology, and much of its most important message for mankind, lies in its power to open and sensitise us each day, each moment, to the unfolding 'energies' and 'power points' of the interweaving cycles of creation.

If the true astrologer is he or she who learns to listen to, to appreciate, and to work with, the creative energies of the moment, then Palden's book will certainly encourage the growth of true astrologers and a real living astrology. The more we can establish an active relationship with those living archetypal Ideas in the light of which the universe itself is produced, the more genuinely creative we can become, learning consciously to choose our path in tune with the time. As Palden emphasises throughout the book, it is not what happens to us that is important but what we make of what happens to us, what we do with the potential offered to us. The kind of increased astrological awareness advocated in this book can assist us to optimise that potential each and every day.

This work is in a sense a handbook for the appreciation of Time. It shows that, even without using the individual birth chart, there is great personal value to be had from studying the ever changing 'climate of ideas', a study normally reserved for mundane astrology. As astrologers have always understood, Time is not simply a measurement of duration, it is that dimension in which the Eternal takes on material form, with all its ever changing qualities. As Plato put it, "Time is the flowing image of Eternity" and "the planets are the instruments of Time". The heavenly bodies as "the first-born thoughts of God" can in this sense be said to mark out the very flow of the Ideas of the Time. The more we can attain to a conscious awareness of those archetypal ideas and processes, the more effectively we can work with them. This book will help in its own way to awaken its readers and students to that daily sense of wonder which awaits all who actively accept the challenge of *Living in Time*.

One word of warning is perhaps in order. The reader new to astrology will need to take in the ideas here presented fairly slowly. This is an ambitious and at times complex book. It sets out to cultivate an appreciation of all levels of Time from the simple rhythms of the lunar month and the annual cycle of the year, right through to the great interweaving patterns of the outer planets which unfold the great formative processes of history. Fascinating and powerful though such intricate analysis can be, it is obvious that nothing less than a state of Cosmic Consciousness would suffice for the effective daily use of all this material by any one individual!

For individuals trying to live their lives more effectively and with greater awareness, the sheer volume of information presented here could at first be overwhelming rather than illuminating. It should not be forgotten that we each have our own unique relationship with the One. With this in mind it will be seen that ultimately the individual birth chart *is* essential to filter out our 'own' tune from what must at a personal level often come through as collective 'noise'. That said, there can be no question that, the more each one of us attunes ourselves to the working of the 'ideas of the time' in the world around us, the more creative, understanding and tolerant we will become of the issues facing humanity, and the more we will be able to help turn to the Good all that befalls us individually and collectively.

Charles Harvey
2 December 1986

this book got written
for you
tucked away in your somewhere
to whom this might be valuable news

if but one person
out there
feels the visionglow
I seek to share
drinks of this fountain from which I have drunk
and finds nourishment
the cycle completes

for this is but a passing on
nothing is new
yet perhaps it will help you remember

when we all are true to ourselves
as microcells in a vast universe
there will be no 'problems'

and this is a little virgoid contribution
to that end

may it bring benefit
on all levels!

What this book is about

This book is about developing a sense of timing. The main focus in cultivating this sense is awareness, a receptivity to what's in the wind, what's going on within and what appears to be the underlying meaning of life's remarkably variegated experiences. There are many paths to awareness, and each of us follows our own heart in following the path appropriate to us. Here we are using the language and symbology of astrology by which to identify the facets of time, and thereby become aware of what's really going on in life as we experience it.

Astrology is useful in this process of identification, because it is precise and well used, encompassing many approaches to reality, and is a language spoken by many, and increasing numbers of people. In generations to come, it will most probably move into centre-stream as a language for understanding time, change and things psychological and subtle. Even if you are not particularly interested in devoting your life to absorbing astrology thoroughly — a committed path — it is undoubtedly worth picking up its basics and using them in your own life, in whatever way is useful for you. This book is thus for you who are interested in the passage of time, in energy-working and natural religion, in seeing astrology in a new light, or in simply being aware of what's going on in your life.

Timing

Here we are talking about subjectively-experienced *time*, which is an elastic, a-rational flow of feeling-tones, head-spaces, angles on life, partial insights into whole reality, phases and chapters, experienced both on an individual and a collective basis. When we usually talk about time we refer to clocks and calendars: "I'll meet you at the station at two-thirty on Wednesday 26th April". Clock and calendar time is a socially-agreed mode of time-measurement, based on the coming and going of the day and the seasonal year, which we use to coordinate our activities in a complex, urban world.

The *time* we are looking at here is more qualitative than quantitative, as in the usage "The times are changing". Here we refer to an identification we might make of the essential qualities of the period we live in — a subjective assessment, but nonetheless real for us. And often it is the case that many people find themselves sharing subjective assessments with others, thereby imbuing such assessments with claims to reality.

It is very useful to come into tune with the nature of time, because it can make our lives easier. This happens because we can fit the immediate moment into a context, a wider scenario, which gives us a sense of direction and purpose, such that we become aware of life being a process. This matters a lot during *bad* times, because when things are hard, when life is an uphill slog, it feels as if it is going to go on like that for ever, and that the difficulties we perceive are going to bug us indefinitely. It matters a lot during *good* times as well, because, even though we might be enjoying ourselves, it helps to know that (apparently) good times, like (apparently) bad times, don't go on for ever, even if we might want them to. This scraping of our expectations and extrapolations against ever-changing reality, both internal and external, is what makes up the stuff of life, very much characterising our human condition.

Sooner or later we realise that we are here, most fundamentally, to learn, and that if we consciously dedicate our lives to doing so, everything we experience becomes a success and an ongoing stream of good fortune: for even if everything seems to be going *wrong*, our learning from life makes it very *right*, valuable, and fundamentally happiness-producing. For happiness, peace, light, freedom, health, love or whatever it is we seek, is a state of being, which derives from within ourselves rather than from the fortuitous arrangement of sought-after circumstances in which we expect, according to our life-education so far, to feel happy.

Astrology can give not only a better understanding of what's going on, but can give us an initiation into working time-energy actively. If it is possible to identify experientially what mars energy is like compared to jupiter energy, or even to distinguish what is likely to be the case when these two energies combine, then it is possible to enter into dynamic involvement with these energies in order to allow them to come through us more clearly and effectively.

Moving in phase with the time, or even adding to its qualities by manifesting situations and creations to outwardly express those energies, we move into a deep union with the power of life itself, intuitively, engaging deeper movements in our everyday lives. It's like surfing: once adept in the art, a surfer stands there and stays on balance, to be transported far and fast by the wave-energy available freely to any conscious partaker of it. So let's get out our psychic surf-boards.

Astrology suggests that life is a process, and that the travelling of the road of life is what it's all about, even though we regularly get caught up in the notion that the reaching of the end of that road is what's desirable. Astrology points out that time is *cyclical,* and gives us the wherewithal to identify the different qualitative cycles at work in characterising any given moment, plus the ability to see the length and context of those cycles, and to move in accord with them, organically.

Itself, astrology is but a simple language of symbols, which, when interrelated and set to work with each other, can describe and help us attune to time, its passage and meaning. These symbols can be perceived and experienced mentally, emotionally and experientially, imaginally and actionally. They contain no judgements of right or wrong: these are entirely supplied by any person interpreting its symbols, and by our own cultural values.

Astrology has traditionally been burdened by many such value-judgements (especially 'good' and 'bad', 'difficult' or 'easy', which might or might not land up being the case on examination of our experience). Astrological symbols describe energy, simply and directly. Our responses to this energy are what make them feel either comfortable and welcome or uncomfortable and adverse. Thus astrology becomes a language of awareness, in that we can come to see how our responses to life colour our experience and influence further experiences leading out of earlier ones.

What I recommend to you in this book is that the best source for learning astrology is *your own life,* and that while astrology books and experts might be helpful in pointing out useful things to you, the words and ideas given out, including these here, in no way replace observations you might derive from your own experience. In fact, a real living *feel* for astrology and time is what's most useful in making astrology work for us in our lives.

So what we're going to do in the pages which follow is look into cycles of time, what they do, how long they last, how they interrelate, and how to see them at work in our own lives, and in the world surrounding us, as we each personally experience them.

We're not looking at birth charts — for some reason astrology has become fixated on them, to the exclusion of this very foundation of astrology itself — and neither are we going to look at fixed definitions of what this means or what that means.

It's over to you to get a living feel of what fullmoons are about, or what goes on when mars opposes pluto, by observing for yourself rather than by indirect learning through the interpretative intercession of an astrologer. Some guidelines will be presented, though, as to how to view things, with the qualification that they should at all times be read *critically*, with an eye for your own experience. In this book, I'm sharing with you what I understand of astrology and life, and if this is useful and stimulating to you, then we have lift-off and all is well. If not, then perhaps this book can help you clarify what your own insights of life and astrology are, by giving something to disagree with!

In the end, the honest aim of all astrologers is to become redundant. Astrology is a tool for getting to grips with the nature of time, but like all tools, it needs eventually to be ditched. It is perfectly possible to develop a sense of timing without using astrology. Any receptive person can sense when the right time is to move forward, and when it is right to hold back — and can learn from previous experience how to be more attuned next time round. But astrology gives us a remarkably accurate means by which to work our way into a keen sense of inner timing, and every aware person would do well to understand at least a little of the basics: lunar cycles, annual cycles and a sense of history and our participation in its creation. There will come a time in the evolution of humanity when such people as astrologers will no longer be needed: our awareness will have developed to a point where we no longer need tools for understanding.

Learning astrology

Absorb astrology at your own speed, relaxed, in your own way. Learn what is applicable to you in your own life, at this time. You don't need to struggle through tomes about the zodiac or other astrological concepts: it is best to learn about those signs or factors which matter to you *in the present time*, for you will come to the other signs in due course when you need to connect with them experientially. It isn't necessary to program your memory-files with descriptions of what venus square jupiter or mars in libra mean, for all you will land up with is a full and heavy head. But it is distinctly fruitful to look into what is currently valid for you and what will help you resolve questions you have in front of you, for you will absorb astrology in a *living* way, in relation to life and experience, beyond words, in the heart of your being.

Get what you need out of astrology and enjoy it! You're doing this voluntarily, out of your own personal need to learn from life, and there is no need to concern yourself with what others think, how fast you or they are learning astrology, whether you understand it right or whether or not you're good enough at it. If you are lousy at figures, leave them until you feel right to tackle them, and persevere, for you will find that since you are self-motivated in your astrological studies, you will be able, in your own time and own manner, to motivate yourself into mastering what previously seemed difficult. This is an opportunity to learn something for yourself, for posterity, something which will have definite benefit for you and those around you. It's a question of multilevel absorption of astrology by the *whole* of your being, rather than head-cramming.

The wonderful thing about astrology is that it can bridge our thinking mind and our deeper self, our left and right brains, our feminine and masculine sides, psyche and world, our personal dualisms. Many of the best astrological insights come after we have given up the books, tables and studies, and are driving the car, sitting on the toilet or lying in the sun by a waterfall — conscious mind relaxes, and allows the unconscious space to work.

The unconscious doesn't think thoughts: it sees things in wholes, and grasps things in visions, 'grokkings', flashes and experiences. Perhaps you've just had a tiff with a loved one or the dog, and you're feeling a bit shocked, and you suddenly realise, yes, that's it, venus is in square to mars, and you've just acted it out! The unconscious works by associations, images, urges, flavours, meanings, knowings, sensings, dream-stuff, and it is well for us to allow it to talk its own language, and to utilise it as a resource for living, rather than an impediment to the survival and furtherance of our ego and its intents.

Use your head to take in the words, but then let it all drop, and allow the rest of your being to really grasp, wholistically, what the astrology is all about. Or, conversely, go to therapy groups, meditations, mosques, oak trees, or find your illuminations up a mountain, then use this or another book as a way of backing up your experiential gleanings with a dose of astrological structuring. Unlike academic subjects, astrology is multidimensional, bridging schisms and allowing room for all sorts of people to use it in their own way.

Astrology is a multilevel language which far outstrips modern languages in its expressiveness, when it comes to understanding the nature of the psyche or the underlying nature of time and change. As when learning a new language, we enter first into a phase of thinking in and translating back to our mother tongue. With practice, a new mode of language dawns, where we find ourselves thinking in the new language, without need for translation. If you willingly beaver away at absorbing astrology, in as many ways as you can, you will find that it all falls into place in time, and that it will become a second language which stays with you throughout your life.

Birth charts

In this book, we are hardly touching astrological charts, but we do come to look at personal changes at the end of the book, for which you will need an astrological chart. You don't need to know what your chart *means* — this is actually a lifelong exploration — but you do need the astrological information contained in it. If you do not already have an astrological chart then try to find someone who will calculate one for you, or find a friendly computer to crunch the numbers for you. Unless you have a particularly strong urge to learn calculation, it is best to leave it until you feel ready (and until you find another book with the instructions in!). When you are ready, go into learning calculations, and if you find this difficult, see if you can get someone to help you: this is the left-brain side of astrology, which involves thinking in simple logical steps, a good counterbalance to right-brain experiential and imaginal stuff.

We start the book, however, by looking at lunation cycles, annual seasonal cycles and planetary motions, for which you need no astrological chart. This is loaded with enough potentiality to keep you occupied for years, if you so choose. We start in the realm of the transpersonal, the collective, the natural, and land up in the realm of the personal. It all weaves together by the end of the book. Take from it what you need.

Cycles of Time

Astrology didn't begin with birth charts: these have become significant primarily in modern times, for we have been gradually individualising throughout history to the extent that we now perceive ourselves as separate from everyone else, and separate from our world, and therefore have a deep need to examine ourselves as individual entities, spurred on by the challenges and questions we encounter in our own lives. Astrology began as a science for understanding the nature of time, and the harmonic movement of all things through change.

The ancients perceived the cyclic seasons of life, and sought to learn how to work with these cycles, knowing that if they caught the right time for particular activities — migrating, planting crops, culling, getting pregnant, lying low or doing great things — they would be able to carry out these activities easily and without hitches. They were so much at one with their world that they realised that if they did not *ask* the seasons to roll on and bring their benefits, then the seasons would cease doing so. This might seem a bit silly, but the ancients had a lot more *sense* than we, and they knew themselves to be not only recipient participants in the divine plan, but active ingredients in it as well. They knew the right times for conception, and therefore had no unwanted children, and they knew the optimum times for planting and harvesting and therefore had nutritious and productive crops.

We needn't seek to emulate the ancients — we need to seek what they sought. They timed and placed their sacred ceremonies carefully and with great effort, building stone circles and landscape temples which enhanced energy flows in earth and cosmos, bringing about wellbeing and ease of living, channeling the flows of the cosmos and consciousness such that they moved in accord with time. Moving in accord with time has the added advantage that universal energies back up human efforts. It makes life simpler yet mightier, more effective and aligned with our intent. Nowadays, governments and institutions cannot even reliably manage the economy, and everything is only just in control. Have we progressed?

The ancients observed and mapped out the cycles of time by observing the motions of the planets and their interrelations with the orbital and rotational antics of Mother Earth. Nowadays we have a simplistic notion that, somehow, the planets up there, millions of miles away, beam down rays which somehow affect us down here, as if we were puppets on etheric strings being interfered with by the cosmos. This is a narrow, cause-and-effect way of looking at things which doesn't credit us moderns with much intelligence or insight.

When we talk about cosmos and wholes, we refer to the notion that a whole is a unity, in which its parts are functioning in harmony with its overall movement and flow. In other words, the energy which we ascribe to planets is actually *down here on earth*, within the very nature of our existence, even closer to us that this page is to your eyes. This energy modulates and flows in patterns and tides, and it just so happens that the motions of the planets of our solar system move in accord with this same underlying energy here on earth.

This means that since life on earth is rather complex, and since the underlying energy patterns within all forms are apparently intricate and subtle, we can benefit from using the motions of the planets as indicators of the nature of time and change, since they and we are part of the same wholeness. Looked at this way, astrology makes a lot of sense. What's going on up there is not as important to us as what's going on down here, but examining what goes on up there is very useful as a way of getting a clear picture of the underlying factors and influences in our lives right here. The proof is in the pudding: use astrology and you will find that it works and serves you in creating a more coherent and meaningful life.

Choice

We are not victims of fate, time or anything else, unless we use outside influences — planets, God, governments, football teams, neighbours, the cat or the weather — as scapegoats for our own hangups. When things go well, I did it, and when things go badly, they did it, according to our normal conditioning (though for some it is the other way round!). We have the power to become *creators* in our lives, through owning our actions of thought, word and deed, and taking responsibility for our causative involvement in the intricacies of the life process. And what living astrology can teach us is that in order to become creators, we need to learn to move in accord with time.

Paradoxically, *creation* involves *acceptance of what is*, for there are things we *can* change, and things we *cannot* change. Types the likes of you and me have the freedom and capacity to be masters of our *responses* to the objective world, such that we no longer fall victim to circumstances. If it is raining when you wake in the morning, and you are addicted to the idea that it *should* be sunny, then you suffer, and become a victim to surrounding (rainy) conditions. If however, you *accept* the rain and make of your life the best that you can in that context, you might well find that miraculous things take place as a result. This book was born on a rainy day!

Receptivity thus gives birth to creativity. And a creative approach to life enhances our receptivity. Acceptance is different to victimhood in that it implies a choice, a fundamental decision to take into ourselves our experienced world and live with it. This gives a handle on reality, an attitude of mindfulness which allows things to be as they are, and which ceases imposing wishes, intentions, illusions and prejudices on life, others and the world. With this, we can get our fingers into the dynamics of life, co-creating, with the universe (of which we are a part anyway), situations, spaces and outcomes which are in phase with universal need. Yin and yang cannot do without each other. Neither can we and the universe!

A personal note on change

This book isn't just about astrology. It's about a whole world-view. I stand the risk of being seen as opinionated or laying on an ideological trip, but something in me says it is right to take a stance. The stance I am taking is that we are at a very critical point in history, and I don't believe that you have to be an astrologer to see this. Nowadays, it is necessary to do a thorough ostrich job to avoid seeing what's going on in the world, and unfortunately, this is the case for many.

We humans can bring about change either through our wisdom and foresight, or through being forced to do it. We seem to have habituated ourselves to the latter option, and now we are getting ourselves shocked into change. I believe wholeheartedly that every single department and detail of life is, sooner or later, in for a very fundamental change, and that no stone can be let unturned, and no person can escape this transformation. There have been crises all through history — invading Mongols, infectious diseases, white men with guns, declines and falls, you name it — but this current world crisis has a new dimension to it: everyone is involved, and the stakes have reached life-and-death pitch for the whole planet. It's really exciting, for we possibly have more choice available to us now than we ever have had. And no one is going to save us except ourselves!

If you stand outside a therapy room full of people catharting, it sounds as if the Devil has taken over: wailing and moaning and gnashing of teeth and all manner of suffering fill the air. Come back an hour later, and all is calm, and a wonderful feeling of love and okayness emanates from those who, shortly before, were manifesting sound effects from the depths of hell. I believe that the world is approaching catharsis, and already the moaning and groaning is easily heard — in the room next door, in distant lands, and in our own hearts. What happens in this catharsis and what finally precipitates it is anybody's guess, but I feel that the time is now and very soon. And we have the choice, individually and collectively, to make this a creative or a destructive catharsis.

I believe that we have the capacity to make it through this initiation, intact and as a human family. I'm glad to be alive in it, and if I have to die, the work goes on whether or not I am in a physical body: what matters is that we *make it* through this quantum jump, and that we use the circumstance to learn, in the deepest place in our beings, what we are here for. And then we need to get on with it.

Now I don't expect everyone to agree with these views, and I cannot insist that they reflect truth: they are my *beliefs*. They are founded in a good measure of questing and soulsearching, pain and insight. I know that there are many who share roughly similar views, and am privileged to live amongst a caucus of such people in Glastonbury (England) with whom I have had a good number of experiential previews of future potential for the human race. I honour my fellow-travellers in Avalon for their courage in choosing, each as an individual, to hasten future human evolution in their own lives, at great personal cost, and celebrate with them the joy and love which is distilled from the devastation of the past and the sharing of the present. I know that there are many others around the world like this, from Siberia to Chile, from Avalon to Bodhgaya, from New York to the mountain fastnesses, and you are probably one of these soul-siblings too. The tidal wave is surreptitiously growing, and no army, bank, government or secret service will be able to stop it.

I cannot write an astrology book without weaving in this world-view, for I find little motivation to impart simply astrological information, however interesting it may be. The seed for this book came from a bunch of women who had been doing good protest and consciousness-raising work at Greenham Common, a cruise missile base, who had twigged that lunar cycles were important: they asked me, an astrologer, to fill them in on what I knew about such things. Running camps and gatherings for astrologers, shamans and seekers at Glastonbury, I became aware that there was a large body of interest and awareness around understanding subjective time, and particularly around specific times when transformative work can be done with enhanced effects.

Astrologers, meanwhile, were not addressing themselves to these questions: for some reason, only a few astrologers seek to enter into actually *working* the energies they identify in their use of the craft. So along came this book, beliefs and all, and I dedicate it to all of you who know in your hearts what must be done, and seek to find ways to do it. If my reality-bubble can in any way be of use for you in yours, then the purpose of these pages, the trees who sacrificed themselves for it, and the people who have been a part of the weaving of these words, is fulfilled. Travel well!

1 Gyrating Spheres

This chapter is a basic runthrough on the astronomy of astrology. If you want to, you can skip it for now (but scan through it to see what it covers) and come back to it when you need to. We're going to look at our solar system and how it looks from earth.

Planet Earth

We live on a smallish but colourful planet we call Earth, third child of the Sun, our local star, which is eight light-minutes away (93m miles, 150m km). The nearest *major* neighbouring star, Sirius, a sister to our sun, is eight light-years away (525,600 times the earth-sun distance). The physical distances involved are enormous. It makes our little lives on earth seem puny. Nevertheless, to us, life on earth is a Big Thing.

Our solar system represents a macrocosmic analogy of an

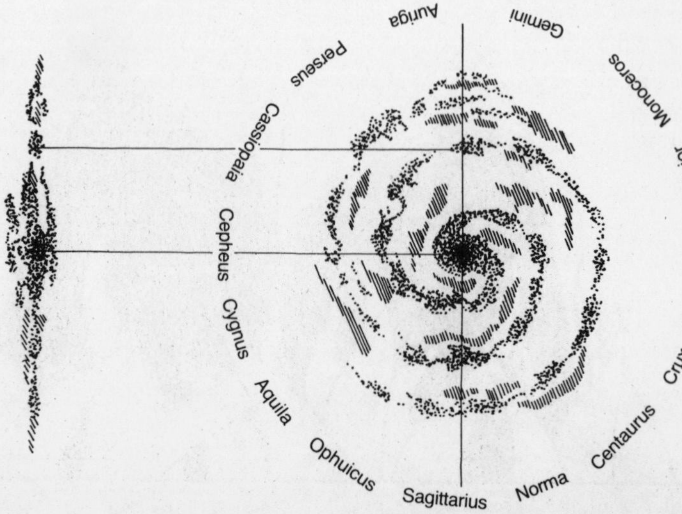

The sun's position in our galaxy. The constellations on the plane of the galaxy, as seen from earth, are named around the edge. Side view of the galaxy on left

individual human. A human is made up of a collection of different psychological components, which we can call *subpersonalities*, and the 'orbit' of these subpersonalities around our real self is analogous to the orbit of the planets around the sun. The planets move visibly over time, and thus are indicators of things which change through time (such as the subpersonalities which variously command our beings at any moment in our lives). The stars, however, have not moved appreciably in relation to each other during the entire course of human history, and thus they cannot be used if we are studying time and change.

Earth is a being, just like humans except much bigger, with its energy-centres, meridians and acupuncture points, a spirit, psyche and physical body, and taking care of her is one of the main issues of our time. She rotates on her own polar axis, like a spinning-top. This gives us the impression that the sun, planets and stars rotate around us each day, as if they were decorating the inside of a vast heavenly sphere, half of which is sky-blue, and half of which is dark, bejewelled with stars. Using earth as our frame of reference, the cosmos rotates around us, but looking at earth from an outer-space viewpoint, earth is rotating on her axis. This is another psychological analogy: we tend to believe usually that the world around us rotates around us, when in fact, the world is fine as it is, and we are the ones who are spinning!

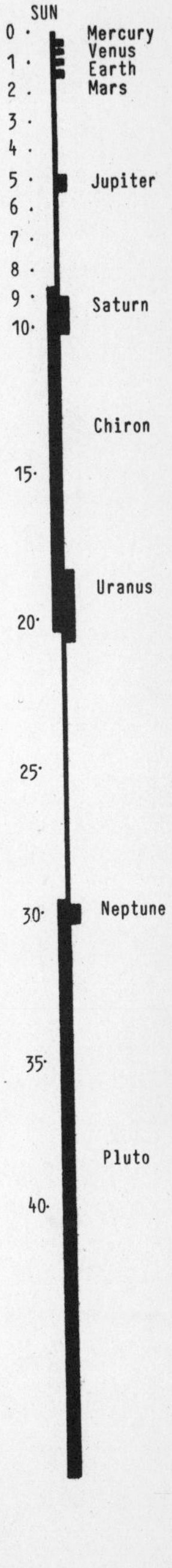

Sun and the solar system

Sun is a being too, a parent to earth, far bigger, made up of a hot gaseous/plasmic thermonuclear physical body. It is one of billions of suns in our galaxy, which takes a lenticular, spiral shape, with a vast centre, dense with suns and all sorts of activity. We live 15,000 light years from the centre of the galaxy (one light year is 60,000,000,000,000 miles). Even though this sounds like a ridiculously long distance, it is significant only within the context of our own galaxy. It is one of a cluster of galaxies, of which there are, in turn, many, and no one really knows whether these clusters of galaxies actually form parts of larger clusters and systems. The distances and time-scales involved are so immense that to us they might as well be infinite: living on a densely-physical planet like ours involves squeezing ourselves into a time-scale and a space-localisation which is seemingly infinitesimally small if we looked at it from a 'God's-eye' view. The history of human life on

Distances of the planets from the sun. The two most eccentric planets, chiron and pluto, vary greatly in distance from the sun, while the other planets have only small variations. Distances are expressed in Astronomical Units (AU), where the sun-earth distance = 1AU earth is like a grain of sand on a beach, and the personal history of each of us in terms of the whole of human history is likewise. So if you think it might take you a long time to read this book, think again!

Back to the solar system. The planets are lit up by the sun, and are a very different thing to the stars or the sun. They orbit around the sun at varying distances — earth is quite close — on a more or less flat plane. This gives the impression from earth that sun and planets move along a narrow belt of the sky, which we call the *ecliptic.* Most of the planets are in nearly-circular elliptical orbits. Exceptions to this are the planets mercury, chiron and pluto, whose orbits are eccentric and elliptical, inclined somewhat to the ecliptic, giving the impression that, in the course of their orbital cycles, they move above and below it. All the planets orbit in the same direction, seen from earth as west to east along the ecliptic (while the daily rotation of the earth makes the whole lot go east to west, as a sphere, at a greatly faster rate).

The ecliptic is divided into twelve equal segments, or *zodiac signs,* each of which is subdivided, for measurement purposes, into 30 *degrees* (12x30° = 360°, a full circle). Thus, we can state the position of a planet at any moment by giving the degree and sign — for example, mars at 12° taurus or jupiter at 27° libra, which in astrologese is written ♂ 12 ♉, or ♃ 27 ♎.

The signs are *not* constellations of stars, even though a series of constellations along the ecliptic confusingly share the same names. Over history, the signs and the constellations slowly shift in relation to one another (at a rate of 1° every 72 years, one sign every 2160 years, the whole zodiac in 26,000 years), owing to the wobble created on the spinning motion of earth by the combined effect of sun and moon. This cyclic shift is known as the *Precession of the Equinoxes,* describing a cycle lasting 25,000 years, which is subdivided into the great zodiacal ages, each lasting 2160 years. When the constellations and zodiac signs picked up the names they have today, in ancient Greek times, they were one and the same,

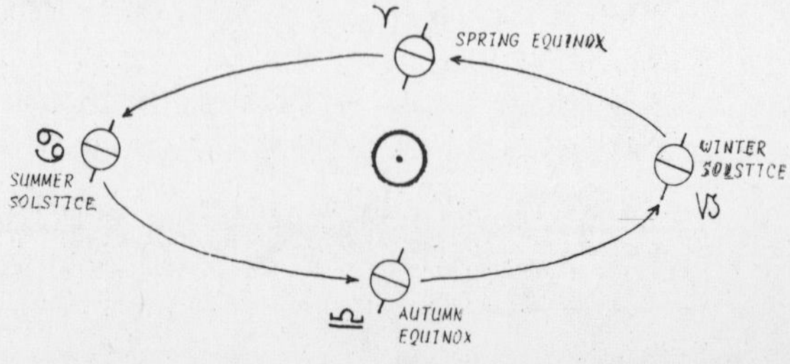

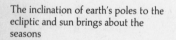

The inclination of earth's poles to the ecliptic and sun brings about the seasons

but this *precession* has now moved the constellations approximately one sign.

The signs are rooted in earth experience, in earthly time-coordinates, the *solstices* and *equinoxes*, which are the anchor-points of the four seasons — and the seasons matter a lot as far as earthly life is concerned. The seasons are brought into being because the earth, with her poles leaning 23.5° from perpendicular to the ecliptic (or the earth's equator leans at 23.5° from it), exposes her north pole to the sun for half a year, and her south pole for the other half, as she orbits annually around the sun. In other words, in temperate countries, the sun moves higher and lower in the sky, seasonally. The orbit and the polar leaning are slightly out of synchronisation with each other by around one minute of time each year, which is what causes this precession: in other words, as history moves on, spring equinox takes place regularly each year at the same point in the earth year, while the backdrop of stars behind the sun (if we could see them) slowly changes. The main point is, though, that the signs are not the same as the constellations, and that we use the *signs* in astrology, for they are related to earth experience, the real stuff of life as it matter to us and affects us.

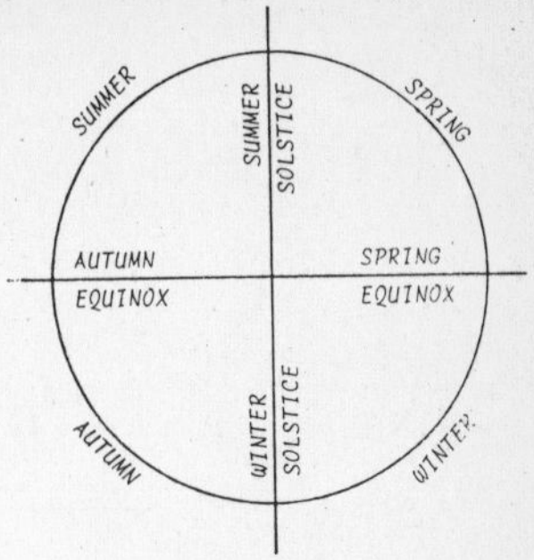

The quarter points and seasons

In the northern hemisphere, the summer-solsticial signs, gemini and cancer, ride high in the sky (regardless of whether or not the sun is there) and the winter-solsticial signs ride low, increasingly the further north we move. [Unfortunately for readers in Argentina, Southern Africa, Australia and other southern-hemisphere lands, this book is northern-hemisphere chauvinistic, written by one who has not yet checked out how everything feels, astrologically, in the southern hemisphere. Apologies and salutations — use a little deduction and imagination, and this book will still prove useful to you.] This means that if the moon or any planet is in a summer-solsticial sign (gemini or cancer) it will ride high in the sky,

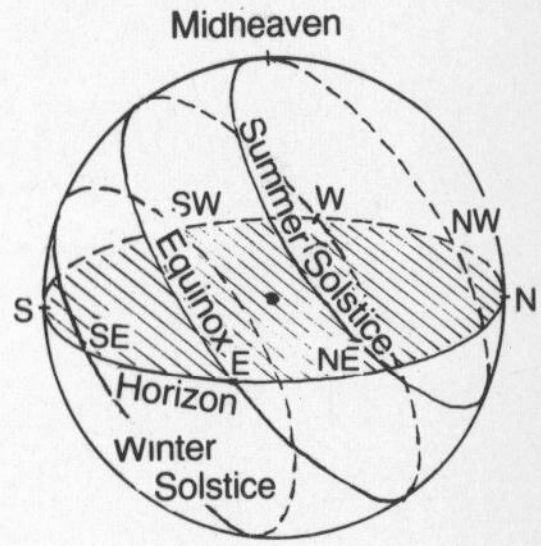

The height of the sun in earth's sky at the four quarters of the year

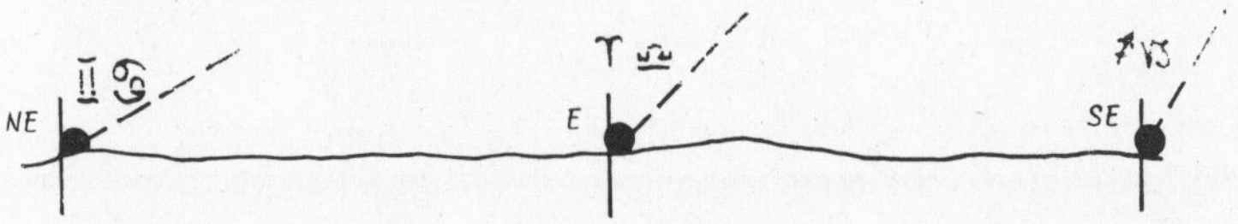

Rising points of the sun at different times of year, looking eastwards at the centre of the diagram. The ecliptic itself oscillates daily back and forth as successive signs rise, regardless of where the sun is in the zodiac. This variation in rising points increases as we go north, until it goes bananas at the Polar Circle, 66 1/2°N

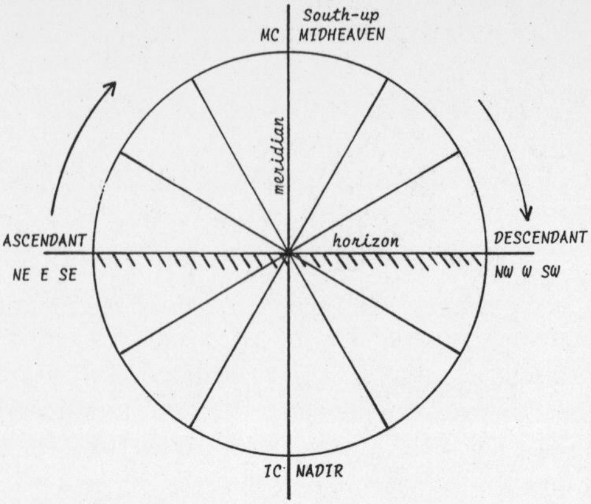

The four angles and twelve houses

and if in a winter-solsticial sign (sagittarius-capricorn), it will ride low — thus, in the late eighties, jupiter, which is moving toward the summer solstice signs, will year by year be climbing higher in the sky, while saturn will remain low, hanging around the winter solstice signs. You can check this out by keeping an eye on the heavens: jupiter will be best visible by night in northern hemisphere autumntime, and saturn in summer, until the early 90s.

Put another way, if sun, moon or a planet is in a winter sign it will rise in the SE and set in the SW, and if it is in a summer sign, it will rise in the NE and set in the NW. If in one of the equinoctial signs (pisces-aries or virgo-libra) it will rise eastwards and set westwards. This oscillation on the horizon increases the further north we go, such that north of 66.5° north latitude on earth (the Polar Circle), sun, moon or planets do not set while they are in summer solsticial signs, and never rise when they are in winter solsticial signs (which is a very remarkable experience to witness!) The ancients made their zodiacal measurements through keeping track of the rising and setting points of sun and moon on the horizon, as seen from carefully-located and designed places such as stone circles, standing stones or mounds, aligned as sight-lines.

Cycles

Astrology is all about cycles of time and solar, lunar and planetary motion. These cycles take on different durations and patterns.

★ The diurnal cycle

The fastest cycle in use in astrology is the cycle of daily rotation of the earth on her own axis. In a birth chart, the *four angles* (Ascendant-Descendant and Nadir-Zenith) and the *twelve houses* show the relationship at any given time (such as at the moment of birth of a person) between earth and the zodiac. This cycle of relationship lasts 24 hours. Wherever we are on earth, half of the heavens are above us and visible either as dark night sky or daylight sky, and half of the heavens are below the earth we stand on, obscured by it. This changes rapidly, hence the importance of the exact time and place of the birth or event in question, as basic data for the calculation of a birth chart. The sign on the *ascendant* (eastwards, where sun, moon and planets rise) changes every 1-3 hours, depending on what sign it is.

★ The lunar cycle

The second fastest cycle we use is the cycle of the moon. Earth and moon are a twin planet, co-orbiting around each other (although the barycentre, or centre of gravity, is still within the earth about 1060 miles, 1700 km below the surface, 2940 miles, 4700 km from earth's centre). Moon moves around the zodiac in 27 days 7 hours (on average). She is by far the fastest-moving heavenly body in our sky. She moves through a zodiac sign every two to two and a half days, according to her speed (itself dependent on her closeness to or distance from earth).

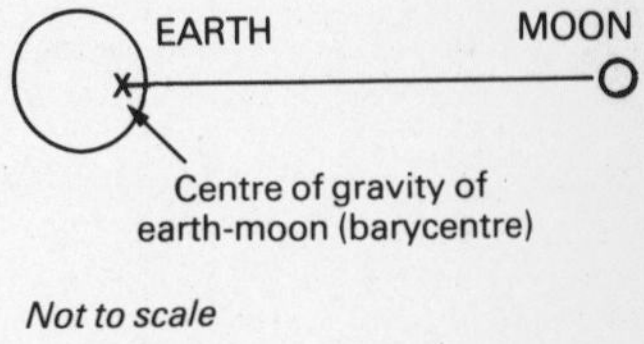

Earth and moon co-orbit around a common barycentre, which, while it lies inside earth, is not at earth's centre

★ The lunation cycle

The light of the moon is reflected sunlight which is continually changing in shape or *phase* because the moon, moving round earth, is continually changing her angular relationship with sun, the source of light, and earth, the place we are looking at her from. This cycle of *lunar phases* (a whole cycle being called a *lunation*) is longer than the cycle of motion of moon around the zodiac because, in the course of 28 days, the sun moves through one sign of the zodiac too: this is like the hands of a clock, where the minute hand has to move through about 1 hr 5 mins worth of movement to catch up with the hour hand and cross or *conjunct* it. Thus the cycle of phases, the lunation cycle, lasts 29 days 12 hours, over two days longer than the average cycle of lunar motion through the zodiac. More about this in the next chapter.

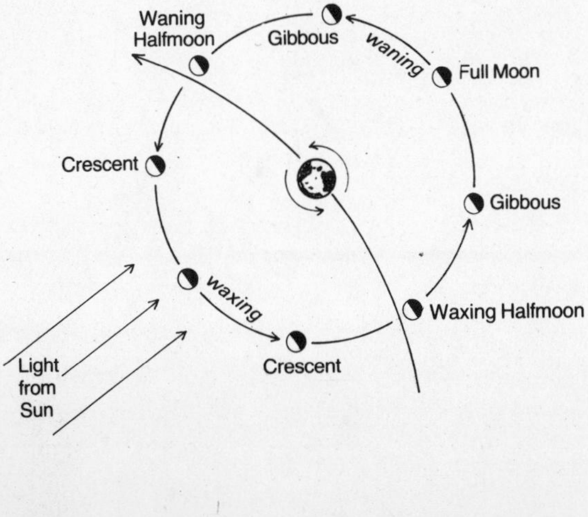

★ The annual solar cycle

The next-longest cycle we use in astrology is the cycle of the year: sun moves through the zodiac in about 365 days, and is directly related to the seasons. A year is subdivided into twelve astrological months (each starting on 20th-23rd of any calendar month — our calendar is not accurately astronomically-based) of thirty-odd days. While the cycle of seasons is obvious to all of us, the underlying energy-currents within it are not so obvious, since we are trained to ignore or overlook such energies and tides. Re-attuning ourselves to them is what we need to do.

★ Planetary cycles

Then we come to the planets, which have various lengths of cycle, ranging from one to 250 years.

Mercury (☿) and *venus* (♀), which both orbit the sun inside earth's orbit, appear from earth's viewpoint always to hover around the sun as it moves through the zodiac. Sometimes they conjunct the sun, and are invisible to us, and other times they can move up to 28° and 47° respectively away from it, either ahead or behind in the zodiac. This means that when mercury or venus are ahead of the sun in the zodiac, they are visible in the evening westwards after the sun has set, and when behind, they are visible in the morning eastwards before sunrise — mercury is rarely seen, because its light is often overpowered by dawn or dusk, but venus can be very bright, sparkly and prominent at different times as a morning or evening 'star'. Sometimes each of them moves faster than the sun through the zodiac, sometimes slower, and sometimes they appear to go backwards — although in fact this is an illusion created by their being on this side of the sun, passing between

The orbits of venus and mercury. When they move on the same side of the sun as earth, they appear to move retrograde. Seen from earth, they appear to accompany sun around the zodiac, oscillating ahead of or behind it and periodically conjuncting it

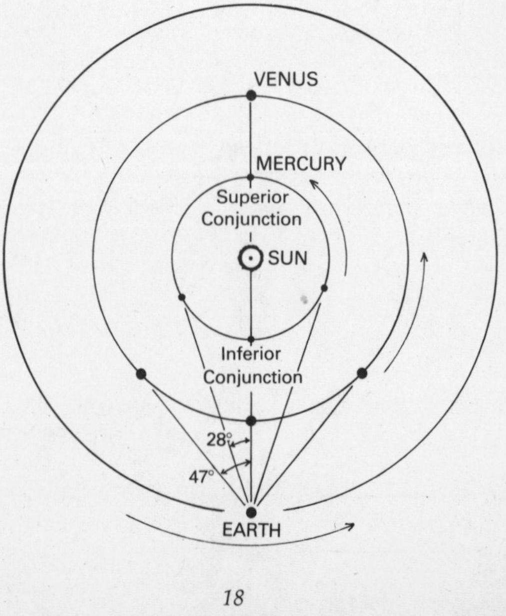

us and it, appearing to move temporarily in the opposite direction to the sun.

The planets outside earth's orbit move around the zodiac each in their own wise. *Mars* (♂ , red and quite bright) takes 1 year 10 months or 687 days, *jupiter* (♃ , very bright, blue-white and often sparkly) nearly 12 years, *saturn* (♄ , dull, tarnishy yellow, not so bright) takes 29 years, *chiron* (⚷ , a newly-discovered planet, invisible to the naked eye, as are all those which follow) takes 51 years, *uranus* (♅) 84 years, *neptune* (♆) 165 years and *pluto* (♇) 248 years. Again, each of these planets can appear to move *retrograde* (backwards) at various times, this time because we are on a moving observation platform and effectively overtaking them, making them appear to move backwards just as an express train can make a slow train moving in the same direction look as if *it* is moving backwards. Mars is retrograde for 60-80 days every two years, and all the other planets are retrograde for 4-5 months per year, around the time when each of them is opposite the sun as the latter swings around the zodiac (or, more accurately, when earth swings round between the planet and the sun). The visible planets amongst these, mars, jupiter and saturn, are at their most prominent each year around this time in the night sky.

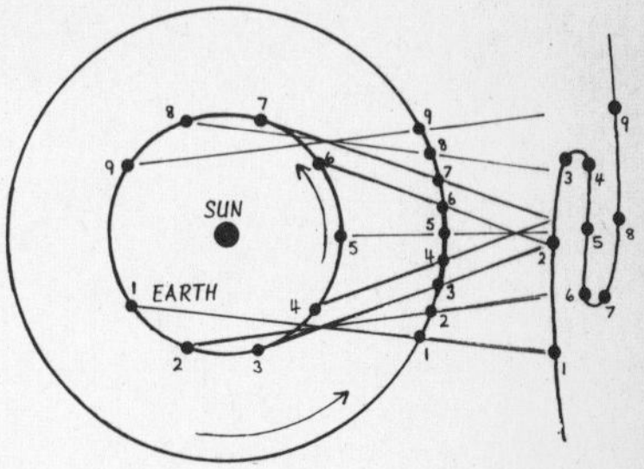

What happens when a planet outside earth's orbit appears to go retrograde. Follow the sequence of numbers

Cosmic clocks

All this means that astrology is using a kind of clock or *orrery* (a mechanical model of the solar system) with eleven hands. Telling the time by this clock is not as easy as it is with a normal analog clock, and thus the language of astrology has developed to help us. The basic language involves *planets, signs, aspects* (angles between planets at any time) and *houses* (related to earth's orientation to the planets and signs), and there is a family of astrological shorthand symbols to do astrological work with. The interrelations between the various planetary cycles (for the sake of simplicity, sun and moon are often called planets, even though they each are of a completely different order to the planets) thus start becoming very interesting. These interrelations are especially noted by taking the zodiacal angles (aspects) between any pair or number of planets, and the aspect and planets and signs involved are taken into account and assessed, to derive an understanding of the nature of the 'energy-weather' at any moment we care to look at.

Birth charts

An astrological chart is a sort of slice out of time, as if someone said "Cut!", and drew up a map to show how earth, sun, moon and planets stood at the exact moment chosen for that chart, as seen from the position on earth of the observer. The place on earth is important, in that two people born exactly simultaneously on opposite sides of the globe (for example Britain and New Zealand or California and Afghanistan) will have exactly the same planetary positions and interrelations, but completely different house-orientations of those positions, one with the sun perhaps rising, the other with it setting. A four-minute difference in time, or a one-degree difference in longitude (east-west measurement of position on earth) will make for a one degree difference in orientation, which can be a critical difference if, say, the signs on the ascendant are on the point of changing. Often astrologers forget that a birth chart is a time-slice: in this book we are looking into the overall flow of time, the original stuff of astrology.

Describing the nature of time

A useful term we shall use is that of *energy-weather*. Just as the weather is made up of a combination of factors which interrelate with one another (warmth, wind, rain, whatever), so also the energy-weather, a subtler and less visible totality, is made up of interrelating factors. In astrology, we name these factors, give them symbols, and play around with different ways of relating them to each other, and deriving meaning therefrom. Any one moment and its energy-weather is characterised by a complete pattern or gestalt involving earth, sun, moon and all the planets, and is broken down into several main components which serve to describe their inter-relationships:

★ the positions of sun, moon and planets in the zodiac signs — for example, sun in aries (☉ ♈), or mars in leo (♂ ♌);

★ their positions in relation to each other, measured by the aspects between them — for example, venus trine saturn (♀ △ ♄), or mars sextile pluto (♂ ✱ ♇);

★ the relationship between the zodiac and the particular place on earth we are looking from (involving the rotation of earth), mapped out in the four angles and the houses — for example, sagittarius rising and libra at the zenith;

★ the relationship between the planets and the angles\houses (closely related to the last component) — for example saturn in the second house (♄ II) and jupiter at the nadir (♃ ☌ IC).

Throwing together all of these factors, and sorting them into a synthesised whole, partially logically, partially intuitively, a skilled astrologer can 'tell the time'. If that time is the time of birth of a person, then that astrologer can say things about the energy-potentials inherent in that person's life, the energy-weather that person chose to be born into. This is based on the notion (which we shall examine again later) that the beginning of a cycle (in this case, birth into life) has within it the seed-potential of the whole cycle. However, just as when you look at a seed, you can visualise what the end-product, the plant or tree, might look like, the precise form that plant or tree takes depends on its own inbuilt growth-programs unique to itself, plus environmental factors which influence the organism as it grows, so the seed-potential of a person must be measured together with uniqueness-factors (soul-factors), and with earlier-life experiences in order to be able to offer worthwhile counsel to any person, using an astrological chart.

In this book, however, we shall be largely passing over the question of houses in a chart. I have mentioned houses here in order to familiarise you with their existence when you come along to looking at your chart later in the book. Since the houses are related to the rotation of earth on its own axis, a fast cycle of 24 hours, which only the more detail-obsessed astrologers would look at in a *timing* context, we shall be leaving them.

Now if all this has thoroughly lost you, don't worry, for you can come back to this chapter as the whole astrological picture starts forming more coherently. A vision of the motions of all these rotations and orbits comes of its own accord in due course, as your understanding of the parts of the astrological jigsaw grows. It can help to spend some time with a flask of tea and a blanket, lying on the ground at night, observing the planets and stars over the course of a year, to help that vision come. You don't have to do this, but it helps, and can give quite a lift. Astrologers nowadays use a book of computer-calculated tables, called an *ephemeris*, which shows the exact positions of the planets for each day, and such a vision can come to the inner eye through working this way too.

The main point to note is that all things move perpetually, and they move in cycles. These cycles never repeat in their inter-relatedness exactly: time is forever unique. This is the basis of astrology.

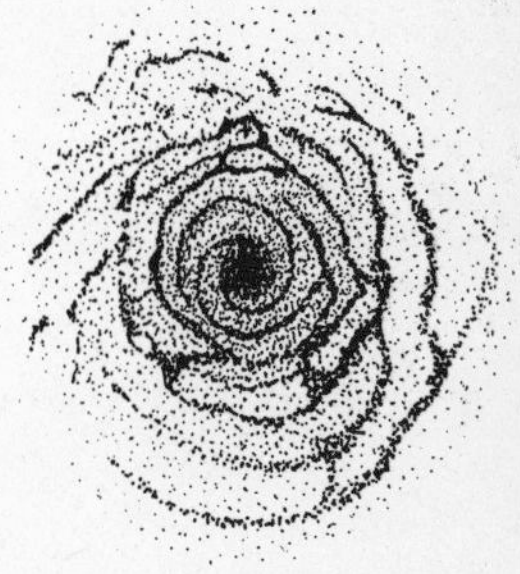

Home

If this has thoroughly lost you, don't worry, for you can come back to this chapter as the whole astrological picture starts coming together.

2 The lunation cycle

The moon is an excellent starting point in learning the astrology of timing because it provides us with directly noticeable situations and atmospheres which we can experience and use as living evidence and material: it is an initiator into the secrets of time. It trains our sensitivities and clues us into some of the isnesses to which a living astrology alludes.

The moon's own motion around the zodiac is one thing, and its phases are another. The first concerns the moon's own motion through the signs of the zodiac, conjuring different shades of influence and tone, while the second concerns its motion in relation to sun and earth (the lunation or synodic cycle), an energy-cycle.

Lunar zodiacal cycles

It is well worth keeping track of moon's zodiacal motion — it passes through a sign in 50-odd hours — for you will soon come to recognise a spectrum of lunar flavours. Take note particularly of the times when the moon changes sign, for a distinct change of atmosphere can take place. A change of sign is called an *ingress*. You don't have to wait long for successive sign-changes, either. For example, when the moon is in ♎ it feels fine to relate easygoingly to others and to enjoy following along with the general drift of what everyone is up to, but when the moon moves into ♏, it is time to face up to things that need doing, to bear with raw facts and persevere. Moon in ♐ brings out the fun in us and extends our horizons, while moon in ♑ asks us to get on with doing what we said we would do, focusing and making things really work. So on it goes: if you observe lunar movements through the signs for a few lunar cycles, you will quite quickly start getting the feel of it and how to respond to it.

This zodiacal cycle lasts on average 27 days and 12 hours. Because the moon swings closer and further from earth (the extremes of this movement are called *apogee*, further, and *perigee*, nearer) during its cycle, it sometimes moves faster, sometimes slower, through the zodiac signs. For this reason, the fullmoon can sometimes look larger, sometimes smaller, as well.

Security

Moon plays a key part in affecting our daily-life responses to things as they arise — our moods, frames of mind, underlying urges and the collective atmospheres around us. A sign-change of the moon infects us with subswells, standpoints, humours, modes and vagaries of being which pass quickly (in hours or a day) but which, at the time we have them, feel total and pervasive, as if we always had them and always will. These are feelings which are often unclear and non-specific, but they particularly affect our feelings of alrightness or discomfort with life, on a momentary basis: if you examine yourself consciously over the course of a day, you will find that your moods and approaches to life change several times between waking and going to sleep, and these 'humours' can immensely affect our way of dealing with life.

Note, however, that the moon does not directly *steer* these moods: our feelings of okayness or agitation, centredness or scattering are our own — the moon is associated with our responses to impartial and essentially neutral atmospheres. A moon in gemini might well create a buzzy, active-minded or dualistic nuance, but what we do with this is our creation: we can choose to go with the energy of the time, or to be hoodwinked by it to respond mechanically to life situations without insight or awareness of what we are creating. Are we fully and awarely present in the driver's seat of the vehicle we're driving?

The greatest steps each and all of us take in life and the carving of our life-story are invariably focused in periods of minutes and hours, and tuning into lunar effects helps us grasp the significance of short moments in the total play of life. Plus the quality of consciousness we need to develop in order to move into a more harmonious and uncomplicated involvement with the here and now.

Lunatics all

The moon's phases (its *synodic* or *lunation* cycle) are not its business alone: they derive from the interrelation of moon, sun and earth, and are independent of the sign the moon is in at any moment. Sun provides the light which moon changingly shines, and its position relative to sun and earth dictates the phase moon shows us. In this sense, moon mediates between sun and earth, filling in the details of the earth-sun relationship.

Sun brings us the seasons of the year, but moon times and qualifies them. Just as the minute hand of a clock gives a precise reading of the time — and catching the 2.35 bus requires an accurate time reading — so moon gives precise timing in the seasonal changes on earth. The small details and intricacies of life add together to make the whole of life, and the buying of a book, the starting of a journey or the occurrence of an accident take place in minutes, not hours or days: these small incidents have a big effect, and form the junction-points in life's ongoing path.

Astrologically, sun symbolises our essential being-nature, the selfness that we are, and its mode of expression as a creative force. Earth symbolises the body we live in, and its senses, the vehicle through which the experiences of incarnate life are had. Lunar energy interposes between these two, affecting the way that selfhood interacts with world situations as they arise, here and now. Just as the sun in the sky can be obscured by clouds (changing our earth experience immensely — note that clouds are very close to earth), so the enactment of our life path can be obscured by all sorts of small things — traffic lights, the ways of others, kids, money questions, our own self-obstructing habits, lunchbreaks, thoughts and flaps, obsessions and malaise and all manner of diversions. Life becomes an interplay between getting our own way (☉) and accepting *that which is*, in front of us (☽), and our capacity to deal with this paradox greatly affects the success we make of our lives, and the happiness deriving therefrom. Many of us allow the daily-life demands of life to dominate our lives entirely, becoming slaves to circumstance, such that the uncovering and persual of life's true direction is lost, buried or forgotten. Others of us project our intent upon the world unreceptively, in a way which creates a wake, or which fails to connect realistically with what's really going on, such that the ends we seek are either not achieved, or our actions create side-effects which complicate matters. Life is an interplay of creativity and receptivity, solar and lunar power. Interestingly, sun and moon appear to be the same size in our sky, even though, astronomically, they are beings of an entirely different order.

The lunation cycle is thus an interactive cycle in which intentions and purposes, whether clearly lived out and experienced or not, meet up with realities, particularly through the intercession of our habitual and learned responses to life. In other words, you are driving from A to B (an expression of intent) and meet a herd

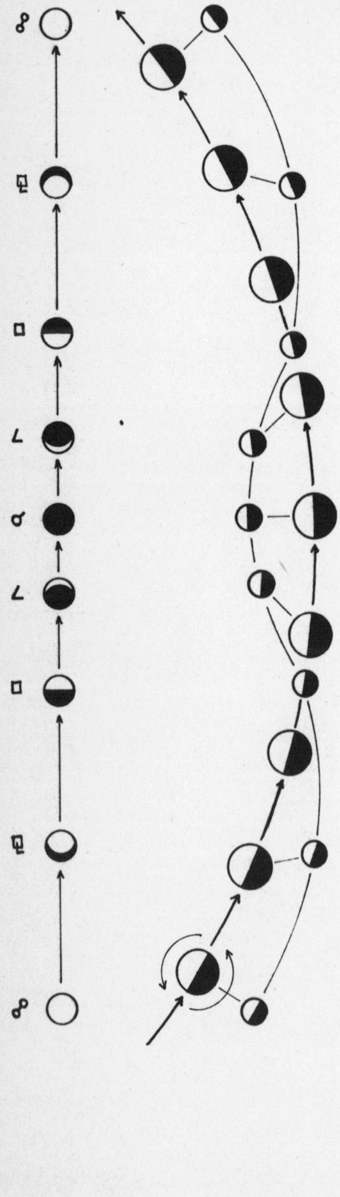

The phases of the moon

of cows blocking the road (an objective fact), and your reactions to this situation can affect your life: it could be a relaxing joke, a minor annoyance, a cause to pause, an outrageous imposition, or even a causative factor in a major mishap three days later!

These reactions will, more often than not, be influenced by past experiences of a similar nature (any programs stored down in subconscious memory which relate, for example, to being thwarted, responsiveness to the moment, expectations, self-esteem, love of nature, whatever). These might cause positive responses — for example, letting things be and allowing facts to be facts, while enjoying the other possibilities the situation might yield — or negative ones — such as getting annoyed, giving up, having it out on an innocent bystander or using a lot of fuel restlessly revving the car engine — and these responses are essentially our own choice, even though we might not consciously exercise that choice.

Riding cycles

The *lunation cycle* (or cycle of phases) lasts 29 days and around 12 hours. Each cycle begins at *newmoon*, when the moon is invisible and in the same place as the sun in the sky. It reaches a climax at *fullmoon*, half way through the cycle. And each cycle, of which there are 12-13 in a year and about 125 in a decade, has its own story to tell, its own issues which are featured and explored. Each lunation is flavoured according to the sign in which the opening *newmoon* takes place — when the newmoon is in ♑, then the whole lunation will be involved with capricornian kinds of issues, even if the sun moves into ♒ part way through. Such a lunation will underlyingly concern issues of realism, social role-formation and fulfilment of obligations, ongoing routines and grounded functioning, even though the sun's ingress into ♒ will change the slant on this question to issues of making things different, looking into the future or changing old routines.

It is very valuable to clue into the under-the-surface themes inherent in each cycle: retrospectively seen, they are very simple and straightforward, taking us through learning processes or life-developments, by revealing to us different aspects of the same question. If the cycle is, for example, about working hard, then sometimes it will be joyous, sometimes productive, other times a bane and a labour, all in the same cycle, revealing to us facets of this part of life we call work.

During the pattern of unfoldment in each cycle of lunar phases, all sorts of ins and outs have to be investigated — they are oscillations and wobbles around a partially-visible emerging question. It is as if we were circumambulating the question at hand, seeing it from different viewpoints, problematic one day, pleasant and hopeful the next, as a future potential and then as a past fact, dull then colourful, rough and then smooth. If you observe meditatively how your standpoints change during the course of a lunation, in relation to whatever major question underlies that lunation, you'll see what it is about. For life is not only about what is happening to us: it is also about how we are internally experiencing it, and thereby responding to it. Our initial instinctive or programmed responses might be different from our later considered responses, and the salient question is whether we acknowledge and take charge of our reaction patterns, or whether we blame life for what's going on.

We can use an awareness of the moon's antics to look into our own. It is not the moon which steers us, so much as our programmed past, our unconscious memories. When life confronts us with challenges and crunches, we have an opportunity to change our responses, release old patterns and open to the wonder of the present moment. For, at root, life is a flow which provides us with every kind of experience we need, at exactly the time and in the way we need it, regardless of what we tell ourselves we need. The never-ending internal rapport of reactions, chunterings and grindings which we go through each and every moment of our lives is habit, and blocks our appreciation of what is available to us in each moment.

The four *quarter phases* of the moon (new, halfmoons and fullmoon) particularly test our fundamental sense of okayness or agitation about life as it is: they are marked in most diaries, and are worth watching, for starters. By doing so, we can come to observe ourselves, and thereby gain insights into how to drop all this exhausting internal rhetoric.

Hemicycles

A lunation has two main halves or hemicycles: the *waxing hemicycle*, in which the future is being opened up out of the context of the past, and the *waning hemicycle*, when the past is being worked with as a foundation for the future. When moon waxes, new possibilities, scenarios, lifetracks and situations are emerging, and when it wanes, already-established forms and arrangements have to be lived with, made use of and completed. It waxes after newmoon, racing ahead of the sun until it opposes it (occupies the opposite side of the zodiac) at fullmoon and fully reflects the sun's light, modified, onto earth at night. It wanes after fullmoon, catching up with the sun by newmoon. In the meantime, the sun has moved through approximately one sign of the zodiac. Consider the hands of a clock and the times of their successive conjunctions (12.00, 1.05, 2.10, 3.15 etc), if you don't understand how the lunation cycle works.

Sun has a yearly cycle with twelve main shades to it, shown by its movement through the signs. Moon has its own zodiac cycle of 27 days. Moon acts as an independent but related factor in bringing these two cycles together in the cycle of phases. For example, each time the moon moves through ♉ throughout the year, it will be in a different phase, owing to sun's own motion, shining its light on moon; similarly, newmoons and fullmoons will wander, by zodiac position, backward in the zodiac as time goes on, usually having one of each during sun's sojourn in each sign, but sometimes having, say, two newmoons in the same sign, at the beginning and end, at least once every year.

Keeping track

These soli-lunar panegyrations are best followed by using the astrologers' holy book, an *ephemeris*. We'll be looking at ephemerides in chapter five. Of course, keeping an eye on the heavens, at the rising and setting of sun and moon, and the changing of moon's phases will get you in touch with *how it looks* in real life. The ancients, and not-so-ancients too, used to make careful measurements and keep tallies of time in order to keep track, but now we have books available which give exact readings: something has been lost and something gained, as with all 'advances' in human ways!

Now we shall trace the main elements of the lunation cycle in detail. See if you can observe them at work on a daily basis, using your own life and surroundings as the material with which to learn how to move in tune with lunations.

The Lunation Cycle in detail

★ NEWMOON (☽ ☌ ☉). When sun and moon conjunct, an old cycle ends and a new one begins. Moon is invisible, being in the sky with sun at daytime and under the horizon at night, with its dark side facing us. The new time-cycle starts with a feeling of immense possibility: here we stand, just being, in the way we are, clear of past grooves yet unstarted on the future. In this beingness are the seeds of the new, and starting new activities is auspicious now. Ideas, plans, expectations, new chapters, preparation of the ground or facing inevitable possibilities can be the keynote — or it might well be time simply just to be, for once, to reclaim ourselves and our own private lives. Energy can sometimes be low, sometimes zippy and charged with potency, but after observing a few newmoons, you will notice their characteristic flavour.

The sign in which the newmoon takes place is worth looking at, for both moon and sun are featuring this sign. Sometimes we can feel vacuous and vulnerable at newmoon, and sometimes we are raring to go: either way, what starts now reaches a climax in two weeks' time at fullmoon: what begins as a potential seeks to become actual, and what comes from me-in-here must move into relationship with that-out-there during the waxing hemicycle. The newmoon period lasts two days either side of exact newmoon, and although there is an energy- or perspective-change at precise newmoon, the whole period is one of beingness, transition into a new storyline, or a new quirk on an existing one.

★ CRESCENT MOON (☽ ⊻ ☉). Two days after exact newmoon, the crescent moon becomes visible westwards after sundown. Things are beginning to take shape, and utter potential is beginning to form into either stimulating or daunting possibilities. Details are emerging which give shape to the future. On the third day, when ☽ forms a 45° angle to ☉ (☽ ∠ ☉), choices need to be made, and beingness is moving into doingness. Developing avenues are either enthralling or appalling or somewhere between, but a commitment must be made to some definite tracks into the future, and wilder possibilities must be thrown out. Get clear, for it is necessary to invest decisive energy into anything if things are to take off.

Four days after newmoon, when moon is 60° from sun (☽ ∗ ☉), things start moving fast, developing and gathering momentum, and we are either getting where we need to go or having to deal with the eventuality that things are on the move anyway — it all depends on whether we are the active or passive ingredient in our lives! This phase, when moon is a fatter crescent, and setting later after the sun, is flowingly, even compulsively productive, and much is afoot. Possibilities widen and move into increasing tangibility, and the enjoyment of progress can make this time rewarding.

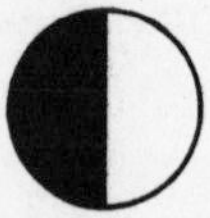

★ WAXING HALFMOON. Seven or so days after newmoon, moon forms a 90° angle to sun (☽ □ ☉), and now sails high in the sky as the sun sets, rising around noon. At halfmoon we must really *do* something, make things *work*, make choices and face facts, whether we like to or not — or we must accept that some things aren't working and must be discarded to make space for things that do work. Life can present us with obstacles without or problems within, and the overall feeling is one of overall unclarity, yet an imperative knowing of what we must do, immediately, in order to deal with the facts of the situation. It has all been set up, consciously or unconsciously, and now we just have to get on with it: we're moving into a new stage of development. Often new elements or problems can surface suddenly, squeezed out of our unconscious or the unknown, changing things radically — even though, philosophically seen (afterwards!), they fit in with the unfolding scenario and were meant to happen.

Imperatives and realities are the halfmoon question, and facing up to them is what is best to do. It is a time for work or transition, overcoming blockages, making things move, or squaring up with the truth of the situation. Here arises the question of whether we are *creators* of our lives, willingly shouldering what we should bear, or *victims* to it, needing the world to force us to face things. The halfmoon period lasts one day either side of the exact 90° aspect, and much can be achieved at this time. A transition is being made between *subjective*, what-I-want-of-life viewpoints, and *objective*, what-life-will-actually-furnish realities.

★ GIBBOUS MOON. If the halfmoon slammed us when we weren't looking, then the next few days we spend getting over it and dealing with, or avoiding, the consequences! If we used the half-moon to get to grips with things, then the momentum gathered goes a long way. Two days after halfmoon, moon and sun form a 120° angle (☽ △ ☉), and things tend to go easygoingly and floatily. This is a pause for a rest and rethink, a space allowed for creative input or reflection, or for simply allowing things to unfold on the strength of earlier effort. Life is lighter if we have grappled well at halfmoon, and if we haven't, it takes on something of a void or sluggish, droopy flavour. Wider perspectives can regain ground, and fun can be had. If action is what you seek now, let things be as they will, for this is not a time for *making* things happen — action times come again soon. Things will connect only if we *allow* them to, not if we seek to push them.

Moon is now growing larger, and when it is 135° from the sun (☽ ⚼ ☉ , 10-11 days after new-moon, 3 days before fullmoon), realignments and prioritisations must be made: a sharp and busy energy surges up, which forces us to look at the relevance of current realities in connection with longer-term perspectives and implications. Un workable intentions should be honed or dropped, and workable developments should be committed to outward-manifestation, concretely. Here our personal dreams and schemes meet the world *as is*, and a jousting of realities occurs. This is a good time for letting go of preconceptions, in order to allow the universe to support us in achieving what we need to achieve. The fullmoon period is building up, and energetic tension is growing.

★ FULLMOON. The fullmoon period lasts four days, two days either side of the exact opposition of moon to sun (☽ ☍ ☉, 180°). It starts when moon and sun are 150° from each other (☽ ⚻ ☉), when moon is almost full, rising before sundown: here we get a crisis of perspective, for things take on a different light and context, and it can feel as if we are no longer clear on what we are doing and why. Yet we know that we need to stand by what we have created and carry it through, as much as reality will allow, for the stage is set and the lights are up.

If we are unsure as to what we are doing, we can develop a feeling of emptiness, lostness and disorientation. If we are hanging on to fixed ideas they can become questionable and void, or life events bring them into question. If we are recept-ively playing things by ear, yet are clear on our priorities and underlying intent, things tend to come to a head: this is it, the time is now, or imminent. Pre-fullmoon can be either a time of intense suspended animation or one of frantic activity to get things right and on line, and the whole world is quivering to the energy. It is a time for letting go internally, suspending judgements and dropping stances, accepting what truly *is*, in the moment, and allowing life to go as *it* will, for the truth will out, regardless.

Fullmoon is electric, zingy and riddled with contradiction and paradox, sometimes highly-str-ung and complex, sometimes calmly loaded; but always, at exact fullmoon there is a fundamental energy-change and perspective-flip, which can make for a remarkably different situation afterwards — although the difference is often *within us*. Moon rises as sun sets, and moonrises at this time can often be critical, tense or headachey, until it swings above the horizon. After fullmoon, high energy can fall flat, or subdued energy can erupt or explode; clarity can lapse into dreaminess or unknowing can move into profound understanding. It is not without reason that tradition has it that Sakyamuni

Buddha attained enlightenment on the fullmoon — he did it by breaking his previously tight rules.

Fullmoon is a prime time for spiritual-psychological breakthrough and growth, facing what's really real (which we might only discover at fullmoon), letting go of old hangups, accepting the present and generally sorting out our relationship with others and the world around. Be aware of your reactions to life around fullmoons, and ask yourself if they are truly appropriate or fruitful ones, otherwise you can lose yourself, separating your own world from the world around and leading to little fruit. This is the climax of the lunation cycle, starting a new hemicycle in which contexts, forms, results and effects matter. Sun and moon are in opposite signs, and contrapose the messages of those two signs in dynamic paradox: the question is, how do we get the contrasting elements of these signs to work together?

The *waxing* moon was dedicated to exploration, opening channels, expressing our wishes and finding our personal identity: the *waning* moon now asks us to join the human race, make our lives useful in the context of what the world needs, set up lasting structures for our efforts to live on when we have moved on, complete what we have started, and also derive the benefits which we deserve from our contributions and creations. And if we have omitted to develop a sense of selfhood, a contribution, a statement, or if we have not taken responsibility for our lives, then the waning moon becomes a period when the world takes us over, forcing us to let it have its way, and we must follow along.

The fullmoon period lasts until moon and sun are again 150° apart (☽ ⚻ ☉), except now moon is moving on the home stretch. Moon's light is waning, and it rises later each evening. During these two post-fullmoon days we digest the impact of the fullmoon and prepare to move on with the outcomes we have created, whether it be intended or inadvertent. The deed is done. This is a time of new understanding, of lessons learned and new orientations begun. At the end of this period, we either feel clear as to what we must next do, or we feel lost and dissipated, awaiting our apparent fate — it all depends on how we create our lives.

★ WANING GIBBOUS MOON, otherwise known as the *disseminating* moon. When moon is 135° away from sun (☽ ⚼ ☉), three days after exact fullmoon, the world wants something of us, or offers something to us, and it is time to gear up, make commitments, and start doing what we say we shall do. What we have set in motion we must carry though, or we must prepare to face the music if we don't. Here the social contract is signed, and we are a part of it. If we cannot carry things through, or do not like what's on offer, we tend to feel adrift, excluded from life, victims of demands, and while we might seek alternatives, they often cannot emerge now unless they are truly appropriate. We must sign on the line and do it, or fix up with others what is to be done if we do not do it. We are all a part of each other, and the system is interdependent: we are needed.

On the fourth/fifth day after fullmoon, when moon moves into a 120° angle to sun (☽ △ ☉), things move into an easier, relaxed mood, even though they can still be moving quite fast, and space opens out to allow new meaning, new contacts and a here-and-now creative edge to enter. During the waning moon, the world affects us greatly, and at this phase our relations with world relax and take on new significance. It is time to catch up on things fallen behind, to potter, and to follow along with what's going on.

★ WANING HALFMOON. The halfmoon period (☽ □ ☉) lasts two days. This is the time to fulfil our agreements with others and the world, to really *do* it, to carry through our side of the bargain and our obligations. Halfmoon brings a focusing of energy on the task at hand, or, if we avoid this, it brings a crunch, where the world confronts us with our assets and failings — the car breaks down, people give up on us or give us hassles, things become impossible, or it rains when we wanted sun. Either way, we are faced with the truth of how we fit into our world, and the outcomes of our acts to date stand before us, sometimes rewardingly, sometimes harshly. Our lives are in the hands of others, for our chance has already been, and if we are victims, we can suffer. What is done is done and is well.

At the waning halfmoon, the past is beginning to end, and a glimmer of the future is peeking out: in the involvement of the moment, with its lessons and outcomes, the future is reborn as a seed of possibilities for a future cycle. Having created a context for our lives, and a role in which we are accepted (or rejected), a question pops up: what have I got from all this, and where does this lead me?

★ WANING CRESCENT MOON. At this phase, moon rises before dawn, thinning as the days pass. When moon is 60° from sun (☽ ✱ ☉), about 9-10 days after fullmoon, we move into a productive time where things are working, moving along the lines they are now habituated to move along, and we expect things to be as they are likely to be, and life expects us to be as we have ordained for ourselves. We are all in it together, moving along as an arranged whole. Progress is being made, and things are as normal. Underneath, new possibilities (or worries), previously unseen, emerge out of the established flow of events, and new understandings develop, perspectives on the past and present. This is a time of before completion, of finishing touches, or receiving the payoffs from our labours. Momentum is strong, moving along the lines we have created and agreed with others. Even if our actions can be seen to have failed, positive outcomes can emerge.

When moon moves to 45° from sun (☽ ∠ ☉), it is clean-up time, let-go time, time for resolving old arguments, dropping old grudges, clearing up the mess and summating things: for the time is coming soon to move on into a new chapter, and the sometimes relentless wheel of change still turns. We are called upon to release our acts to the world, and allow them to become history, a ground to stand on, not an environment to be in. We must complete things, tie things up and drop them, give them away. What we once identified as our own is no longer so. This can give immense clarity of purpose, or a sense of perspective over the longterm drift of our lives, or release, a lightening of a burden.

Still, however, there are two-three days before newmoon — the old-moon phase, ☽ ⚺ ☉ — when the thinning crescent, rising before sun at dawn, disappears. Many are the issues to contemplate, and the distant as well as the recent past comes in to help us integrate our experience and commit it to memory-files, as new hopes and intentions for the next step emerge out of the dust of the old. Side-issues need sorting through, things need cleaning, polishing, mending, fixing, and the resources we have demand attention. Habit prevails, and the waiting for the old to end is on. Old moon is sometimes a low-energy time, thoughtful, a phase for living with the past as past, and simply being, letting the dust of life settle. Sometimes it can be busy, if things demand finishing, or if future possibilities need preparations, or foundations need building: things now need sorting out before it is too late. The old moon, while past-dominated, hatches within it future possibilities.

★ NEWMOON (☽ ☌ ☉). After all this cyclical hyperactivity, it is well to spend some time just being, living in our own space, doing, or not doing, things we ourselves feel are best. This is a transition, and things cannot be hurried. Seeds are germinating, but have not yet taken any distinct form, and need tender nurturing. Things might not happen in great quantities at newmoon, but the *qualities* of our thoughts and feelings, and the omens presented by events have great relevance. If things are lined up to be carried out, it is well to begin them at newmoon. If things in the past have been busy, and the future is unclear as yet, it is well to bear with it and allow things to emerge. A new awareness is coming through, a new cycle, and a change of perspective is common at new moon, setting off a new tone and set of themes which will develop into the future. Life goes on! And at this stage, the overall picture of life can present itself to us, as if we were temporarily outside the process, looking in.

Lunar energy

Tuning into moon and its phases has great implications. It is not only a way to familiarise ourselves experientially with lunations, cycles and the astrological language, but it also facilitates big changes in the way we handle life. In tune with moon we can move into a new sense of *flow* with life. Lunar phases time the unfoldment of larger changes, and, especially at critical moments, it is very useful to know the astrology of what is going on, so that we can live and make our choices clearly, see our experiences in the larger context of cosmos and naturalness, and understand some of the hidden meanings in life. Consciously living with lunar energy opens the cracks between the worlds, and we can engage deeper levels of reality in our lives, in a very practical way: when it is time to act, act, when it is time to lie low, lie low — this is the simple order of life, which hasn't changed since people like Lao Tzu wrote such advice 2,500 years ago.

For women, awareness of lunations is very important. Once, menstrual and lunation cycles were synchronised — in ancient times all women ovulated at fullmoons and menstruated at newmoons (as far as I understand) — and women were in active touch with a deep power, a power to be in tune with their bodies, hormones and psyches, in a wavelike way which men cannot experience. There was no population problem, no unwanted birth, no worry about contraception or infertility. Women were in tune with the secret of their beings, and asserted full influence in the life of the human family: it will be a major transformation in the world when womankind regains this harmony. Lunar and solar energy need balancing.

It helps men to tune into the moon as well, not only to understand women better, but also to put them in touch with their deeper sensitivity, their a-rational side, their innocence, humanness and naturalness within, the anima. A man in touch with his inner woman can move the full power of his masculinity without needing to be macho or prove his strength: his strength lies well-rooted in his ability to be sensitive and vulnerable (qualities to which men are traditionally taught to avoid giving energy), and yet to adeptly survive without the need to protect himself from imagined possible assault on his self-determination, strength or integrity. Without opening to the feminine, whether a woman or a man, we cannot *receive what we need* out of life, feel nourished, at home, alright, a full member of humanity, here in the world.

Observation

To start with, watch what goes on for you around new and full moon. Diaries give their dates, but ephemerides are better. Observe what goes on within you as well as around you. Seek not to form judgements or conclusions: simply *watch*, and pick up experience. To move in accord with moon means that we need to open up an *umbilical* feel for life, in a part of us where thoughts are of little relevance.

Watch your reactions to life situations as they arise: resistances, acceptances, control and relaxation, efforts and allowings. Note the changing paradoxes between what you *seek to happen* and what *actually* happens, and note the ways you deal with them. Take a look at nature, especially at everything related to *water* (cloud, rain, water flows, tides, plant growth, water within your own body), for major moonphases time the outbreak of changes which the sun seasonally brings (flowers blooming, birds migrating, leaves falling, weather changes) through influencing water. Watch road traffic, the behaviour of animals and children, the people on the train, the cat, pot plants, patterns of sleep, patterns of thought and phases in your relationship with others.

When you have the gist of what fullmoons and newmoons are about, look into the halfmoons, and gradually expand your observations to a sensing of the whole lunation cycle. As time goes on you will find that something in your body-consciousness starts moving, giving you reliable messages which your brains would never see. The lunation cycle is a goodly potted cycle to look into, for it is rapid and repeating, and illustrates how other astrological cycles work. While no two lunations are the same, there is an underlying pattern to all lunations and all cycles, and there is also a pattern of responses within you to them.

Eclipses

Keep your eyes peeled, when poring over your ephemeris, for *eclipses*. Only sometimes are they visible, either because what is visible might be taking place under the earth (a 50/50 chance), or because it is not an exact enough eclipse to be visible as one. Moon is eclipsed only at fullmoons (when earth's shadow falls on the moon, lasting up to 1 hour and 20 minutes) and sun is eclipsed only at newmoon (when the moon passes in front of the sun, a rare occurrence, lasting up to 8 minutes).

Despite visibility or lack of it, there is an energy-condition which accompanies eclipses. They are *extraordinary* new or full moons, which can prove to be major turningpoints. Around the time of an eclipse, things go still, and a pensive, lurking quality pervades the airwaves, as if all things were waiting for something significant. Eclipses take place when the moon and sun conjunct or oppose one another close to the moon's *nodes*, which are the points where the moon's plane of orbit around earth intersect earth's plane of orbit around the sun. The nodes move slowly backwards (retrograde) through the zodiac, making a complete cycle once every 18.6 years. This is called a *metonic* cycle, which the ancients used to count as significant, in that it gave a time-period which spanned one generation. People who felt that the ancestors lived on through those who are alive, and who had a strong sense of longterm timing spanning generations and lives, counted the metonic cycle carefully.

The zodiac positions of eclipses, which tend to take place at two periods at opposite sides of each year, move slowly backwards with the nodes. Wherever the nodes are, eclipses will be, whether approximate or exact ones. Either way you can tell the *feeling* of an eclipse, visible or not. Thus different zodiac signs get singled out for featuring through eclipses — always opposite signs. Opposite signs essentially work with the same basic question from different viewpoints — as if they were two sides of the same coin. Eclipses bring out the contradictions in opposite signs, and on a spiritual/psychological level, ask for resolution of conflicts into unity. Try to observe the *energy-weather* at eclipses, and to use them consciously as times when it is auspicious to get clear on intents, perspectives, deep choices, moving through watersheds, or to allow the forces of life to indicate the best way forward. They are excellent times for ceremonies and meditations.

Moon reveals facets of life which we normally keep subconscious, giving us inroads into the secret fluxings behind everyday events. The sensitive inner child within us, wide-eyed and open, is waiting to come out. Anachronistically, when it does, we start truly growing up.

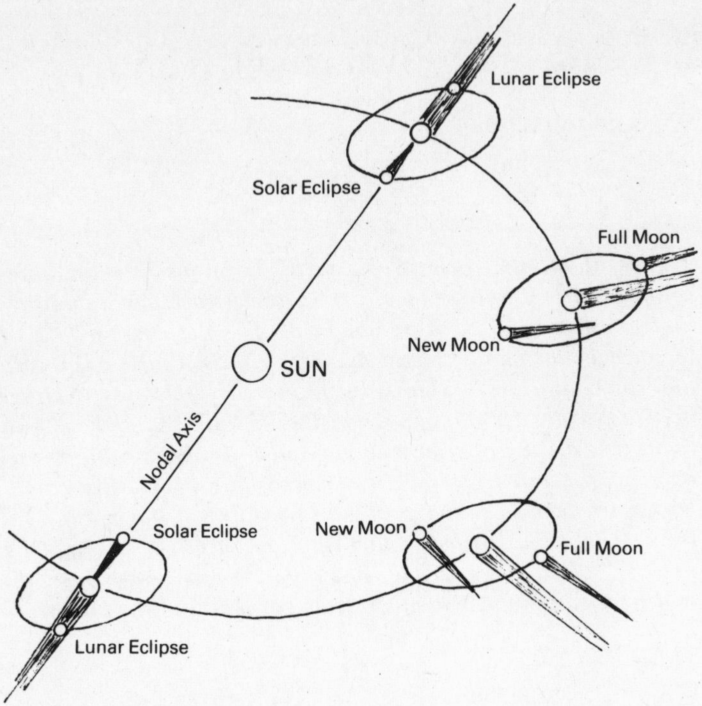

Eclipses occur when a new or full moon takes place on the axis of the lunar nodes (☊ ☋) – where the orbital planes of earth around sun and moon around earth intersect. They take place at two periods in the year, and these periods vary gradually according to the slow retrograde motion of the nodes through the zodiac

3 Ancient festivals and the four seasons

This is about the cycle of the year. To move into an inner affinity with it brings us closer to the power behind nature and gives us new creative potential. For the energy-cycle of the year is not just a calendrical affair: it is a cycle of growth and consolidation fundamental to our very existence. Neither is it just a matter of changes in the availability of heat and light: it is a cycle of subtle energy which is very usable in our own lives, a participation in the breathing of Mother Earth. For we are as nits on her skin, and need to transform our lives from being parasitic to participatory. And observing the ancient festivals is one way of doing this, an inner basis on which we can move into our role as gardeners of the planet.

Years

We tend to take the cycle of the year very much for granted, viewing it *calendrically* rather than from an *energy* viewpoint. Which means that we miss out on the undertow of life and omit to use the available energy of time to guide us and help us in the achievement of our purposes. If we moved in harmony with time, we would move in harmony with each other as well, and life would unfold more organically, in phase with overall energy-conditions. Like surfing, moving through life is dead easy, if we catch the wave and know how to ride it: thus the question arises, how can we recognise the wave-pattern, and how can we develop and sustain the consciousness to be able to perceive it and stay with it?

The seasons are brought about by earth's relationship with sun, in which she exposes each of her poles to it for half of the year as she orbits around it. Outwardly, sun gives earth light and heat, and the seasons come about as a result of the meeting of the yang, solar energy, and the yin, earth substance, with moon mediating through regulating water flows. Inwardly, however, there is an *energy-weather* cycle which activates the life-force within the earth being, and within ourselves. It courses through the subtle meridians of the earth and underlies the very blueprints of life itself.

The ancients recognised this, and took it upon themselves to invoke favourable seasonal change, in the knowledge that change is the essence of earthly life, and rhythm is the breathing of life-force, of the prana or ch'i of earth and all who live on her. This solar life-force is what gives us the urge to live, chase our dreams and actualise the fullness of our potential. The sun in us is at the centre of our being, and is our fundamental *raison d'etre* and source of strength, a potentially vibrant, shining place within us which can make something good out of any life circumstance.

The sun moves around the zodiac in a year, exposing us to living experiences of different underlying realities inherent in life as it moves through the signs. There are twelve *signs* of the zodiac, and these are anchored in four *quarter-points* in the year, the two *solstices* and two *equinoxes*. The twelve signs outline the qualitative undertow of the seasons, archetypally. An archetype (in para-physics, an L-field) is an image or model of fundamental patterns behind and within all happenings and situations, and is experienced by our unconscious or deeper self. In other words, life experience is a combination of circumstances *out there*, and inner states of being: it pays well to observe the changes of these inner states in the collective psyche, and in our own lives, as we progress through the year.

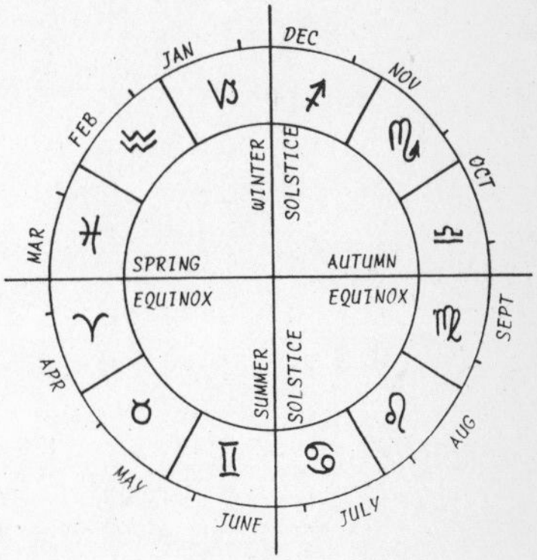

The solstices and equinoxes: gateways of energy potential and archetype

Interestingly, nature itself manifests its changes according to an eightfold pattern, marked out by the four quarter points and the midpoints between these. The energy *principles* behind each year are represented by the twelve signs, but the *manifest* changes are represented by an eightfold subdivision of the year. The ancients, who were more interested in the cyclical facts of life than we are, used a fundamentally eightfold zodiac, as evidenced in many stone circles and sightlines in ancient remains in Britain and elsewhere. Let's look at these eight annual subdivisions. These periods were bounded by points in time, marked by festivals, which we call the *quarters* and *cross-quarters*.

The four and the eight

The Solstices. These are, quite simply, the two exact points in the year when the days are longest and shortest — that is, when the poles of earth are maximally inclined toward the sun, or when sun is directly above the two tropics (of Cancer and Capricorn) on earth. Energywise, the solstices are times of pause, in which a movement of change from one light condition — long days or long nights, emphasised for people living further from earth's equator in cooler latitudes — to the other stops and reverses. These processes of light-change bring forward energy-changes too.

When the light is increasing, from winter to summer solstice, all individual entities are finding and expressing their own identity, or *individualising*, and when the light is decreasing, from summer to winter solstice, nature and life as a whole is integrating itself into interrelated unison, or *wholising* (sometimes called socialising or universalising). You can observe this in your own life if you keep an awareness of your internal changes throughout the year.

The solstices occur around 21st-22nd June and December (the variation being due to our unnatural calendrical system initiated by Pope Gregory). At winter solstice, individual things and people experience their belongingness to the whole, yet start on a journey of exploration of their individuality, which lifts off at the spring equinox (20th-21st March) and reaches its peak of growth by summer solstice. Within completion lies a new beginning, however, and from summer to winter solstice, lifting off at autumn equinox (22nd-24th September), all individualised beings journey on a process of reintegration into belongingness to the whole, the family, the ecosystem. In the three months after each solstice, the change is bubbling under, giving new context to the prevailing energy of the time, and at the equinoxes, the change surfaces, becomes conscious and acted out.

The solstices are characterised by a feeling of stillness or pause — a contrast to the rushing changes which take place in autumn or spring, preceding them. They give us a chance to stop and take stock, to assimilate all that has been rapidly developing, and to make a transition into *stasis*, into a state of being rather than a state of becoming. They are gateways of consciousness, where the simple fact of our being alive becomes worthy of celebrating. At summer solstice, we celebrate our individuality and our personal stance on life, our creativity and the joy of being alive in the relieving openness of early summer. Winter becomes memory, and summer becomes fact. At winter solstice, we celebrate our membership in the family and tradition of the human race, our togetherness and reunion, and the wealth of goodness we have accumulated, each in our ways, to carry together through the winter.

As gateways of consciousness, winter solstice becomes a pause to perceive the seeds of future growth, to gather intent and make our resolutions for the future (New Year's resolutions being a modern leftover of the ancient solstice custom, moved to another date, the Gregorian New Year), while summer solstice becomes a pause in the midst of the potent life-process, a gathering of intent around what we are going to *do* with what we have moved into since winter solstice. Since winter solstice is lifeless, it symbolises all that is changeless, formless, concealed, potential, and in northern climes, candle and fire rituals represent the quiet surviving of the life-force in the midst of the darkness. Since summer solstice is buzzing with life and activity, it symbolises all that is living, transient, productive and vibrant, in which the fire is represented in warmth and sunshine. Light within and light without: these two different aspects of the life-force are vital to an understanding of natural religion and the cycle of the year. What has been achieved and created has indeed been done, and at these points we come to accept *what is*, and get on with it.

Thus, if you seek to move into inner harmony with the underlying motion in the year, observe the solstices consciously, and use their energy-state with a tone of reverence, and you will find yourself opening up to the fundamental pattern of the year.

The Equinoxes. These are the midpoints between the solstices, when the length of days and nights are changing fast, but are equal in length, sunrise to sundown. These are times of transition and rampant change. At spring equinox the restraining influences of the whole give way, and individuals take it upon themselves to go forward in their own interests, mutating and growing as they each can. At autumn equinox, individuals, somewhat tired of their own separateness and its implications, begin to join together and feed energy into one another, in the pursuit of shared interests, relationship and togetherness. This alternating current of energy, in which we seek to find ourselves, then seek to find our place in the scheme of things, only to find out that we again need to find ourselves, is the very stuff of life experience.

Thus, while the solstices mark pauses in the life cycle, at which times it is auspicious to take stock, and to orientate on coming developments, the equinoxes mark midpoints in the action, in the movement toward becoming-something-else, times of transition. The equinoxes are highpoints in the tide of change, realignments from living out the effects of past states to moving into potent future-unfolding states. Solstices are times of potential, of seed-laying, and equinoxes are times of action, movement and germination. Yet solstices are times also of completion and fulfilment, while equinoxes are times for releasing past ways, in order to make space for what is to come.

Often, things are too busy at the equinoxes for the same kind of observances as the solstices allow: it just so happens that in the natural scheme of things, there is little to be done at the solstices, while at the equinoxes, things are moving fast. They are times of gear change, engagement in the life-process, stepping out. All of these are magical times well worth noting: look at what goes on for you at the quarter-points, and listen to the experiences of others around you, and you'll get a taste of what we're talking about. You will find that the most potent time for observance of these festivals is the hours and two days *before* their exact timing. The exact timing can be found in an ephemeris.

There is nothing hidden or mysterious about the quarters: the only veils between us and understanding the quarter-points are the veils of our own awareness. Astrology can be learned directly from life itself — which is the way the first astrologers did it. And they found that, second to the lunation cycle, the annual cycle and its quarters was most vital to come into active, conscious involvement with. Thus it is that many people now are instinctively starting to observe these festivals. Interestingly, a surge of interest in them took place when the planet neptune was sitting for a few years on the winter solstice point in the early 80s: in the later 80s, uranus sits there, and is likely to feature them in a new light.

The Fire Festivals.
It takes time for energy to filter through into nature and actuality. This is where the *cross-quarters* come in: these are the midpoints between the quarter-points and mark the times when nature and form respond concretely to the energy-changes which came into motion at the quarters. The zodiac is measured in terms of 360°, and the quarter points are 90° from each other, while the cross-quarters are 45° from the quarters, and sun moves at more or less 1° per day. The ancients, at least in Europe, where seasonal changes of light and dark matter a lot, used these cross-quarters as festivals to celebrate and participate in the power of nature and her expressions. They tended to use consciousness rather than technology by which to interact with their world.

Calendrical quirks have shifted these festivals away from their original astrologically-auspicious times (just as Yule or Christmas has been shifted to three days after winter solstice), which are the times when sun reaches 15° of one of the four so-called *fixed* signs (which I prefer to call *fixing* signs). The astrologically true quarter points thus take place around 2nd-7th May, August, November and February. However, the ancients were not as calendrically-fixated as we, and they often used to shift the festivals around a little to coincide with a new or full moon, or any other astrological *power-point in time* which was around at each particular festival. In fact, the ancient Celts used both solar and lunar calendars, in parallel: these calendars would go through a cycle of relationship with one another, which lasted 18-19 years, a so-called 'metonic cycle', at the cruxpoints of which would be special festivals of longterm significance.

Outwardly, there are visible seasonal changes at the four cross-quarters, and inwardly there is a quality of realism to life, a feeling of breakthrough in relation to the theme being explored underlyingly in each season.

It is important to get the distinction between the quarters and the cross-quarters. The quarters represent change-points in energy-potential, both inwardly and in terms of light in the physical world. The cross-quarters represent change-points in manifest energy, inwardly and in terms of visible seasonal changes: the peaks of the four seasons show themselves at the cross-quarters. Thus, although the light starts increasing at winter solstice, this change is noticeable only at the following cross-quarter, Candlemas in February, and although spring starts at the equinox, it manifests itself fully, in flowers and throbbing growth, at Beltane, the May cross-quarter. And so on.

The cross-quarters used to be known as the Witches' Sabbaths, times when the inner intents of consciousness-workers such as witches (the word derives from the same source as the word *wisdom*) became reality, times when such a person needed to allow things to come to pass, or to facilitate the manifestation of what is inevitable. The times for fixing our intent are the solstices, and those for adjusting or reaffirming intent are the equinoxes. At the cross-quarters, it was necessary to enhance the developing energy in the yearly cycle, to make the steps forward into actualisation of intent which previously were on the level of potential.

Conscious energy-working is a process of bringing things from the dream-level into the reality level, and of uniting with the flow of natural energy in the world in order to enhance it and be supported by it. In ancient times, people would gather together at times like these, in order to meet each other, celebrate and focus their awareness collectively, in order to keep the human family working in tune with the times. People are starting to do this again now — not for the romantic purpose of emulating the ancients, but because they sense that this is auspicious and necessary, even if the reasons for doing so might not be intellectually clear.

Tuning into these eight points of the year we can move into harmony with the whole integral cycle of the annual solar cycle. We are entering into active involvement with life-force and its cyclical modulations. And thereby our lives are enriched. Try it. It sheds new light on the four seasons, as well, especially on the underlying effect the seasons have on us as a worldly learning process: the seasons take place not only out there in our world, but also in here in the psyche of us all, regardless of whether we are open or shut to it.

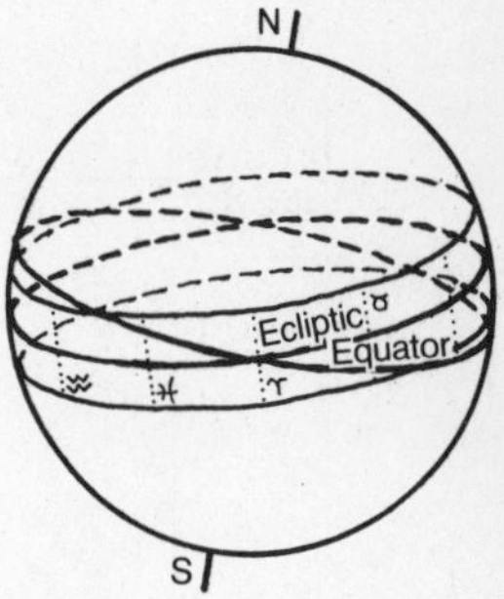

The ecliptic and the celestial equator cross at the equinox points

The Four Seasons.

In the climes where most people live, we have four distinct *seasons* — people like the Lapps had eight — and each of these has its hidden flavour. Living as we do in heated and lit buildings and towns, we tend to think we behave more or less the same in any season, but we do not — it is just that we don't notice it, for our consciousness habitually goes not very deep. We could start anywhere in the annual cycle, and since these words are being written at autumn equinox (1985), we can start there.

★ **Autumntime.** At autumn equinox, an awareness of the relationship between self and other becomes important: summer has ended, and nature is beginning to batten down. Increasing darkness and cold, not yet serious, but making its presence felt, is impinging on nature and people, making them aware that they are part of a larger wholeness, which at this point is asserting its primacy: individual entities must respond and adapt. This in-principle realisation of the need to explore our relationship with whatever is around us is actualised at the cross-quarter (in Britain, called Hallowe'en or *Samhain*, the time when sun is at 15° ♏), around 5th-7th November, when the dark and cold is definitely a fact: leaves fall off the trees, migrating birds have gone, frosts come, and animals go into hibernation. The implications of our interrelatedness and co-involvement become actual and very real, while at equinox they were unexplored, but a possibility to be tried out.

At this time, humans must accept, regardless of our wishes, that winter is approaching, and we must face up to the fact that together we stand, divided we fall, and that the freedom and bounty of summer is gone. This is facing-facts time, and out of the loss of ease and individuality arises a reborn selfhood, rooted in belonging to a family, to society, to tradition and social mores. Dark and cold is definitely a fact: leaves fall off the trees, migrating birds have gone, frosts come, and living things go quiet. The implications of our interrelatedness and co-involvement become actual and very real, while at equinox they were unexplored, but a possibility to be tried out.

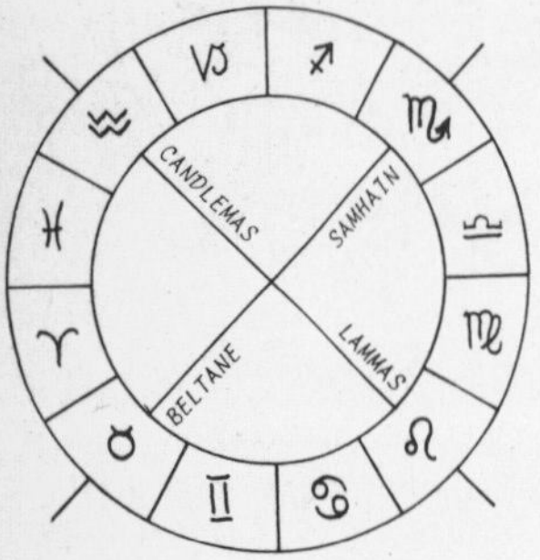

The cross-quarters or fire festivals: gateways to manifestation and seasonal change

The ancients held a fire ceremony at Samhain to recognise that while the solar light is dying, the light within is reborn: this is a time of death of the old, yet within it is the *eventual* promise of rebirth of the new. It is a time of forced adjustment (like death, something we cannot choose, but must accept when it comes), which, once accepted, reveals a new set of possibilities, a new power in life, the power to survive and make something good by being a part of something larger.

From Samhain to the winter solstice, we explore this new reality, starting with its hard facts and ending with a celebration of our social nature: Yule. The heart-warming advantages of early winter, with crisp air and the first snows and warm fires to come home to show themselves just before winter solstice.

★ **Winter.** To deal with winter, we must consolidate and come together. This is done at winter solstice, at which time darkness is maximal, an established fact, and no longer increasing. It is a time for celebration, for, together, we have made it through some difficulties of adjustment to each other, and find ourselves still here, together, as a unity of relatives of blood or soul. The fruits of the past season are shared and eaten, even to excess, after a solsticial pause for awareness or prayer, for the seeds of the coming year are laid here — even though it is dark, the light is from now going to grow.

Winter is here, and to survive it we must carry through our routines, social agreements and obligations, sensibly, to ground and solidify our beingness, to consolidate ourselves after the activity of the summer. Summer gives meaning to winter, and vice versa. And while autumn was a time of *becoming*, winter is a time for *being*, for working with what *is* and living in it, benefiting from what it can offer in the knowing that it is unavoidable.

After 45 days, however, it becomes evident that the light is growing, and a twinge of restlessness is in the air: it is still cold, but a change in the light is becoming apparent. This is the winter cross-quarter, (called Candlemas, or Imbolc), when the sun is at 15♒, by which time winter has been around long enough for us to start looking forward again to something else. Our beingness and acceptance of winter realities are giving way to an urge to become something else, to change things, to move toward the springtime mode. Yet the winter quarter is not yet over, and forces us to accept that we cannot simply have our way, and that in fact the coming change is so great that we must be held in arrested progress in order for us to move into it on the right footing. So the back end of winter, up to equinox, is spent fulfilling our obligations to the social contract, accepting that everything has its time, and that completion must come before new avenues can open up. A time of reality-adjustments, starting at Candlemas and reaching a peak just before spring equinox.

★ **Springtime.** Up to spring equinox, we have to accept the restraints and continued obligations which winter and our relatedness to everyone else place on us, and find out the true, deep reasons why we need to progress along our *own* path: we need to do so because social change comes from individual impulse, and because social institutions suffer inertia by their very structuring. At equinox, however, life-force suddenly rises, the cork pops, and seeds germinate and grow above ground, fertilised by the water released in the thaw: likewise, we feel empowered to strike out on our own, to take risks, drop our self-restraints, and simply get on with it, motivated by an urge to *make things happen.*

This assertive push takes on momentum over the ensuing weeks, but it is not until the spring cross-quarter (Mayday, or Beltane), that things really move: flowers bloom, birds sing and nature is alive with bounteous fertility. In ancient days this was another fire festival, when folk celebrated the upwelling of life-force in full flower: the sap rises, and people have the urge to play and frolic. This was also a festival marking the distinction between male and female, the separateness which in joining perpetuates the race and creates the greatest pleasure: heaven warms and earth blooms. From Beltane (5-8 May, 15 ♉) until summer solstice, everything is pellmell and in action, and every individual species, every person, is going for it, growing into their full

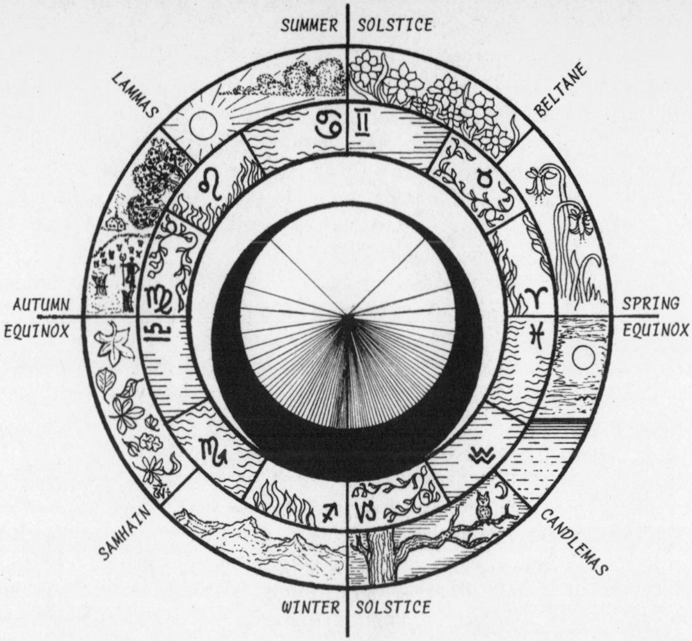

potential, unrestrained, free to grow in ideal conditions where there is space for everyone. Yet this seeming separation of once-united people has its twinge of pain too, but there is no time to care, there's too much to do! And everyone is determined to do it. On the approach to summer solstice, the lightest time, everything goes bananas.

★ **Summer.** Rampant growth, self-expression and progress make for a cacophony which can be a bit too much: at summer solstice, within the factuality of light and warmth lies the hint of a reversal. While everyone may pause for celebration of life in the gap between spring and harvest, stay up all night and flirt with pleasure and variety, an urge sets in to settle into some kind of coherence: if every plant and every human is to realise its full potential and fruit, some focused effort is needed. The hay needs making while the sun shines.

The heat grows as the summer cross-quarter approaches (Lammas or Lugnasadh, at 15♌), and nature ripens, the young grow, and each individual person explores the maximum possibilities inherent in her or his reach, almost selfishly. Green moves to gold, and summer becomes a normal reality. Summer, like winter, is a time of *beingness*, of living in a state which has already been established: it's all about each of us doing our own thing. But we individuals collide and interfere with each other in our apparent freedom, and underneath all this, at Lammas, lies a hidden concern that perhaps it has all gone too far — yet also, we must exhaust our need for individuality before we can do anything else.

After Lammas and before autumn equinox comes the harvest, when the results of all this growth must be dealt with: we must bear in mind the future and the hard times which will come unless we lay in while we can what we need for winter. Individualism is a fact, yet there creeps up a weariness, a sense of being stuck in ourselves, and a growing desire to find out how others have it, to explore relationship and the benefits of cooperation. Late summer becomes lank and less lively, and the urge for change is brewing. Much has happened, and a pause to assimilate it all (not dissimilar to the reality-adjustment just before spring equinox) takes place just before autumn equinox, before the change starts in actuality. This change breaks out at autumn equinox, where the potential in relationship is seen: the sacrifices inherent in it are not yet looked at, but the motion is there, and in time, by Hallowe'en, the full implications of membership in the social whole surface, and a transformation comes.

Transformations

Transformation takes on two faces: death at Hallowe'en (in Britain, Guy Fawkes' night is a remnant of the fire festival) and growth at Beltane. Existence or beingness takes on two faces too: consolidation at Candlemas and creative self-expression at Lammas. The solstices and equinoxes thus mark points in time when energy enters the world, and the cross-quarters mark points where it becomes fulfilled, a reality. Candlemas is a time for gently cultivating light and energy, a transition toward becomingness and an invocation of the life-force, a rebirth of its potency. Beltane is a time for bringing forth life, and finally breaking free of the shadows of winter, in order to go forward in a fulsome burst of growth, extension, variation and expansion. Lammas is a time of climax, the peak of growth and the first sign of death, the time for ripening, collecting and harvesting, and Samhain is a time of indrawing, uncovering the inner secrets of the life-cycle in the absence of its outer forms. Fires were lit to represent life-force and its capacity to transform and enliven, yet at each cross-quarter, the fire represented a different aspect of life-force. Thus the symbolism of the year was played out in a natural religious form.

Increasing numbers of people who are now seeking to return to the roots of religion are finding a pull of memory to mark the quarters and cross-quarters in some ceremonial or conscious way: it is as if Mother Earth is calling back her children, after their long sojourn into the starry, earth-transcending heavenly spiritual paths, which, through history, while bringing worthy teachings and enlightenment on many fronts, have also brought with them war and ignorance, an ungrounded myopia wherein spirit has separated from earthly life.

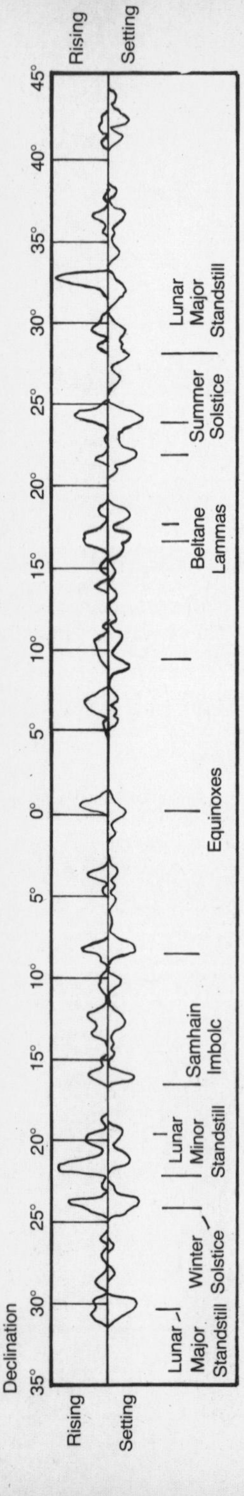

Try it for yourself: at one of these power-points in time, visit a special place, an ancient site, or a hilltop or woody glade, and lend your spirit to the time, and see what happens: you will find an empowerment, a peaceful strengthening, which awakens new life and adds new vision.

Stone circles and ancient sites in Britain and elsewhere show that the ancients set great store by this eightfold subdivision of the tides of the year: they did this because participation in manifest form was a vital process to them. Alignments at ancient remains in Britain also point to a sixteenfold subdivision of the annual cycle, measured by alignments to rising and setting points of the sun at the various times of year.

The twelvefold subdivision now used in astrology arose when cultures developed materially to the level where people became interested in the *psychology* of living, in the underlying images of energy which they experienced when they had made some separation between themselves and their environment. They had the time and insight to look at deeper, less manifest forces at work behind creation. Twelvefold zodiacs are the work of materially-civilised people: hence the zodiac in use today is traced back to the Chaldeans of the Tigris valley, who evolved the seeds of our culture which were passed to us through Greeks and Romans.

Yet the twelve signs are rooted in the four quarter points, just like the eightfold system: the solstices mark the beginnings of the zodiac signs ♑ and ♋, and the equinoxes mark the beginnings of the signs ♈ and ♎. The eightfold and the twelvefold bevel into one another, and from the viewpoint of living with the flow of time, it pays us to notice both. The exact times of the quarters and cross-quarters can be culled from your ephemeris. And one day, you will be able to tell when these times are without it!

Moving into an inwardly sounder flow of harmony with the time-energy in the annual cycle has several effects. It allows us to live our lives more effectively, not only from the standpoint of getting things done, but also from the standpoint of awakening within ourselves. It's not so much to do with nature-worship — although in our time, a spiritual connection with nature and its changes can be enlightening and necessary — as to do with living in accord with all levels of our being. We cannot simply impose our will upon our bodies, on life or the world, for the results land up being disastrous — illness, confusion, things going 'wrong', meaninglessness and fundamental insecurity. The new life which

Regularity of incidences of stone alignments to the rising and setting points of sun and moon, found by Professor Thom amongst 300 ancients sites in Scotland we are seeking (or being forced by inevitable historical forces of our own making) to evolve has to do with rapport between what we want and what we've got, between intention and the subtle small things of life, the yang and the yin. Moving into conscious participation with natural time-cycles has implications which are immense. And the beginning place is awareness. Now.

4 The zodiac cycle

Within the cycle of the year lies a cycle of prototype images which have a dynamic effect on us all. Clueing in on the zodiac gives us a chance to perceive the inner archetypes at work behind all life and form, giving us a subtle basis of timing out of which to work our way through the labyrinth of life. There's another dimension too: by seeing clearly the energy-weather we live in, we can see and be beyond it, increasingly centred in the timeless. The timeless is found through acknowledging our living in time, for there is no escape from the wheel until we can love it. The root-archetypes in that wheel are the signs of the zodiac.

There's a season for everything

Evolution (individualisation) and *integration* (wholisation or socialisation): these are two main undercurrents behind the zodiacal year. From solstice to solstice we enter into a journey of progression from one state to another. Neither individualism — the prevailing life-experience of summer, between the equinoxes — nor wholism/socialism — on the winter side of the equinoxes — is the ultimate experience, for both exist in relation to the other, and the story of life is involved with exploring the paradox which both create. We need to *belong*, to be involved in something larger than ourselves, and we need to follow our *own* course, yet we also need to learn from the outcomes of both, for we incarnated on this planetary school to experience paradox and extremes, in order to learn how to find a middle way, which leads beyond.

Within everything lies its opposite: beyond the yang and the yin lies the essence, the source of the flow. If we have had a fullsome summer, we can enjoy winter as a contrast, and we need summer in order to loosen out from the gruelling side of winter. Spring implies autumn, and autumn is a prerequisite for spring. We appreciate things when they are not there, and tend to behave as if a transient state were always the case when it is here. We tend not to see things in terms of the part they play in the totality. A fundamental illusion astrology has laboured under for too long is that some signs are better than others: in this lies an ignoring of the contribution each sign plays in the whole.

In *winter* we learn commitment, focusing, involvement and how to fulfil the roles we have wittingly or unwittingly cut out for ourselves. In *spring* we need to learn how to take life in our own hands, follow our aspirations, develop ourselves, move forward (if necessary alone) and open up new variants in ourselves. In *summer* we learn how to live out our selfhood to the maximum, regulate our own energy, create, and become aware of our own personal contribution to life. And in *autumn*, we need to become aware of our place in the world, our need for interrelationship and togetherness, face up to what is wanted of us, become involved, carve out our role through trading off energy, and face facts which we might have previously overlooked.

Backward and forward, round and round: when looking back over the years, we no longer see this oscillation, but we do see the net motion in the year as a whole: shorter-term consciousness is like a bug sitting on the rim of a wheel, while longer-term consciousness is like a watching eye at the hub. Interlacing the beingness-in-the-state-we-are-in at summer and winter with the becoming-something-other-than-what-we-already-are at spring and autumn, we create our existence. Within the shorter-term perspective of one year, this movement of consciousness is very meaningful, although, seen over a period of years it is insignificant, but steps in the context of a larger cycle embracing many years.

Modes

Each season contains three signs. The first in each, starting at either a solstice or equinox point, is a *cardinal* or initiating sign: in these we are getting into the new mode of being of that season, investing energy, establishing new modes of being or moving, seeking to make things happen. The second sign in each season, with a cross-quarter point in the middle of it, is a *fixing* (or fixed or carrying-through) sign: in these we make the meaning of the season work, and do what is already set up to do, making things actually happen and going through the experience of engagement with whatever reality is presenting itself to us at the time. The third sign is a *mutable* or assimilating sign, ending at a solstice or equinox point: in these we complete, digest and make sense of what is done, before the next step comes, laying the groundwork for the next

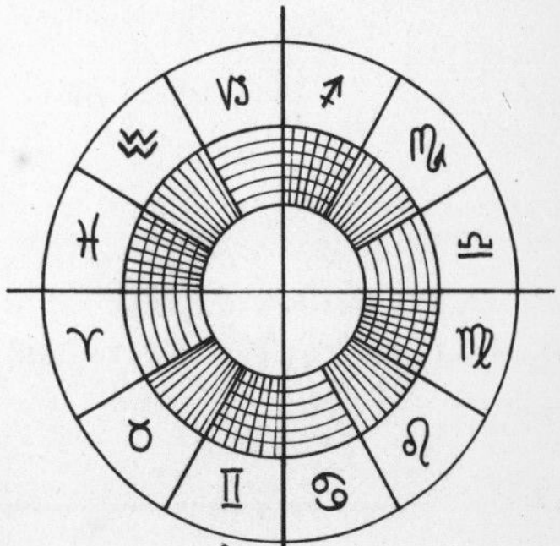

development. These are called the three *modes*, and signs opposite and at right-angles to each other are always of the same mode.

Since the zodiac is a whole cycle, it has no start or ending, despite what traditional astrology says about ♈ being the first sign (a somewhat male chauvinistic notion, ideologically justifying the dominion of individualism) and ♓ being regarded as the last sign. Since in a book we have to string out ideas along a line, though, we have to start somewhere, and in order to give credit to the sign ♓, which has always landed up being the last and probably least understood sign, we shall start this time with ♑. Since life-force has died back at winter-solstice, lying hidden under the ground and within our beings, there is some reason for looking at the cycle this way, as long as we don't get stuck in this (or any) way of thinking.

The zodiac signs

Winter. Winter is a solidifying, form-oriented season, started off by the sign *capricorn.* ♑ faces us with the fact that we have set up a situation (since summer) which we must accept and work with, perseveringly and systematically. We must carry out our *role*, fulfil our niche in the human family. Winter solstice or Yule (now Christmas) is a time for family reunion and the following of tradition as a socially stabilising factor. Things are as they are, regardless of what individuals might want, and if we cannot accept this, then we risk being left out in the cold: the approval or disapproval of others, and our responsibility in the fulfilment of what is expected of us dictate this. We're all in the same boat, and sink or swim together. Social forms give continuity and resilience to collective life, so we might as well get on with it, for in these, we find protection while the light is low. ♑ is the soil in which the seed of the individual plant lies dormant, waiting.

Aquarius, however, has a tinge of boredom with things as they are, and wants to see things differently. There is a spark of promise in the air, for the light is increasing: yet it is too early, and winter is still here. While our eyes are looking afar, our feet haven't moved. ♒ seeks to change convention with ideas of a new social contract, of future possibilities. A restlessness grows: ♒ seeks to encourage everyone to do their own thing, together, for then it can do its own thing too. A heady time, where collective values can override individual ones, aquarius is a time for concerted action, aimed toward an ideal goal. But it does have some difficulty accepting the isnesses of life: they *ought* to be different!

New possibilities need to await the right time, though: this is what *pisces* says. Social mores and agreements restrict individual movement, and ♓ teaches us to see that there is more at stake than meets the eye. The bottom drops out of what is known and agreed, fixed, and the void gulps our illusions. Deeper preparation is needed: the thaw is here, but spring is not, yet. We must prepare our ground through soul-searching, listening to greater and subtler things, learning patiently to await our time, when the universe will allow and support our endeavours. A selfless atmosphere prevails, in which we are obliged to accept ourselves as little atoms in a great universe. New vision arises, and an understanding of the fundamental dynamics behind life and its living dawns, for ♓ is a sign of *power*, root-power, hidden power — it is a revelation of the true nature of the mystery of life, if we have the strength to look and see. Calm equanimity, applied timelessness and the quelling of restless urges are what ♓ teaches. Otherwise the alternative is frustration and confusion, helplessness generated through incapacity to see the underlying meaning of things.

Spring. Then comes spring equinox, and suddenly the sun is out, and seeds are sprouting: the power of creation is unleashed, sometimes with a bang, sometimes creeping up from behind. We throw off inertia, shrug our shoulders and stop waiting for everyone else and compromising ourselves to the rules and expectations winter brought. Doubt and hesitation are now out of time, and it is now right to head for what we want. If in ♓ we have not uncovered a vision, life propels us forward anyway, and we are ripped away from our comfortable past. *Aries* is an energy sign, rampant and spilling out: forethought and caution are restrictive, while self-determining action and forward progress are auspicious. This is it: we just have to do it, or we'll get left behind, for everything is growing, pushing out above ground, and new things are being born. Evolutionary energy is breaking loose.

The decisions are made, and it all has started up: now *taurus* must carry it through on a thunderous momentum of growth, fertility and development. Flowers are out, nature is seething and humming, the past is gone, and breakthrough is here. It's wonderful, delicious, and this is even more *it* than ♈ thought. This is living, doing, moving, the very purpose of life, and nothing will stop it. Everything has now to move on, for it is too late to change course or back down. Enjoy it while the going is good: follow your own path, make that step, for we are now on our own, and the tide is flowing fast. Get out of my way before I run you over! Purposeful, sustained and dogged motion are what ♉ teaches us. And enjoying the good things of life, the fun and cream buns.

Singleminded action is all very well, says *gemini*, but look at what you're missing! There's a world of variety, fun, colour, alternatives, experiences and ten thousand things to play around with. I can go anywhere and do anything, try things out, and act out every possibility that comes up in the moment, like a bee in a kaleidoscope of flowers. Anyone who tries to call me out and obstruct me is just a square. Why get stuck in serious responsibilities? ♊ maximises on stimulation, new situations, babble, flutter and buzz, and everything is wonderful. Sure, it's complex, but who cares? ♊ drops all the heaviness and purposefulness of preceding signs, and takes on the world. Yet often, in this sign, the extent of choice, and the duality and division which life presents can be a hurdle only the clear-thinking can cross. Nevertheless, summer solstice is a celebration of being alive, so let's have fun! Evolutionary motion has reached its peak.

Summer. Hold on, says *cancer*, this is all a bit too much: so much is happening, I can't deal with it. Amidst all this panegyration, I must find a safe space from which to operate, for infinite variegation cannot go on forever, and I might be caught unawares, without anything to hold on to. This creation business has to *lead* somewhere, and I must nurture what is most valuable and cut out the rest. Things stabilise out and mature in ♋, for now summer is an established fact, and won't last indefinitely. And besides, all this action is trampling on my personal sensitivities, and my own interests are at stake. ♋ teaches us to cherish what is most valuable, and to look after ourselves and our interests, in the midst of all the summery goings-on.

And *leo* teaches us to express it, bring the growth process to fruition, act out our own personal truths and be ourselves, fully, even to the extent of imposing it on others. We must make something of these ideal conditions, and I know what the best thing is to do: follow me, everyone, for this is our moment. ♌ acts out the play of life, dances the dance for all to see, believes in itself, and does it, really does it. Welcome to my party, everyone! Underneath, though, there is a concern as to whether everyone else actually wants to come, or is taking any notice — ♌ is beginning to become aware that I myself need others to validate me. While the sun is high and the summer is hot, there is no time to worry: I'm just doing my own thing, and that's what's right for me. Evolutionary tendencies have reached their peak of expression — yet meanwhile, integrative tendencies are setting in, just as evolutionary ones were doing in ♒, the opposite sign to ♌.

Then *virgo* picks up the pieces, and does the

washing up when everyone has drunk their fill or even vomited up the results. ♍, in late summer, is aware that forethought, caring, meticulousness and consideration matter if anything is to be practically achieved. The harvest must be brought in, stored and processed. I myself have little significance if I cannot make a contribution which is valued by others. ♍ is tired of being itself, and seeks a role. To be valued, I should do the sort of things others omit to do, for the purpose of my life is to serve the whole. It's all very practical and thought-out, carefully dealing with the consequences of past actions, and making something out of them for the future, for posterity.

Autumn. Everything's alright, really, answers libra — why don't we become friends? A lot can be done if we work together, and I'm sure we can smooth out our differences — it's not all that bad. I don't mind what we do: what would you like? It's nice to share our lives, and we can work it out, for something more than both our added energies comes out of our coming together. Life is tough, but we can make it *good*, make things look as if everything's really alright. ♎ seeks to fit in and adjust to others and the world. But the anachronism is that there is far more than meets the eye to relating: self and other can clash if one of them takes the upper hand. Through experience of imbalance and extremity, ♎ seeks to find a comfortable compromise, yet can rarely itself define what that is — the views of others must be given an ear before I can formulate my own position. Which of course is flexible, depending on how things go. Integrative forces are setting in.

Libra doesn't want to look at many of the more uncomfortable truths about life, even deliberately avoiding them, but *scorpio* feels it deep down. Ouch! The world is killing me, and I hate it — but I should grin and bear it if I'm going to survive. In ♏ the social contract is forged, for you are me and I am you and we are all together, whether we like it or not. This is the crunch with reality, and it brings up a lot of naked crunches. Darkness and cold abound, and I have only myself to rely on, so I must grit my teeth and engage with life, at whatever cost, and with great resolve, for there is no alternative, and the wheels are already in motion. I must take it on myself to face this (often horrendous) reality. There's a beauty in it though, underneath, a hidden truth which gives access to the working dynamics of life. For in the end, we're all in this cess-pit of life together. Even the rawest realisms have their compensations, and the more engaged we are in confronting them, the more we'll uncover those payoffs. Let's go through it, and see if we can get to the other side.

What! *Sagittarius* loves life and the possibilities it reveals. The world is gratifying and enriching, and you shouldn't be got down by a few hard times. They pass. Let's celebrate and make the best of it, eat, drink and be merry, for it's not all that bad. Crisp air, evening fire, new routines to develop: hey everyone, let's get on with it and see things another way! There are lots and lots of things to do, ideas to share, people to meet, places to go. If I give to you, you can give to someone else, and it'll return to me in the fullness of time — and we'll all benefit together! Your wellbeing is mine, and mine yours, so what's stopping us? ♐ explores the bounty in social life and the great wide world: why get locked up in ourselves when there is all this to enjoy? The sagittarian feast peaks at winter solstice, and from the dawn of time people have come together to find out what's been going on with everyone else. The work of the year is over, and we now have time to rest and find benefit. Energy is reintegrated or socialised at winter solstice — and the full expression of this comes through ♒, just at the time when evolutionary forces are again picking up.

One cycle ends, another begins

Not quite, says ♑: we actually need to settle down and be practical. Yes, but let's not get bogged down, says ♒, let's change things around. Not so fast, says ♓, it's not quite a simple as you think. Yes, it is, says ♈: it's just a matter of doing it. And really carrying it through, says ♉. And trying out all the alternatives, says ♊. No, it's all too much says ♋, I'm staying where I am. What you lot need, says ♌, is a good dose of my magic recipe for the elixir of life. Perhaps, says ♍, but look what we land up with: we're all overlooking the small things of life, which really matter. Why is everyone arguing, says ♎, when we could be having a nice time together? No one sees how raucous and superficial they are, says ♏: they're all avoiding the brass tacks of the situation. Rubbish, says ♐, there's plenty of space for everyone and plenty to enjoy. And the funny thing is that everyone is right and everyone is wrong.

Hangups!

♑ can get stuck in mindless drudgery, ♒ in rebelliousness and refusal to face facts, ♓ in confused, powerless resignation, ♈ in desire to control things and be on top, ♉ in self-indulgence and doggedness, ♊ in hyperactivity and dilettantism, ♋ in self-preoccupation and defensiveness, ♌ in expecting everything to go its own way, ♍ in nitpicking puritanism and overconcern, ♎ in evasion of real issues and indecision, ♏ in resistance and resentment, and ♐ in running away and over-indulgence. It all depends on how we use our opportunities !

Just watching

There are many ways of experiencing the different signs throughout the year, and year to year you will find your responses to them change. These words are useful stimuli and pointers, but they cannot substitute your own experience: we could write long tomes on the art of bike-riding, but in the end when you are on a bike and riding, the ability to ride it comes from a wordless place within you. A direct feel for time and its modulations through the signs is what is needed if we are to live in accord with it, use it and let it channel through us to make our lives happier and more fruitful. Let the cycle of the signs percolate into you over time!

It is interesting to watch the energy-change when ☉ moves from one sign to another (an *ingress*). This can happen somewhere between 19th and 23rd of each month, and the exact time can be found in an ephemeris. At the end of a sign, things get a bit stuck in the mode of that sign, and when a new sign comes, a new atmosphere dawns quite markedly. Things then settle into a rhythm, such that in the middle of a sign it can feel as if that atmosphere were always the case. Yet in mid-sign, its message is coming through strongly, becoming habitual, even excessive or running in a groove as the end of the sign approaches. Then the atmosphere or energy-weather lifts and changes again, and the cycle moves on. It's all a question of underlying atmospheres.

The cardinal signs tend to be at their strongest at their beginnings, the fixed signs in the middle and the mutable signs at their end. Which brings us back to the quarter points and the cross-quarters, the ancient festivals in which things show their changes. The zodiac signs suggest underlying themes, pictures of possibility in the unfoldment of life experience, which bevel into the crux-points of demonstrated seasonal energy at the eight festivals.

We could go through the signs again and again, revealing different facets of their nature. The wonderful thing about them is that they truly cannot be contained in simple definitions, and every time we try to do so, they reveal a new quirk which hadn't been specified earlier. In this way, getting to speak the language of astrology has a fundamentally transformative effect on our way of seeing things. Symbolism in astrology presents us with onion-layers to peel off as we grow and progress: new meaning in astrology ceases to reveal itself only if we stop truly living!

Take a year to observe the ins and outs of the zodiac signs. Observing the moon passing through the signs gives a clue — a much faster motion — to the undertones and strands of the signs, but they are best comprehended by following the motion of the sun. The other planets move through the signs each at their own rate, and give backup to these observations. For it is a living *feel* for the signs which really makes the difference between head-knowledge, however profound, and a gut-level knowing of what to do about things when faced with real life situations and the predicamentality of living in them.

5 Using an Ephemeris

An ephemeris is a book of tables which show the positions of the sun, moon and planets, usually for each day, at a stated time. It is the main tool of the modern astrologer. If you are getting involved with astrology you need to get hold of at least one ephemeris, and below we are going to look at two of the most useful ephemerides, so that you can read and use them. Ephemerides are cosmic timetables for a continually-fluxing train of energy-weather.

The term *ephemeris* comes from ancient Greek, and means 'book of days' or 'book of changes'. It is the major sourcebook for the astrologer, because it helps us keep a watch on planetary movements and antics over time. Here we are going to look at two widely-available ephemerides: *Raphael's Ephemeris,* useful for its portability and detail, and the *American Ephemeris,* commendable for its accuracy, good value, details and the length of period it covers, a century.

It is important to get hold of at least one of these ephemerides as soon as possible, and eventually to get both. Without them you would be unable to do your own research or apply the ideas given in this book. Raphael's Ephemeris is published once a year to cover the coming year, is light, small and easily carried in a bag for everyday reference, when you are sitting in the bus or twiddling your toes. It costs little, and holds a lot of data. But when you get along to looking at longer-term planetary motions, and calculating charts, you need tables to cover all people alive today, which the American Ephemeris fulfils well, at a reasonable price for what you get (£12.95 in England in 1985): this book covers the century, and caters for all but the most senior citizens.

An aside about other ephemerides. If you happen to have available another ephemeris and want to use that, some are good and some not so good. Accurate and workable ones available are the Concise or the

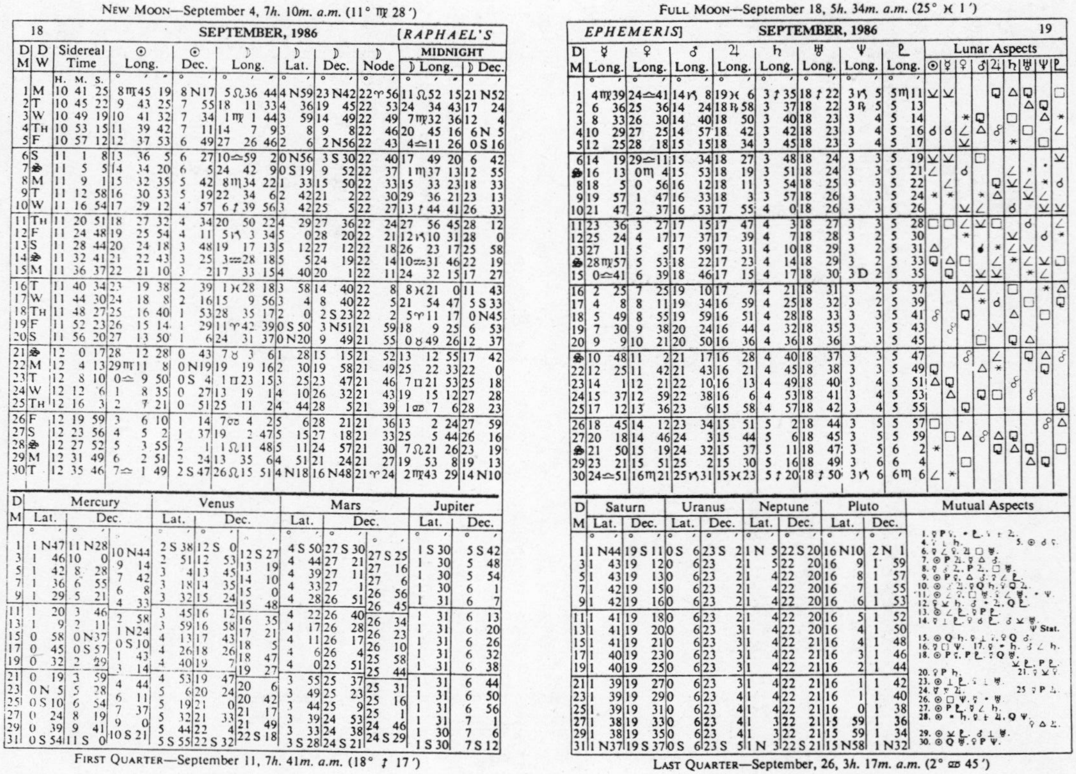

New Moon—September 4, 7*h.* 10*m. a.m.* (11° ♍ 28′)

Full Moon—September 18, 5*h.* 34*m. a.m.* (25° ♓ 1′)

18 SEPTEMBER, 1986 [RAPHAEL'S EPHEMERIS] SEPTEMBER, 1986 19

First Quarter—September 11, 7*h.* 41*m. a.m.* (18° ♐ 17′)

Last Quarter—September, 26, 3*h.* 17*m. a.m.* (2° ♒ 45′)

A page of *Raphael's Ephemeris.* Check the planetary positions on 11th September (Chiron was at 20 ♊, not shown in Raphael) to see what a grand cross looks like in an ephemeris. The lower part of the page is of little use to most astrologers. *Mutual aspects* gives basic information which then can be checked in the *Complete Aspectarian.* Note major moonphases, times and positions, at the top and bottom of the page

SEPTEMBER

Day	Aspect	Hour	Min	
1	☿ P ♀	0am	47	
M	☽ ⚼ ♅	7	40	b
	☽ △ ♄	8	4	G
	☽ ⚼ ♃	9	6	b
	☽ ⚺ ☿	9	47	g
	☽ □ ♇	11	10	B
	☽ P ♅	4pm	35	B
	☽ ⚺ ☉	6	33	g
	☿ ✱ ♇	6	41	
	☽ P ♆	9	7	D
	♀ ± ♃	9	34	
2	☽ ⚼ ♆	11a	47	b
Tu	☽ △ ♅	0pm	20	G
	☽ P ♄	2	59	B
3	☽ ✱ ♀	2am	58	G
W	☽ ⚼ ♂	9	26	b
	☽ △ ♆	3pm	47	G
	☽ □ ♄	4	53	B
	☽ ✱ ♇	7	47	G
	☽ P ♀	7	53	G
4	☽ ☌ ☿	4am	15	G
Th	☽ ☌ ☉	7	10	D
	☽ ∠ ♀	8	40	b
	☽ P ☿	11	31	G
	☽ △ ♂	1pm	33	G
	☽ □ ♅	7	44	B
	☽ P ☉	8	12	G
	☽ ☍ ♃	8	14	B
	♀ ⊥ ♄	8	19	
	☽ ∠ ♇	11	8	b
5	☽ P ♃	0am	47	G
F	☽ ⚺ ♀	1pm	38	g
	☽ P ♇	3	43	D
	☉ ☌ ☿	5	32	
	☽ □ ♆	10	0	B
	☽ ✱ ♄	11	16	G
6	☽ ⚺ ♇	1am	59	g
S	☽ P ♇	6	14	D
	☿ ∠ ♀	8	52	
	☽ ⚺ ☉	4pm	57	g
	☽ ⚺ ☿	6	49	g
	♃ □ ♅	7	56	
	☽ □ ♂	8	14	B
	☽ P ♃	9	16	G
	☽ P ☉	10	26	G
7	☽ ✱ ♅	1am	1	G
Su	☽ ∠ ♄	1	45	b
	☽ P ☿	2	2	G
	☿ △ ♂	6	50	
	☉ P ♃	3pm	38	
	☽ ∠ ☉	9	5	b
	☽ ☌ ♀	9	56	G
8	☽ ∠ ☿	1am	4	b
M	☽ ✱ ♆	2	28	G
	☽ ⚼ ♃	2	47	b
	☽ ∠ ♅	3	6	b
	☽ ⚺ ♄	3	54	g
	☽ ☌ ♇	6	28	D
	☽ P ♀	8	13	G
	☿ ☍ ♃	1pm	6	
	☿ P ♃	2	1	
	☿ □ ♅	4	15	
9	☽ ✱ ☉	0am	52	G
Tu	☽ ✱ ♂	1	26	G
	☽ P ♄	3	21	B
	☽ ∠ ♆	4	16	b
	☽ △ ♃	4	20	G
	☽ ⚺ ♅	4	55	g
	☽ ✱ ☿	6	50	G
	☉ △ ♂	1pm	3	
	☉ P ☿	1	17	
	☿ ∠ ♇	6	5	
	☽ P ♆	6	56	D
	☽ P ♅	10	55	B
10	☽ ∠ ♂	3am	41	b
W	☽ ⚺ ♀	4	42	g
	☽ ⚺ ♆	5	51	g
	☽ ☌ ♄	7	27	B
	☽ ⚺ ♇	9	54	g
	☿ Q ♄	2pm	59	
	♀ ⚼ ♃	7	9	
	☉ ☍ ♃	9	16	
11	♀ ✱ ♆	0am	2	
Th	☽ P ♂	1	28	B
	☽ ⚺ ♂	5	46	g
	☽ □ ♃	6	53	B
	☽ □ ☉	7	41	B
	☽ ∠ ♀	7	43	b
	☽ ☌ ♅	7	57	B
	☽ ∠ ♇	11	22	b
	☉ ∠ ♀	11	30	
	☉ □ ♅	11	45	
	♀ ∠ ♅	11	48	
	☽ □ ☿	5pm	21	B
12	♂ Q ♇	3am	41	
F	♀ ⚺ ♄	6	49	
	☽ ☌ ♆	8	36	D
	☽ ⚺ ♄	10	24	g
	☽ ✱ ♀	10	36	G
	☽ ✱ ♇	0pm	44	G
	♂ ✱ ♃	1	43	
13	☽ ✱ ♃	9am	2	G
S	☽ ☌ ♂	9	45	B
	☽ ⚺ ♅	10	38	g
	☽ ∠ ♄	11	48	b
	☽ △ ☉	2pm	2	G
	☉ ∠ ♇	3	2	
	☽ P ♂	7	50	B
	☿ P ♇	11	0	
14	♀ ☌ ♇	1am	50	
Su	☽ △ ☿	3	15	G
	☽ ∠ ♃	10	10	b
	☽ ⚺ ♆	11	16	g
	☽ ∠ ♅	0pm	2	b
	☽ ✱ ♄	1	17	G
	☽ □ ♇	3	33	B
	☽ □ ♀	4	19	B
	☽ ⚼ ☉	5	18	b
	♆ Stat.	7	38	
	♂ ⚺ ♅	7	50	
	☽ P ♅	7	54	B
	☿ ⊥ ♇	8	30	
	☽ P ♆	11	54	D
15	☽ ⚼ ☿	8am	22	b
M	☉ Q ♄	10	17	
	☿ ⊥ ♀	11	10	
	☽ ⚺ ♃	11	29	g
	☽ ∠ ♆	0pm	50	b
	☽ ✱ ♅	1	38	G
	☽ ⚺ ♂	2	8	g
	☽ P ♄	3	10	B
	♀ Q ♂	6	36	
	☽ P ♀	10	6	G
16	☽ ✱ ♆	2pm	44	G
Tu	☽ ∠ ♂	4	49	b
	☽ □ ♄	5	2	B
	☽ △ ♇	7	14	G
	☿ □ ♆	8	42	
	☽ △ ♀	10	59	G
17	♂ ∠ ♄	1am	6	
W	☽ ☌ ♃	3pm	12	G
	☿ ✱ ♄	4	9	
	☽ □ ♅	6	0	B
	☽ ✱ ♂	8	4	G

The *Complete Aspectarian* gives exact times of aspects. Some of these aspects are minor ones, worth ignoring. Bs and Gs are worth ignoring too

Complete Planetary Ephemeris, die Deutsche Ephemeriden, Golgge or Metz, plus a new one from Para Research, but it is very *important* that you check whether they are calculated for *noon* or *midnight* GMT (for they vary), since a twelve hours difference in time causes the earth to rotate 180° on its axis, and ☽ moves 6-8°, a critical difference where a casual mistake can have big results. It doesn't matter which ephemeris you have, midnight or noon, as long as you know *which* you have, and apply the appropriate calculations when you come to them. There are also some tables available which give inaccurate figures, and these should be avoided — the Compleat Astrologer and Waite's Compendium are examples. It does not pay to have a cheap and incomplete ephemeris such as these. Most ephemerides do not give the positions for ⚷ (except the American Ephemeris which gives a reading for once a month): for ⚷ the best source is the *Chiron Ephemeris,* available on its own.

Raphael's Ephemeris

This is a small 40-page booklet, mainly occupied by double-page tables for each month, showing planetary data for NOON GMT each day. You will need to buy one each year (get someone to give it to you for Christmas!), but it's worth it, for it shows every item of interest you should need in any year. (1986 price in England £1.25).

Toward the back of the book are further tables of special use. These are:

★ 'Daily Motions of the Planets', useful in chart computations, but you can skip over it for now. It shows the motions of each of the faster planets during any 24 hour period.

★ 'Phenomena', with some useful times and data, much of which is quite advanced and specialised, but give it a look over to see what is there.

★ The 'Complete Aspectarian' is very useful, for it gives all the aspects formed between ☉, ☽ and planets in great detail, with their timings — some of the data given is of little use, for it shows greater detail than is necessary for most astrologers, and the column with Bs and Gs, signifying 'bad' and 'good' aspects is worth ignoring, for it is based on a somewhat victorian or even medieval world view in which there are many value judgements of little use in modern growth astrology.

The Complete Aspectarian needs using selectively, so that you avoid landing up in a muddled mass of detail! In this book we are emphasising the *major aspects,* and it is best to focus at first on ☌, ✱, □, △ and ☍, moving into ⚺, ⚻, ∠ and ⚼ as and when you feel good to do so. Pass over the other aspects given (such as quintiles and parallels). Many of the lunar aspects can also be passed over, because they pass so quickly, but ☌ s and ☍ s by ☽ to the planets are well worth watching.

★ 'Distances apart of all Conjunctions and Oppositions' shows the strength of these critical aspects. Each planet, except ☉, wobbles slightly north and south of the ecliptic (plane of the solar system), thus meaning that when, say, two planets conjunct in zodiacal longitude (eg. at 12 ♉ or 25 ♒), they might still be a few degrees away from one another, because one might be north and one might be south of the ecliptic. This does not invalidate a ☌ or ☍ — it merely qualifies it with a subclause on strength of the aspect, in relation to other ☌ s and ☍ s of the planets in question during other cycles over time. A largish distance apart will tend to signify a weaker ☌ or ☍ than a small one, and a deadly accurate one (such as an eclipse of ☉ or ☽, or an 'occultation' by ☽, passing over a planet) will tend to be strong and crucial.

★ 'Times when the Sun, Moon and Planets enter the Zodiac Signs' is an *ingress* table, and is very useful to watch (see chapter six).

★ Sunrise and Sunset tables can be useful, but are not used in normal astrological reckonings — they are more useful if you are spending a lot of time outdoors, and are affected by such things.

★ The Tables of Houses, using the Placidus system, are of marginal use. It is better to have a complete book of Tables of Houses. We won't be looking at chart calculation in this book, so these are of no relevance to our current purposes. Pass over them for now.

★ Proportional Logarithms are useful in chart calculation, but are of no use right now. They can shorten the calculation process, but are an optional tool.

Much can be learned through regularly leafing through Raphael! This book is particularly useful to be able to whip out when you are musing over something (as astrologers are wont to do) and need to check out what is happening astrologically.

Note that Raphael gives readings for NOON GMT. If you live elsewhere than in the GMT timezone, then you can quite easily make mental adjustments to the times given in the Ephemeris: find out how many hours difference there is between your timezone and GMT (modernly called UT, Universal Time, to take away the imperialistic undertone), then *add* that figure to the times given in Raphael if you live east of Greenwich (eg Europe, India, Australia), or *subtract* if you live west (the Americas). Ireland uses GMT, and the EEC countries are one hour ahead of GMT. If you have the clock time in your own country, and want to convert to GMT, then *add* the timezone difference if you are *west* of Greenwich, and *subtract* if you are *east*. If the date changes in the process, check that you are reading correctly from the tables — for example, if the time is 6am on 27 October in

TIME WHEN THE SUN, MOON AND PLANETS ENTER THE ZODIACAL SIGNS IN 1986

JANUARY			FEBRUARY			MARCH		
2	☽♎	*8pm45*	1	☽♏	*6am19*	2	☽♐	*2pm52*
5	☽♏	*0am44*	2	♂♐	*6am29*	3	☿♈	*7am32*
5	☿♑	*8pm42*	3	☽♐	*9am31*	4	☽♑	*5pm56*
7	☽♐	*2am46*	5	☽♑	*0pm 2*	6	☽♒	*9pm43*
9	☽♑	*3am42*	7	☽♒	*2pm35*	9	☽♓	*2am49*
11	☽♒	*5am 2*	9	☽♓	*6pm33*	9	♀♈	*3am32*
13	☽♓	*8am40*	11	☿♓	*5am21*	11	☽♈	*10am 4*
15	☽♈	*4pm 4*	12	☽♈	*1am21*	11	☿♓	*5pm27*
18	☽♉	*3am14*	13	♀♓	*3am11*	13	☽♉	*8pm 4*
20	♀♒	*5am35*	14	☽♉	*11am38*	16	☽♊	*8am23*
20	☉♒	*8am46*	17	☽♊	*0am17*	18	☽♋	*9pm 4*
20	☽♊	*4pm12*	18	☉♓	*10pm58*	20	☉♈	*10pm 3*
23	☽♋	*4am14*	19	☽♋	*0pm39*	21	☽♌	*7am37*
25	☿♒	*0am33*	20	♃♓	*4pm 6*	23	☽♍	*2pm39*
25	☽♌	*1pm47*	21	☽♌	*10pm24*	25	☽♎	*6pm22*
27	☽♍	*8pm50*	24	☽♍	*4am57*	27	☽♏	*8pm 5*
30	☽♎	*2am10*	26	☽♎	*9am 7*	28	♂♑	*3am47*
			28	☽♏	*0pm 6*	29	☽♐	*9pm20*
						31	☽♑	*11pm25*

APRIL			MAY			JUNE		
2	♀♉	*8am19*	2	☽♓	*2pm31*	1	☽♈	*4am44*
3	☽♒	*3am12*	4	☽♈	*11pm 1*	3	☽♉	*3pm45*
5	☽♓	*9am 4*	7	☽♉	*9am59*	5	☿♋	*2pm 6*
7	☽♈	*5pm13*	7	☿♉	*0pm33*	6	☽♊	*4am26*
10	☽♉	*3am37*	9	☽♊	*10pm26*	8	☽♋	*5pm16*
12	☽♊	*3pm51*	12	☽♋	*11am18*	11	☽♌	*5am11*
15	☽♋	*4am42*	14	☽♌	*11pm15*	13	☽♍	*3pm17*
17	☿♈	*0pm32*	17	☽♍	*8am44*	15	♀♌	*6pm52*
17	☽♌	*4pm 9*	19	☽♎	*2pm40*	15	☽♎	*10pm37*
20	☽♍	*0am24*	21	☉♊	*8am28*	18	☽♏	*2am35*
20	☉♉	*9am12*	21	♀♋	*1pm46*	20	☽♐	*3am35*
22	☽♎	*4am49*	21	☽♏	*5pm 1*	21	☉♋	*4pm30*
24	☽♏	*6am15*	22	☿♊	*7am26*	22	☽♑	*3am 0*
26	☽♐	*6am16*	23	☽♐	*4pm56*	24	☽♒	*2am51*
26	♀♊	*7pm10*	25	☽♑	*4pm15*	26	☽♓	*5am14*
28	☽♑	*6am42*	27	☽♒	*5pm 1*	26	☿♌	*2pm16*
30	☽♒	*9am 7*	29	☽♓	*8pm55*	28	☽♈	*11am35*
						30	☽♉	*9pm55*

JULY			AUGUST			SEPTEMBER		
3	☽♊	*10am32*	2	☽♋	*6am 3*	1	☽♌	*1am 8*
5	☽♋	*11pm19*	4	☽♌	*5pm26*	3	☽♍	*10am 5*
8	☽♌	*10am55*	7	☽♍	*2am44*	5	☽♎	*4pm33*
10	☽♍	*8pm49*	7	♀♎	*8pm46*	7	♀♏	*10am15*
11	♀♍	*4pm23*	9	☽♎	*10am 4*	7	☽♏	*9pm11*
13	☽♎	*4am39*	11	☽♏	*3pm35*	10	☽♐	*0am40*
15	☽♏	*9am58*	11	☿♌	*9pm 5*	12	☽♑	*3am28*
17	☽♐	*0pm34*	13	☽♐	*7pm16*	14	☽♒	*6am 7*
19	☽♑	*1pm10*	15	☽♑	*9pm22*	15	☿♎	*2am28*
21	☽♒	*1pm18*	17	☽♒	*10pm44*	16	☽♓	*9am27*
23	☉♌	*3am24*	20	☽♓	*0am52*	18	☽♈	*2pm34*
23	☽♓	*3pm 0*	22	☽♈	*5am28*	20	☽♉	*10pm26*
23	☿♋	*9pm51*	23	☉♍	*10am26*	23	☉♎	*7am59*
25	☽♈	*8pm 4*	24	☽♉	*1pm37*	23	☽♊	*9am14*
28	☽♉	*5am12*	27	☽♊	*1am 0*	25	☽♋	*9pm44*
30	☽♊	*5pm19*	29	☽♋	*1pm39*	28	☽♌	*9am39*
			30	☿♍	*3am28*	30	☽♍	*6pm56*

OCTOBER			NOVEMBER			DECEMBER		
3	☽♎	*1am 2*	1	☽♏	*2pm19*	1	☽♐	*2am 8*
4	☿♏	*0am19*	3	☽♐	*3pm19*	3	☽♑	*1am28*
5	☽♏	*4am35*	5	☽♑	*3pm49*	5	☽♒	*1am23*
7	☽♐	*6am48*	7	☽♒	*5pm29*	7	☽♓	*3am50*
9	♂♒	*1am 0*	9	☽♓	*9pm30*	9	☽♈	*9am50*
9	☽♑	*8am53*	12	☽♈	*4am15*	10	☿♐	*0am34*
11	☽♒	*11am45*	14	☽♉	*1pm25*	11	☽♉	*7pm11*
13	☽♓	*4pm 4*	17	☽♊	*0am26*	14	☽♊	*6am42*
15	☽♈	*10pm13*	19	☽♋	*0pm46*	16	☽♋	*7pm 9*
18	☽♉	*6am36*	22	☽♌	*1am25*	19	☽♌	*7am44*
20	☽♊	*5pm16*	22	☉♐	*2pm44*	21	☽♍	*7pm30*
23	☽♋	*5am37*	24	☽♍	*0pm46*	22	☉♑	*4am 2*
23	☉♏	*5pm14*	26	♂♓	*2am36*	24	☽♎	*5am 4*
25	☽♌	*6pm 2*	26	☽♎	*8pm58*	26	☽♏	*11am 6*
28	☽♍	*4am19*	29	☽♏	*1am13*	28	☽♐	*1pm19*
30	☽♎	*11am 4*				29	☿♑	*11pm 9*
						30	☽♑	*0pm54*

Ingress table – very useful!

New Zealand, it will be 6pm on 26 October at Greenwich, and the tables should be read for that date. Raphael is accurate for 1pm in Germany, 2pm in Finland and Greece, Egypt and South Africa, 5.30pm in India, 10pm in Sydney, Australia, 7am in New York and 4am in Los Angeles. You will get used to such mental juggling as you progress! If you want an accurate sourcebook on time zones and changes, try *The International Atlas* or *The American Atlas* (USA time changes only) by Neil Michelson's Astro-Computing Services.

If you are living in Britain, then there is no timezone problem, but there is the question of Summer Times, or Daylight-Saving Times. This applies also to other countries, and is particularly complex in USA, where not only states but also counties have their own ordinances and rules. Practicing astrologers have to furnish themselves with a set of Time Change books to deal with the question. However, in most of Europe and in ex-British Empire countries it is not too complex. You need to find out if there is/was Daylight Saving Time at the date on the year in question and then simply subtract one hour from your clock time to get true zone time. If you are reading out of the ephemeris, then add one hour to get your clock time. Each year, Raphael has the dates for British Summer Time for that year in the front of the book.

The American Ephemeris

This is published either for Midnight GMT (00 hours at the beginning of the day) in a red cover, or for Noon GMT in a white cover. It doesn't matter which you have, (it's mainly a matter of whether you function better using the 24 hour clock, or using am/pm) as long as you are clear which one you have! The same rules apply regarding time zones and daylight saving times (DST) as outlined above.

The data for each month is given all on the same page. This ephemeris is not as detailed for day-to-day perusal as Raphael is, but it has the advantage of containing all the important pieces of information you need for ongoing chartwork — and it covers a century. Explanations of the layout of each page are at the front of the Ephemeris. Buying Raphael for a century would cost you ten times the price of the American Ephemeris, and you would land up with 100 booklets to house! The American Ephemeris is a worthwhile investment, for you could get at least 50 years of use from it! It is not easily portable, though: Raphael is best for carrying around.

What to look out for in your Ephemeris

As life goes on, certain astrological things are worth watching out for, and below is a list of major factors to keep your eye on regularly. In other words, astrology encourages an attitude of watching and noting. Don't push yourself to grasp everything at once: allow yourself to get bewildered every now and then, and trust that all will come clear in good time. Give yourself six months to get the gist of what it is all about — let things sink in. Don't be daunted by the time you need to give it, for the most worthwhile insights into the mystery of life are well worth putting some time and energy into. In fact, this watching of ephemerides and 'sniffing the air' is addictive!

LONGITUDE **OCTOBER 1993**

Day	Sid.Time	☉	☽	12 hr ☽	True ☊	☿	♀	♂	♃	♄	♅	♆	♇
1 F	0 38 57	7♎49 50	10♈ 8 30	16♈ 3 55	4♐29.6	29♎52.7	11♍29.4	2♏38.4	21♎17.1	24♒14.6	18♑13.9	18♑22.8	23♏40.2
2 Sa	0 42 54	8 48 50	21 59 19	27 54 54	4R20.6	1♏13.7	12 43.0	3 19.1	21 30.0	24R12.1	18 14.1	18 22.8	23 42.0
3 Su	0 46 50	9 47 51	3♉50 55	9♉47 40	4 13.8	2 33.5	13 56.7	3 59.9	21 42.8	24 9.6	18 14.4	18 22.9	23 43.9
4 M	0 50 47	10 46 55	15 45 28	21 44 40	4 9.6	3 52.1	15 10.4	4 40.7	21 55.7	24 7.2	18 14.7	18 23.0	23 45.7
5 Tu	0 54 43	11 46 1	27 45 41	3♊48 56	4D 7.7	5 9.3	16 24.2	5 21.6	22 8.6	24 4.9	18 15.0	18 23.1	23 47.6
6 W	0 58 40	12 45 9	9♊54 55	16 4 6	4 7.6	6 25.3	17 38.1	6 2.5	22 21.5	24 2.7	18 15.5	18 23.3	23 49.5
7 Th	1 2 37	13 44 19	22 17 3	28 34 17	4 8.6	7 39.7	18 52.0	6 43.6	22 34.5	24 0.5	18 15.9	18 23.5	23 51.5
8 F	1 6 33	14 43 32	4♋56 22	11♋23 50	4R 9.7	8 52.6	20 5.9	7 24.6	22 47.4	23 58.5	18 16.4	18 23.8	23 53.5
9 Sa	1 10 30	15 42 47	17 57 10	24 36 50	4 10.0	10 3.9	21 19.9	8 5.8	23 0.4	23 56.5	18 17.0	18 24.0	23 55.4
10 Su	1 14 26	16 42 4	1♌23 10	8♌16 27	4 8.8	11 13.4	22 34.0	8 46.9	23 13.4	23 54.7	18 17.6	18 24.4	23 57.4
11 M	1 18 23	17 41 24	15 16 47	22 24 7	4 5.7	12 20.9	23 48.1	9 28.2	23 26.4	23 52.9	18 18.3	18 24.7	23 59.5
12 Tu	1 22 19	18 40 46	29 38 13	6♍58 37	4 0.9	13 26.4	25 2.2	10 9.5	23 39.4	23 51.2	18 19.0	18 25.1	24 1.5
13 W	1 26 16	19 40 10	14♍24 40	21 55 29	3 54.9	14 29.7	26 16.4	10 50.9	23 52.4	23 49.7	18 19.7	18 25.5	24 3.6
14 Th	1 30 12	20 39 36	29 30 0	7♎ 7 0	3 48.3	15 30.5	27 30.7	11 32.3	24 5.5	23 48.2	18 20.6	18 25.9	24 5.6
15 F	1 34 9	21 39 5	14♎45 9	22 23 7	3 42.2	16 28.6	28 45.0	12 13.8	24 18.5	23 46.8	18 21.4	18 26.4	24 7.7
16 Sa	1 38 6	22 38 35	29 59 30	7♏33 2	3 37.3	17 23.8	29 59.3	12 55.4	24 31.5	23 45.5	18 22.3	18 26.9	24 9.8
17 Su	1 42 2	23 38 8	15♏ 2 35	22 27 8	3 34.0	18 15.7	1♎13.7	13 37.0	24 44.6	23 44.3	18 23.3	18 27.4	24 12.0
18 M	1 45 59	24 37 43	29 45 55	6♐58 20	3D32.6	19 4.0	2 28.1	14 18.7	24 57.6	23 43.2	18 24.3	18 28.0	24 14.1
19 Tu	1 49 55	25 37 19	14♐ 3 59	21 2 42	3 32.8	19 48.5	3 42.6	15 0.4	25 10.7	23 42.3	18 25.4	18 28.6	24 16.3
20 W	1 53 52	26 36 57	27 54 27	4♑39 23	3 34.0	20 28.6	4 57.0	15 42.2	25 23.7	23 41.4	18 26.5	18 29.3	24 18.5
21 Th	1 57 48	27 36 37	11♑17 45	17 49 55	3 35.4	21 3.9	6 11.6	16 24.0	25 36.8	23 40.6	18 27.7	18 30.0	24 20.7
22 F	2 1 45	28 36 19	24 16 18	0♒37 23	3R36.3	21 34.0	7 26.1	17 5.9	25 49.8	23 39.9	18 28.9	18 30.7	24 22.9
23 Sa	2 5 41	29 36 2	6♒53 41	13 5 44	3 36.1	21 58.2	8 40.7	17 47.9	26 2.9	23 39.3	18 30.2	18 31.4	24 25.1
24 Su	2 9 38	0♏35 47	19 14 5	25 19 14	3 34.4	22 16.2	9 55.3	18 29.9	26 15.9	23 38.9	18 31.5	18 32.2	24 27.3
25 M	2 13 35	1 35 34	1♓21 42	7♓21 58	3 31.3	22R27.2	11 10.0	19 12.0	26 28.9	23 38.5	18 32.8	18 33.0	24 29.6
26 Tu	2 17 31	2 35 23	13 20 29	19 17 40	3 26.9	22 30.7	12 24.7	19 54.1	26 42.0	23 38.2	18 34.2	18 33.8	24 31.8
27 W	2 21 28	3 35 13	25 13 55	1♈ 9 35	3 21.8	22 26.1	13 39.4	20 36.3	26 55.0	23 38.1	18 35.7	18 34.7	24 34.1
28 Th	2 25 24	4 35 5	7♈ 5 0	13 0 27	3 16.5	22 12.9	14 54.1	21 18.6	27 8.0	23D38.0	18 37.2	18 35.6	24 36.4
29 F	2 29 21	5 34 58	18 56 12	24 52 30	3 11.5	21 50.7	16 8.9	22 0.9	27 21.0	23 38.0	18 38.8	18 36.5	24 38.7
30 Sa	2 33 17	6 34 54	0♉49 35	6♉47 41	3 7.4	21 19.2	17 23.7	22 43.3	27 34.0	23 38.2	18 40.4	18 37.5	24 41.0
31 Su	2 37 14	7 34 51	12 47 0	18 47 45	3 4.4	20 38.4	18 38.5	23 25.7	27 46.9	23 38.4	18 42.0	18 38.5	24 43.3

Astro Data	Dy Hr Mn
☽0N	1 22:23
☿0S	12 9:35
☽0S	15 19:47
♃□♅	16 16:42
♃□♆	17 9:53
♅ D	27 12:24
☽0N	29 4:22
♆ D	30 6: 6
♄□♇	9 6:47
♃△♄	12 19:27
☽0S	13 6:22
♃⚻♇	14 0:25
♀0S	18 20:52
♅☌♆	25 6:33

Planet Ingress	Dy Hr Mn
☿ ♎	11 11:19
♀ ♍	21 14:23
☉ ♎	23 0:23
♂ ♏	27 2:15
☿ ♏	1 2:10
♀ ♎	16 0:13
☉ ♏	23 9:38
☿ R	25 22:40
☽0N	26 9:57
♄ D	28 3:37

Last Aspect Dy Hr Mn		☽ Ingress Dy Hr Mn
2 7:12	♇ △	♈ 2 21:21
5 1:34	♄ ✶	♉ 5 10: 9
7 13:34	♄ □	♊ 7 22:16
10 3:24	☿ □	♋ 10 7:37
12 1: 6	♇ △	♌ 12 12:51
14 6:32	♄ ☍	♍ 14 14:20
16 3:10	☉ ☌	♎ 16 13:44
18 6:46	♀ ✶	♏ 18 13:15
20 12:40	♀ □	♐ 20 14:53
22 19:32	☉ □	♑ 22 19:54
25 1:41	♂ □	♒ 25 4:19
27 4:23	☿ △	♓ 27 15:13
29 14:37	♇ △	♈ 30 3:29

Last Aspect Dy Hr Mn		☽ Ingress Dy Hr Mn
2 4:28	♄ ✶	♉ 2 16:13
4 16:42	♄ □	♊ 5 4:27
7 3:18	♄ △	♋ 7 14:42
9 10:47	♇ △	♌ 9 21:34
11 14:41	♇ □	♍ 12 0:36
13 20:35	♀ ☌	♎ 14 0:47
15 15:15	♃ ☌	♏ 16 0: 1
17 14:53	♇ ☌	♐ 18 0:23
19 21:33	☉ ✶	♑ 20 3:42
22 8:52	☉ □	♒ 22 10:49
24 14: 7	♃ △	♓ 24 21:17
26 22:39	♇ △	♈ 27 9:39
29 17:18	♃ ☍	♉ 29 22:20

☽ Phases & Eclipses Dy Hr Mn		
1 2:33	○	8 ♓ 41
9 6:26	☾	16 ♊ 35
16 3:10	●	23 ♍ 16
22 19:32	☽	29 ♐ 48
30 18:54	○	7 ♈ 37
8 19:35	☾	15 ♋ 32
15 11:36	●	22 ♎ 8
22 8:52	☽	28 ♑ 58
30 12:38	○	7 ♉ 6

Astro Data

1 September 1993
Julian Day # 34212
Delta T 57.1 sec
SVP 5 ♓ 20'36"
Obliquity 23°26' 21"
Chiron ⚷ 29♌38.2
☽ Mean ☊ 7♐33.1

1 October 1993
Julian Day # 34242
Delta T 57.1 sec
SVP 5 ♓ 20'34"
Obliquity 23°26' 21"
Chiron ⚷ 3♍29.8
☽ Mean ☊ 5♐57.8

The *American Ephemeris* for Sept-Oct 1993 (midnight). At the bottom of the page are various useful bits, which are explained at the front of the ephemeris. Chiron positions for the 1st of the month are shown in the bottom-right box. Lunar Last Aspect boxes help you to find void-of-course moons. AstroData shows aspects formed by the slower-moving planets only

★ Observe *newmoons* and *fullmoons* at first, with their timing and the zodiac signs they involve, and later, progress on to halfmoons and a general awareness of other phases.

★ If ☽ interests you, watch its ingresses into signs as well. This is very much a day-to-day affair, and if you have the time and attention to do it you will learn a lot about signs, the moon, yourself and life. Conjunctions and oppositions of ☽ to planets are also quite useful to keep and eye on, but it is not worth bothering with other aspects formed, unless you are a moon maniac or a sucker for details (which I was when I was first learning astrology — I ate it for breakfast!)

★ Watch for *solar ingresses* into signs — the true months, energywise — and note the atmosphere 2-3 days before and after. Also note the *solstices, equinoxes* and *cross-quarter days.*

★ Observe *ingresses* of other planets into the signs, and their passages over the above points. Even if you do not grasp what they do, and cannot sniff anything as it is happening, note these times, and you will find things fall into place after a while. It takes time to fit everything together, but it works.

★ Keep a watch on the *aspects* forming between ☉ and planets throughout the year. Sun completes a full cycle with regards to each planet during the course of the year, and ☌ s, ☍ s and □ s are a good starting point for observing this.

★ Look into all other aspects formed between planets, for these will clue you into both the planets and the aspects and the areas of life they cover. To minimise information overload, stick at first to the main aspects.

★ Look out also for the *stations* of planets — the times when they stop and turn either retrograde (R) or direct (D) — for these are times when they are coming through strongly.

Outlines of what all these things do and imply are scattered throughout this book, but it is worth taking note that these are guidelines, tuning tips, rather than replacements of the real thing. It's like drinking whisky: it is much more effective to do it rather than read about it! For then you have real live experience. And like drinking whisky, you won't understand immediately what's going on, or see the experience with the kind of perspective which you will gather as time goes on, but on the other hand, by doing it, you go through the motions of gathering that experience, and it all matures in time. Investing this time is well worth it, for astrology gives us tremendous help, increasingly, as we progress through life, grow and see new things, and accumulate a developing knowledge of the subject at the same time. Learning direct from life experience has no substitute. The flow of time needs your conscious participation as much as you need it and its guidance!

6 Pure energy: the planets

So far, we have been looking at the two* lights, *sun and moon: the time-energies behind these are basic and central to the here-and-now living of our lives, and every enquiring human, by rights, should know something about them. When we come to the planets, however, we are dealing with more sophisticated or specialised forms of energy. The planets never display their energy in pure unmodulated ways, however, for they are continually toned and filtered by the zodiac signs they pass through, and by the aspects, or angular relationships, they form with other planets. Here we are going to look at these planetary energies, but note that these descriptions, to help you tune in to them, are somewhat abstract, since no one planetary energy can be experienced in isolation or unmodified at any time. Just as most people in our lives experience us with clothes on most of the time, altering our expressed beingness considerably, so the planets also wear facets of their energies, revealing themselves to us only in different guises. Sounds complicated, but you'll get used to it!

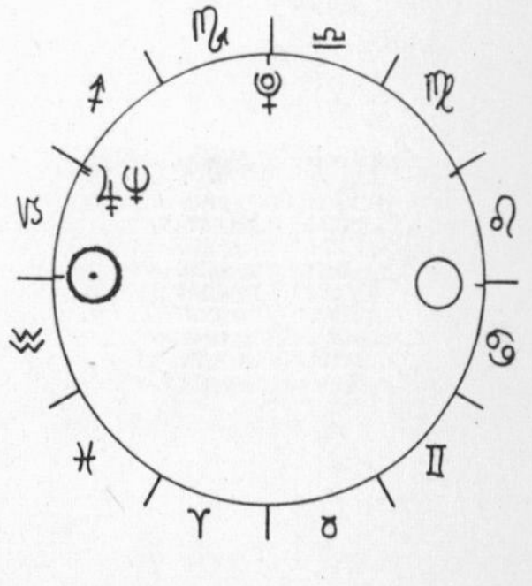

18 January 1984: five planets making an ingress. Pluto changed signs six weeks before, and on 19 January both jupiter and neptune entered capricorn *on the same day*. Meanwhile, at fullmoon, sun and moon were both ingressing into opposite signs simultaneously

Tapestries of time

To reiterate, what we are looking at here is earthly, subjective time-energy. It just so happens that this time-energy, using the earth and earth-mind as a resonator and energy-transformer, moves and changes in unison with the motions of the planets. This time-energy presents us with atmospheres and psychic climates within which we carve out the stories of our lives, and the human race as a whole carves out its history, according to the choices we make within the context of time, its possibilities and limitations. There is no direct cause-and-effect relationship between planets and energy or between energy and what we do with it.

It is as if the planets were strands of energy, of different colours and flavours, which become woven together through the transfor mations of time, to create pictures or totalities, wholenesses of subjective climate, to which we all variously respond, each in the best way we can. Astrology becomes a way of deciphering the way in which these energy-strands are interwoven, and the way in which, at any moment, certain strands are prominent, while others provide the background.

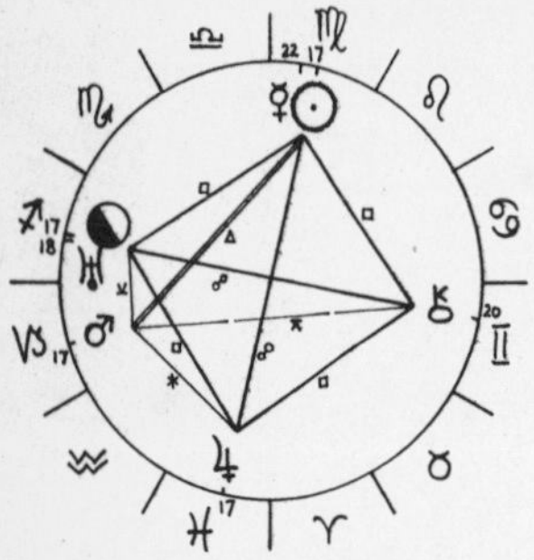

11 September 1986: a grand cross involving four planets, sun and moon. Mars interjects also with aspects to the others from capricorn. The broken line indicates an inexact aspect

Even though the planets are at work all the time, there are occasions when it is possible to single them out, in order to take an experiential sounding. The times when individual planets reveal themselves most strongly are:

★ When they change sign, a distinct change of atmosphere comes about, within the area of life which that planet tends to affect — as in the case of the sun, an *ingress* brings a fresh and open change after the taste of a planetary energy becomes a bit sour, clogged or worn when the planet is at the end of the preceding sign. Ingresses, especially with the slower-moving planets, represent times of qualitative choice, when we have options to change our mode of approaching things and processing energy passing through our lives: these options present themselves when the planet is in the last 2-3° of a sign.

★ When one planet forms an *aspect* to another planet (or a few). An aspect is a specific angular relationship between two planets travelling the zodiac — we met them when we were looking at the lunation cycle. When two planets interact by aspect, they thrum and resonate with each other in a distinguishable way, setting up a third energy which is the 'chemical' outcome of the reaction they are going through. More about aspects later, in chapter 8.

★ When a planet is at a *station* (this doesn't apply to sun and moon) it comes through strongly. A station is a point in time, and a place on the zodiac, where a planet appears to stop moving, turning either from *direct* (forward) to *retrograde* (backward) or vice versa. This is the moving-train effect pointed out in chapter 1. A stationary planet usually makes its presence felt for at least a matter of days around the precise time of the station — an ephemeris will give this time to the nearest minute.

★ It is also possible to look at the effects of planets on a more personal level by comparing the movements of the planets in the heavens with the positions of the planets in a birth chart, a technique called *transits*. We shall be looking into this at the back of the book, in chapters 17 and 18.

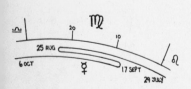

August-September 1990: one of mercury's retrograde periods, with dates of ingresses and stations

For now, it is best to limit the amount of these factors you examine, in order to avoid astrological indigestion. It's a matter of building up your insights gradually, without giving yourself too much to examine. Ingresses and major aspects are good to start

Transits 1978–82

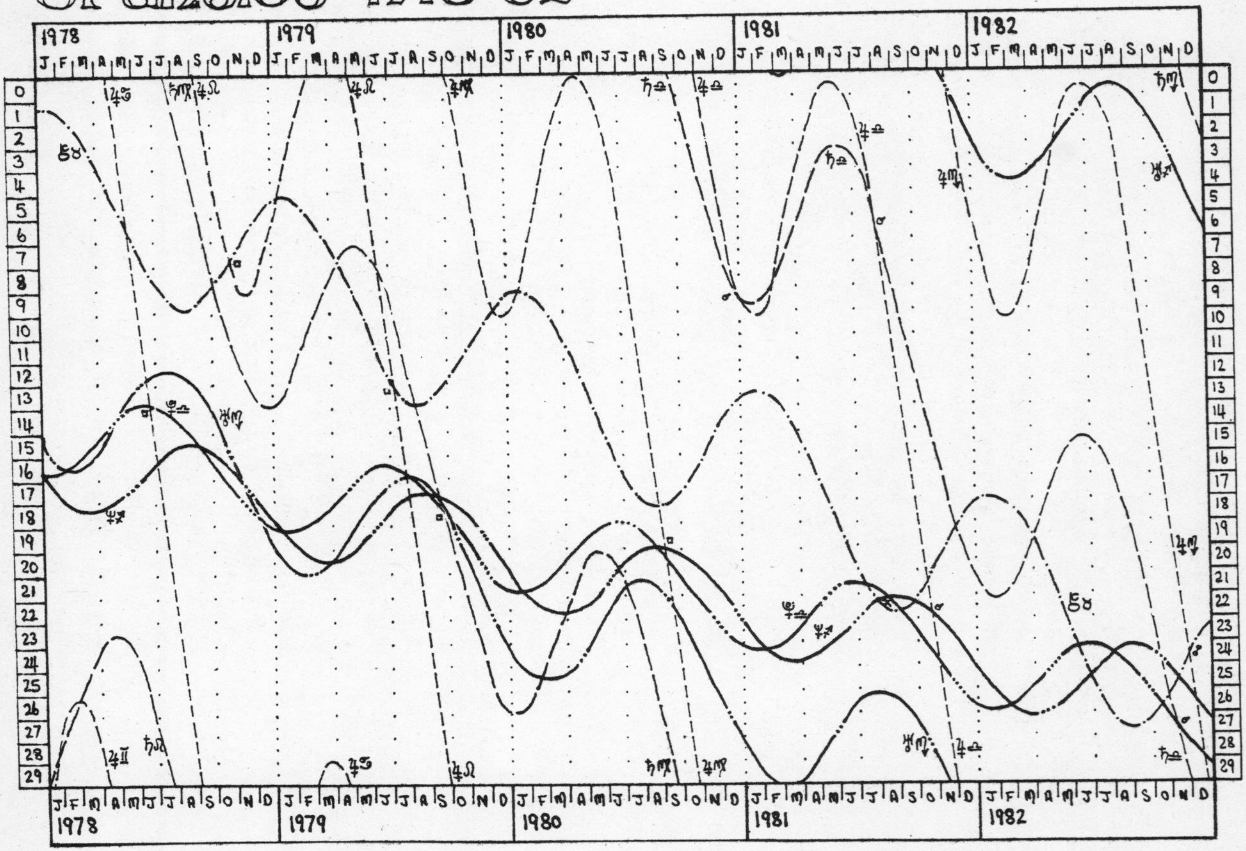

A graph showing motions of the slower-moving planets over a five-year period. Along the vertical axis are the degrees of all signs, and along the horizontal ones, time, in months and years. Each planetary path is identified by planet and the sign it is moving through. When lines intersect, an aspect is formed: ☌ ⚺ ✱ □ △ ⚻ or ☍. Such a graph as this can be used in transit work, as outlined in chapter 19 with. Leave transits until later. In your perambulations around the pages of your pet ephemeris, however, keep your eye on ingresses, major aspects and stations, and simply observe, without seeking to form too many conclusions: by building up a stock of conscious experiences, the whole lot will sink in.

Planetary zodiacal cycles

These are their cycles of motion around the zodiac. They vary greatly in length and behaviour patterns. Moon affects us primarily in hour-to-hour and day-to-day contexts, although new and full moons can feature issues which have longer-lasting import. Sun, mercury and venus affect us on day-to-day and week-to-week levels, and mars on week-to-week levels usually: as you can see, the time-contexts these influence depend on the planets' speeds. Jupiter and saturn affect us on month-to-month and year-to-year bases, while chiron, uranus, neptune and pluto affect us in terms of longterm life-issues. See chapter one for more details.

Thus we have different levels of time at work, and it all depends on what kind of perspective we are seeking to have — shorter-term or longer-term. Later in the book we shall look at longer-term changes in history, in chapter 15.

However, all these levels of time and significance interlace one another. For example, ♇ can spend 12-35 years in a sign (currently moving fast), bringing up issues of longterm value and meaning. Yet, the faster planets form aspects to ♇ on their own journeys round the zodiac, thus pulling longterm issues into shorter-term contexts. Thus, an underlying historical change, having significance in terms of centuries of evolution, can be focused into a particular time as an intensified work-out, the significance of which reveals itself only slowly. An example of this is the ♅ ☌ ♇ of 1965-6, where immensely longterm changes, both in consciousness and technology, surfaced as a disruptive outbreak in those few years, when the significance of what took place then will take at least 170 years to work through full cycle (at the next conjunction around 2130**AD**).

Thus different layers of time are at work, and we and the world move through these layers at various different times, sometimes living through times of short-term significance, and occasionally being bombarded with times of longterm meaning. We hardly recognise this as we go about life, but these interweavings of duration take place, and it help to be able to identify them and to use these times to their best advantage.

What kind of energy each planet embodies

Here we are looking at what kinds of energy, atmosphere and situation are likely to arise when a planet becomes strongly featured in the overall energy-weather. You'll find that you cannot grasp all of them at once, yet you'll be able to identify the workings of some of them in your own experience immediately. We tend to respond actively to some planets, and find it difficult relating to other ones, depending on how much they resonate within our own beings, and how much we have awakened these resonances within us in the course of our lives.

Usually, books present the planets in their order of distance from the sun, starting with mercury and ending with pluto. Here we're going to look at them in a different way, thematically. The planets can be grouped into four main groupings, which are well worth contemplating. We're not going to follow this grouping, but you might care, on second reading, to read through the planets in a different order from the way they are presented in this chapter.

The four groupings are:

★ the *lights*, sun and moon, which work in the here-and-now, existentially, through the yang and the yin within us;

★ the *functional planets*, mercury (on a +/– 1 year cycle), venus (+/– 1 year) and mars (2 years), which work through our mentality, feelings and will respectively, in the context of daily-life ins and outs in ourselves, the world, and our relations with both;

★ the *social* or *identity-forming* planets, jupiter (12 years) and saturn (28 years), which work through our sense of selfhood and world-purpose and their manifestation;

★ the *transformative* planets, chiron (51 years), uranus (84 years), neptune (165 years) and pluto (+/– 250 years), the planets which work through the group psyche, affecting historical undertones and archetypes, and their emergence into consciousness.

That said, we're now going to look at the planets in a different order. This isn't a system or something you should follow religiously: it is merely another way of looking at the planets — frankly, it's what I felt like writing at the time of writing! Here, I'm pointing out some energy-similarities between planets, which, at a stretch, can be regarded as different octaves of related kinds of energy. You can rest assured that other ways of looking at the planets are possible too.

Grokking it

By *grokking*, I mean that capacity within us to comprehend and relate to what goes on in our inner and outer experience. Three connected themes here: mercury as a mental experience-processor, jupiter as a belief-system builder, and uranus as an illuminator and stirrer.

★ ☿ **MERCURY.** Closest of all planets to sun, ☿ appears to hover around ⊙, as seen from earth, staying always within 27° of ⊙, ahead of or behind it in the zodiac. Its only aspect with ⊙ is a ☌, which can happen either when ☿ is direct, overtaking ⊙ in the zodiac (behind ⊙ from us), or retrograde, moving temporarily in the opposite direction, (in front of ⊙ from us).

☿

When ☿ is active, things get zappy, and there is much to-ing and fro-ing, chatter, brain-rattling, tickertape and nervous energy. ☿ activates our minds, in their capacity to receive, store and process life-information and ideas, and in their communicative capacity. Lungs, speech organs, hands and eyes are involved too, as well as the stomach. Language, rationalisations, travel, all media of communication, and wind are all transmitters of ☿ energy. So is this book. Our nervous systems and intelligence are activated by ☿. Mercury splits things, people, places and thoughts into separate entities, and then interrelates them by creating linkages. Observe your active mind, the flight of birds, the road traffic and people's propensity for interchange while ☿ is active.

★ ♃ **JUPITER.** The biggest planet of our solar system (it wasn't far from becoming a sun, in its early days), bright in our sky (best at the solar opposition), ♃ stays in each sign for roughly a year, turning retrograde for 4 months each year. Jupiter is enhancing and furthering, extending and enriching energy. Being much slower than ☿, it works with a different level of issues: power in society, self-esteem and beliefs in ourselves, and progress and bounty in nature.

♃

Jupiter, when waxing strong, urges us to cross the great water, make steps forward, reach out and externalise ourselves. It stimulates activity, bravado, confidence and intensity of social energy. The basis of this is our beliefs, accumulations of experience and acquired knowledge, underpinned by a choice to construct our realities according to a certain fundamental philosophy of life. As our beliefs and confidence grow, as we grow up, so does our capacity to *out* ourselves, acting creatively, stimulatively, positively and fruitfully in society and the world. When ♃ is strong, society as a whole throbs with energy, issues, fads, developments and not uncommonly excesses. Belief can overshoot realities, or it can enhance them, depending on our capacity to *grok* what's going on. In the end, a reality is only such because it *works* for us: our sense of reality, of how we stand in relation to the great wide world, is formed through the working of ♃ energy.

★ ♅ ***URANUS.*** One of the distant planets of the solar system, ♅ spends 7 years in each sign. It works through a deeper level of psyche, by stirring things up, disrupting, hyper-activating, rattling us and creating eccentric, extreme or polarised conditions. It rips us, people and nature away from the old, and tests the validity and flexibility of all forms and structures, in our conditioning, in society and out in the woods. It awakens the knower within: that mode of consciousness which operates a-logically, intuiting and envisioning wholenesses, which somehow land up being proven right. ♅ seems at first to drive everything off course, but, when the truth is out (sometimes a difficult process which we resist, because it disturbs our sense of reality and expectations), it is easy to *see* that things have moved more *on course* than they were before.

Sudden, impish, abnormal, differing, dissenting, extremist energy abounds when ♅ is broadcasting. Things can heat up and blow, and secure knowns can shatter: underneath, in group psyche, new life-energy seeks to erupt, stopping things from becoming too entrenched. Since the majority of us are well taught to preserve our egos and support our institutions, this can be difficult, but uranian energy can also be inspired, electric, futuristic, clear and sharp when channeled openly. Individuals often take it upon themselves to embody these impulses of change for society as a whole, embodying the archetype of breakthrough. In our own lives, if we omit to open ourselves to uranian energies, our unconscious will manifest someone in front of us who rips up our normalities and gives us a whacky wobble. To work through into relatively perceptible atmospheres, uranus has to work through one of the faster-moving planets, for example by aspect.

Feeling it

By *feeling*, I mean three things: one is our capacity to sense, feel and image, the second is our sense of okayness or happiness with regard to being alive, whatever is happening, and the third is our capacity to experience feelings arising in our hearts. Three planets are involved here: moon, venus and neptune, the feminine planets.

★ ☽ ***MOON.*** Moon is by far the fastest mover of all the 'planets'. It is our twin sister planet, part of earth, co-orbiting. Moon energy engages our umbilical feelings of alrightness or agitation in many and subtle ways. Our sense of security is wrapped around our feelings about and past experiences of situations where we are vulnerable, subject to influences within or without which can destabilise us. The more we open up, the more we feel okay in whatever situation arises, however threatening it might be. Our *in*security comes from stored subconscious memories of what happened before when similar prompts arose to those arising now. These memory-programs are drummed in through habituation or trauma, mostly at birth and in our first years, though also later too, and we tend to act out these programs automatically, without being conscious of them. Thunder = fear, hunger = must fill stomach, goodbye = loss, money = happiness, emotion = danger: we all have whole banks of programs going on inside us, activated by different promptings from lunar atmospheres, life situations and subjective sensings. Thus we carry our past around with us.

Lunar energy is instinctual, and working our instincts depends on how friendly we are with our bodies and the child within us. Like a mother, instinct knows best. Every moment of every day we are presented with choices to run our old patterns of response, or to allow ourselves to respond to life from a new and open viewpoint. It's good sense to do the latter, yet we tend, unless challenged, to do the former — until we become conscious of what we're doing.

Moon energy, when working strongly, thus takes us through various and changing angles on life, changing feelings toward situations. It works through sensitivities or lack of them. We are challenged by ☽ to *allow* things to be, to be sustained, nourished, cared for, supported and fulfilled by the world, by people around us, and by our own capacity to trust. These issues crop up in the smallest of details, in moods and situations which last but hours, rapidly-changing, on a very daily basis. Have you watched the way you eat your food, how you relate to going to the toilet, how you meet the day or how you respond to the phone ringing or dogs barking?

★ ♀ ***VENUS.*** Venus orbits inside the orbit of earth, and follows ☉ around the zodiac, like ☿, except moving up to 47° distant from ☉ as it travels through the zodiac. While ☽ energy is umbilical, ♀ energy moves through our hearts. When flowing well, we feel happy, contented, loved and loving, open, creative and colourful, and when blocked, we feel separated, sad, cool, alienated, closed-up or hurt. Through our hearts, we feel union, with ourselves, with others and with the more pleasing aspects of the world, drawn to what we like, and averse to what we dislike.

When ♀ is strong, things are soft and likable, verdant, inclusive and enjoyable, bringing out the love aspect in life. Music and tone, beneficence and trust are venusian qualities — as are the absence of these, when ♀ is being blocked or challenged in energy-weather.

★ ♆ ***NEPTUNE.*** Neptune moves through one sign every 14 or so years. It embodies a higher octave of feeling, spiritually rather than circumstantially generated. Through ♆, all boundaries are melted, and insight and expansion of consciousness heal the pain which such dissolution can bring. When ♆ is strong, all knowns disintegrate, and the ground drops away from beneath our feet. Inappropriate notions, reality-bubbles, identities, structures and arrangements become invalid and fall away, leaving an empty space in which heart is the only guide. Neptune is an awakener, through literally disillusioning us, moving us into a new space.

A ♆ atmosphere has a weird, spacey quality to it, where it's difficult to know exactly what's what. Things become still, and the void opens up. Misunderstandings and non-comprehension arise. Things go out of gear. Yet within this a new reality reveals itself. ♆ activates the imagination, our inner capacity to use images and convey them by subtle means through creative arts. It feeds our inner life, if we will but give it attention. Without attention, imagination can play tricks on our grasp on reality — mystically, ♆ calls into question any sense of reality at all. For it can attune us to the Ultimate, or nullify our known universe — depending on which way we are receiving it. Neptunian times are strange and disorienting, but go with it, and a new sense of space and openness can come through.

Doing it

Here we shall look at mars, chiron and pluto. We could include ♃ here as well, in its power aspect — so contemplate ♃ in this context as well as the above in which it has been presented.

★ ♂ ***MARS.*** Mars orbits on a two-year cycle, turning retrograde only once in that cycle. It works through our assertiveness, our ability (or inability) to get what we want and make things work *our* way. When mars energy comes on strong, we have a driving urge to make things move, get some action and strengthen our own cause: this can bring up feelings of frustration, anger, resentment, restlessness or thwartation too, if we are disposed to feel such things. Sod the rest of them, I want things my way! In the weather, ♂ brings hard rains or fierce winds, and a tense atmosphere prevails: whether this goes anywhere depends on whether the energy is either favoured or blocked. Mars energy is about standing up for ourselves, applying ourselves, engaging with life, exercising muscle and *clout*, jousting with our dragons. It is baseline sexual energy, firing desire, seeking orgasm — whether in lovemaking or in relating to the world. Things accelerate when ♂ is strong, and a relentless, ruthless force can come into play — which sometimes clears the air and causes some distance to be covered, and sometimes leads to trouble, hurt or the overlooking of finer considerations. One who knows ♂ well knows also how to temper will by applying firm patience, focused effort and action where listening and response are still possible. Mars energy makes things move and overcomes obstacles.

★ ⚷ ***CHIRON.*** This newly-discovered planet, orbiting between ♄ and ♅, and eccentrically crossing the orbits of both — ♅ when in ♈, where it stays for 8 years, and ♄ when in ♎, which it rushes through in 1 year — still has to reveal its energy-qualities to us

⚷

clearly. ⚷ concerns another mode of action from ♂: while ♂ urges action on behalf of self, ⚷ urges action on behalf of the cosmic whole, as if we were chess-pieces on the world-board. ⚷ urges change and activity on behalf of cosmic/general need, engaging our personal gifts, knacks and intuitions in resolving very concrete, yet paradoxical questions, which have *both* personal and transpersonal significance. Like ♅, ⚷ works through the *knower* within us, challenging us to drop our preconceptions and rationality, and encouraging us to follow that spark of enlightened action within us which does exactly what is most appropriate, from many viewpoints at once.

Chiron forces the master-victim question, and our capacity to resolve riddles with no precedents. It brings out our magical abilities — the defying of expectations, the creation of miracles, or the ability to find and follow the shortest path through the maze. When ⚷ is strong, we are presented with accumulations of problems and dilemmas, seemingly impossible to resolve, which can be masterfully broken through a contextual shift, an expansion of awareness and an opening of our brilliance and genius — or often, plain old simple sense, previously not seen. Strange things take place, yet they have their meaning in the whole picture. When it all seems impossible, and when we give up, we open to ⚷, and find the key which opens the door blocking our path. Everything which happens in connection with ⚷ seems to be *meant to happen*. Synchronicities and uncanny flips and breakthroughs, inner guidance and deeply-engaging predicaments characterise ⚷ at work. Our work is to facilitate the universal flow through us: for when working in harmony with this elusive yet immanent Force, our ability to create masterpieces out of apparent flops grows, leading to outcomes whereby general and personal benefits are beveled into one another.

♇

★ ♇ ***PLUTO.***. Pluto is another eccentrically-moving planet, moving inside neptune's orbit briefly, when in ♏ for twelve years, and moving far away when in ♉ for 36 years. Pluto precipitates the eruption of the deepest truths, the inevitable stored-up force which accrues from all our previous cover-ups, ill-considered acts, misdeeds, evasions and dishonesties. It brings out the darkness we carry round, and the ugliness and violence in the group psyche — yet in doing so it offers enlightening breakthroughs, an alchemical flowering into a new state of being.

Pluto has uncivilised libido energy, rampant, often uncomfortable, wild and totally *living*, urgent, obsessive and cathartic. When ♇ is strong, life-and-death issues come up, and primal energy tests our capacity to survive and make the big transformation. It is the root of sexual energy, and of power, and while its apparent uncontrollability can be fearsome, adepthood in working ♇ power can bring a capacity for inner control and immense centredness without crutches or crap. Its force generates resistance and fear, but inevitably this is but the prelude to breakthrough, going with the power of the universe, the onward-moving force of history which cannot wait for us to carry on living our secure, routinised lives. Pluto blows it for us (and even for nuclear reactors, if necessary) and precipitates the new. It is the last word on change: this is *it*, when ♇ is at work.

Being it

In the modern world, *beingness* is a quality we overlook: we are judged by what we *do* (or fail to do). Yet beingness is the seat of our doingness: what we *are* cannot be taken away from us. Who we are, our sense of selfhood, of the way we in our individuality elect to manifest our beings, is an area which has now become very important: many of us are feeling that we have spent enough time and energy being good, worthy citizens, doing what is judged by others and society to be worthy and acceptable, and seek to find our real selves, our light and true purpose, which in the end is what matters. Here we shall look at sun and saturn.

★ ⊙ ***SUN.*** Just as sun is a star, which holds the solar system in orbit, so the sun within ourselves is that 'cubic centimetre of awareness' within which holds us together as integral human beings. The sun represents our potential to shine, to *live*, to hold to our centre and be our true self. Often the sun can be obscured by clouds: we compromise ourselves in order to make things easy, in order not to stick our neck out. We lose ourselves in what is required of us, especially in relationship. Yet by doing so, we lose track of our spirit, the spark of our individuality, and we make things difficult, complex, unflowing. Through unveiling the sun, we enliven ourselves, find ourselves, grow and find our Way.

⊙

Sun represents such a basic form of life-energy — the kind which keeps us wanting to be alive — that it isn't possible to be too specific about it. It pulls together all the facets of our being and keeps us functioning as an entity with identity, with a sense of having somewhere to go, and a purpose to be fulfilled. It isn't about being selfish, for paradoxically, being ourselves facilitates the overall unfolding of life, and naturally tends to connect itself with what is right for others too. Being ourselves, we do what is already in the scheme of things, moving with the Tao of the world.

When solar energy is strong, life, nature and people move on, develop, find energy to grow, propagate and create, bloom and reap fruit — though being a yang energy, it can also create excesses, where we can impose our own wishes, prejudices, projections and intentions on life, missing out on the need to be receptive to what life is offering us. Firm and central, the wise person follows her/his path, ever aware of the world around, always including others and imbuing them with their own sense of selfhood, tuned into the pulse of the universe as it shows itself to her/him.

♄

★ ♄ **SATURN.** Saturn stays in each sign for about 2 years, and is the outermost planet visible to the naked eye. When ♄ is at work, we have to face up to the crunch, get to grips with realities and account for ourselves. We have to come to terms with what we fear and avoid, because their perpetuation limits our progress and growth, cramping our life-energy, creating failure, disability, lack, degeneration, guilt and negativity. Saturn is about concrete realities, and presents us with all the inevitable consequences of our acts and self-restrictions: all the difficulty we encounter through it is our own self-creation. But ♄ faces us with our creations, forcing us to become conscious of them and the way we set them up. Thereby, we consolidate our sense of self, by structuring our lives, prioritising what is most important and coming down to ground level. Through ♄ we have to state clearly who we are, where we are going, and what our terms of trade are with others and the world.

Saturn challenges us to get on with our life's work, to overcome our limitations by deliberately limiting ourselves to a particular chosen path, for thereby we muster the energy and focus to find our freedom and realise ourselves. We are offered a choice to take responsibility for ourselves, to own our failings and self-obstructing patterns: if we dutifully obey others' expectations, obligations and impositions (brought to us particularly by authority figures who appear to have the power to greatly affect our lives), ♄ duly keeps us within these confines until we get straight on our own path. Fear and guilt maintain the status quo: yet the status quo, particularly in times such as now, is not necessarily appropriate to the healthy functioning of the world. ♄ is one of our greatest friends, for while it dresses in dour clothing, it enlightens us with a real truth which other planets cannot do.

When ♄ is strong, energies of other planets can be repressed or restricted. Yet this containment makes life-energy gather strength over time, and stimulates future growth: if we will but choose to express that energy. ♄ works in society through institutions, laws, hierachies and power structures, be they Popes or governments, or admonishing fathers or teachers. Obey the rules, and you will find favour: disobey, and you will be punished and cast out. In such a way we are kept under control. Yet ♄ energy can be transmuted, such that we take on ourselves our own responsibility, and define our rules according to our own sense: ♄ welcomes change if it is sincere, committed and thorough, grounded and workable, but until it is, the rules hold. In nature, ♄ brings about hard conditions, challenges the strength of treetrunks and rocks, weeds and prunes out the weakest species in order to prosper the stronger ones and eventually help nature maintain itself. Sometimes it brings the axe, or wipes out old forms: it tests the limits of all things in order to keep them from excess, waste or lethargy. Hardship is a test, but it is in the end furthering to life and new growth.

Planetary modulations

As we established earlier, the planets are forever modulated in the way they express themselves. As follows.

★ As the planets move through the signs, they focus their energies around certain definable issues, ways of working, assets and problems, underlying themes and overt potential outcomes. The motion of a planet through a sign is itself a subcycle, a story with a beginning, middle and end, the foundations for which were explored in the preceding sign, and the results of which reveal themselves in the following sign: this can be understood if you develop an overview of the issues and developments which have come into focus while a planet you are watching has moved through a sign. Although it demands some waiting, ♃ and ♄ demonstrate this storyline sequence well, for their sojourns in signs (1 and 2 years) are long enough to see the story.

★ The planets feature each other by engaging each other by aspect. The main aspects are initially most revealing. Each year, sun forms a whole cycle of aspects to most planets (except ☿ and ♀), which are well worth observing. Planetary interaspects, with varying periodicities, also give good tastes of what they are about. We shall be looking into aspect cycles next.

Retrogrades and stations

☿ turns retrograde three times per year, for 3 weeks each time. ♀ is retrograde for 6 weeks every 19 months, and ♂ for 6-11 weeks once every 2 years. All the other planets (except ☉ and ☽) are retrograde for 4-5 months per year, while earth swings in between them and sun.

A planet is particularly powerful when at its *station*: you can feel it clearly. When moving *direct* (forward), its energies move through us in a relatively straightforward way, passing in, through and out of us (unless we obstruct them) in evolutionary, expressive ways, 'as per normal'. When a planet slows down, the energy loses impetus, beginning to twist up, becoming habituated rather than motivated, losing vivacity, originality and colour. When it is *stationary* ('stationary turning retrograde', St.t.R) there is a general snarl-up and blocking, out of which a questioning emerges, a questioning of the way we do things, of the point of it all, and doubt and uncertainty creep in. Our actions seem to become voided and incapacitated, and a re-examination of issues arises. Watch next time ☿ turns!

When a planet is accelerating retrograde, there is a relaxation of energy, and out of this can dawn a new perspective, an acceptance, peaking when the planet conjuncts (in the case of ☿ and ♀) or opposes (in the case of all other planets) the sun — that is, when earth, planet and sun line up in the solar system. After this transition a new sense of surety develops, a feeling of increased readiness to move afresh, to create, move in a clear direction and explore a new possibility.

When the planet slows to stationary again (St.t.D) all is poised, and a surge of energy grows, propelling us forward into intentional and resolved activity, growing in energy up to the next conjunction with sun, cyclically. After this conjunction, the energy begins to run on momentum, becoming regularised and taken for granted, until the ensuing retrograde period churns things up again. The universe keeps us on our toes!

Dreamweaving

The archetypal resonances of the planets are forever modified and changing in tone, strength and feature as time moves on. Gradually we are building up a picture of how this works, and how time moves.

Life is a strange mixture of fact and dream, to the extent that what we often accept as facts reveal themselves to be dreamstuff too: our illusions and knowns sooner or later get blown. We create our lives through what we think, say and do, multilevel, and much of this goes on unconsciously. Within the context of time-energies available at any moment, we create both the objective realities of our lives and the subjective components of how we experience them. In other words, even though affluence, progress, success or popularity is generally regarded as a Good Thing, to one person is is so and to another it is not, and it can also be that different halves of ourselves carcinogenically conflict with each other at the same time. A heavenly place can become hell, hate can become love, and pain can become pleasure. All things change in subjective significance through life.

Our choice (often unconscious) of how to experience things is the same stuff as dreaming. For no matter what is going on, we are continually inventing interpretations, reactions, preferences and prejudices to suit our subjective needs. We get caught up in confused graspings of reality, caught in our own *stuff*. But as ♆ teaches us when we dig down into its secrets, all of what we call reality is actually a string of constructs, beliefs concerning what is real and desirable or not. Reality is real only if it works for us and yields results. As we move through life we find that old realities become invalid and cease working, losing their realism. We eventually reach a stage where we realise that nothing is ultimately real.

This becoming so, life becomes of the nature of dreaming, and dreaming takes on a reality equal to our 'normal' waking reality. We're all dreadfully asleep, but astrology, one path to awakening, is a way of realising that time does not bind the timeless spirit, and that all things are relative to the way we are experiencing them. Thus we are weavers of a tapestry of dreaming, and can act in the world much more clearly, knowing it is all a dream. Our possibilities for using the power of consciousness to dream into existence and work new dreamlike realities increase, and our effectiveness in the world miraculously grows. For in the end we are here to learn, and to co-weave the dream which this world is. Perhaps astrology, on its deepest level, is about learning how to dream creatively. Somehow we have to create a new world: our dreams seek to become manifest. We are all, to some extent, reincarnations of Walt Disney!

7 Wheels within wheels: interplanetary cycles

Each and every planet works with each and every other planet, interweaving energy to create time and the possibilities inherent in it. The planets do this by moving through a cycle of relationship with each other — one fast and one slow — the stages of these cycles being called* aspects. *Aspects are recognised angles between planets, forming sequences in cyclical form. Here we are looking at cycles, so-called* synodic cycles, *and some groundwork on aspects, before going into a full outline of the shape of a cycle in chapter 8. This and the next chapter are a bit dense and complex: return to them again after some time has elapsed, and allow yourself on first reading simply to get a picture of the whole issue of aspects.

Cycles

When we were looking at the zodiac in chapter 4, we were looking at a *zodiacal* cycle, in which a planet moves in relation to a fixed frame of reference, the zodiac. The zodiac filters planetary energy to bring to us underlying themes, viewpoints, atmospheres, possible scenarios and feeling-tones, distinguishing chapters in the story of each planet's journey round the zodiac. But planetary motions through signs do not necessarily create the energy changes which have the power to set in motion events and distinct breakthroughs: aspects do this.

Aspects are part of a *synodic* cycle, in which, like the hour and minute hand of a clock, two planets move in a cycle of relationship with each other. This cycle begins when the planets conjunct (☌), located transiently in the same place in the zodiac (as when clock hands are at 12.00, 1.05, 2.10, 3.15 etc). It comes to a climax when the planets are in opposition (☍) to one another (as when clock hands are at 6.00, 7.05, 8.10, 9.15 etc). Other stages mark different points along the way.

Successive conjunctions take place in different signs. While the faster planet of any two might fulfil its zodiacal cycle in a certain time (for example, ♂ in 1 year and ten months), it might take some time to catch up again with the slower planet, which by this time has moved along at its own rate (for example, ♂ conjunctions with ♃ take place roughly every 2 years and 2 months. In the 1980s and 90s, for example, successive conjunctions of ♂ and ♃ take place at 15° ♓ (Dec 86), 0° ♊ (March 89), 11° ♌ (June 91), 15° ♎ (Sept 93), 18° ♐ (Nov 95) and 24° ♒ (Jan 98), about six times in a zodiacal ♃ cycle of 12 years. The zodiacal lunar cycle is 27 days 7 hours, while her synodic cycle is 29 days 12 hours, on average: there is a time-difference of degree between a zodiacal and a synodic cycle.

The ♂ - ♃ cycle relates to tides of assertiveness, male sexuality and assertion of power in the group psyche, which is a very different business to that of the lunation cycle. The synodic cycle of ♂ to ♇, by comparison, (relating to a deeper source of assertiveness which brings in the death and transformation of the old, and the forcing forward of the inevitably-new) takes place a little quicker, even though it is a ♂ cycle, because ♇ moves slower than ♃, and thus successive ♂ - ♇ conjunctions will take place in only just a little more than a zodiacal ♂ cycle — in the above time-period, 86-98, ♇ will have covered but one sign, while ♃ will have moved through the whole zodiac. The ♃ - ♇ cycle, in turn, lasts around 13 years.

In astrology we have a wide range of cycles from 29 days (☽ to ☉) to around 490 years (♆ to ♇). Lots of scope! More within our reach, ☉ / ☿ / ♀ to ♂ cycles last around 2.4 years, ♂ to slower planets just over 2 years, ♃ - ♄ cycles 20 years, ♃ - ♅ 14 years, ♃ - ♇ 13 years, ♄ - ♅ 45 years, ♄ - ♇ 35 years, and so on. Transits involving ⚷ and ♇ can be extremely variable over time, because each of these orbit so eccentrically that it is difficult to generalise. We're thus playing around with a whole range of interlocking and quirky cycles, which give a lot of scope for ongoing wading-sessions through your ephemeris!

It can be mind-boggling to our thinking mind (left brain) and illuminating to our visionary mind (right brain) to visualise all this interrelated movement going on. There's a beauty to it which at least equals that of watching ocean waves! *Give some time to developing this vision, for it is vital.*

You can do this several ways on a practical level: ★ keep a constant eye on your ephemeris for a year, and form regular pictures of the distribution of the planets round the zodiac, and what they are doing to one another; ★ the more technically inclined can draw or follow graphs of planetary motions, (of which there are examples in the book) by sketching in the motions of the planets for a few months or a year on some graph paper; ★ or you can draw yourself a big circle (or paint a zodiac mandala) to stick up on the wall, then, using mapping pins, you can move the pins round daily or periodically for, say, a year, reading positions from your ephemeris — you could even go mad and build a mandala on the ground, using log stumps or stones for the planets: do whatever stimulates you most! ★ following *transits*, which we look at later in the book, is another way of moving into relationship with planetary motions.

Hemicycles

A *hemicycle* is a half-cycle. We can look at a complete cycle in terms of two different kinds of hemicycle.

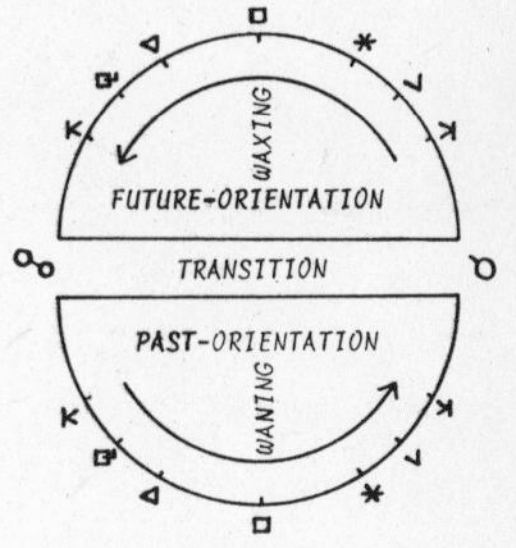

Waxing and waning hemicycles

★ The *waxing-waning* hemicycle is interesting because it illustrates the developmental, evolutionary/integrative side of cycles. The *waxing hemicycle* starts at the ☌ and ends at the ☍. During this time the faster planet is moving away from the slower one: this is a process in time where new potentials are explored, where dreams and intentions emerge from in-here to out-there, an evolutionary motion. The *waning hemicycle* starts at the ☍ and ends at the ☌. Here, the faster planet is now catching up with the slower: this is a process in which the externalised identity consolidated at the ☍ seeks and fulfils a context in the overall scheme of things, an integrative motion. Consider the growth of an annual plant: it first grows and takes shape, rising to flowering, to declare its own selfhood, then it gives forth its pollen or seeds, and eventually its very leaves or even stalk, to further future cycles of growth.

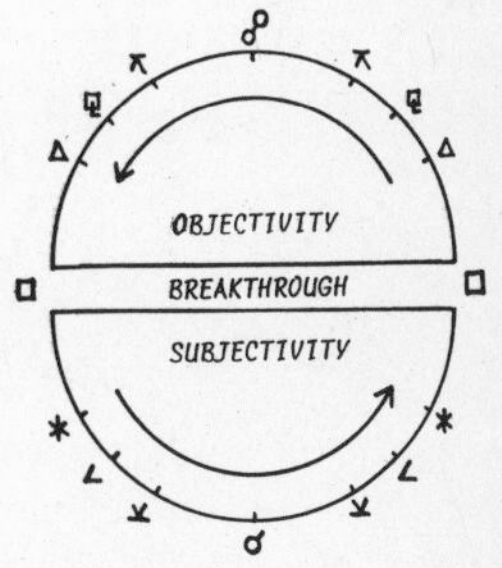

Subjective and objective hemicycles

★ The *subjective-objective* hemicycles illustrate the various facets of a certain state of being or awareness. Subjectivity is a me-in-here standpoint, in which personal aims, plans, ways of interpreting life and defining self prevail. The *subjective hemicycle* has its focus at the ☌, but spreads out either side to two points halfway to the ☍, called the square (□) aspects (see diagram). Objectivity is a me-in-relation-to-all-that, or me-as-a-part-of-that, standpoint. The *objective hemicycle* peaks at the ☍, and itself spreads out to the squares. Thus, between, for example, the waning □ and the ☌, we are finding out who we are through filling our created role in the world, while between the ☌ and the waxing □ we are exploring our own terms of reference: both are different aspects of selfhood. While between the waxing □ and the ☍, we are meeting the world and its specifications, and between the ☍ and the waning □ we are exploring our membership in the world and society.

Combining these two hemicycles, we can define four quarters to a cycle. From ☌ we are 'doing our own thing', from waxing □ we are encountering the world and entering into rapport with it, from the ☍ we are being a part of everything, and from the waning □ we are rediscovering ourselves through fulfilling and finding personal meaning from our involvement and roles.

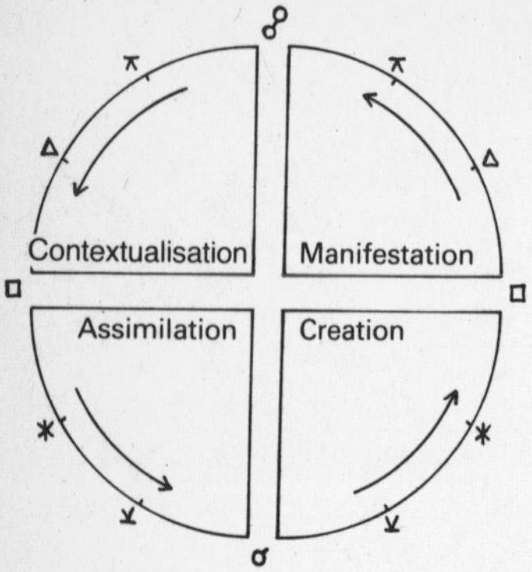

Four aspect quadrants

Aspects

Aspects are recognised angles of relationship between any two planets where we can identify certain describable kinds of energy-interchange between them. They are stages on the journey of relationship around a whole cycle. A cycle starts with a conjunction (☌) and then moves through various stages: ⚺ semisextile at 30°, ∠ semisquare at 45°, ∗ sextile at 60°, □ square at 90°, △ trine at 120°, ⚼ sesquiquadrate at 135° (90° + 45°), ⚻ quincunx at 150° (called *inconjunct* in America) and ☍ opposition at 180°. The general principle behind them is a subdivision of the cycle of 360° by a number such as 2, 3, 4, 6, 8 or 12. In more advanced astrology, all sorts of numbers can be used, yielding sometimes quite weird angles (such as 51°25′, 1/7 of the circle), but we'll leave these out here. Here we shall look at the above-named aspects, the most important ones.

A cycle has within it four main stages: childhood/beginning, youth/development, maturity/application, and old age/completion. Gestation of the new takes place within the completion stage, for, as the Chinese were wont to point out, an end is only the prelude to a new beginning. This is another way of looking at the fourfold subdivision of the cycle mentioned above. The transition-points between these four stages are vital humps to cross, and when they involve slower cycles, they are points of initiation (☌ , □ , ☍): an initiation takes place (when we are willing to go through it) when we face up to truths about our life and situation and go through a squeeze or a crunch, fundamentally changing our way of being and way of working with life, becoming a new person.

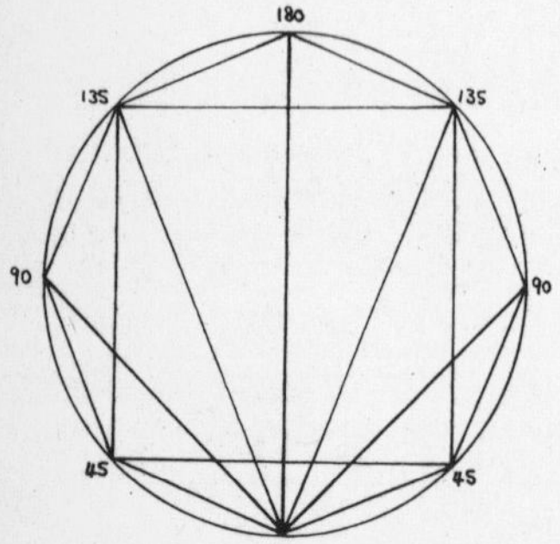

The octile family: ∠ □ ⚼ ☍

These initiations can be very major ones when slow-moving planets are involved, for the test can be drawn out over a longer time, such as a year, and can involve major life-questions. Lesser initiations punctuate our lives too, such as when ☽ periodically brings up a crunchy situation lasting one evening, which, while brief, can still give us a goodly shake and wobble. These small and punchy crunches and scrapes can often serve as critical points in larger initiations, for often the greatest of changes can focus on something on one evening or in one night-time dream, even though the whole process might be going on over years.

Challenges and developments

Aspects are spread out throughout a cycle in a regular fashion — at least, the major ones which we shall look at here are so — at intervals of either 30° or 45°. A glance at the diagram will illustrate this. Each of the aspects has a symbol in astrological shorthand, and when we mention two planets in aspect to one another, we say, for example, 'moon sextile jupiter' (☽ ∗ ♃). That is, the faster planet, doing the aspecting, comes first, then the aspect, then the slower planet, being aspected. Note these for example: sun trine saturn (☉ △ ♄), mars quincunx uranus (♂ ⚻ ♅), but then moon trine sun (☽ △ ☉), sun opposition mars (☉ ☍ ♂), saturn semisquare uranus (♄ ∠ ♅). The whole sequence of aspects follows in the next chapter.

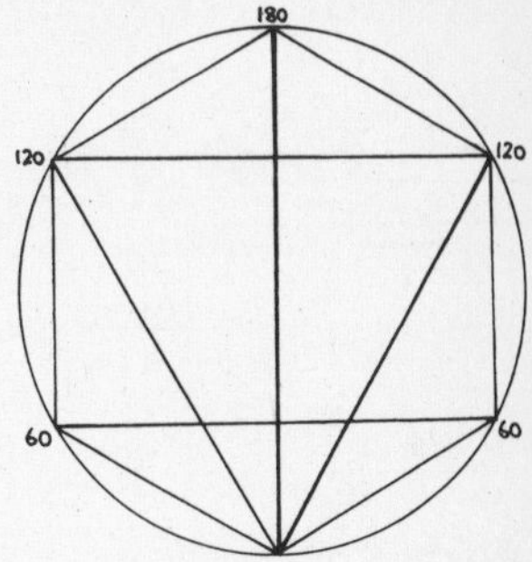

The sextile family: ∗ △ (☍)

The *fundamental* aspects (☌ and ☍) mark the beginnings and climaxes of cycles, and have major implications relating to the overall meaning of each and every cycle; the *challenging* aspects (□ , ⚼ and ∠) represent something which must be climbed over, worked at, broken through, confronted, decided upon or released; the *flowing* aspects (△ and ∗) represent an opening and widening out, a relaxing, an evolution and a development; the *incidental* aspects [my term], (⚺ and ⚻) introduce new elements into the game, incursions from the unknown, which change our experience of things. Each of these kinds of aspect plays its part in the pattern of a cycle, and their sequence is significant.

It all very much depends on how we deal with things. Challenging aspects are very positive if we are willing and ready to work at things, for they encourage us to do just that, while flowing aspects can imply a feeling of stuckness and inability to motivate a change if we are inactive or lazy. Our experience of each cycle is greatly influenced by the way we are *using* our lives: sometimes it can be very beneficial to be ill, and other times it can be very difficult having everything we want!

Where it stops, nobody knows

Cycles do not exist separately from one another: they lead on to and from each other, and serve as each other's past and future. Often it is the case that issues dealt with in one cycle go under and reappear in a much later cycle, which then thematically feeds back not only to the immediately preceding cycle, but also to earlier cycles. Also, cycles exist within larger cycles. This becomes an adventure in perspective! At the times when we are able to stand back from life, digest and look at things, we come into contact with the larger cycles at work in our lives. The life process moves ever onward, and these pauses in its somewhat relentless movement act as timeless breaks in a never-ending process of historic unfoldment.

As you come to understand the pattern in a cycle of aspects, you'll notice that there is a distinctly coherent undulation to it which makes a lot of sense. The grand design has it that we can go through digestible variations in experience, with sufficient challenges to keep us on our spiritual toes and enough relaxations to allow us to be at ease with life. Some aspects are fundamental, some challenging, some flowing and others incidental: thus life presents us with a series of time-processes which are very well designed!

Astrology is a relatively sane way of grasping the ungraspable, reaching into the unknowable. Whilst we can give a description and impression of the form of a cycle, as we are about to do, it is, to be truthful, not as easy as this to limit things to a nice but rigid definition. When using astrology, we are moving into the realm of *nagual*, riddle and paradox! Thus, if you watch what happens during a succession of fullmoons, you will notice that they are both similar to each other, and extremely different. That is, the underlying pattern is there, for all fullmoons are soli-lunar oppositions, and have a definite undertow to them which can be recognisable even if you don't have your ephemeris around, but the precise flavour of each fullmoon can be quite variable. In other words, use this book, and any other, as a catalyst to help you attune to what we're talking about, but form your own conclusions, from your own experience! For this is the only way to true knowing.

Orbs

While each aspect is a specific angle (like 30°, 60°, 90°), it represents a stage, a milepost in the unfoldment of a cycle. But like mileposts along a road, they represent but markers along the cycle to show us where we are: in fact, a cycle is a continuum. Each aspect has a field of influence around it, where it can be said to be having an effect: this is called an *orb*. Just as any event has a buildup, a specific time of occurrence, then an aftermath, so it is with aspects.

Orbs vary in wideness, according to the nature of the aspect. There is debate amongst astrologers as to how wide we should have orbs. One discrepancy in this debate is that many astrologers seek a definite orb, a degree where the aspect markedly starts or finishes. This is not lifelike, for energy unfolds gradually, just as the colours of the rainbow phase into one another gradually, and cannot have clear lines of demarcation. So in this book, the values given for orbs are twofold: the smaller orb denotes the area where a definite effect from an aspect can be detected, while the larger one denotes the area where rumblings are felt which might not at the time be noticeable, although in retrospect or under subtler scrutiny, they can be recognised. An example is the pre-fullmoon period, which can be felt for two days (up to one sign, 30°) before the exact fullmoon.

To complicate matters, orbs are widened or narrowed according to the planets involved. Generally, orbs are widened when ☉ and ☽ are involved in any aspect, and narrowed for slower planets. Suggested orbs for both aspects and planets are summarised on the symbol page at the beginning of the book. When assessing an aspect, therefore, use your judgement as to the width of the orb, and if in doubt, consult your own experience and make your own decisions as you progress!

Application and separation

These are astrologese for aspects which are *forming* (the faster planet is moving into aspect with the slower) or *moving apart* (the faster is leaving its aspect with the slower).

As an aspect is applying, the two planetary energies are juddering against one another, seeking to form a relationship, to come into gear: this can mean some friction, jarring, jangle and difficulty until the aspect is formed. In addition, we tend to throw into the bargain our own resistances and anticipations, which heighten this grating. A lot of the *work* is done during the buildup to aspects: people who resist growth and change exert much energy stop it happening, and people who accept it go through some resistances but yield to change as the aspect nears exaction, while people who seek to *induce* change often go through hell some time before it, only to land up thriving on it all when the aspect is close. Resistance tends to give way to acceptance around 1-2° before the exact aspect. For some an aspect can be very fear-inducing, stimulating resistance at all costs, since change is seen as a threat to security: at best, such people might loosen up after the pressure dies down when the aspect is separating, and at worst (not uncommon) no movement is made at all, heels are dug further in, and misfortune, illnesses and unhappiness set in sooner or later.

Aspect energies come into their own around exaction, and an alchemical reaction takes place, bringing about change, transition or movement. Once this is done the aspect starts separating, and a process of digestion and assimilation follows, in which the dust settles, and the new state is integrated, normalised and utilised. As the aspect separates, what was once future and potential becomes past and established. At times the integration process can take some time, especially if concrete life-forms need changing (like a move of house or a marital separation), or if there has been considerable shock, confusion or disarray around the time of the aspect. Usually things become clear and established when the aspect is around 2-3° separating.

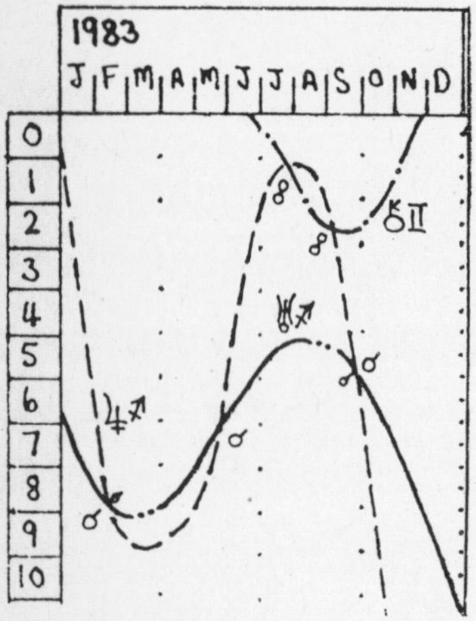

Three passes of a ♃ ☌ ♅ in ♐ in 1983. Note also the ♃ ☍ ⚷ : jupiter was getting caught up in a gradually-applying ⚷ ☍ ♅ which became exact from 1986

Retrograde waltzes

Particularly with the slower planets, two of them can move into aspect, then one or both can turn retrograde, move out of aspect, then back in again. This makes for a three-step process in which changes are strung out over a period, made into a lengthy process. The *first* formation of the aspect then becomes a news-bringer, in which we move into an awareness that a change is needed or pending or desirable: it ends the old situation, but inaugurates a limbo. At the *retrograde*, second aspect, there can be a feeling that things are literally going backwards, and a struggle or energy-droop can ensue, wherein, semiconsciously, the resolve to make the change is generated. The change, the beginning of the future state, takes place when the *final*, direct pass of the transit takes place.

Occasionally, with ♆ and ♇, this can take place more than three times: ♆ and ♇ have been in an ongoing ⚹ to one another, passing into and out of aspect many times over the last few decades, for ♇, currently at its fastest, is keeping pace with ♆, even though its overall cycle is much longer — this has been an important historical aspect, bringing about an ongoing emergence of new ideas, developments and innovations over a long term.

Following cycles

Shorter-term cycles are not too difficult to follow — lunations and annual cycles don't involve too much waiting. It is worth observing them as they are happening, and in advance and in retrospect also. This means keeping your ephemeris with you (Raphael's is best for this) and keeping a regular watch on the motions of the planets, checking what you see in the ephemeris with what you experience in your life and around you in the lives of others, nature, the weather, the cat or whatever interests you. It's a matter of learning to tune in to the collective psyche, and the underlying tendencies in nature and the world.

Longer-term cycles are different. It starts getting really interesting if you have been studying planetary movements for a decade or more, but it isn't very encouraging to be admonished to wait so long! There are escape routes: if you come across a slower aspect (for example, ♃ □ ♄ in 1986, ♄ ☌ ♅ in 1988, ♃ □ ⚷ / ♅ plus ⚷ ☍ ♅ in 1986-7) it is possible to look back through your ephemeris (the American Ephemeris is best for this one) at previous dates when earlier aspects in the cycle in question took place. In this way, the significance of the current aspect can be seen in terms of past developments. Look back over the past (at some time when you are feeling relaxed and recollective) at longer term cycles, and see what you can make of them by comparing their timing with things that happened. Later in the book we shall look at ways in which you can look back over your own life, at its own cycles, breakthroughs, turning-points and flowerings, using *transits*.

Cogs in the cosmic machinery

Different interplanetary cycles bear different levels of significance and effect. The general rule is: the slower a cycle or the planets making it, the more fundamental and deep it is in effect. Even though a fullmoon can, at the time, feel as if it is the end of the world or a major soulquake, fullmoons come and go. They can play a part in a larger energy-process, if they connect aspectwise with the slower planets involved, and can sometimes make for cruxpoints and crunches which bring longer-term, deeper issues to the surface — for example, the Chernobyl nuclear reactor blew its top on a fullmoon close to conjuncting pluto, playing a dramatically specific part in a longer-term ♇ in ♏ unfoldment lasting from 1984-96.

The ♅ - ♇ aspect cycle is a very different thing from, say, the ♀ - ♂ cycle. It's necessary to sort out therefore what the different levels of cycles are, so that you can form an idea of the significance of a specific aspect or cycle you might be observing:

★ cycles between outer planets have historical significance affecting centuries and generations, anent the surfacing of new thought-forms, realities and possibilities in the collective psyche and the lives of nations and the world;

★ cycles between ♃ or ♄ and the outer planets have historical significance in terms of decades, particularly affecting the way deeper thought-forms are materialised, and institutional and social changes are wrought, interlacing deeper issues with world issues;

★ ♃ - ♄ cycles involve practicalities, organisational realities and concrete social issues, with turning-points every 5-6 years, and new cycles starting every 20 years (featured by assassination attempts on US Presidents!);

★ ☉ - ☿ - ♀ - ♂ cycles to outer planets repeat once every 1-3 years, featuring the surfacing of deeper issues (outer planets) in more fleeting yet discernible terms in interpersonal issues and atmospheres — aspects last 1-3 weeks in their effects;

★ ☉ - ☿ - ♀ - ♂ aspects to ♃ - ♄ act similarly, focused on personality-level issues — these cycles are somewhat longer than those in the above point, because ♃ and ♄ move faster than the outer planets, requiring more chasing by ☿ , ♀ or ♂ ;

★ cycles between ☉ , ☿ , ♀ and ♂ last only months or up to 3 years, evoking feeling-tones, motions of energy, shorter-term changes and conditions which feel significant at the time, but which melt into lost detail in a longer-term perspective;

★ cycles between ☽ and any other planet last but a month, yet major aspects between them can bring about occasionally powerful yet brief (1-2 days) atmospheres and occasions, and can be well worth noting.

It's a matter of choice as to how to focus your interest: some look into immediate, shorter-term cycles (especially because they are experientially quite definite and concise), while others are interested in longer term flows and issues arising in connection with them. Of course, isolating individual cycles is not possible, for everything takes place in the context of everything else, but an awareness of the different levels of cycles at work helps sort out what energy is what when you're in the middle of a life-situation and trying to make sense of it. Periodically, all sorts of multiple interactions or sequences of astrological events take place, forming interestingly different patterns, atmospheres and trains of experience. Keep your astrological eyes peeled, your nose to the wind and your ephemeris within easy reach!

Panegyrations

Imaging up a picture of the whole living, breathing motion of the solar system can be a boggling experiment. But it is possible. If you first get a sense of the periodicities of the planets and their order from the sun, you can then image the whole system in its parts. Take the sun first, and develop a good picture/experience of it as a star and a being; then image mercury, venus, earth, mars, jupiter, saturn, chiron swinging eccentrically, uranus, neptune and pluto individually, taking your attention off the previous planet yet maintaining a sense of a presence of it still there, moving on its course. The planets orbit anti-clockwise when seen from 'above' the solar system. When you have reached pluto, widen your perspective, and re-image planets, moving back in toward the sun, including them one by one into the whole scenario. If you lose the image, you can reclaim it by persevering with re-imaging planets, taking them in one by one, until a whole sense of the solar system takes shape. It is possible to allow the planets to dissolve into light, and note their colours/feelings, then to take this light into yourself, such that it fills your body. Stay with the state you have developed, and rest in it, before surfacing.

The solar system is a living, breathing being, with an incredible beauty to its manner of moving. This imaging is easier to do than what is necessary in order to be able to see how the planets look from earth! In days of old, an astrologer would serve a training of many years in order, amongst other things, to develop a living, moving picture of the motions of all cycles and movements we look at in astrology. S/he would spend many nights for years and years observing the stars, planets and moon, and the rising and setting of the sun for an inner grasping of the movement of the solar system stimulates a genuine spiritual experience. Try it!

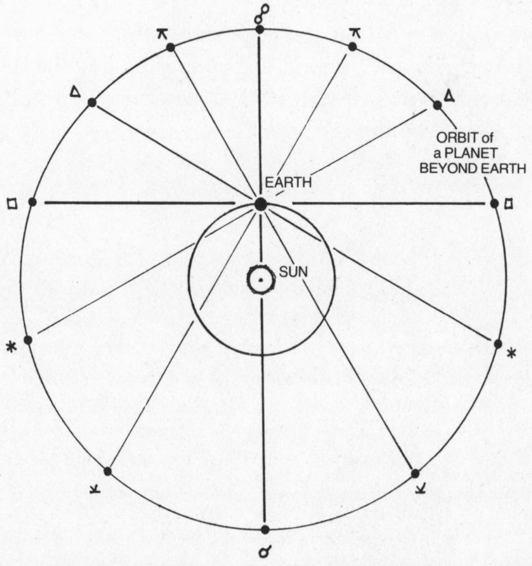

This shows the way that aspects between sun and any planet outside earth's orbit actually look from a solar viewpoint. Earth actually moves itself, at its own speed, as well as the outer planet, so this diagram is a simplification

8 Facets of the diamond: the cycle of the aspects

The nature of life is such that we are enabled to circumambulate the quintessential core of truth of life (whatever that is!) by experiencing facets of it. Life is itself a cycle passing through many stages — if we experienced childhood, youth, maturity and old age at the same time we would not only get confused, but would also miss the main gist of what living on a planet is all about. Thus we have time-cycles, which interface spirit with the dense stuff of bodily living, in gradual doses. Now we are going to look at the cycle of aspects, the blueprint of all synodic or interplanetary cycles.

Apart from the conjunction and opposition, there are two of every aspect in this cycle, one waxing and one waning. When waxing, a faster planet is moving away from a slower planet, until it opposes it, and then starts waning towards it.

The aspect sequence

★ ☌ **CONJUNCTION:** 0°, orb 7/20°. *Transition, ending and beginning, energisation.*

A very powerful aspect, known to the earliest astrologers, since conjunctions are obvious and easily visible in the night sky. This aspect marks the transition into a new cycle, ending the old and starting the new. The ☌ is a statement of utter potential, a condition of beingness, the beginning of germination. Nothing in the cycle is happening as yet: it is simply that the combined energies of the two planets are co-expressing themselves. What this tastes like depends on what the two (or more) planets are: ☽/♀, ☽/♃, ☿/♀, ♂/♃, ☉/☿, ☉/♃, ♃/♆, ☿/⚷, to name a few, work usually quite well with each other, while ☽/♂, ☽ or ☉/♄, ☿ or ♀/♇, ♀ or ♂/♄, ♄ to ⚷/♅/♆ or ♇ have some more difficulty, since their principles stir up friction or discomfort with each other — these comments are not fixed, however, for timely difficulties can be easy and beneficial, and easy-moving energy can sometimes be unproductive or wasted, and at every moment we *choose* how we create our realities.

Conjuncting energies tend to move from within us or our own little universe to consciousness and the world, without any great awareness of this happening, or of the potential effects, rebounds or implications involved: it is purely an expression, eruption, out-

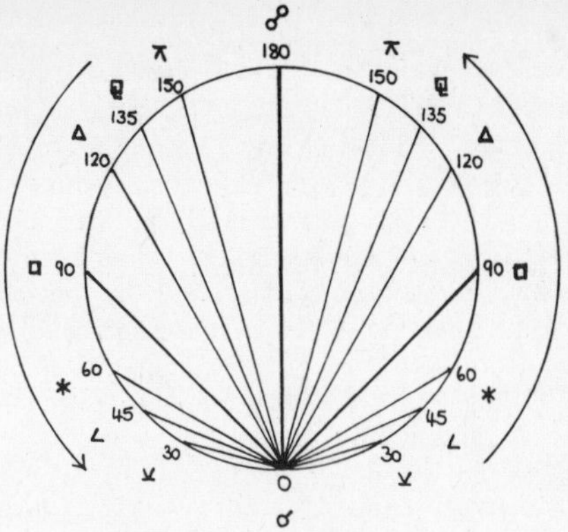

The cycle of the main aspects

pouring or unintentional, undirected state of energy-being. They also imply a larger than normal freedom of choice, an opportunity to reformulate our manner of approaching life, or to change our responses to situations: fundamental patterns of being can change here if we feel primed for them. Qualitative changes can occur, and atmospheres around us can thoroughly change flavour, and the space we are coming from within us can sometimes make a radical flip. Conjunctions have a here-and-now flavour, with sometimes a strong *in-betweenness* to them. We tend here to go at life feeling stable in ourselves, as if the world were our playground. Any disruptions to our beingness usually come from within at conjunctions: whatever happens is a direct mirroring of our state of mind.

★ ⚺ **SEMISEXTILE:** 30°, one sign, orb 2/3°. *Emergence and germination.*

This is an 'incidental' aspect in which our state of *beingness* is moving into motion: *becomingness* is gathering momentum. Things emerge into more definite possibility-profiles, especially since new material is entering the situation, sometimes disjointedly or seemingly irrelevantly, but showing its meaning in the end. Things just start *happening,* without any clear direction, and new avenues open up which weren't clear before. Whatever comes up at this stage might not seem to have value or use, but its very *existence* at this stage means something. At this stage we receive strong omens of coming developments. It is an opening up, but is still early in the cycle.

★ ∠ **SEMISQUARE:** 45°, 1 1/2 signs apart, orb 2/4°. *Orientation, initiation, commitment.*

This is a challenge to link in what is now developing into a longer-term scheme of things, both drawing on the past and with a view to the future. Things happening or needing attention now have wider implications in many directions over time. A sharp and acute awareness of underlying issues at stake dominates, and decisions and initial commitments-in-principle must be made: a narrowing of potentials, setting out of terms and a choice are necessary to set the trends for the future. Often immediate concerns are unimportant, but longterm intentions demand immediate focusing, prompted by current events and the outcomes they look like leading to. This is an initially internally-stressful aspect, but is very rewarding if we invest our energy wisely at this stage. It asks for clarity and precise planning and orientation to make use of it.

★ * **SEXTILE:** 60°, two signs apart, 3/6° orb. *Progress, developments, activity.*

A busy, flowsome aspect where things are really moving or calling for energy. If you are tooled-up, things are going with a swing, if not faster than manageable. Options are widening, people are joining in, things are happening, and it seems as if all is going well. The sextile is too active for us to think too much on things — the why and the how are a low priority — and ends justify means. We're on top of things, and our capacity to exploit the situation is peaking. Skills, abilities, imagination, openings and adjustability are all working well. We are getting towards where we want to go, the present is full, and the future is promising. The automatic expression of energy with this aspect can make for negligence and rashness, though, and it is necessary not to be too caught up in expectations about the potential benefits of the action, for awareness of the issues at stake and the potential consequences of current acts *is* important, even if but background awareness.

★ □ **SQUARE:** 90°, three signs apart, orb 5/10°. *Encounter, work, facing facts.*

Hold on, not so fast — things aren't quite that simple! We also have to face up to things we would prefer, perhaps, not to encounter. We have literally to square up with the world and make things really work — no messing around. If we are avoiding or evading things, they hit us now. If we are prepared to engage with life, this is our first *big* hump to cross. This is a good time for hard work, for paying bills, fixing things, making those choices and fulfilling an obligation to ourselves to carry out what is necessary in order to manifest our vision — or wrestle free of tricky situations we have set up. It requires acknowledging our own part in things, our faults and responsibility, 'owning our stuff', for otherwise we tend to project our hangups outwards so that others or situations represent them for us, and we find ourselves in conflict with them. Intentions meet facts: you're waiting for that cheque and a bill comes instead, or you're driving to town and the car breaks down.

There is little clarity or perspective available here: there is simply the task at hand and its isness. There is scope for an argument with life, so perseverance is called for. Patience is applied timelessness, and application of our attention to the task at hand is creation. Nitty-gritties must be sorted out, even if it keeps us up all night. Squares can face us with our blockages, failings, vulnerabilities and unawarenesses. If we will look at them, we can make great progress, but if not, we have a crunch, and can make a mess of things, with complex results. We have to become more objective, face up to the world around. Delaying is no good, for today is the time. At squares it is always clear exactly *what* we need to do, even if the reasons *why* are unclear. Our intentions are at stake, and we must work them through into the world, reassess them or drop them, for practical reasons, whichever option is best.

★ △ **TRINE:** 120°, four signs apart, orb 4/7°. *Freeflow, okayness, space for understanding.*

This is an easygoing aspect, a freewheeling glide: a holiday or busman's holiday if we have worked hard, or an oblivious drift if we have evaded things. Things work well or fall into our lap as a result of previous effort, or we can lose our grip on things if we have not grappled properly with the □. There is time to look again at what we are doing, lick our wounds, lie in bed, simply enjoy fantasising and coming to a wider understanding of everything and its implications, doodle or have fun. Or it can be a matter of simply carrying on with what we are doing, yet enjoying it more. Things can't be pushed at the △ — it is far better to allow them to unfold as they will, for if we push, we might either waste energy or fall over because there's nothing there to take up the pressure.

It's a time for loosening out, assimilating experience, free exchange, letting be. The △ is a stabiliser. Energy is allowed to emerge for doing other things, creating new approaches, seeing different facets of what's been going on and what is to come. Sometimes things can become flat or apathetic or drop away if expectations are too high, or if there has been previous failure or non-progress. But if there is accumulated momentum, they can move easily and well, developing of their own accord, and life takes on a pleasant hue. This isn't a time for radical changes: it is more for developing along tracks we already are moving along, with some extensions and variations. Openness, tolerance and space, relaxing old stresses and letting new colour, tone and taste come in: it's time to sing your song just for the singing of it. Trines and Sundays go together very well! While this is a time of relative ease, though, watch out for laziness, for there is an awakening coming.

★ ⚼ **SESQUIQUADRATE:** 135°, 4 1/2 signs apart, 2/4° orb. *Choice, readjustment, resolve.*

Longterm considerations are at stake again, for it is now time to refocus, to consciously adapt to new circumstances and to look again at what we are doing, why, and whether it all fits in with what was originally intended or what is seen as the likely developing reality or goal. If we are to allow our intentions, or the flow, to work, we need to let go of some of our predispositions, our old patterns which block life-force, our tensions, expectations or rigidities. *We* are the *source* of any difficulties here, if we cannot accept realities as they are revealing themselves at this stage:

we are being tested on our abilities to rearrange our plans, adapt, see things from new angles. Such adjustments facilitate our growth: the universe supports us if we are attuned. This aspect encourages clarity through letting go, clarity which allows us to create what is possible in the circumstances that have developed. If we drop unnecessary baggage and recommit ourselves to what really matters, as much as we can see this at this stage, then we're laying open a creative path through the period of the opposition.

★ ⚻ **QUINCUNX (Inconjunct):** 150°, five signs apart, orb 2/3°. *Tangents, perspective, letting be.*

The waxing ⚻ is intimately tied with the ☍ process. Here we have an incursion from the unknown — things start happening, or inner nuances develop, which hadn't been bargained for, and there can be some difficulty getting everything to connect. When in ⚻, two planets tend to have a *non-relationship* — not even particularly a conflict — and one tends to dominate the situation, with the other coming in through side-channels, sneakily or unconsciously. If we are moving on the flow of things and can allow the unknown into our lives and trust it, remarkable things can develop: here the challenge is to *actively let it be*, wait and see, allowing what *will* happen to take place and positively joining in with it when it does. If we have unmoving aims and expectations (identification with one of the planets, perhaps) then other factors come into play, which sometimes can be confounding or compromising.

This is the great cosmic merry-go-round, where if we are insecure and doubtful, we can lose our way, while if we are inwardly open, things will work out, plus more, in ways which will reveal themselves in time, often at the ☍. The ⚻ brings us a crisis of perspective and trust! Sometimes larger issues are initially invisible or incomprehensible, but still, they are there, and we have to act on trust in the life-process, an innate knowing that whatever happens will be right.

★ ☍ **OPPOSITION:** 180°, six signs apart, 10/20° orb. *Confrontation, transition, a big difference.*

When two planets oppose each other, one is on one side of the earth and the other is diametrically opposite — obviously a very powerful configuration. This is the climax of a cycle, and the truth will out: our intentions, dreams and schemes meet wider reality (group psyche or world environment), with a resulting validation or invalidation of our ways and activities and being, or something of both. The known meets the unknown, and either a resolution or a clash emerges — especially during the buildup to the ☍. Here there is an acute awareness of the relation between this and that, self and other, wishes and facts, and the joining or dissonance of the two.

Through conflict great power is found, either as definite effects deriving from our beingness or activity, or as a learning experience and enlightenment, or both. This conflict happens on the buildup, and the outcomes emerge at the exact ☍. The balancing act required needs instinct, experience and receptivity rather than knowledge. The extent to which we released our hold on things at the □ influences our balancing immensely. Work and play, female and male, events and dreams, past and future, spontaneity and responsibility: whatever the dichotomy is, it comes up in full technicolour clarity. Whether we can face this and resolve it is *our* business, and a lot of qualitative choice is available in the immediate moment for it: it all depends on our ability to resolve conflicts within ourselves, instead of projecting them out into our environment and blaming others or events.

This is a session in *owning* our own faults, and using situations to learn and move forward. Making a clear decision here can sometimes be difficult, but something must be done, for things can take on an urgent quality, where the best strategy is to cool down, quit fretting and listen to our hearts.

While there can be ripping and wrenching going on, there can also be great peace and insight which brings a transcendence of the issues of the cycle, a seeing of the overall meaning of it and life, together with a re-entering from a new standpoint. For this insight is invaluable, since at an ☍, a new context is emerging. We have the chance to become someone quite different during these climactic turning-points. For this is the beginning of the *waning hemicycle*, in which context, environment, society and our place in the scheme of things — and the use we make of them — are the main issues.

Painting a picture is of personal benefit in the doing

thereof, but the picture's full meaning and purpose is fulfilled when others look at it and enjoy it. Building a house becomes fulfilled when someone moves in and lives in it. Transforming clay into a cup finds significance when the tea to put in it is brewed. The waning hemicycle is a consummation, a dedication of our works to history and the world: what we have established, developed, accumulated and evolved seeks to be carried through into completion. The waning hemicycle is the *yin* side of the cycle.

This tremendous transition and workout, squeeze and leap can make life very different after the ☍. But while the exact ☍ can mark the watershed, the whole area around the ☍, before and after, is the *process* — and the hottest time can often be when the planets are applying to ☍ 4-7° out. Once this transition has been gone through, willingly or not, wittingly or not, the tracks are set for what must be carried out as a result of earlier developments: it is time to fulfil our *contract* with life and the world.

★ ⚻ **Waning QUINCUNX:** 150°, five signs apart, 2/3° orb. *Finding a context, seeing clearly, joining in.*

Here is another yawning of the great unknown, except this time, instead of the unknown impinging on the known, the known is seeking to *find a place* in the as-yet-unknown. It's like applying for a job, or the journey before you reach your foreign destination, or making a bid for something. Here, we need to find a context into which to fit, or a context can open up and we need to see it. This is often a question of attuning to what the world wants of us, what is required or is the most obvious thing to do or be. In this crisis of perspective, we risk losing ourselves, and need to remain clear about what we ourselves are seeking out of life. Like its opposite, the waxing ⚺, this is an *emergence* aspect, yet the context differs. Here, we need to be sufficiently self-aware to avoid moving into a sheepish following-along with others mode, for in doing so we are relying on the right choices of others, and if everyone is just following along with each other, a directionless morass can result!

★ ⚼ **Waning SESQUIQUADRATE:** 135°, 4 1/2 signs, 2/4° orb. *Getting stuck in, engagement, interaction.*

If the ⚻ was the application, this is the interview. An orientation and commitment must be made, and our capacity to fulfil our part in the social contract is being tested. As with the waxing sesqui, there is an acute awareness with sharp edges, but here we must mould ourselves to the world, to playing its game. We are pawns in this game, and must play it, because we're there. Our personal priorities and claims have diminished significance, yet we must keep them in the back of our minds, since we need to be conscious of our terms of trade and limits of willingness. The world needs us to make its issues our own. In the ⚼ we are admitted to the club, but in being admitted, we take on obligations. Soon we must carry them through.

★ △ **Waning TRINE:** 120°, four signs, 4/7°. *Going along with things, belonging, harmony.*

What things are like at this stage depends on how we have treated the post-☍ period. If the ☍ weakened us, then we tend to go along with the drift of life, doing what it and others tell us to do. If it strengthened us, then we are creators within the larger context of life, and life and creativity move well and effortlessly. The △ thus becomes either a rather flat drift and energy-subsidence, or it becomes a time when the flow of things works for us and the world carries us along favourably. There can be an indolent side to it too, which doesn't lead to anything productive, but can be restful.

People accept us, are used to us and everything can move along happily and as a matter of course. Normality prevails. Things are as they should be — even if we might have difficulty accepting this. There is space to breathe and enjoy the developing results of our efforts, to allow things to move along as they are doing, on momentum. If we happen to be unwilling partners in the social contract, we tend to comply passively, for want of anything better. All things move along in their channels, and the world has its way. Not a great time for major changes! But a time for smooth developments.

★ □ **Waning SQUARE:** 90°, three signs, orb 5/10°. *Effort, dedication, breakthrough.*

This is a crisis of context: we run the risk of losing ourselves in involvements, obedience, drudgery or slavery. Carrying on because 'that's what I've always been doing' can get disrupted, and we are challenged to release our attachment to normality and everydayness. Things must be faced, for our own individuality is re-emerging — consciously or unconsciously — and if we overlook this in deference to maintaining the status quo, we are likely to land up fulfilling what is expected of us without using our own initiative, looking at methods and implications or feeling personally involved with what we're up to. New elements — which can trip us over if we refuse to see them — oblige us to account for ourselves, make the sale, go at it, *do* something. What needs doing usually presents itself clearly and immediately in the form of a concrete challenge, obstacle, breakdown or riddle: perspective is not usually plenteous, but imperatives make themselves obvious.

Our own immediate needs arise forcefully — yet paradoxically, we must first discharge our obligations to fulfil them, in order to bring the old to completion. Addiction to the fruits of our labours renders us a prisoner of fate, rules, mores and expectations: yet by seeking the personal payoff gained from fulfilling what we said we would do, we can energise ourselves for the next move. Here the seeds of the next cycle are laid, even while there is still a quarter of the present one to get on with. We must complete what we have set up, yet through this sometimes exhausting dilemma, we begin to find our own path, seen in the context of our involvement with all around.

★ * **Waning *SEXTILE:*** 90°, two signs, 3/6° orb. *Activity, feedback, completing.*

Busy times, times of reward. This is the golden handshake, if we have fulfilled our involvements. If we have not, this is the karmic backlash. Either way, we receive the results of our actions, and a lot is moving. We are a part of everything, recognised and accepted, and the world turns around and we with it. Productive and creative, this aspect runs on momentum and on effect, and the past either supports or weighs us down. We are seen for our role, not for our selfhood, and the satisfaction or lack of it we experience here depends on us. We have the opportunity to graduate towards a new chapter of development, or to move into victimhood and move along with what is demanded of us: this is a fundamental question lurking in the background now. There is much energy at work, the finishing touches of the cycle are being made, and time waits for none.

★ ∠ **Waning *SEMISQUARE:*** 45°, 1 1/2 signs, 2/3° orb. *Release, voting, sorting out the past.*

Longterm issues again: what are we going to do with the future, and what have we, in the end, gained from the past? Time to extricate ourselves, take that step, and separate ourselves from what we have been identified with previously — otherwise life will rip us away someday, and we secretly know it.

Each of us is an individual in need of our own life. Regardless of what has happened before, it is time to shrug shoulders, learn from the past and commit it to the history file. This is an assertion of selfhood — or alternatively, a stripping away of the props we've used to hold us up — and it is time to choose to move on. By learning our lessons, releasing our guilts or regrets, sorting out all that was unsaid or undone, forgiving and forgetting, we can find a new freedom and clarity, start over with a clean slate. It is time now to finish things off, hand in our notice, and drop whatever we might have been holding on to. It is also time for clearing up messes or unspokens before they go under into the repository of forgotten faults, to linger there until another time comes for repeated lessons to be learned. If things are now uncompleted, we have to realise that we shall have to come back to them another time: issues are changing, and history eats the present gluttonously.

★ ⊻ **Waning *SEMISEXTILE:*** 30°, one sign apart, 2/3° orb. *Reminiscence, rounding up, new angles on old themes.*

A time for contemplation and understanding, quiet recharging, drawing inner fruit from our experiences, forming conclusions, integrating, reminiscing and assimilating. Absolute finishing touches, and foundational preparations for what comes next are in time now. The past exerts a strong moulding influence, but within this we can dig out new vision and orientation, lay the groundwork for... what?

Throwing out all that is useless, repairing and updating what is useful, we discover yet new meaning to life, hidden secrets which weren't conscious when we were in the middle of things. Our own personal viewpoint is reclaiming attention, and often forgotten things, linkages, memories, tendencies can come up to test our will to move on. This is a time for weighing up all things, perhaps honing down initially-wild dreams, perhaps realising our dreams could be wilder. Doubts can creep around in the ruminations and potterings, yet through this we sort out, by ☌ time, our sense of direction and priorities. Between now and ☌, it is time simply to be. To use the time of beingness for doing whatever, in the here-and-now, is good to do. This end-of-cycle period is a final completion, in which the past still lingers in its hold, but does so relevantly, for issues and conclusions arise which are valuable ground-bases for future growth.

★ ☌ **CONJUNCTION:** 0°, orb 8/20°. *New beginnings, potential, beingness in what is.*

When all is said and done, it is our beingness which matters: what we actually are, not what we tell ourselves we are, is the material we carry with us into a new cycle, starting at the ☌. The isness we are decides how the new cycle opens up: visions, intents,

fears are all stuff of imagination, and demonstrate little of the main body of who we are and what we can do. The ☌ is a major transition, and the scenery of life takes on a different slant, often quietly, but fundamentally. A great vista of potential opens up, perhaps welcome, perhaps daunting. Either knowing where we're going, or waiting to see what comes, future or past is at this time but hypothetical in significance, for the Now and its events and omens are *what is*. Life goes on, and only in the present *as is*. Not unlike the ☍, this aspect provides a chance to see beyond the cycle, to come to an internal overview of life's underlying secret, hidden in the timeless.

Beginning and end, renewal emerging from death. What we think, feel and see at the ☌ has a powerfully formative effect on our future, and awareness helps greatly. This is a subjective self-awareness, yet it has a feeling to it which can be balancing and balanced with regards to the world, if we are attuned to ourselves. For we ourselves have within us the whole universe.

The final meaning of what we have experienced as we move through a cycle integrates itself long after the cycle has ended, after we have forgotten the sequence of events, thoughts and issues which went on in the cycle. This integration is a soul-digestion, an assimilation of personal history, and a throwing of it into the great ocean of infinity. For what has happened to us is of little relevance: it is what it has *done* to us, and what we have *made* of it, which leaves its mark, a clutch of qualities which we evolve as we pass through the labyrinthine intricacies of life.

9 Nuances: more about the signs

The planets manifest their energy-principles in all sorts of hues, tones and manners of phrase, filtered according to the sequence of the zodiac signs. There is an underlying pattern to this sequence, which we shall be looking at now. These are the **genders, modes, elements and planetary rulerships.** ***Understanding these, we come into a clearer grasp of the way the zodiac signs behave as they do.***

The zodiac signs

These reprocess planetary energy. The signs themselves reveal psychic patterns and life potentials, which, when functioning freely and openly, are all balanced and whole in themselves, and have their own ways of manifesting enlightenment. But they each have characteristic ways of becoming obstructed, corrupted, twisted and hampered as well. When you observe the workings of the signs you will see both characteristically advantageous and disadvantageous qualities at work, even at the same time. Yet these pros and cons are of our own creation, related to our own convenience, wishes and expectations: the signs themselves represent qualities of energy-processing which are in themselves unprejudiced and neutral in their preferences, just like a cloudy day with sunny periods.

It is interesting to pay some attention to *life statements* connected with the signs. Each sign has its characteristic life-statements, or attitudes of heart and mind which somehow fundamentally summarise what that sign is about, or the kinds of experiences which get associated with them. Life statements themselves are human things, associations with certain kinds of energy: they can express different facets of a sign's qualities, and different open or closed responses to them. Thus, for example, ♑ life statements can be "yes, but we *ought* to do what we said we would do", or "if you keep on working at it you'll get there in the end", or "what would people say if we were caught like this?" or "I'm feeling stuck and can't leave what I'm doing, even though I feel like dropping it". Aquarian life-statements might be "I wish I could be different from who I am, for life would be a lot better then", or "people are always trying to tie me down, when they ought learn to let go" or "if only everybody got together and stopped leaving it all to me, the world would be a much better place".

It is necessary to look deeper than the surface to see sign energies coming through, for sometimes people can behave quite the opposite to what one would expect with a sign — yet, underneath, they are working with the same issue. For example, in response to ♑ energy, there might be a strong feeling of rebellion against anything which smacks of authority, or a semiconscious aversion to being held to roles or tasks: "Oh, well if he thinks he can expect me to work extra today, I'm going to take the day off, just to teach him a lesson". Or in response to ♒ energy, someone might say "I can't be bothered with all these big ideas, I'm going off to do my own thing" or "these people think they're being so wonderful with all their committees and sharing, but they don't realise my sensitivities are getting trampled on!" In other words, a sign represents a gaggle of *issues*, or charged notions or archetypes, towards which different people can react in different ways, depending on their current disposition.

Similarly, typical situations arise, where the flavour of the sign is getting acted out. In ♊, couple relationships can go through sometimes ruthless temporary situations, because each person wants to do things their own way, or in ♍ people can set about getting their lives in order and tidying up. Spontaneous socialising can break out in ♐ after a focusing on nitty-gritty realities during ♏. When ♄ moved into ♐ in late 1985, a worldwide terrorist flap suddenly brought up a widespread fear of international travelling, and the American and European space programmes suffered a major setback due to the crashing and destruction of their launching shuttles and rockets. Sometimes these kinds of symbolic events can be so literal in their adherence to astrological changes that it is rather uncanny witnessing them: one wonders why, after so long, astrology is not in wider use, to warn of such things.

These life-statements and omens can be *picked up* by a symbolically aware eye and ear. Similarly, it is worth keeping an eye on our own thoughts and feelings, for we ourselves can provide all the cues and prompts to enlighten ourselves on the working realities to which astrology alludes. It is a matter of lateral association, keeping ourselves tuned to symbolism hiding within events, big and small: if the milkman delivers the milk late when ☽ is in ♓, he is perfectly in tune with the cosmos, and there's nothing amiss! He'll be back in gear when ☽ moves into ♈ — unless there is something bigger going on.

Substrata. From outside to in: zodiac signs, elements, modes, genders, traditional planetary rulerships

Substrata

The signs are linked with each other in so many patterns. Here we shall look at the contributory factors which interlace the zodiac: the *genders, modes and elements,* followed by *planetary rulerships.*

There are two genders, *yin* and *yang* (female and male), of which there are six signs each, alternating in sequence; there are three modes, *cardinal, fixing* and *mutable,* of which there are four signs each, running in sequence; and there are four elements, *earth, air, water* and *fire,* of which there are three signs of each. Twelve is a wonderful number, since it subdivides to produce an interesting geometry. First, we shall look at the relationship each sign has with all the others.

By looking at signs *sequentially,* as a cyclic series, we see how each sign affects that following, and feeds out of that preceding. A sign tends to *react* somewhat to the sign before it (just as generations of people do), to avoid the pitfalls the last sign fell into. Yet it also stands on the ground the previous sign laid, working from that sign's experience. It tends to look down on its predecessor, underrating the latter's contribution — probably a self-justificatory ploy. Meanwhile it does not *see* or acknowledge the possibilities that the following sign

can open up, and yet is unconsciously seeking to become like it, move towards what to that following sign is normal reality. This contrasting of successive signs takes place within a certain leeway, for while they contrast one another, they are also intimately linked, their themes leading on from one another. You can observe this contrast of theme quite easily when a planet makes an ingress into a new sign: the atmosphere changes sharply and discernibly, while there is also a distinct feeling of sequentiality.

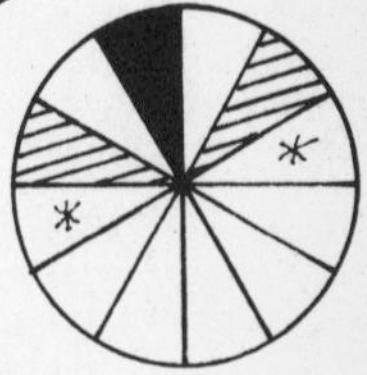

Signs at ⚹ to one another (next-door-but-one neighbours) are different from each other in emphasis and approach, but share similarities of energy and viewpoint, tending to support one another quite fruitfully: they share the same gender, and a different element and mode — thus, for example, ♍ and ♏ each internalise experience and inwardly dwell on its ins and outs as a matter of habit, the first to understand and intelligently adjust to it, the second to get to the bottom line of gut-level truth and deal with it, hence being able to work easily with one another if two planets are activating each other between these signs.

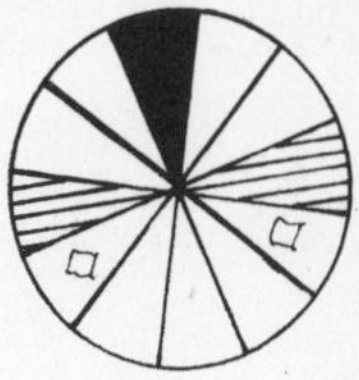

Signs at □ can either conflict or meet in work with each other, facing up to things which for other sign combinations might be uncomfortable or unproductive: they share the same mode, and have a different gender and contrasting element — thus, ♈ works with courage and willpower, while ♋ works with security and sensitivity, energies which can clash or undermine each other, yet while they conflict, both are necessary to each other to overcome each others' weaknesses.

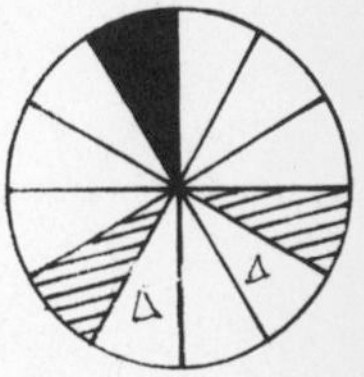

Signs in △ have a similarity of aims and ways, a natural harmony of being which is mutually reinforcing, not very dynamic but easygoing: they share element and gender, but not mode — thus ♑ and ♉ both are earthy, grounded in approach and set on their course through life, yet the former is motivated by reasons of social propriety while the latter is motivated out of an urge for self-determination.

Signs at ⚻ to one another suffer non-communication and dissimilarity: they have different modes, genders and elements, and find difficulty forming any common ground — thus ♓ tends towards selflessness and beliefs of personal insignificance and universal participation, while ♌ tends toward self-centredness and a belief that the universe revolves around it. This dissimilarity of issues can go either way, and doesn't have to be a problem, as long as there is some clarity around what the issues are and what they entail.

Signs in ☍ to one another work as opposite sides of the same question, and each has the other hidden within it, and can learn a lot from the other. Each calls the other into question, yet the meeting is dynamic and charged with potential: they have the same mode and gender, but are of a different element. Thus ♐ takes a wide world-view, and generously believes in altruism and beneficence and friendliness, while ♊ takes a changeably detailed world view related always to itself and its immediate environment, looking after its own life and being affable when nothing is demanded.

Yet together this lot form a family!

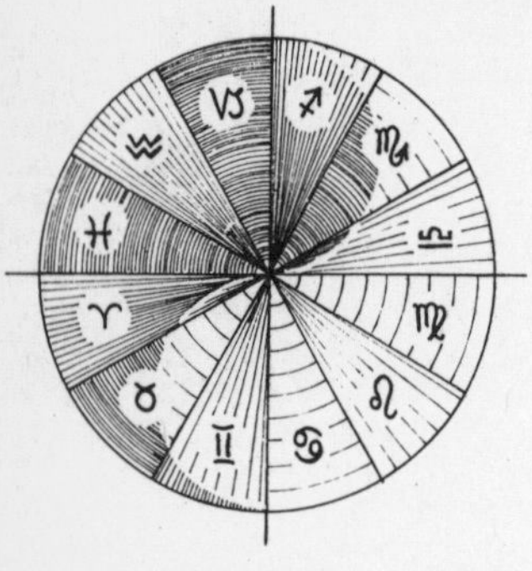

Yang and yin

Gender

Signs alternate through the zodiac, yin and yang. *Yin* is the feminine principle, and works through the water and earth signs, the givers of shape: these signs assimilate what *is* and work with it, make sense of things, ground and channel them. They operate receptively, giving substance and stabilisation to energy-impulses coming from yang. *Yang* is the masculine principle, and works through fire and air signs, the movers: these signs create anew, energise and stimulate motion and alteration. They operate actively, giving life and mobility to the forms embodied by yin. Yang and yin, ancient Chinese terms, are used here, because they do not have the same sorts of loaded connotations which can accrue around terms such as masculine/positive and feminine/negative. Yang and yin point to the two genders within each of us, regardless of the bodily forms we have taken on as males and females. Yang and yin complete one another, and through their joining, creation comes about. The signs alternate gender in order to keep a balance of energy.

The yin signs exercise beingness, while the yang signs exercise doingness/becoming. The cardinal signs, which start each season, endow that season with a gender. Summer and winter, begun at the solstices, can both be seen to be yin signs in that they represent a state of beingness, living with a given situation which has already come about and is there to be got on with it. Spring and autumn, beginning at the equinoxes, can be seen to be yang seasons in that they inaugurate a process of becoming, of changing into something other than what was, creating a new state of being. Thus an intricate pattern builds up, even when looking only at the genders.

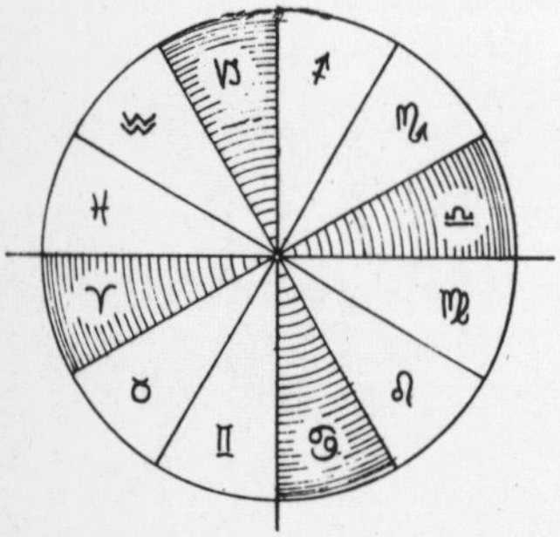

The cardinal signs

The three modes

There are four crosses of three different modes, *cardinal, fixing (fixed) and mutable*. These crosses involve signs at opposition and square to one another: they work with each other to create transition and 'chemical' reaction, each in their own way, in the zodiac. They represent modes or *styles* of operating in life. Each modal cross has a sign of each element — and each triangle of elements contains representatives from the three modes. Each modal cross has two yin signs opposing one another, and two yang signs at square to them, opposing each other.

The *cardinal* signs work to summon and concentrate energy, the particular energy represented by the element involved. They find, define and initiate the action, start motion in a particular direction. They seek to *make* things become as sought, make facts catch up with principles or potentials, and get involved in things. They bring character to the seasons they initiate. At the beginning of each cardinal sign, a process is started in an urge to develop into the state of being represented by the element involved, and by the end of the sign a feeling develops that things are happening, moving along — yet still, the real work must be carried through. Thus winter, initiated by ♑ is an earth season, even though the work is carried on after ♑ by + aquarius, an air sign, and ♓, a water sign.

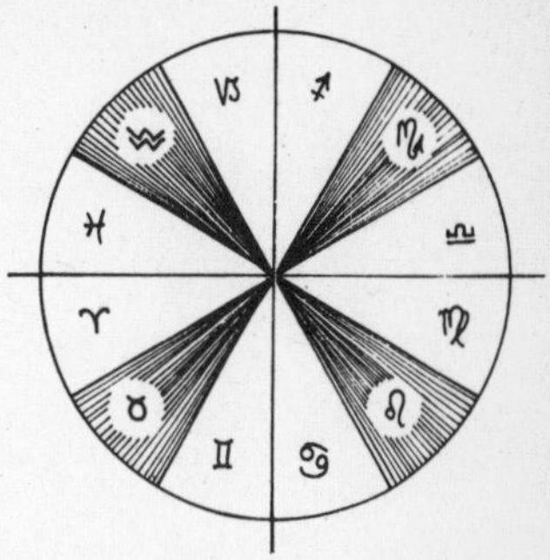

The fixing signs

This real work is tackled by the *fixing* signs: they must fix the energy already in motion, in order to ensure that it achieves something. They are intensely involved with what is already present, given, what has come to pass. Here potential becomes actual, something to live with, work through, make something of. The element involved shows what has to be lived and worked with. At the beginning of the fixing sign there is a sense of engagement, in the middle (at the cross-quarter point) the activity is happening and the work *must* be done, now or never, while at the end the full implications are grasped and the work must be stabilised and nailed tight. Thus, while ♒ seeks to make things different, and to institute a new idealised order, it is working still with earthy, consolidative themes as an undertow, and regardless of its wishes, must recognise earthy factualities.

The *mutable* signs adjust, regulate and perfect what has come to pass. The fixing signs have been too *involved* to see clearly the fullness of all that has come about, while the mutable signs release their hold on things and stand back to gain perspective. They put things in a context, see things anew, finish things off, clear up the mess, add finer touches and ensure that some lasting benefit is accrued from the activity-melee which the cardinals started and the fixing signs made happen. They also learn from mistakes made, develop an overall view of how to understand and better things. They ask questions and develop answers. At the beginning of mutables there is a releasing of tension leading to questioning, at the middle corrections, perfections and reflections are made, and at the end there is a waiting and preparing, a generating of future perspective and foundation-laying. This sets the prelude to the following cardinal signs.

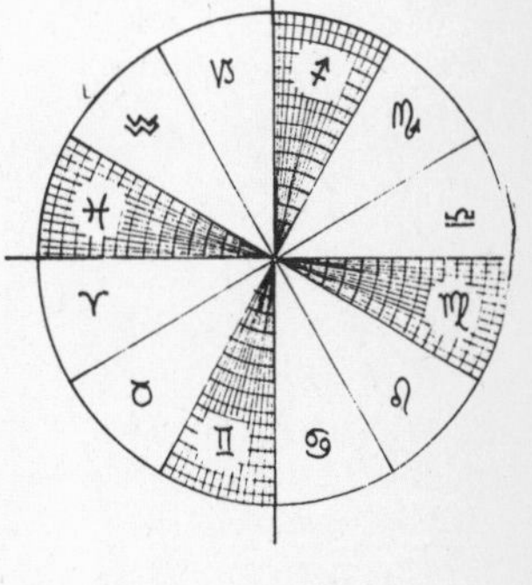

The mutable signs

The different modes find different kinds of difficulties. *Cardinal signs* are fine at starting things, but can get addicted to *making* things happen, a kind of restlessness or drive which sticks, regardless of objective developments. There can be a habitual moving on without completing things, believing that initiating things, or personally *getting involved* is all there is. They can become tied up in feeling that the situation as it is, is insufficient, or seek to impose intentions and wishes on life. Letting go of the future, of attempts to arrange things as wanted or thought best, is a good cardinal sign therapy.

Fixing signs can get stuck in the doing of things, the living out of involvements, without being able to stand back and see *why* they are doing it. They justify things by saying that they must be done, but cannot disentangle themselves sufficiently to see that they can be done another way, or might be well left to sort themselves out. They have trouble releasing standpoints, their hold on things, fearing loss of identity if they do not have the commitments around them which they feel they must adhere to. A relentless driving force can come into play, which does not necessarily adjust easily to changing circumstances.

Mutable signs can build up complex reasons why they are as they are, using rationalisation as a way of covering up what's underneath. Releasing, letting things be and dropping things can become a habit which is mistaken for enlightened behaviour: rather, it can be a *habit* of yielding, where a greater tenacity might be in order. It's all relative for a mutable sign, and changeability can be an attachment, an excuse for not facing things full on. The flexibility of the mutables gives space for new energy to enter the situation, however, and for fresh atmospheres to start brewing, as a prelude to the following cardinal sign.

The four elements

The modes and elements represent the warp and weft which makes up the tapestry, the set of linked issues and archetypes which characterise the signs, which work as sieves letting through specific facets of a planetary energy.

The modes represent stages in the wave-motion of a cycle, while the elements qualities of energy in themselves. The *fire signs* represent the principle of energy or light, vivifying and bringing out into the open whatever energy is around, amplifying it. The *earth signs* represent the principle of solidification and organisation, structuring and gelling energy, making it work. The *air signs* represent the principle of mobility and interrelation, intermixing, loosening up and ideationally distinguishing this from that. The *water signs* represent fluidity, melting and the soaking up of energy, sensitising, joining and causing energy to flow together and become its essential oneness. Strictly speaking, there is a fifth element, ether, which represents space, consciousness and the emptiness within which all forms play, but astrology does not formally build this in to the zodiac, since it is formless and all-encompassing. The four elements symbolise the four states of matter: plasma, solids, gases and liquids (respectively), each with its way of embodying energy in form.

Earth. Well, it's all very well everybody going round getting inspired, clued up and falling about relating and catharting, but what about the real, down-to-earth things which need doing around here? In astrology it is often forgotten that the earth path is as spiritual and enlightening as any other: in fact, it suggests *concrete* inner progress, for in ploughing through earthy experiences we *really* have to prove our mettle, drop our fancy ideas and presumptions, and *get on with it*. Life would get very complicated if things were not practically organised, such that we can know that they *are* going to happen, be delivered, arrive on time or be be known to be accessible: erratic, fitful activity achieves but gusts of progress.

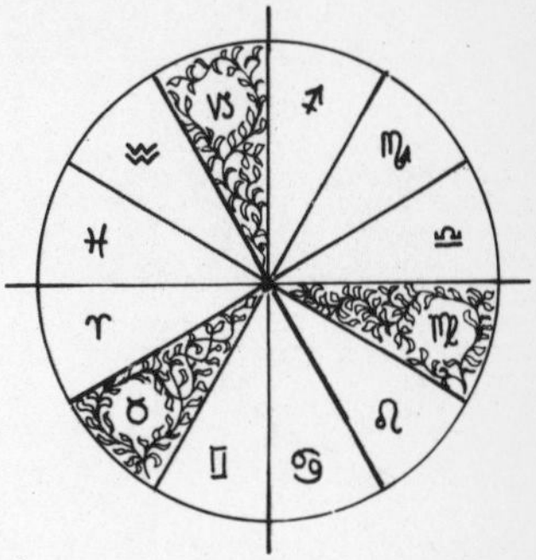

The earth signs

We need houses to live in, and the crops need growing, and the bills need paying. Earth signs are not directly about these activities, but concern the *state of mind* which is required if we are going to keep things such as these on the move ongoingly, and come to grips with concrete issues. We have to develop a constancy, a focus and a discipline, a grounded approach to life if things are going to work, and we need to make decisions and commitments, fix times and terms, prerequisites and parameters. Everything needs fixing up properly, say the earth signs.

The earth signs are about deciding our course and sticking to it, persevering: even in relaxation and enjoyment earth signs are like this, times of habit, even indulgence, but times which have their pleasures which can be made the most of. Earth signs find out how things work, functionally, mould them, build them up, alter them, knock them down and sort the rubble, shift things to where they are most usefully kept, to their completion. Like farmers, we have to learn to keep on going, regardless of what fancies or whims cross our minds, regardless of our emotional states. In earth signs we have to apply commonsense to keep the world ticking. No messing around. Or, at least, not too much.

Like water signs, earth signs involve receptivity, yet there is not the same vulnerability: their innate stability keeps us going. But underneath, the smallest nuances can matter, and responsiveness matters. Earth energy does not budge if resisted or threatened, but keeps on chipping away at things. Changing course is valid only when it is proven that it is most sensible to do so. It seeks to make things last, to preserve the experience and to go into things fully. There is a need to foresee eventualities and the probable reality of future things, and be ready for them. Energy can get stuck though, through a lack of nimbleness. Perseverance leads to results, but it also costs in terms of lost freedom or joy or love. There is more going on than meets the eye, and there are greater possibilities than those already attained or demonstrated, and more alternatives than those routinely followed. Gilt-edged securities have their value, but earn profit slowly.

Air. The air signs contribute mobility to any planets which move through them. While earth signs, which precede them, are committed and solid in their approach to life, the air signs are detached, and look at things afresh, from new angles. They loosen up stuck energy, and toss issues between extremes or alternatives, widening out the possibilities inherent in life. They perceive choice, and while they are often not in a position to execute what they have seen or chosen and stick by it, they unearth the options, so that energy can be liberated, let loose, to explore situations spontaneously and freely.

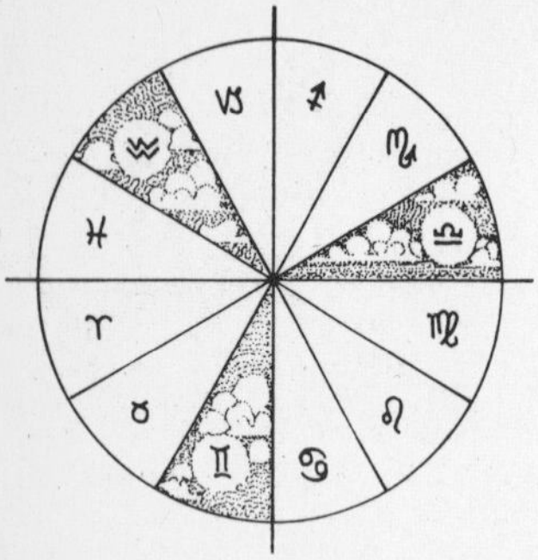

The air signs

The air signs are relativistic: there is a tendency to react to whatever is the given case, and to take the opposite, or a contrasting, viewpoint, for the sake of opening out the issues involved. When that fixed standpoint changes, a quick adjustment is called for, in relation to whatever is going at the moment. In this way there is an element of fickleness or dilettantism, a staying on the edge of things. This is certainly a favourite air-sign ploy — avoidance of the heavy stuff, the real muscle of any situation — but the air-sign initiation is also about finding a middle course between extremes, stabilising energy yet also allowing it to fly free, as it will, in the moment. Paradox and seemingly irresolvable opposites!

Air signs follow ideas and philosophies, and use these as the yardstick on which to judge things. Sometimes these thought-worlds or projections take over from objective reality — because of the tendency to complement givens with opposites — but also their projections into the world can have important consequences in terms of changing things. The three air signs are all placed at points in the zodiacal sequence where sideways changes, perspective and adjustment are needed in order to facilitate movement, distribute energy, bring fresh breezes and induce flexibility: placed between earth and water signs, they dry out all sogginess and muddiness.

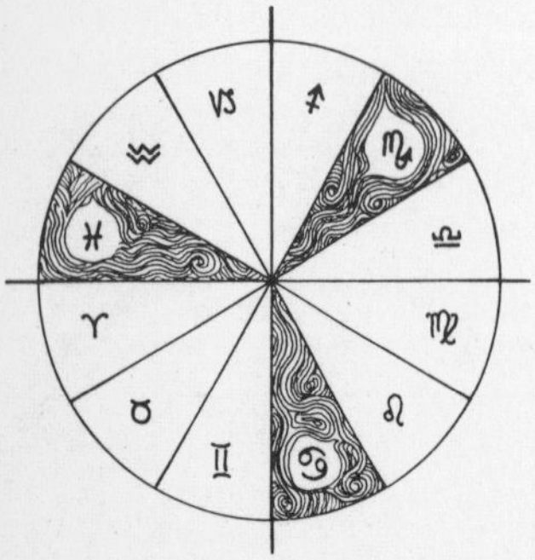

The water signs

Water. Out of the detachment of the air signs arises the *involvement* of the water signs. Standing back from experience takes something away from it, for it is the very *experiencing* of life which is its essence. We humans have a deep need to be *affected*, moved and permeated by what happens in our lives, for existence is not merely a theoretical proposition deserving observation, it is a whole experience which is here to move us, open us and influence us from inside out. We need passion, immersion and dedication, direct feeling of life and its ins and outs if we are to find real benefit, say the water signs.

Water signs bring out our sensitivities and vulnerability. Thus, a measure of protection from the onslaught of life is needed, otherwise, while being affected by it, we might also be overwhelmed by it and lose our way and be obliterated. Water always flows back together: it follows a downward direction to reunite all its tributary parts and become one with itself, the sea. The ocean is the vastness of the unknown or unknowable: from the air we can see all things, except what lies under the water — and there is more ocean than land on planet earth! Through our finer sensitivities we derive new experiences of depth and profundity: simple, small things matter, and care for genuine human qualities and feelings makes human life more human. The water signs are subjective, even to the extent of being overly self-preoccupied, but they represent the personal, intimate, fragile and unguarded treasure of life, a hard-won and easily lost asset.

In water signs we feel ourselves to be one with all things: yet we have to fight to retain a sense of self in a cruel world. When the world loses its harshness and jagged edges, the water signs flow out openly and bring warmth and unity to all, and qualitative benefits accrue. But when the icy blast is on, the water signs hold on tight to what is there or what feels safe, with a tenacity which is strengthened as the pressure grows, until bursting point and implosion. At this very point, the essence of living is let out: when the tears roll, people are awakened, yet when the pretences are maintained, the meaning of life is lost. For life *needs* meaning, and all beings need closeness, belonging, community, family and care, if their existence is to become fulfilled: objective, quantitative realities have little meaning when feelings are involved.

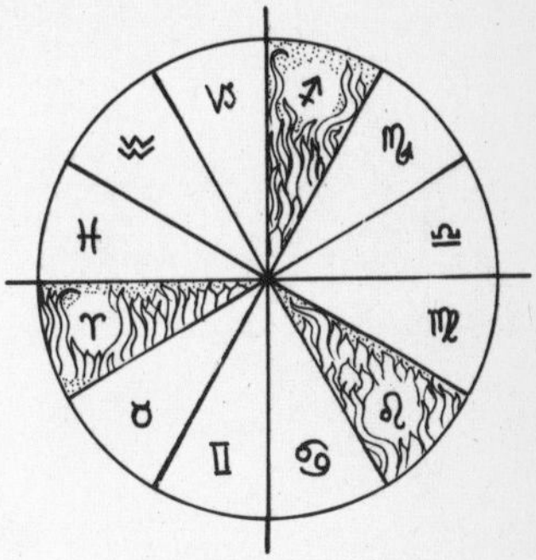

The fire signs

Fire. Fire energy converts forms into living energy quickly, totally and indiscriminately: it does not hang around and wait for permission, the right conditions or the support of the majority, for it just burns, and once started, cannot be stopped. The fire signs energise things, make them move, roll, transform, come out, blossom, explode and *happen*. Fire is individualistic, and wants progress, now. Resistances and obstacles are not recognised, except as challenges to be overcome, and cause for *action*. Fire brings out issues, expresses creativity and initiative, sets things up, starts things or makes them work through to the goal.

But it also goes fast, and does not pause long enough to take in the situation. There must be action *now*, and the trail of destruction left behind can counterbalance the new opportunities which have been created. Nothing is hidden, and there are no reservations. Fire energy does not rest. Energy can be fitful, wholly enthusiastic or wholly depressed, volatile and yet inspired with genius. Results happen. The direction is upwards — which is why the earth signs follow them to remind us of the ground we need to stand on if we are to soar high. Yet the fire signs also whip up a spark of life and courage to get us out of the doldrums and spongy morasses which we can fall into in the water signs. The fire signs change things.

Contrary to watery self-involvement, the fire signs are other-involved — and paradoxically, the water signs care for others and the fire signs care for themselves. There's nothing wrong with me, says the fire sign, for I am a wellspring of all things good, and everyone will benefit (even if they don't think they will!) This rightness, confidence and power is the enlivening aspect of the fire-signs — yet also, the things overlooked, whizzed past and avoided are important too, and sensitivity and listening can balance fire energy into an energy which really works and gets far.

The four elements are very useful ways of looking at the zodiac, and simplify an otherwise apparently-complex situation, when it comes to looking at how each planet is modified by the signs. Essentially, all three fire signs have similar energising effects on any planet, but they each have a different mode, and thereby energise each in their own way. Getting to know this basic style of energising, we can then move through to understanding each sign in itself: thus, ♈ (cardinal) creates some distance from the past by independently asserting itself and following the impulse to move forward, and ♌ (fixing) simply *is* and *does* itself by unceasing energy and creativity and ballyhoo, moulding the world in its own way, while ♐ seeks to further the social context by supporting, investing and furthering others in ways most conducive to the general situation.

This interwoven pattern of genders, modes and elements thus makes for a fascinating setup in the zodiac where, even though three main factors are involved, all the signs have their own uniqueness in the way those factors are combined. Next we shall look at a further dimension, which are the planetary connections with the signs.

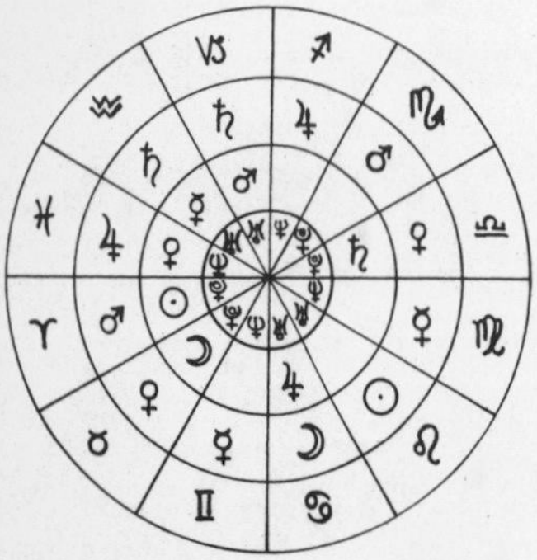

Planetary rulerships: outer circle, the zodiac signs; middle, the traditional rulerships; inner, exaltations; innermost, suggested outer planet connections

Planetary rulerships of signs

The astrological signs are further qualified in their special *rulership* relations with the planets. These not only contribute to our picturing of the signs, but also suggest a system whereby we can understand how the planets work through the signs, or at least, through specific ones.

Astrological tradition, handed down to us through Ptolemy in ancient Greek Egypt, and through medieval channels to the present day, has given us a symbol language and set of manipulations and rules for these symbols which are surprisingly workable today. A few astrologers say they are outdated or chauvinistic (male kind), but I believe that it is our understanding of these rules which needs to change for present day use, not the rules themselves.

It is true to say that a planet has importance and validity in *every* sign of the zodiac, but rulerships and so-called *detriments, exaltations* and *falls* (dreadful archaic terms, but there is no modern replacement!) typify the working of a planet, giving examples or archetypes of the most representative kinds of qualities, assets and difficulties which a planetary energy can manifest through the signs. Also, they give an inroad into the otherwise initially-complex field of planets in signs.

Amongst the personality-building planets (the planets which are visible to the naked eye), ☉ and ☽ each 'rule' one sign, and ☿ -to- ♄ each rule two signs, forming a pattern which is not only interesting but also very revealing. When ☉, ☽ or a planet are in a sign they rule, they are at *home*: they are in a sign which embodies their particular kind of contribution to the energy-tapestry of time. Thus, we can call ♓ a ♃ sign, implying that the energy of ♃ is highly compatible with that of ♓, and that when ♃ is in ♓ (as in 1986), it expresses one of its most archetypal facets, it becomes itself.

Each of the planets is at home in a yang and a yin sign, which reveals a yang (male-archetype) or a yin (feminine-archetype) side to that planet. For example, ♃ is at home both in ♐ (yang), which relates to social and material prosperity, and in ♓ (yin), which relates to inner wealth and vision. We could say that ♋ and ♌, the two signs ruled not by planets but by ☽ and ☉ respectively, are a similar pair, creating a soli-lunar connection involved with simply living existentially, in our beingness.

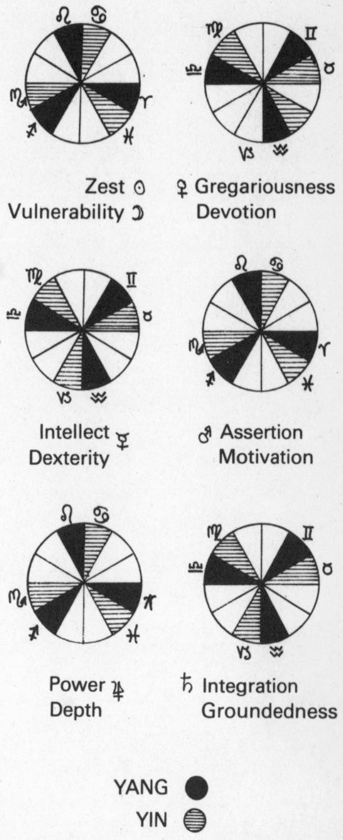

Planetary relationships with the elements

Now in mainstream astrology, the arrival of ♅, ♆, ♇ and now ⚷ into the planetary family has caused astrologers to assign *them* rulerships too. ♅ is at home in ♒, ♆ in ♓, ♇ in ♏, and ⚷ has not found a conclusive home yet (we need to give this question more time!). Some astrologers have forgotten the old rulerships of ♒ (♄), ♓ (♃) and ♏ (♂), rating the outer planets equally to the personality-building planets. It is valid to use *both* the old inner-planet sign rulerships *and* the newer outer-planet ones, for these planets work on different levels, and through each other. The outer planets cannot express themselves clearly into the world except through individual personalities and the personality-building planets, since they work through the unconscious only, in themselves. The inner and outer planets work on different octaves, and thus can complement but not replace one another in rulerships. It seems best at the moment to allow ⚷ to live without a sign rulership — we might be a little neurotic in looking for one, seeking to fit ⚷ into a system it might not want to fit into. I have heard astrologers linking ⚷ to ♎, ♐, ♍ and ♓, all for different reasons, and my personal feeling is to sit on this question for a decade and look closely before forming conclusions.

One interesting pattern worthy of note is that the outer planets each *could* be seen to have connections with at least four signs, which manifest different facets of these planets' workings. This pattern gives credence to old and new sign rulerships, and has some meaning to it. ♅ can be said to hold influence over ♑, ♋ and ♌ as well as ♒, and in doing so, it demonstrates the full profile of uranian influence — for change is facilitated first through *resistance* to change, through buildup of pressure, which takes place in ♑ and ♋. ♆ can be said to influence the four mutable signs, ♊, ♍ and ♐ as well as ♓ — while ♓ has obvious connections with ♆, the three other signs, dealing as they do with reality-systems in their different facets, with mentalistic holding-together (♊ and ♍) as well as intuitive letting loose (♐ and ♓), and with transition, demonstrate different possible ♆ connections. ♇ can be said to influence ♈, ♉ and ♎ as well as ♏: the resistance to change manifested through ♎ and ♉ is as much a part of the change as ♏ and ♈ are. Think about it, for this pattern has interesting implications.

Opposite to the home signs are the so-called *detriment* signs. This is an unfortunate term (like 'fall', later) which suggests a value judgement which is not really there. When a planet is in detriment (for example, ♃ in ♊ or ♍, opposite ♐ and ♓) it expresses itself at least as strongly as it does in a home sign, but it shows some of its excesses or insufficiencies, and the rough edges which need working on if the planet is to move its energy well. So, ♃ in ♊, for example, takes the lust for experience which ♐ has, and turns it into intellectual knowledge, which in turn can lead to heady disconnection from reality and an over-reliance on concepts and rationalisation in place of the hearty belief-power ♐ has. ♃ in ♍ can attach itself to down-to-earth practical considerations, which can lead to great results, but also can block the vision and faith which ♓ works with. In general, signs opposite one another reflect completely different sides of the same question, for *each sign has its opposite hidden paradoxically within it*.

When a planet is in a home or detrimental sign it is strong, demonstrative and typified in its expression, *quantitatively*, in terms of energy-flow, and any issues arising are powerful ones. When a planet is in its *exaltation* or *fall*, however, the message given is not about flow, but about *quality* or *style* of expression. When a planet is exalted, its energy expresses itself in a fine, progressive and subtly skilled way, or has the potential to do so.

Fall signs lie opposite exaltation signs, and when a planet is in its fall, it can tend to express itself in a way which is insensitive, untrusting or reserved. Somehow the goodness of that position *struggles* to get through: yet a fall, like a detriment, gives material to work on, and can be moved into conscious operation as we awaken. For example, ♃ is in exaltation in ♋, through which it expresses itself in a caring, protective, beneficient and sheltering manner (great mother archetype), while when in fall in ♑, it manifests as an overworking, account-bookish, tightly-grounded manner (mean father archetype).

☉ is exalted in ♈, in fall in ♎: the integrative, expressing energy works well in ♈, but in ♎ it all depends very much on what others are up to. ☽ is exalted in ♉, endowing a caringness, instinctual sensuality and enjoyment of comforts, and in fall in ♏, where it does not want to acknowledge or fully enjoy its needs, for fear of letting out a wild dragon of wants. ☿ is exalted in ♒, where abstract thought and enquiry prevail, and in fall in ♌, where it thinks it knows it all and cannot listen. ♀ is exalted in ♓, where compassion and healing of wounds can arise, and in fall in ♍, where we need to *choose* to love and relate, out of reticence. ♂ is exalted in ♑, where it works long and hard, and in fall in ♋, which impulsively wants things *now*, having difficulty applying itself to the procedure of getting them. ♃ is exalted in ♋, in fall in ♑. ♄ is exalted in ♎, where it is judiciously detached and diligent in relating, and in fall in ♈, where fear of loss of self can obstruct progress and involvement.

A planet in a home or exalted sign can bring difficulties if there are blockages attached to that planet, excess or unawareness: it is not an automatic advantage to have a planet at home or exalted. Home signs in particular harbour lack of self-awareness, an *automatic* kind of energy-expression which does not see what it is doing. Exaltations can behave as if *their* way of doing things is the only way, and cannot see beyond it (though this is myopic rather than arrogant). On the other hand, a planet in detriment or fall is faced with the outcomes of its acts, and presents difficulties which foster awareness and a self-correction in behaviour in a willing, seeking person, thus becoming a positive influence once learned about.

Planets and elements

Each planet tends to sit more comfortably in signs connected by element to its home signs. Signs of the same element reflect three different facets of the same kind of energy expression.

Thus, ♃, being at home in ♐ and ♓, fire and water signs, tends to find power in other fire (♈ and ♌) and water (♋ and ♏) signs: ♃ in fire signs demonstrates stimulative energy-expression, while in water signs it demonstrates sensitivity, empathy and understanding. Similarly, ☿ (at home in ♊) in air signs is mental, theoretical and intellectual, while in earth signs (at home in ♍) it is dextrous, skilled and factual.

On the other hand, in signs unconnected by element to their home signs, planets function perfectly well (if channels are open), but find less power or originality. Thus, ♃ in earth signs embeds itself in practicalities, which, while they often do work, they restrain jupiterian zest. In air signs ♃ creates ideas and beliefs which are sophisticated, yet might not be directly applicable. Or ☿ in water signs gets caught up with feeling-sensitivities, both becoming more responsive and losing its impartiality, while in fire signs it forms conclusions and spouts them out quickly, often missing mercurial refinements and making for unwillingness to learn anew.

A reminder: no planet is better or worse in any sign, and preconceived notions of how they are going to work, or whether they will produce pleasant or intolerable results will prove themselves, on observation, to be incorrect. When a planet passes through a sign, it expresses a quality, that's all, and that quality is necessary in the whole scheme of things. Hard times make the good times good, and good times give meaning to the hard times: yet these perceptions themselves relate to the way we individually or collectively are programmed in relation to energy arising through time. Pain and difficulty are directly related to the degree to which we are holding on and obstructing the flow of life-energy.

The zodiacal tapestry

With the background picture given above, it is possible to gain significant inroads into understanding how time moves as the planets visit different signs. It's all a matter of keeping an eye in your ephemeris, noting what happens in your experience when planets change signs, and accumulating a stock of conscious experience, to which you can increasingly refer as you grow and develop in astrology.

The signs represent themes. When a slower-moving planet changes signs, the themes which are counted as important in the collective psyche change. Sometimes events come along to precipitate these theme-changes (for example, although terrorism has gone on for some time, the Reagan-Gadafy power-battle in early 1986 featured the issue, caught the energy of the time, and made it into a big theme, big enough to cause people to change their behaviour as a result — a manifestation of ♄ in ♐).

Thus, while things can be going on over a period of time, they can become charged issues only when there is some planetary energy, modulated by a sign, to support that charge. Government leaks, and atomic leaks (another issue at the time of writing) have been happening for a long time, but the presence of ♇ in ♏ (issues around secrecy and control) and ♆ in ♑ from 1984 onwards have made these issues charged ones: being outer planets, affecting the collective unconscious, events, sparked off by aspects from faster-moving planets, can cause ripples in the collective, where fears, ghosts and insights suddenly arise to jolt people out of their normal everydayness. A theme or charge can be hanging around latently, while an aspect can spark off an event which gives it energy, bringing it out into the open as an issue which everyone has to face.

Theme-changes take place with the faster-moving planets too, but each planet works on its own level, with its own level of significance in the way it affects time and life on earth. If you are in a close relationship, watch how the ♀ cycle affects it: you might find your relationship pulls together when ♀ is in ♋, and becomes more separated when ♀ is in ♌, to be gradually healed when it is in ♍, and to find new interrelatedness when in ♎. ♃, spending a year in each sign, brings up conscious social issues and atmospheres changing approximately yearly: ♃ in ♈ (1987) brings an atmosphere of initiatives, competition and activation, while ♃ in ♉ (1988) encourages ongoing, steadier growth and realism. Watching ☽ is a way of familiarising ourselves of the basic patterns and sequentiality of the signs, because changes of sign take place roughly every two days.

Then there are concentrations of planets in certain signs, or certain kinds of signs. The permutations in planetary movements through time are infinitely varying and very interesting. The concentration of planets in ♑ - ♋ in 1989-90, pinpointed especially when faster planets swing into it, will give excellent experiential data on what these signs are about, on many levels and from many angles. A little astrological deduction would suggest that the capricornian issues the world must look at here concern the way we structurally organise our social and international relations — money and law, institutions, order versus chaos, stability versus disintegration, agreements, constitutions and social purpose — the father principle. The cancerian issues involve the security of individuals and nations, welfare and food, resources, fuel and sustenance, the people and the mother principle. God and Caesar/Babylon suffer wobbles and weaknesses (♅, ♆ and ♄ in ♑) while Goddess and people offer ways forward, openings and solutions (♃ and ⚷ in ♋). The choices for us, as individuals or groups or nations or one world, are to allow fundamental structural change to come about, preferably bring it about, or to resist change, hang on to knowns, and thereby manifest the breakout of unknowns, disruptions, shocks and collapses: do the people serve the system or does the system serve the people? This is a big one.

We all have all of the signs working through us. Planets in our birth charts highlight the issues of certain signs more than others in our own lives, but the archetypal issues of all signs come up sooner or later: selfhood-relatedness (♈ - ♎), self-determination-involvement (♉ - ♏), knowledge/flexibility-belief/power (♊ - ♐), security-organisation (♋ - ♑), me-us all (♌ - ♒), competence-insight (♍ - ♓).

A grasp of this cycle of archetypes can help us understand a lot, and function better. We can then start seeing the part that particular perspectives play in the totality of life, learning to persevere through them, to choose our timings for doing things or working things out, and move into closer accord with the flow of time. It really helps, in manifold ways.

10 Power points in time

A power point in time is a minute, hour, day or period from a week to years when there is a clearly* special *energy-weather condition going on. Astrologically, it can be identified through looking at various synchronous factors such as aspects, ingresses, stations or multiple situations. Time is elastic and a-rational in its unfolding, and temporal power points are times when energy is available for big changes, developments, realignments, releases, energy-raisings and breakthroughs. The greatest power points in time are those when we are able to experience the innate peace and infinite emptiness within life and its ephemerality. Time power points come only now and then, but when they do come, they are worth making use of.

Back to the roots

One of the more important jobs of the earliest astrologers was to identify power points in time in advance, and also to know what to do with them when they came. People then used religion and ceremony as an integral part of their lives, and the inner and outer life was one. Ceremonies, often performed for the most sensible of reasons, would take place at power points, at places and times when it was possible to access deep levels of *existence-consciousness-bliss.*

Astrologers then were also natural philosopher-shamans who were actively participating in the fortunes and evolution of the tribal nation, not just proffering advice: their inner work, with and for the nation, was to access subtle spheres of consciousness where it was possible to work within the group psyche, or enter into creative involvement with the inner psyche or logos of nature, the planet and the deities. This they would do only at times and places which were auspicious, safe and potentially productive: power points.

A deity is an identification of a certain kind of energy. Healthy religions inherently incorporate the notion that deities are imaginal forms which can give us access to an experience of these energies (or in some cases, beyond-energies, consciousnesses). Which doesn't at all deny deities their existence or power: it makes them more contactable and workable with. In astrology, we are lending energy-wavelengths symbols, in order to identify them and perceive their relations with each other — in a sense, deifying them, perhaps somewhat matter-of-factly.

Thus we can simply mention ☿, or ☿ in ♑ in ⚹ to ♀ in ♓, and anyone who knows the symbol-language will get a 'fix' on what we are seeking to convey. Similarly, a Viking would say that Odin was having a fight with Tiw, or a Tibetan would say that Tara was born of the tears of Chenrezig (when he saw that the Wheel of Life yet again, after all his efforts to empty it, was filled with suffering sentient beings). If we had no symbolic identifications such as these, we would find difficulty tuning in to specific energy-spectra and their contributing sources.

Our depth-consciousness, both unconscious (the deep dark) and superconscious (the realms of light), recognises subtle forms through symbol. Every night, when we dream, we are cooking up symbols and scenarios which are not only visual-mental but also feelingful-tangible (in the dream state) or even move into the physical world (in movement and speech during sleep). In transpersonal imaging sessions, people who are new both to imaging (conscious dreaming or guided fantasy) and astrology can, when asked to call up within them an image of ♂ or ♄, come up with images which are surprisingly universal — yet with personalised quirks — without any prompting or suggestion. Some symbols therefore are universal, lying there in the group psyche, waiting to be accessed, and others are personal, revolving within our own psyche. In deeper levels the dividing line, if any, between own and group psyches is very hazy.

Awareness

Many of us nowadays have come to the conclusion that the only really effective way through life is to transform our way of living it, to make it more meaningful, happy, effective, peaceful and trouble-free, and to find our spirit. There are all sorts of ways of changing ourselves available now, but all of them move in a similar vein: they put us in touch with what is going on inside us, so that we can come to know who we are, how we tick and how we fit into the grand design.

The funny thing about awareness is that our contact with it comes and goes and takes on different qualities and facets, but for each of us there are particular times when we make significant breakthroughs in awareness, and we experience ourselves to be changed by them. These can be crunches and confrontations or enlightenments or simply relaxations, but what characterises them particularly is that they have a quality of timelessness to them.

When we experience timelessness, clocks can be ticking away, but we are working on a different level from clock-level, time-bound consciousness: a few minutes can go by and seem like hours, or a day can go by seeming only moments long. This is *time-stretching*, something which is a natural consequence of consciousness expansion (for example, 20 minutes meditation can have the effect of several hours rest or days or weeks of mental-emotional spadework, and judicious drug or alcohol use can also radically change our time-perception). When time stretches subjectively, we have an *opportunity*, for at such moments, we are able to reprogramme our beings, to resolve knotty wind-ups, heal ourselves or create miracles which we never thought would be possible. Deeper levels of consciousness are not geared into the same biological/planetary clocks as our bodies and daily-life waking minds are. Yet a lot can take place for us in an hour or even a microsecond, which can affect the rest of our lives fundamentally. Birth is one example.

If we learn to identify these access-points to deeper consciousness, or to recognise them when they arise, we can *use* them. Otherwise, they can use us! Just as it is valuable to catch a talk, group, orchestra or performance when it is in your area, so is it very valuable to catch power points in time — these times when stretchings and inner changes are available — when they come. By *catching* I mean being aware of them, and making ourselves available to their benefits: we don't have to *do* anything in particular. It can help greatly to visit the sea on a fullmoon or to sit quietly under a tree as ♃ turns retrograde, for then we will be able to allow the universal flow to work, prompting us transformatively. If you are driving a car or doing the shopping, it is possible still to tune into them, but funny things can happen, and it can be out of context to be doing what we are doing: we need to be a little less distracted, mental, self-preoccupied and a little more receptive and open than usual.

More than just ancient remains

We all do little ceremonies to add significance to our lives, even if it concerns the way we pour the coffee, the early-morning routine, the handshake or the graceful wielding of a Visa card. We can use ceremony also to raise our awareness. I greatly benefit from visiting ancient sites around the country, power points in space, putting myself into a receptive mode, and ceremoniously acting out a dialogue with the place, the Great Spirit, or my inner self.

The characteristic quality of a space power point is that we find, when we leave, that we are in a significantly different, more positive, clear and relaxed state than when we came — we have changed level, and not all places have the capacity to affect us in this way. Dowsers say that the presence of water domes underground (blind springs) create the kind of energy-field which makes for a power place. The ancients sought out these powerful places, and built temples, erected stones or mounds, and did esoteric work to enhance them, out of a recognition of their value in getting us in touch with root and core questions, pure energies and spaces of mind and heart which are beyond the normal. Power points were places of ceremony, uplift and atmosphere, where inner work took on a different dimension of effectiveness. People would gather there periodically to join together in shared inner experience.

When I arrive at a power place, I deliberately arrive slowly, pause before entering the site, ask inwardly whether it will accept and welcome me (they are beings like us, with a consciousness of their own), enter respectfully, plant a little offering as a symbol of my love for life, sit quietly and listen within. Sometimes I feel an urge to circumambulate the site, to sit in a certain spot, to sing, to touch my forehead to the ground, to fast or to feast, or to carry out all manner of weird antics: whatever arises, spontaneous or only loosely planned, gives my life a feeling of enrichment and deepening, of belonging and clarity, of connection with the Mystery and of underlying significance. I find that my perspective changes, and the problems I might have come with resolve themselves, or the unclarities or unhealth transform into a new feeling of connectedness.

Combining a visit to a power point in space with the observance

A power point in space

of a power point in time makes these infinite moments all the more potent and moving. Time *stretches* more, and our real selves can surface from under all the garbage of our daily consciousness. Dowsers testify that the aura can expand radically at power points, opening up to nature and the universe — and at the same time our awareness becomes one with the flow, and is cleansed. We need but to receive this state unto us. For it is outrageously natural. An old Bantu song goes: "Listen more closely to *things* than to *people...*".

Power points in time

There are major and lesser power points in time, and if you allow your life to move more or less in tune with things, with a receptive inner ear, you will find you are intuitively on-line to catch them and make the most of them. Some of them are visible in advance, and others come upon us when we're not looking, presenting us with immediate questions to which the best answer is Yes. Those which come upon us can often precipitate difficulties or obstacles: a force takes us over and changes things, like getting stuck in a traffic jam, and being forced to sit patiently, or like cold symptoms arising, forcing us to slow down and take care of ourselves.

An example of a pretty major visible power point. For the past couple of years I have been organising gatherings for people interested in earth mysteries and astrology, and a camp was planned for springtime, for the ancient British fire-festival of Beltane. A look in the ephemeris yielded a very definite choice of dates for it — a major power point in time. Such major power points in time often have a few different astrological phenomena taking place synchronously, and this was no exception.

On 4 May 1985 was a fullmoon, and fullmoons are very good for any kind of consciousness-raising activities. This one, however, was upstepped by several other things: first, the fullmoon took place when ☉ was at 14 ♉, and ☽ at 14 ♏ — this was therefore a combining of cross-quarter timing with fullmoon energy, a marrying of solar and lunar cyclical peaks; second, the fullmoon was an eclipse, which happened to be rising over the eastern horizon just as it was coming into effect — a lunar eclipse is an extra-strong and exact fullmoon when everything goes still and a strong sense of the timeless takes over for its duration. Third, this fullmoon formed an exact □ aspect to ♃ at 15♒, creating what is called a T-square, an ☍ with two linked □ aspects forming a right-angled triangle — a powerful injection of hearty ♃ energy, of hope and forward movement, with an emphasis on working it through into the isness of daily life, brought by the challenging aspects involved; fourth, the fullmoon also fell at a

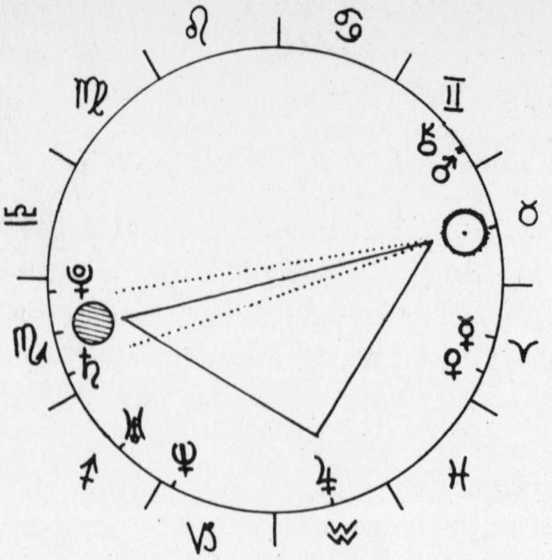

4th May 1985: Glastonbury Earth Mysteries Camp at Beltane

strong *midpoint* between ♄ and ♇, bringing in their combined truth/breakthrough influence — that is, ♇ was at 3 ♏, and ♄ at 25 ♏, the midpoint between which was, lo behold, at 14 ♏, exactly the position of the eclipsing fullmoon; fifth, a ♂ ☌ ⚷ in ♊ the following day, adding a flavour of activity, bridging gaps and an opportunity for healing differences; sixth, ☿ in ♈ was forming a ∗ to ♃ and a △ to ♅, adding a taste of open-mindedness and insight.

Any seasoned astrologer can see that a combination of this kind of energy is worth using for something — and we did. And it worked. At the time of the eclipse — the five-day camp was timed to have the eclipse at the middle — 170 people, open and tuned up through 3 days of preparation, stood watching and participating in it, awe-inspired. Everyone was going through a deeply stirring reaffirmation of their livingness and hope for both themselves and the world, simultaneously making many deep decisions, new linkages and experiencing a quality of love which dawns only sometimes. For some it was a major opening. The experience, even though it lasted in itself but an hour, went down in memory as *one of those* which those present are likely to remember all their lives. People later reported it as a major breakthrough time. That evening far outshone everything else that went on during those five days.

Such energy was not available for the Beltane camp in the following year — so we had to choose a time which was *good enough* for our purposes, in the knowledge that such power points are only occasionally available. What happened though, was interesting: the week before the camp there was a fullmoon closely conjuncting ♇ in ♏, a power point which was a little too early for the camp. On this fullmoon, the nuclear reactor at Chernobyl, USSR, exploded, causing a shiver of fear to run through the world, and not least through the 'green' kinds of people attending the Beltane camp! The whole camp became a processing of fear, powerlessness and emergent chaotic unconscious reactions, not to mention the detectable feeling of the radiation. The result, after a week, was a feeling, again, of break through: everyone had come to a resolution of their own reactions to the event, and the experience had become a major turningpoint in our dedication to Life, and our willingness to accept and creatively work with whatever catastrophically arose in the world in future. A temporal power point had precipitated an event which had awakened deep archetypes in the group psyche, which in turn stimulated an opening up and strong affirmation of commitment to the path, amongst 120 people — the psychic influence of these 120 people feeds back into the collective psyche, connects with that of others working similarly, and a climate for positive outcomes can be augmented or created, transpersonally.

To me these two experiences were major validations of the notion that careful timing of events such as this can create effects far beyond what otherwise might happen. Either careful timing, or intuitive hunches. For it is an alignment of human activity with cosmic energy, and both feed into one another. One wonders what sort of wider effect arises from people joining together to attune and inwardly transform energy at power points in time: such an effect is not something to seek intentionally to create, but it is certainly a by-product which is worthy of acknowledgment. It was indeed a synchronicity that Ronnie Reagan was in Bitburg in Germany at the time, trying to score political points, but landing up making a pointless blunder and undermining his integrity.

It is not easy to convey the essence of these sorts of experiences in words — poetry might do better — yet you yourself will have similar experiences to recall. One of the funny things about these stretchings of time and dives into deep consciousness is that they are difficult to *remember* in an ordinary daily-life way of being — yet, when we re-experience similar modes of consciousness, the memory and its significance returns as if it were only yesterday, part of a continuity of consciousness of its own.

Let's look at another power-point in time, of a lesser magnitude, and responded to inadvertently this time. Even astrologers fail to consult their ephemerides now and then, and this was the case for me on 3rd October 1985 — I had been 'too busy', writing this book! My partner and I were getting on with our lives, and while there were a few important things which needed to be done, we didn't at the time have the inclination or energy to carry them out. Until *that* day. When we awoke, on what was *expected* to be a perfectly ordinary day, everything came up immediately — both of us awoke in a dreadful mood, defensive and frustrated, and we had a tiff. We both turned away from one another, irritated.

Some work had come to me the evening before, and I had to get on

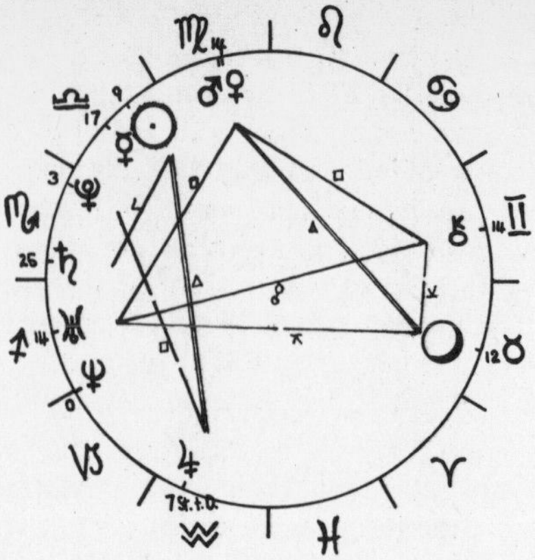

3rd October 1985: a blustery day when things budged

with it. My partner, meanwhile, feeling as if she wanted to get her teeth into something, anything, and moved by the energy, simply drove off, hired a van, and disappeared to the other side of the country, only to reappear that evening, having collected some effects which she had needed to bring home for some months. We had by now forgiven one another at a distance, and realised that the tiff of that morning was not through any faults either of us might have felt the other had, more through the emergence of something within both of us. It is quite common that if there is energy arising from within, of which we are unaware, or which we are resisting, agitation takes over, destabilising us in order for the energy to erupt out.

Her arrival with her things spontaneously sparked off a complete rearrangement of the furniture in our office, long overdue and needed — a whirlwind of frenetic activity, done in a day rather than an expected 3-4 days. Meanwhile, the space we had had from each other had caused us both to realise that we had got on top of one another (a common problem in close relationships!), and we decided that we needed to do something about it, which in the following weeks, we did. Locked energy in our relationship was thereby released, and both of us were the happier for it.

In retrospect, then, we had argued because each of us was unconsciously preventing the other from getting on with things, and allowing the other to prevent us doing so: we had both awakened with a deep strong urge to get on with things, and needed to act swiftly, of an urge, unplanned. So it all happened.

What took place astrologically? ♀ and ♂ were conjuncting at 16♍ (close to her ☽ and my ☉, in our respective charts), and together forming a waning □ to ♅ at 14♐, lending some whacky emotional/activity energy to the situation, with a few sudden surprises. +Jupiter+ was turning, on that day, from retrograde to direct, in ♒, letting off a surge of energy toward getting things moving in preparation for probable later ♃ developments in months to come, and ☉ was forming a waning ∠ from 10♎ to ♄ at 25♏, forcing a decision — 'voting with our feet' — which was connected with completing past issues in order to clear the way for future developments.

The energy-weather (it had also been blustery and stirring weather outside!) had given us the opportunity to deal with some issues — in the physical form of moving round furniture and effects — which we had been hanging back on for some time. And it had churned up some sudden feeling-energy which made us aware that we had been lapsing into an unintentional stultification of relationship. As such revelations often do, the initial form had appeared negative, when in fact the issues and outcomes were positive, a learning and a facilitation of flow. But we could also have resisted the opportunity: both of us could have held on to one another for fear of possible loss of love, while also making life worse for one another by restricting each other's growth. We could have picked up that furniture at much greater expense of time and money, if we had not allowed spontaneous flexibility in, and we could have made life more difficult in the office because we hadn't changed it around according to need. But we did what we did, and the effect was fruitful. We were unconsciously responding positively to a power point in time. We both laughed when a check on the ephemeris put the whole affair into context! It shows that you don't *have* to be an astrologer to be in tune with time.

These two examples show how such power points work. There are bound to be plenty of examples you can call upon in your life as well. Power points are there to be used. They never return in the same way again. And they give special inroads into the mystery of life. The ancients used them consciously, for the benefit of the human family, for nature, earth, heaven and deities, while we often overlook them, respond inappropriately, or drastically resist them: wars break out at power points in time too. We choose how to use time. The question is: is this choosing inadvertent and by default, or is it fully conscious?

There was an interesting power point on the weekend of 8-10 February 1986, when Halley's Comet reached its closest point to the sun in its 76 year trajectory, conjuncting the sun in ♒, at a newmoon, with ☿, ♀ and ♃ also in ♒, and a wide ☌ of ♂, ♄ and ♅ in ♐. I went to an exciting astrologers' conference that weekend, which started off a new trend in cooperation and co-consultation between astrologers in Britain: all went well, and the astrologers had the will to make that step, and were well ready for it. Charles Harvey, Chairman of the Urania Trust and one of the conference organisers, wrote to me about it, describing the way it 'fell together'. "When in December 1985 I noticed this new moon I realised it would be an ideal opportunity to launch the Urania Trust's fund-raising campaign with a

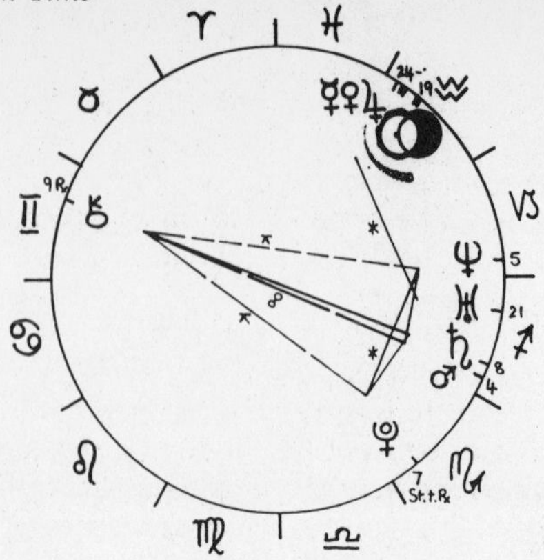

9th February 1986: a time for conferring and group process, with Halley's Comet thrown in

suitable press conference. We decided to put on some lectures. Overnight a full-blown Conference materialised! In the event in less than 6 weeks we got over 500 people to that weekend in the middle of winter. It was a great success, but the press conference and the fund-raising aspects were almost non-existent." A classic example of how something which seems *meant to be* can come about — often using pretexts for the starting of the venture which later land up being irrelevant, yet being a pathway into the manifestation. In magical work such as this, where we are picking up on what the universe wants, we need to be flexible in the way we see and steer things, if universal support is to come through well!

On checking the newspapers soon after, I found that, in Britain alone, some 15 conferences and major meetings were reported for than weekend, ranging in results from positive group action through to bickerings and total fallout: obviously many organisers in many places had chosen this weekend for all sorts of ostensible reasons, but nevertheless, such a congruence of intent in different subgroups of society (ranging from the Conservative Party to the Urania Trust for astrologers) came to pass, and different outcomes were generated by the different groups. That was a heady, whizzing weekend: a conference on the weekend after would have missed the energy.

If you watch out for temporal power points from this time on, you will find all sorts of variants taking place over time. We are in a period of history now when many interesting energy surges are taking place: their power is becoming magnified because humanity is now on the edge of a big change, and is primed for all manner of changes, shocks, crises and great-leaps-forward, and thus a medium power point can become major in significance because the stakes are so high! The most longterm historical changes, however, are more like power-periods, rather than points, although within these power-periods, lesser power points will accentuate themes and dynamics, acting as subwaves in the big wave.

11 Identifying temporal power points

There are all sorts of different kinds of power points in time, with different qualities, magnitudes of import and duration: some pinpoint one day as crucial, while others can spread over several years. Different timescales are involved, calling into play significances from last month or from 160 years ago. And their effects can have repercussions which vary in all the little and big departments of life, in every sphere: after all, astrology is a study both of energy, and of the way we humans deal with it.

Magnitudes of power points in time
There are different levels of power point, working in the context of different timespans. There are no hard and fast rules about this, but here are some suggestions. We'll start with the rarer ones, and move to the commoner ones.

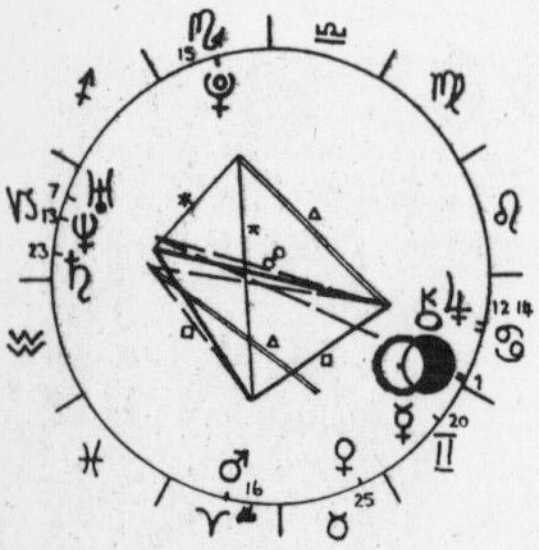

Summer solstice 23 June 1990: a magnitude 1 power point. Broken aspect lines signify an inexact aspect still worth bearing in mind. Note also that six planets are in their home signs, and ♃ is exalted

★ Mag 1. When two of the transformative planets ♅, ♆ and ♇, or even three, form an aspect or make a synchronous ingress, we have a major historical power point, in which fundamental new strains of energy emerge, totally new, not merely a development of what was going on before.

Around 550**BC** there was a multiple ☌ of all three, hapwise at the time when Buddha, Pythagoras, Elijah, Mahavira, Confucius and Lao Tzu were alive (closely followed by strings of seminal thinkers and cultural changes in succeeding centuries), planting the seeds for a new world order. More currently, we have a ♅ ☌ ♆ taking place in 1993. Such aspects can be strengthened — for they often last over a period of years in immediate effect — by the swinging of other planets into the configuration. Thus, 1989-93, ♄ also goes through a ☌ to ♅ and ♆, and ♃ and ⚷, themselves conjuncting, jointly form an ☍ to them: a major five-planet line-up. This is a big one (more about this in chapter 9).

Major outer planet configurations work to restock the collective psyche with new impulses, thought-forms, innovations and images, lying as seeds in the unconscious, waiting for individuals and groups to cotton on to them and embody them in living form as an initiative or new development. These spread out, over years, generations and centuries, until what once was a dream becomes everyday normality. In this way, deep impulses filter through into cultural and material form, and turn the pages of history. Thus, the power-period between 1890 and 1907, involving a major line-up on the ♊ - ♐ axis, brought forward virtually all of the basic ideas and forms which character-ised the 20th Century: flight, petrol engines, telecommunications, wide-spread use of electricity, the splitting of the atom, Darwinism, Relativity, socialist movements, Theosophy and eastern religions, to name but a few things. The effects of these have unfolded in the decades following.

★ Mag 2. Around June-August 1980 a configuration of slow planets formed, comprised of a ⚷ ☍ ♅ at 18 ♉ and 19 ♏, two ⚺ aspects to ♅ and two ⚻ aspects to ⚷ from ♆ at 20 ♐ and ♇ at 19 ♎ (called a *yod* formation), all of these being aspected by ♄ and ♃ over these months as they moved through similar degrees of ♍, themselves approaching ☌ (forming △ to ⚷, □ to ♆, ✱ to ♅ and ⚺ to ♇. Throw in a few extras such as the eclipse newmoon at 18 ♌ on 10th August 1980, latched in with a simultaneous ♂ ☌ ♇, and we had a very interesting situation! Needless to say, we all survived.

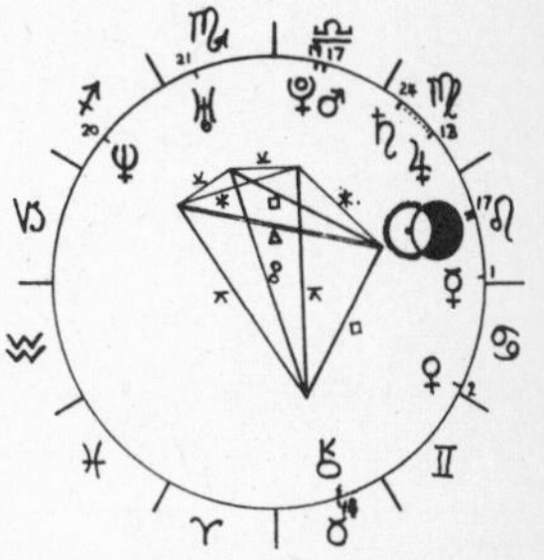

A partial solar eclipse 10 August 1980: magnitude 2. An outer-planet yod, with a more temporary T-square and a ✱ △ ✱ triangle thrown in: what was going on for you at this time?

This was a more complex configuration than the multiple ☍ mentioned above, yet it formed a chord of energy which was significant for many: a time of choosing life-paths, getting clear on the most appropriate path to pursue, and sharpening the issues of the time. From this time on, many of the 'alternative' world-views, activities and lifestyles came out into the open, moving into the social mainstream: healthfood shops started opening on the main streets of everytown, Greenham activated women, complementary medicine emerged into public view, and awarenesses which had been lurking underground since the 60s began a long process of moving into mainstream (likely to be mainstream when the ♅ ☌ ♇ of 1965-6 becomes ♅ □ ♇ around 2014 — a long time, but short in historical terms. The kind of configuration seen in 1980, involving as it did several of the slower planets, has historical connotations timing the emergence into tangibility of seeds planted earlier, like that of mag 1, but mag 1 power points form very distinct, major turningpoints, climaxes and transitions, featuring ☌ and ☍ aspects in particular. These are different levels of magnitude of historical configurations. More about this in chapters 15 and 16.

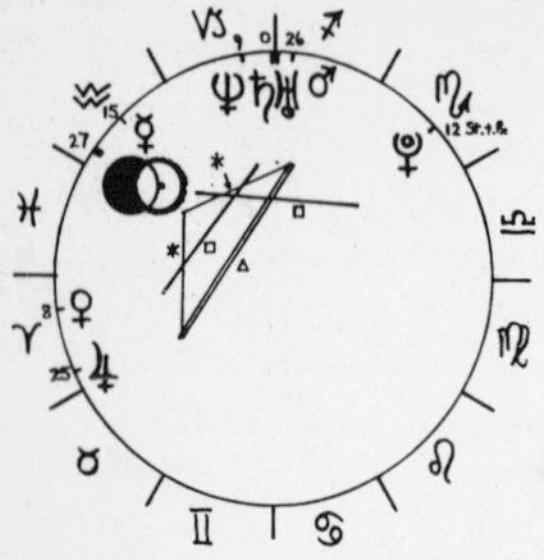

17 February 1988: magnitude 3. A ♄ ☌ ♅ on the winter solstice point is upstepped by ♂ and a newmoon two days after the ingress-conjunction

★ Mag 3. When ♃ or ♄ form a strong aspect to one of the outer planets, we have a power point which has significance in terms of shorter-term cycles, and which has visible effects over weeks of time, or months. If other faster planets swing into this, if there is a new or full moon involved, or if this aspect is combined with an ingress (as with a ♃ ☌ ♆ exactly on 0 ♑ on 20th January 1984), then it will be strengthened, more acute in power. These kinds of aspects draw deeper currents from the transformative planets, from the unknown, into the realm of the known, of society, structures, politics, culture, and around quite concrete issues.

Worth watching are the ♄ ☌ ♅ in February 1988 (an ingress too, at 0 ♑) and October 88, and the ♄ ☌ ♆ in February and November 1989 — while these take part in the larger configuration in ♑ - ♋ of the early 1990s, they can also be examined in themselves as they are taking place. These two configurations offer possibilities for major reforms, or likelihoods, in the context of resistance to change prevalent nowadays, or disintegrative events of a concrete kind, threatening established structures severely. Saturn to outer planet cycles last 35-40 years, and jupiter ones last 13-15 years.

★ Mag 4. The interaspects of ♃, ♄ and ⚷ are well worth watching, especially if featured by added energy from other planets or phenomena. Here we are dealing with cycles involving decades, and aspects affecting periods of weeks and months. ♃ and ♄ conjunct one another once every 20 years, while they interact with ⚷ variably, since ⚷ moves eccentrically.

An interesting configuration came up during the writing of this book, in March 1986, where ♃ formed a □ from ♓ to ♄ ☍ ⚷, ♐ to ♊. During this period, many people underwent major dilemmas over money, committees, organisational questions, and the grounding of visions. During this time, also, the Euro-American alliance went through interesting rumblings, showing cracks in what until then was being regarded as an everlasting partnership of interest. In 1987-8 ♄ pulls into a ⚷ ☍ ♅, further accentuating the theme of organisational changes.

★ Mag 5. When there is a multiple line-up or configuration of faster-moving planets, perhaps bringing in the odd slower one too, a lot of energy can fly around: this can make it a peak time for certain kinds of activities, or for certain issues to arise in the world. The quality of energy in a multiple configuration varies according to the planets and aspects involved.

A few examples: on the fullmoon of 5th April 1985, ☉, ☿ and ♀ were in ☌ at 12-15♈, ☍ ☽ at 15♎, and activating ♃ at 11♒, ♂ at 15♉ (a cross-quarter) and ♅ at 17♐, involving many aspects and a lot of frenetic rushing around! Another was a newmoon-plus-three-planets, plus Halley's Comet, all in ♒ in February 1986, a hot time for groups, conferences and all manner of associations to work out their issues, and a strange time for being alone (chapter 10).

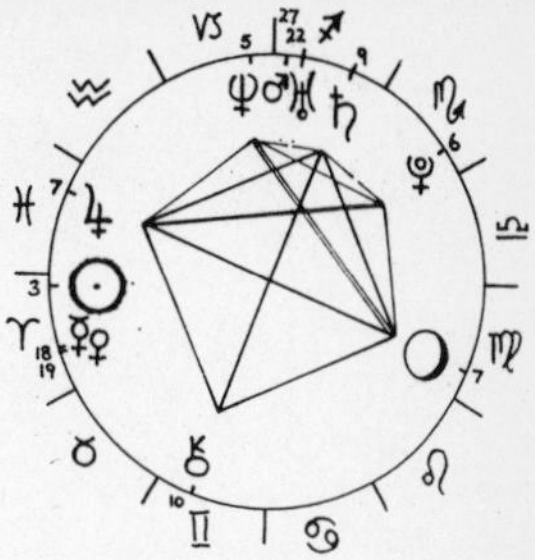

24 March 1986: magnitude 4. A grand cross forms briefly, a few days after spring equinox and before fullmoon: otherwise, it's a longer-term T-square. There's a cradle there too. Not all aspects formed are drawn in

During the big outer-planet multiple ☍ between ♑-♋ mentioned above, a smaller configuration comes into play to feature the larger issues in a very specific way: the newmoon on 26 March 1990, with ☿ conjuncting it in ♈, forms a □ to the major oppositional axis, while a ♀-♂ conjunction in ♒, squaring ♇, unrelated yet synchronous, joins in, to make what could well be, for those few days, an intensely hair-raising situation! This could be a situation where many connections are made and unmade, communications issues are rife, and social pressures of an emotionally-charged kind reverberate in all corners of society, creating jangle and fuss, yet within it, possibilities of a breakthrough in legislation or decisive events affecting nations and organisations.

Another example is the 'Hopi Prophecy' date of 17 August 1987 (still in the future while this is written). Here, ☉, ☿, ♀ and ♂ are all conjuncting closely in ♌, forming △s to ♃ in ♈ and ♄-♅ in ♐: this could be both dangerous (an outburst of fire energy) and extremely exciting. Here, according to the Hopi prophecies, "144,000 Sun Dance enlightened teachers will awaken in their dream mind-bodies... and become a major force of the light to help the rest of humanity to dance their dream awake. A Sun Dance teacher is any human being who has awakened, who has balanced their shields [integrated themselves psychologically], who has gained the dream mindbody and who honours all paths, all teachers and all ways...". What we see here is a possibility for all those who have definitely moved into a mode of being able to manifest their dreams and infect others with them to 'dance their dance', and bring about a major shift of consciousness and therefore reality. This is likely to be one of a growing number of instances where many different consciousness-raising events are taking place all over the world simultaneously, activating a collective consciousness effect in the world psyche — regardless of whether instigators or participants are aware or not of the Hopi prophecy. In the normal world it is likely to emerge as possible clashes, scandals and upsurges, where positive elements emerge from within the apparent furor of milling people and energy. It remains to be seen: stay tuned. I shall be out in a field running an Oak Dragon Music and Dance Camp for 350 people: do something yourself to raise positive *and grounded* energy at this time. Note also that a few days after, all of the planets in ♌ will all move into ♍: with the Oak Dragon we are holding an Arts and Crafts Camp to move *in phase* with this change!

★ Mag 6. Powerful new or full moons. These can be so because there are one or more other planets involved (not too uncommon, a few times per year), because it is an eclipse, and thereby extra strong, or because the new or full moon is falling on a critical zodiacal point (for example, the fullmoon of 21 June 1986, which took place but hours after the exact summer solstice). These energy-peaks last for days only, but can be highly energetic and significant in a shorter-term perspective.

You will find that such times can unlock an energy which then emerges further as time progresses — an example was the ♏ new moon of 1986, which unlocked a powerful confrontational energy, manifested publicly in a chemicals spill in the Rhine, an outburst of AIDS paranoia/consciousness, the exposure of the British government and secret service in an Australian court and the exposure of the US government over sending arms to Iran, and funds to right-wing Contras in Nicaragua.

Eclipses. The moon wobbles 5° north and south of the ecliptic during its moonly journey, but if a new or full moon takes place exactly when ☽ is crossing the ecliptic, it will be lined up so precisely with ☉ that it either passes in front of ☉ at newmoon, partially or occasionally totally obliterating it, or passes into the shadow of earth at fullmoon, being eclipsed by it. Eclipses always turn out to be extra-strong turningpoints, extra-significant lunations, and at the precise time of them, nature slows down, the atmosphere calms, and we have an opportunity to have access to the timeless: at a lunar eclipse we have the opportunity to see a full cycle of ☽ phases in around one hour, a profound experience to have if you are in a good position to observe and celebrate it. The periods (of around two weeks) between successive eclipses (new and full moons) can be particularly intense, crucial and energised. What you choose to do at a lunar power point is entirely what is best for you: the important thing is the consciousness with which you do it. It is well worth observing and consciously participating in eclipses: the ancients put great store by predicting and observing them magically (contrary to the image of helpless savages running in fear when the sky went dark!)

★ Mag 7. Simple and single power points, lasting but days, yet, within their own area of life, having considerable significances as peaks of energy, challenges or turningpoints on a shorter-term basis. There are several different kinds of such power points.

Times when the sun is moving over one of the solstice or equinox points, or the cross-quarters, mark major shifts of energy, time and theme in the context of the cycle of the year. Solstices are particularly good times for standing back from life, and looking at what we are *really* seeking from it for the coming year — plus a celebration of our aliveness. Equinoxes are better for empowering and enabling ourselves and others to move forward, make steps, or change our way of being engaged in our lives. Cross-quarters are times when things are really happening: they have a *this is it* feeling to them — in the midst of the action, it is good at these times to reflect on what is behind it all, to check our alignment and attunement, and to carry things through to where they are going.

Sign ingresses often liberate energy by changing the theme and taste of life, and thereby laying open new possibilities, new standpoints, new facets of life previously unseen. These are lesser power points, but can augment the energy of any other phenomenon taking place at the time, giving a shade of meaning which has to do with the contrast of significance of one sign to another. These can be ingresses of ☉ or any of the other faster planets into a new sign.

When ☉ is in a strong aspect to another planet or a few of them — particularly a ☌, ☍ or □ — then there is energy around which is worth joining in with. It can be good to observe these phenomena, and look back at what went on at earlier times in the year when preceding strong aspects were happening. +Sun+ activates the life-energy within whatever issues are tied up with any other contacted planet. This is strengthened when such an aspect is backed up by a noticeable moonphase — often the energy in the time is fully released only when the moon's aspect to the planet(s) in question becomes exact. Solar aspects are noticeable for around 2-4 days before and after they take place.

When ☿, ♀ or ♂ form strong aspects to each other or to any of the slower moving planets, or when they in turn hit quarter-points or cross-quarters or change signs, energy is available in their specific areas of life. Thus, a ♀ ☍ ♂ can make for a general emotional flurry (check the signs involved) wherein relationship issues get heated or pinpointed; a ☿ ☌ ♀ makes for lively interchange, social contact and is a good time for parties or meetings; a ♂ □ ♄ is excellent for hard work or facing up to difficult, grindstoney issues; during a ♀ ☍ ♄ it is good to accept that sometimes we are all alone, and it's alright; when there is a ☿ ☌ ♇ some truths and unspoken messages must be had out, and when there is a ☿ ☌ ♅, so much mental energy is flying around that sleeping, logicalities or simplicity are hard to come by; on a ♂ □ ♃, a lot of force is about, but when there is a ♀ ☌ ♆, things can be peaceful, beautiful and nicely rounded. The effects of such phenomena can be around for a few days, sometimes more, and can influence longterm developments through acting as cruxpoints.

Other contributing factors which create power points in time are:

★ the stations of the planets (when they stop and turn either retrograde or direct);

★ configurations of planets which do not shout loudly from a technical astrological point of view, but which form concentrations in certain signs or types of signs (such as a lot of action in mutable signs, or a focusing on three consecutive signs, or a featuring of signs of the same element, or several separate phenomena taking place synchronously, yet unrelated to each other);

★ arrays without major aspects, but a balance or pattern to them which stands out (such as the general spread of outer planets in three signs, ♏, ♐ and ♑ in 1984, backed up by seasonal visitations from faster planets);

★ ongoing periods when there is a lot of activity in general (such as 13 March to 5 April 1985, when there was an extraordinarily large number of everyday kind of aspects going on, eighteen in all, plus four stations, spring equinox and the back-end of a ♃ □ ♇! Check this out in your ephemeris). To give but a few examples.

All sorts of variants can occur over time. The interesting thing is their uniqueness, and the sometimes uncanny synchronicities of theme or atmosphere which can come about — as if the Grand Old Dancemaster up there were deliberately flipping through his cranial ephemeris and cooking up interesting configurations to entertain those people down there and test their capacity to turn from energy-victimhood to capacity to flow and use the energy available in a creative and progressive manner. Keep your eyes on your ephemeris!

Opening up

There are no hard and fast rules to the identification of power points. It is well to use a flexibility of thought and openness to possibilities when looking for them. Also, it is important not to set out to *predict* what is likely to happen at power points in time: it is far more valid either to seek to see the kinds of *openings* they offer, or to consciously make ourselves receptive to what might arise, when it arises. For here we are seeking to allow the Unknown to come into our lives, and to trust that the power of life, if we open to it, will provide us with what we need, even if we do not see what that is. There is a subtle yet crucial difference between using astrology to stave off anything we fear, and using it as a way of opening to life.

Power points do not even need to be identified in advance. If you are functioning receptively, in your magical self, you will find yourself intuitively using energy-peaks to advantage. Noting power points *retrospectively* helps us learn from life, giving new insights into the significance of things which we have experienced, and also, through this, giving memorable living data by which to learn astrology, and more about time and energy. Looking into the future needs to be done without prejudice, without the need to *want* things to be a certain way. If we are seeking to move beyond ourselves and our normal reality, why should we seek to narrow our lives to expected future possibilities?

Sometimes these power points can be spread out over time, as well — for example, a sequence of astrological events over a few days or weeks, which quicken energy and precipitate situations which demand resolving. Or a sequence of related events, such as ☉ then ☿ moving into ♊, followed by a ☌ of the two, followed by a newmoon involving both, even if they are by then, say 7° apart. Astrological phenomena, as well as life experiences, cannot be looked at in isolation: they link up, even if we see the linkage after the event.

A new way of life

It is well worth contemplating the benefits of planning your life around them — as much as life in the modern world permits. To modern people, Monday Morning is Monday Morning, regardless of the astrological configurations going on, but there comes a point where, if we are going to live sanely, we need to allow our time to be more flexible — otherwise all sorts of mishaps can occur, mishaps which we set up by not paying attention to the subtler things in life, like relaxation, sensitivity, good diet, time alone and time for raising our spirits. It is regularly a good thing to relax for a day or two either before or after a fullmoon, or to work late into the night when ☿, ♂ and ♄ are contacting each other — for then we are able to make use of time more effectively, and our lives become easier. Obeying modern work ethics does not necessarily get the work done faster or easier — it just increases the worry, bustle, complexity and blindness which can disturb our lives daily, adding layer upon layer of complexity at every turn.

In England, there is a sign they place at level crossings, where a road crosses a railway, which says, quite simply: **"STOP, LOOK AND LISTEN".** It speaks for itself.

Working energy

Power points are not only places and times for making personal progress with. We owe it to life and the world to care for them, for the world is not simply a stage upon which to act out our individual movies — it is a being with a life of its own, a being on whose skin we live and crawl around, sucking her blood and tending not to do much in return. And time is not merely a simplistic continuum through which we carve our personal histories — it is a medium of evolution, an ongoing flow of change within which we are enacting the whole of human history and the evolution of consciousness. Every act we make, word we speak and thought we think has meaning in this stream.

Especially at energy peaks. The wholesome thoughts and feelings we can generate at these times have great power, as have the negative ones. And the stillness and timelessness we can find within time is an access point to the fundamental secret of all life. "The Tao which can be spoken is not the eternal Tao: the person who speaks of it does not know, and the person who knows does not speak". Lao Tzu's teaching points to the fundamental secret within astrology, which nowadays is often missed: through living in time, we can come to an ultimate experience of what lies beyond time. This experience has the power to heal all ills.

The ancients used power points in time because it gave them access to the inner planes, a chance to get out of everyday consciousness, and to involve themselves consciously with the causative level of archetypes and spirit. Many power places on earth exist to gather or transmit energy from and to the wider universe, or to do the same horizontally with regard to the landscape around. Some of them — such as 'hillforts', henges and 'burial chambers' — were specifically built to insulate the spiritual practitioner from the complex energies of the landscape and the world, in order to foster the development of psychic abilities or spiritual illuminations. These were used at power points in time, which themselves endow a raising or sharpening of energy, which, when met by deliberate consciousness-raising, can make for quantum changes in all directions. This kind of work involves our own soul and personality, our local environment and those we share such experiences with, the wider world, and the Beyond, simultaneously and multidimensionally.

On a short-term basis, every dawn and sunset is a power point in time. Sometimes they can be major ones for us, leaving an indelible imprint. To extend our hands to the sun and welcome it into our lives internalises it, and opens us to its life-current. Such a common thing, the sun rising and setting, yet sometimes the experience is uncommon and stirring. A simple attitude of reverence for time, nature and the living of life does amazing things: oneness is more than just a nice idea.

12 Configurations

Occasionally, three of more planets form a configuration, all of them forming aspects to one another. These set in motion a surge of energy with a distinguishable flavour, and some of them can be major power points in time. They twang strongly. Here we are going to look through several different aspect structures. Get an overview of the chapter, for it is not necessary to read through thoroughly unless you so wish: but it is a useful chapter for reference.

Multiple aspect structures

When three or more planets aspect one another mutually, they form an aspect *structure*, of which there are several different types. These are usually three-sided triangles, less often, four-pointed structures, and even less often, more complex ones. Any structures forming in the heavens at any time indicate a temporal power-point, where a dominant chord sounds which has a strong signal of its own. There are very definite, clear issues to work with, which can raise the stakes of life immensely. These configurations can give the energy-wherewithal for quantum leaps. When ☽ or another faster planet, swings into these, specific incidents or strong atmospheres can be sparked off, featuring the story of the whole configuration.

Understanding a structure depends on what the aspects are which make it up. If there is a prevalence of challenging or flowing aspects, then their characteristics will dominate. In some structures, there is a mixture of both, such that challenging aspects create action, dilemma and work, while flowing aspects let off the pressure and add talent, ease or naturalness to the configuration. On the other hand, a prevalence of flowing aspects can make for gifts and assets which are present and available, but which also can be taken for granted or unactivated — but one or two challenging aspects thrown in activate the structure and create a measure of acuteness to goad these abilities or resources into action.

Below we work through the main kinds of aspects structures which tend to form between planets over time. Although there are some descriptions given here, indicating what to look for whenever you notice a multi-planet structure forming, the main purpose here is to point out the kinds of structures to be looked for, and to encourage you to sniff the air, and observe what is going on within and around you in your own life at thee times. There are plenty of surprises in astrology: use the below notes as starters, and use your own senses to *get* what a structure is *doing*.

Specific structures

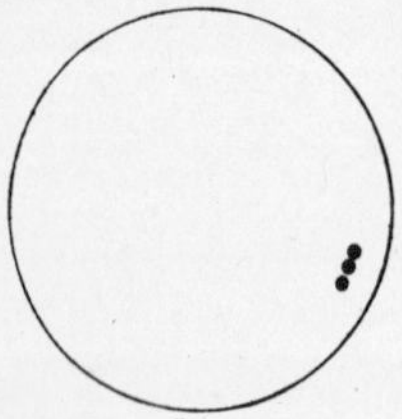

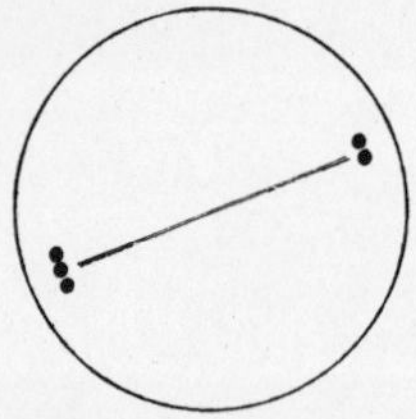

* **Stellium.** This is a multiple conjunction, involving three or more planets within orb of each other (orbs can be loosened out in this case). This amplifies the general ☌ situation, in which there is a lot of energy moving from within outwards, being expressed naturally yet often unawarely, as if everyone were like that and it were perfectly normal. Difficulty in seeing the effect of what is taking place, or the contrast between intents and realities: the world has its own ways which might not accord with our own wishes. Occasionally a slap in the face is needed from life to objectify this aspect. But it is powerful and often leads to big results, if worked well. New beginnings, and the death of the old: the magnitude of this change depends on which planets are involved. A strong power point for work on intent and focusing the dream which will guide us on through the future. An example of this is the stellium which forms around 24th August 1987, where a newmoon at 0♍ is conjuncted (within 3°) by ☿, ♀ and ♂ in ♍ — a time for forgiveness, resolve to clear up the potential mess made during the previous few weeks, and to ground the wildness of the energy prevailing in the weeks beforehand (during which there is a multi-planet grand trine in fire signs).

★ **Multiple opposition.** Here, an ☍ is joined by one or more planets, upping the energy. If there is a weighting to one side, then the predominant side will act usually as the conscious side, and the weaker side will act as a stirrer, lever and irritator, to agitate the predominant ☌ and objectify energy. It depends what the planets are, and how they link up to the rest of the chart. There is often a tendency for polarisation, them'n'us sydromes on the buildup, which might or might not be resolved into agreement at the exact forming of the aspects. There can also be a changing of roles between the apparent sides, or the breaking through of a new reality out of the ashes of the old: something which previously had not been acknowledged. This is a peak time, good for breakthroughs, realignments and transition to the next stage in any developments. A strong configuration, and a time loaded with energy: deep choices are enacted here.

An example is the newmoon of 3rd July 1989 with ☉ and ☽ at 11♋, ⚷ at 8♋, ♄ at 10♑, ♆ at 11♑, ♅ at 3♑ and ♃ at 24♊ (out of orb, but contributive) — a likely decisive time, when strong pressures are exerted by popular demand and social action on the legal, governmental and financial of the world (strongly affecting Britain, US and India, countries with a strong ♋ or ♑ influence). Likelihoods of powerful shake-ups, where being in a position of power is not going to be very pleasant (unless such a person enjoys historical roulette wheels!): those in power who can move with the time and respond rapidly and appropriately to the somewhat crazy energy rife at the time will make great progress. This could be a watershed — one of a few during this longterm line-up.

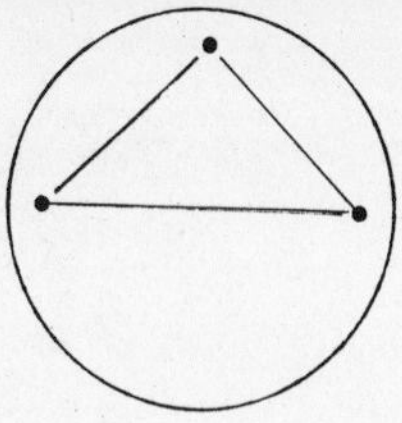

★ **T-Square.** This is an ☍, with a planet which forms □ s to both ends of it, a very challenging aspect. The ☍ lends dilemma and the □ s lend effort/crisis. With such a configuration, a strong energy is driving to break through, overcome extreme limitations or challenges: the choice offered is hard work and breakthrough, or avoidance of the issue and breakdown. It is an imbalanced structure: the □ ed planet acts as an irritator, yet also is the one with the solution. The point opposite this planet is often an area of life which must be attended to urgently or intensely, in order to create a fourth energy which balances the tension and makes for lift-off. The stress and apparent difficulty involved in this triangle makes for action, drive goaded by threat or pain, and circumstances which arise where we unconsciously confound our own purposes, find obstructions, or make things laborious.

A recent major T-square in 1986 had ♄ ☍ ♅, with ♃ in □ to both, straddling the mutable signs: when ☽ swung into ♍, a grand cross was formed. A lot of effort was required to make progress in getting things to work: the answer is found in radical, yet pragmatic contextual shifts of viewpoint. This was about organisational perspectives and infrastructures. A time for decisions. Gorbachev and Reagan made a go at it, but the issues were very big, and the changes of viewpoint involved were threatening to become larger than either system they represented could handle. Yet, the concreteness of both ♄ and ♅ demanded real action, and were precipitating forced solutions, through a growing awareness of the costs and disadvantages of carrying on in the old mode of Big Power rivalry. ♃ in ♓, at the apex of the T-square, introduced a visionary, overall 'what-are-we-doing-all-this-for?' undertone to the hard negotiations, bringing into focus both immediate practical issues and long-term basic questions.

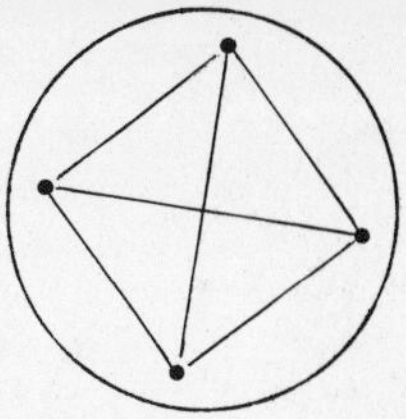

★ **Grand Cross.** This is a step on from a T-square, involving at least four planets in mutual □ to each other, with two ☍ aspects linking them. This is a rare and powerful one, not to be taken lightly, and to be celebrated awarely. Usually, this is about uphill climbs and hard realities, forcing total engagement of energy, leading either to an 'overdrive' situation leading toward resolution and excellence, or a going under, giving up or a catastrophe leading to great learning. Difficult or exacting situations present themselves until the question is assaulted from the front and the bull is grasped by the horns. This is about root- and core-questions.

As with a T-square, the planets concerned will usually be in signs of the same mode, featuring the qualities of that mode strongly — if they are not, there can be complications which befuddle the situation and demand clarity. The presence of a grand cross implies that there is something very special and important happening, even if it cannot be discerned at the time. It is quite simply a question of doing it and breaking through on it. Odds appear to be against, yet these in some way increase the stimulus to get to grips with the situation.

There is tremendous spiritual power behind a grand cross, if accessed: the power to overcome experienced difficulties lies in raising awareness and engaging deep resources in the battle. Inner stillness is important as a way of quieting conflicts and getting clear. This is a breakthrough aspect: when it happens in the heavens, a crunch comes to the world, choices must be made, and things can change radically. This is a quantum leap, calling for total revolution in whatever field the planets and signs allude to. The planets and signs involved point out the issues. Since most grand crosses involve faster-moving planets, they are short and sharp in duration, yet their effects can reach out a long way.

At the time of the above-mentioned grand cross (24 March 86) I was seriously contemplating declaring myself bankrupt, in despair that my intentions and actualities seemed light-years apart — and after busting open my pride and acknowledging the situation fully I realised that there was in fact no choice for me but to carry on, for the longterm prospects (♃ - ♄) were good, and what the issue was really about was about my own psychological capacity to persevere and know that odds-against often imply promising possibilities (a ♅ in ♊ paradox!). I was writing chapter 10 at the time — and this book could have ended there!

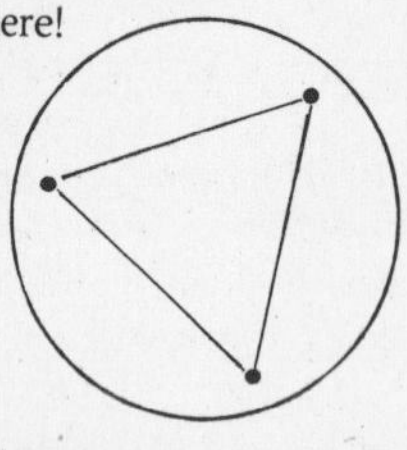

★ **Grand Trine.** Here three planets are in mutual △ to one another. This is strong and very stable: it opens up a natural flow of energy, fortunes or events, endowing abilities, qualities and assets which just seem to *happen,* as if they had always been meant to, even though no-one had thought of it. It gives a measure of ease, beauty and fortune, where the energies of each planet mutually back each other up. Yet there is another side as well: this aspect is so flowing that we might tend not to be aware of the *significance* of what we have available, because the need for it is not seen, or there is a lack of urgency accompanying it. Life is easy enough as it is, therefore motivation to change anything or join in on change is low-key.

But the sheer movement of energy which is released by a grand trine sets things in motion — even things which weren't *supposed* to be in motion, by the sheer erosion and activation brought about by a quickening and opening of energy. Such enhancements can bring out as many social or world diseases as they can bring out benefits, for while there is much healing and relaxing of barriers, emergence of latent or sleepy negativity is encouraged by this energy. When life-energy is rising, watch out for negativity getting released, and make sure it doesn't stick or pollute: in the end, what we call negative energy is but energy which is not flowing freely and naturally. This is a channel-clearing, without stress: but it depends what is in the channels needing clearing! Often the feeling around a grand trine is that the energy is not controllable, that it just happens: focusing this energy can be difficult. It is a time for trust, for opening up to the universe, and *allowing* the right thing to happen.

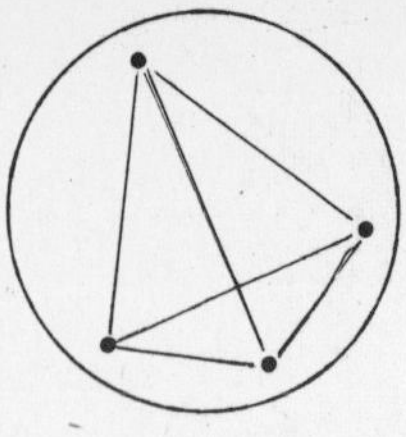

★ **Kite.** If, between one of the △ aspects in a grand trine, there is a pair of ∗ s bringing another planet in (itself forming an ☍ to the third planet), then we have a kite. This is a very moving, flowing aspect, with a measure of the urgency the grand trine doesn't have. Here, the talent and capacity of the grand trine is channeled into a specific task through the ☍ . The presence of the two ∗ s bring in dynamic movement and busy occupation, and the whole configuration, if balanced astrologically and worked well psychologically, points to the possibility for success and progress in great measure, a time of memorable developments. It sails, but is grounded by the ☍ . There is a unified feeling in the air, much energy-buzzing, and a clarity underlying it too: the ☍ gives an objectivity which tends not to become a dilemma because the △ and ∗ aspects help the energy become one and integrated. The issues can be quite large, however, and if there is a tendency to lapse into triney routines, the ☍ , when activated, will force issues through uncomfortably. The planet at the bottom of the kite usually holds a focal role, binding the △ and ☍ aspects.

On 18 August 1987 a kite forms with ☽ in ♊ ☍ ♄ - ♅ in ♐, ♃ in ♈ and ☉, ☿, ♀ and ♂ in ♌, a time when energy is flowing strong (grand trine in fire signs), but is focused by a short-term ☽ ☍ ♄ - ♅ , demanding true independent thinking, flexibility and structured (♄) spontaneity (♅). A good day for staying up all night and making the most of it!

★ **Greater Octile Triangle.** This involves two ⚼ aspects and one □ . This is a *work* configuration, giving a sense of purpose and longterm intention to the time. The ⚼ aspects focus immense energy into using current circumstances as a way of moving toward an *eventual* end: there is a task cut out which we must fulfil, even if it makes life temporarily more difficult. Goals should be reachable, otherwise this eventual goal may never be reached, and the here-and-now should be looked at and learned from as well, for it contains integrative omens and lessons relevant to past and future. This configuration suggests a deliberate, clearly purposeful time. Facing the world fair-and-square.

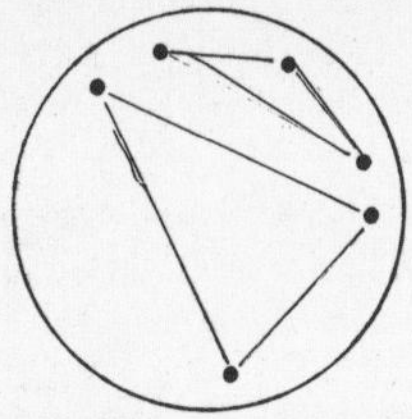

★ **Lesser Octile Triangle.** Here we have a □ and two ∠ aspects. Issues are not dissimilar here to the greater triangle: longterm perspectives are hauled into everything around the planets of this triangle. The difference is that personal intentions dreams and drives prevail, while in the greater triangle overall concerns and the filling of perceived social/world needs prevailed. This triangle elicits commitment, while the former tests it. But there is strong intention here, a sharp sense of distinctions and goals, and the wherewithal to develop abilities into something dynamic and original, evolved through accumulated experience.

An interesting example: during the time of the final correction of this book, I was being faced with an important task — to write some effective advertising copy for the Oak Dragon camps which I am a part of organising. There was no inspiration coming, and I was getting internally ratty about the matter. On Sunday 17 January 1987, a lesser octile triangle came into being: ☿ put itself into a ∠ in the middle of the ongoing ♃ □ ♄ which was afoot at the time. To add a personal note, also, ☿ , then at 2♒ (♃ at 20 ♓ and ♄ at 17♐) was forming a △ to my natal ☿ (at 2♎), and ♃ was nearly ☍ and ♄ was applying to a □ to my natal ♄ (at 21♍). So what's all that about? ☿ entering into a double ∠ aspect to ♃ and ♄ brought in a question of longterm, preferably clarifying, thought about longer-term organisational issues, in general — seeing this, I decided to drop what I was doing in the way of busy-busy activities, and to focus on getting this copy done. During the ☿ ∠ ♄ on the Sunday, I sat around rather dull-brained with one of the other directors of the project, and while we got nowhere in terms of a finished product, we did manage to focus our attention on the issue and bring up some catchy phrases. As soon as it had formed, things started getting clearer, and during the time-gap before the ☿ ∠ ♃ formed on Wednesday 21 January I battled away getting down some useful pieces. But it all suddenly fell together in one swoop during the ☿ ∠ ♄, and I emerged from the process with the copy required. Meanwhile, the transiting ☿ △ to my natal ☿ opened up my communicative abilities, which I consciously put to work in this task. The time was used productively, toward the longterm ends I was working with (which my natal ♄, aspected by ♃ and ♄ in transit, was craving!). ♃ and ♄ thus put ☿ to work: otherwise the time might have been spent mercurialising some other way, talking, reading, thinking or buzzing around — but I choose in this instance to use the occasion for a conscious purpose. It works.

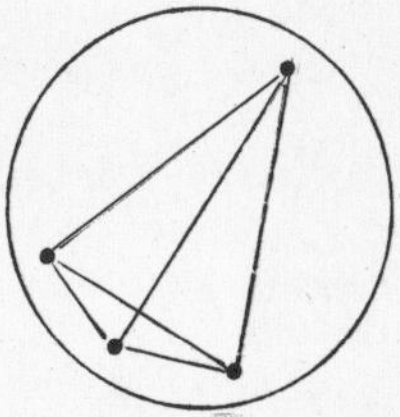

★ **Octile Kite.** This is uncommon and very powerful. This configuration lends a strong sense of destiny, dedication and the development of abilities to a great capacity. It brings out skill and gathered experience, and makes for apt and talented work for causes, for activities which bring no immediate reward, but have big implications. The planets in ☍ focalise the energy. A discovery that there is far more underneath the surface worth working for, or that the time is Now to execute what has been awaited for long. Issues arising fast, precipitating emergencies. Tremendously focused and well grounded. This can also make for a major failure syndrome, wherein obstacles to be surmounted can be seen to be so large that nothing can be done — this is largely a way of seeing things rather than a fact.

Another structure with a similar taste is a T-square, with two ∠ s and one ⚼ thrown in. This puts the slant much more on dealing with immediate issues (T-square), but eventual ends are always accounted in as well.

★ **Rectangle.** Often called a 'mystic rectangle', there is nothing specifically mystical about it. Here, two ☍ aspects are woven together with two △ and two ⚹ aspects. This can make for a time of enormous questions, yet potential solutions which arise

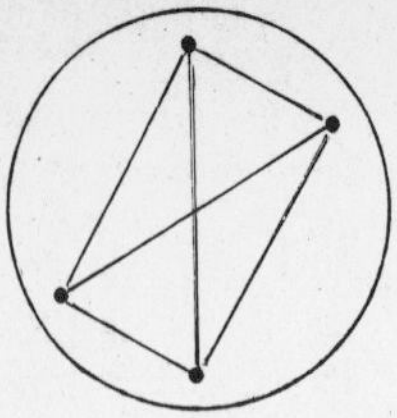

either by default or by apparent good luck. The flowing aspects take much of the tension out of the ☍ aspects. There is much to work out, but it looks as if great things are possible. Abilities and assets search for a cause to be engaged in. Dilemmas can have difficulty being resolved in *usual* ways, but they seem to work themselves out anyway. Letting go is the main way through: the state of mind is often the obstacle, when in fact there is an open road ahead. Here there can be exceptional skills which overcome immense obstacles, through synthesising apparently different elements into an original and appropriate package. The rectangle brings marked results.

An **Octile Rectangle** is also possible, linking two ☍ with two ⚼ and two ∠ aspects. There is a great work to be carried out here, but it can involve immense focused effort for a short time: there is a secret which needs cracking, and the breakthrough is then brought about through a summoning and concentration of energy into the moment, giving a superhuman challenge with potentially great results. Other rectangles can be formed too, for example with ⚻ / ⚺ or minor aspects linking up the two key ☍ aspects — a grand cross is related too. The important thing here is that the ☍ s generate the energy while the linking aspects release it. The ☍ s need focusing and integrating, and the linking aspects demonstrate the talents and assets available for doing so.

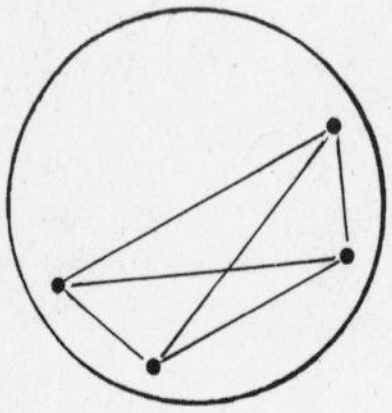

★ **Trapezium.** This is a four-sided figure with two sides parallel. There can be several versions of this, each with their own undertones: □ - ∠ - ☍ - ∠ , ⚻ - ⚹ - □ - ⚹ , ∠ - ⚼ - ∠ - ∠ , △ - □ - ⚹ - □ , △ - ⚺ - ☍ - ⚺ , to name a few. Each of these has its own flavour, but a few patterns apply: the two aspects linking opposite corners of the trapezium will show the main issue at hand, while the perimeter aspects will show media of release; of the two parallel sides, the shorter will show what the energy source is, and what the subjective element is, while the longer side will show the objective means of expression — there is a question of application of possibilities in this configuration; no planets focus the form, but it is necessary to bring all of them together to work as a chord of energy — the resonance or noise created depends on the planets involved, and the conscious use we make of the time; any outer planets involved will point to the most fundamental issues involved — note their position in the configuration. Trapezia crop up from time to time, and when they do, conscious attention needs to be given to the implications offered by the two planets on the shortest parallel side.

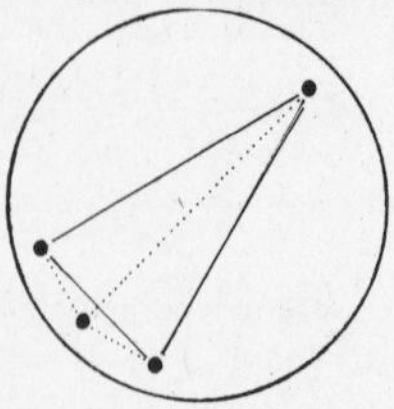

★ **Yod.** This is a ⚻ - ⚹ - ⚻ , and its appearance is not uncommon — especially while ♆ and ♇ have been in a running ⚹ for the last few decades. It features a crisis of perspective, in which the energies of the two sextiled planets find difficulty integrating with that of the apex planet. This dichotomy is not directly a conflict, rather a bewilderingly dualistic and compromising situation. This is an 'appointment with power' in which consciousness and its capacity for *seeing* are tested. It is a secret to be decoded, an intense dilemma, or a visitation from the unknown. This is where intentions refuse to gel with realities: the solution is available as soon as clarity dawns. Allowing things to happen rather than seeking to steer them is what is called for: yet, underneath, there is a new kind of adepthood which brings in a new form of control without holding on, if we can see it.

The yod can be accentuated when an ☍ is thrown in, with two ⚺ aspects too. The ☍ forces the issue, and the apex planet becomes very critical: what it represents needs to be consciously worked, owned and integrated. Hairy situations, with remarkable solutions, once found. This is a form of kite, except there is a strong perspective issue here. A yod formed between ⚷ in ♉, ♇ in ♎, ♅ in ♏, and ♆ in ♐ around August 1979 precipitating (at least in my own circles) strong feelings of personal despair, recognition of darkness, difficulty and fault, and an underlying growth of resolve to *do* something positive about it: this was a forced clarification of issues, internally powerful, emerging into action and demonstration over the years which followed.

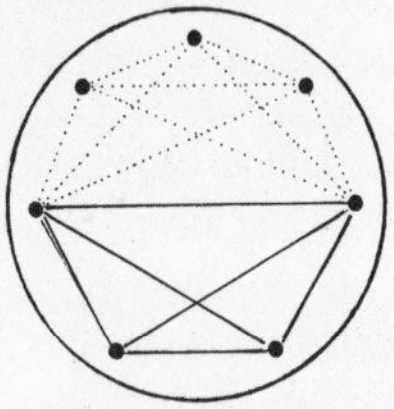

★ **Cradle.** Traditionally, this has three ⚹ aspects plus an ☍, but it can involve any kind of aspects, as long as there is a string of the same aspects at work and at least four points to it. It can also be four ⚹ s and one △. Either way, there is a strong nurturing, brewing, hatching tone to this form, in which the new is created, or the old is creatively enlivened: the midpoint of the largest empty space in the configuration will show the hidden integrative ingredient the key or missing link. This is a facilitative formation. If populated by ⚹ s, it gives birth to a set of skills capacities which have the potential for stimulating great progress and impetus, naturally rooted and innately 'right'. With a formation of three ∠ s plus one ⚼, or four ∠ s with an ☍ skills and formulae are developed through focused effort and a sense of overview: there is a timeless aptness and poignancy to what happens with cradles, when they form. Cradles act as a receptacle for a strong surge of energy and change.

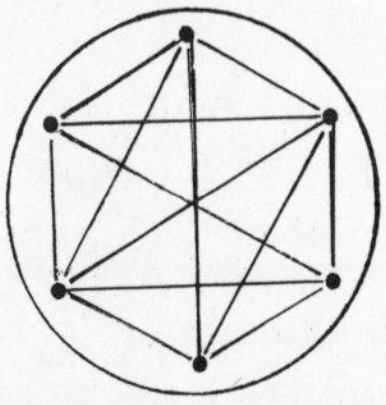

★ **Grand aspects.** These are very rare in occurrence, but can crop up, often inaccurately but all the same powerful during their period of operation. The grand trine and cross are the most common, but it is also possible to meet a grand sextile, grand octile, or a grand minor aspect form at occasional points in history. Try counting how many individual aspects are at work in a grand sextile! At these points in time, a very strong resonance is set up, which, in the character of the individual planets concerned, can make for a power point of supreme proportions. A very special message comes forward from such a time. Many ☍ s are involved, creating an intense and sharp atmosphere, but the peripheral aspects will show how the energy is released — by all-round integration of all of the energies present in the configuration, an alchemic fusion. A grand sextile can make so much happen, so much energy to flow, that it becomes cathartic. A grand octile can set up such a thoroughly challenging dilemma that potential for resolution is infinitely expanded, through sheer pressure: otherwise everything must stop, and death sets in. Grand aspects are very powerful!

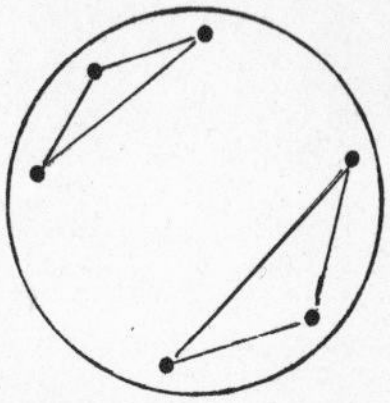

★ **Lesser triangles.** All sorts of different lesser triangles can come to pass, linking three or more planets. Each is an individual case. Generally, the planet not at either end of the longest side holds the key to the form, even though its aspect relations with the other planets might lead to a variety of outcomes: a unidirectional flow can arise where each planet relates easily to one other, relating to the third through the second. There can be symmetrical or asymmetrical triangles: the former will tend to be more balanced and integrated as one energy-chord.

Of the more regular symmetrical triangles there are: ∠ - □ - ∠, and ⚼ - □ - ⚼, both mentioned above as octile triangles; ⚺ - ⚹ - ⚺, a creative conception triangle, in which new perspectives and possibilities emerge into daylight, stimulating both new openings and completions of the past (for example the ♆ ⚺ ♄ ⚺ ♇ which took place in December 1985, fostering outbreaks of xenophobia and parochialism which have precipitated their opposite, a move toward globalism and liberal attitudes, long term); ⚹ - △ - ⚹, a highly flowing form, where everything cruises well and even crises become effortless (for example, March

1986, when there was a ♃ ✱ ♆ ✱ ♇, which unleashed a busy flow of developments involving the setting of future intentions and the channeling through of inner directives quietly and secretly affecting many people's plans for the future).

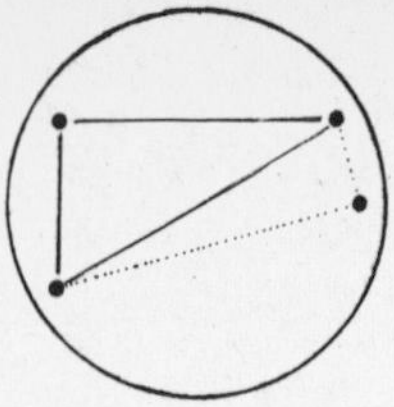

Of the asymmetrical triangles, a few examples: ☍ ⚻ ⚺ shows an impingement of the unknown, bringing new angles into the situation, previously unforeseen or accounted for; ☍ △ ✱, suggesting a dynamically creative interlude and open channel; ☍ ⚼ ∠, a challenger, with knots to work through, yet a clarifier and a worthy confrontation with isnesses; ⚻ □ ✱, a sensitive issue which can press buttons, but can get to the heart of the matter and work through it well; ⚻ △ □, calling in wider-world issues, with regards to agreements and relations of whatever kind is indicated by planets and signs. All of these triangles need assessing on the merits of the planets and signs involved. It is best to openly witness a few, then to break them down into their components in retrospect.

In the case of all these configurations, three or more planets are being hauled into the same basic question. They point to times when the signal (as opposed to the noise) in time-energy comes strongly and clearly. Significant chunks of our being latch into them. The more planets involved, the more significant the energy and change. Whichever planet is in the focal position, this planet must be parlayed with in order to make sense of the time. If there is no clear focal planet, all of them must be engaged together, unless for some reason the configuration is weighted in one direction. Either way, all planets in the configuration must be accessed and worked with, even though some of them might be more readily accessible or friendly.

Configurations are major contributors, when we are looking to identify power points in time: so much energy gets caught up with them. Most often, these configurations include moon, or moon and sun: it is well worth watching those new, half and full moons which engage with other planets, for in the short term these can be crucial and intense, or remarkable in some or another way. When slower planets engage in configurations they bring with them large scale changes affecting centuries of time. An example is the ♅ ☌ ♇ in ♍, opposed by ♄ ☌ ⚷ in ♓, with a △ / + sextile from ♆ in ♏ in 1965-6, which brought a major historical turning-point, a longterm seed-time, (about which more in chapter 16) symbolised by the outbreak of the 'permissive society'(♏), flower power and sex'n'drugs'n'rock'n'roll (♓, an expression of the ♇ in ♌ generation growing into adulthood at the time), the protest movement (♅ and ♇ in ♍) and the emergence of the microchip (♍), as well as the impending first landing of a human on the moon and the rise of Japan as the manufacturing hub of the world (♅ ☌ ♇ symptoms) — all events which boded strong omens for future times.

At each major power point we are offered choices, personal, social and global: to get clear on what these options are is a large part of their resolution, and to develop the willingness to make whatever changes are pointed to is the main point of it all. Change flows naturally when our resistances disappear.

13 Planetary combinations

The planets are forever carrying out relationships with one another. Planetary archetypes in combination set up a third energy or interwoven archetype, which works itself through in varying ways, according to the aspect which is operating. Here we shall look through the ways in which planetary energies combine, at the new issues they set up, pair by pair. By combining your understanding of the aspects with your gleanings from this chapter, you will get a reasonable idea of what to look for when observing an interplanetary aspect at work in real life. This chapter is one of those which you don't need to read systematically through: scan it and dip into it for stimuli.

Planetary pairs

Use these tips as guidelines of what to look for rather than narrow definitions of *what will happen when....* Note that these planetary combinations represent different levels of issue, affecting different time-spans, according to the speed of the planets concerned. Thus, lunar-to-planet combinations will, on the whole, affect timespans of hours or a day, while ♄ - ♇ ones can hang around for a year, and ♅ / ♆ / ♇ ones for up to a decade. Faster-moving combinations tend to bring things to the surface in more tangible terms than slower ones, although slower aspects can reveal all sorts of different facets of the issue, surfacing over time as an ongoing process. How much surfaces depends on the openness we have to the surfacing of issues, a matter of willingness and readiness to be aware.

A lot could be said about every different planetary combination. Also, these combinations modulate differently when two planets are in different aspects to one another. So take these brief guidelines — about which there could be a whole book — as a starter in your own ruminations and observations, and move on from there.

★ ☉ *SUN.*

Moving around the zodiac and forming aspects to other planets, the sun injects life-energy into questions which are outlined by any other planet, and by the sign-positions of both sun and planet. It makes the question important, pressing, actual, and commands energy to be put into it, stimulating our need to grow in and through life. With the slower planets, the solar cycle will tend to be just a little more than one year, bringing questions into life around the underlying issues these planets are digging up. Sun *features* other planetary energies and makes them grow outwards into expression in our lives.

★ **Sun-Mercury:** ☉ and ☿ form only one significant aspect to one another, ☉ ☌ ☿ , since ☿ never moves further from ☉ than 28°. When they combine, thought-processes, nervous energy, linkages, travel and general buzzing go on, and new connections are made in whatever field of life is important at the time. Intelligence, flexibility, mentality, and the capacity to make contact, stay calm and get there are in question. Rattling brains.

★ **Sun-Venus:** ♀ moves only 47° from ☉, such that there can be a ☌, ⚺ and ∠ only between them. This is about heart energy, oneness, loving and being loved, radiating and receiving warmth, caring, belonging and being open to feeling. Issues around closeness, attachment, value, appreciation and roundness prevail here.

★ **Sun-Mars:** This is about assertiveness, action, energy, force, pushing things through, wanting and striving, 'going for it', and strong sexual impulses. Tact, patience, perseverance and understanding can be issues here, together with the recognition of other's rights, sensitivities and even their very existence.

★ **Sun-Jupiter:** This is about assertion of faith, doing things in the belief that they will work and bear fruit, making steps, putting ourselves on the line, doing Big Things. Issues around mutual value, social power, influence, interrelatedness, shared beliefs or differences of belief can arise here, as well as money questions. These two energies combining encourage steps forward.

★ **Sun-Saturn:** This is about focusing, accepting our lot, working hard, dealing with our failure syndromes, doubts and fears, fulfilling our obligations and facing the consequences of things we have done. Issues of accountability, responsibility, limits, sensibleness, structuring and hard realities can come up here. Faith and objectivity are necessary. Plus a wholehearted *decision* to be alive, have fun and succeed.

★ **Sun-Chiron:** Here we are concerned with changing the way we look at things, such that problems transform into gateways to resolution. It is about miracles, using a deft hand, acting intuitively with regards to real-life issues, breaking out of moulds and expectations, manifesting what is needed and overcoming victimhood. Magical work and situ ations. Flips and manoeuvres, knots and balancing acts.

★ **Sun-Uranus:** Sudden changes, electric atmospheres overcoming resistances, about-turns, holding an independent line, deviating from the norm, distancing ourselves, saying goodbye, allowing new influences into our lives, accepting our being stirred up by things beyond our control. Sometimes a shocker, sometimes thrilling.

★ **Sun-Neptune:** Weirdness, 'spacing out', not knowing what's what any more, fantasies, phantasms, phobias, revelations, and new inspirations arising. Issues can come up over disintegration of knowns, illusion-bubbles popping, inability to hold one's own and find space, unclear agreements. Strangenesses!

★ **Sun-Pluto:** Thunderous rumblings, 'this is it', confrontations, heaviness followed by breakthrough, raw honesty, 'stuff' coming up, unwanted rubbish, potent power, charged encounters, secrets uncovered, blood, workouts, clearing the air, do-or-die, transformation. No escape! Issues here often involve fear of the abyss and resistance to change, and fear of deep powerful urges to really *live* and *do it*.

★ ☽ *MOON.*

Lunar aspects form and pass rapidly, connecting us with the here-and-now of real life as it is each day. Here our responses to arising life situations are triggered, and we are given the choice to react mechanically, or to use daily normalities and moods and events as a gateway to awareness of how we meet life. Through ☽ we seek and receive what we need to nurture the life within us. It's about kids, distractions, things simply arising, life as is, and the use we make of each hour. And it is about conditioned memory, and the way we let it interfere with our lives. The profundity of this is startling when we become mindful of all the little

programmed responses we use to get through life: try walking slowly and becoming *totally* aware of the movements in the muscles in your legs, for example!

★ **Moon-Sun:** This is about the way we balance meeting each day and hour and situation with our sense of purpose and direction, the fulfilment we gain out of life by responding to it clearly, and the ripples we set up when we do not. How we meet the here-and-now, and connect with life on earth, in all its phases. Sun brings conscious intentional action to meet with lunar semiconscious responses.

★ **Moon-Mercury:** How we get in touch with our needs, verbalise them, connect our thoughts with our umbilical feelings. Habits of thought and word, automatic thought-responses to life as it arises, repetitions. Feelings we need to express, unconscious messages behind words. Nuances.

★ **Moon-Venus:** Feelings and sensitivities, capacity for loving-caring, warmth, softness, femininity, joining in, niceness, healing through rest and nurture, receptivity, belonging. Issues arise around needing to be liked, loved or needed, attachment and 'followership'. Need for attention.

★ **Moon-Mars:** Assertion to protect self, anticipation of assault, defensiveness, stirring up trouble, vulnerabilities, fulfilment of desires, indulgence, sexuality\orgasm, sensationalism, argumentation, rivalry, jealousy, overreaction. Issues here involve whether to fight or feel hurt and recoil.

★ **Moon-Jupiter:** Wellbeing, fun, ballyhooing, pleasure, creamcakes, comforts, social warmth, forgiving, membership, 'in' groups, motherliness, generosity, anything goes, understanding, goodliness. Issues around attachment to 'goodies', waste, overdoing it and habituated unawareness. Comfort and joy.

★ **Moon-Saturn:** Doing without, solitude, foregoing needs, out of contact, social distance, sacrifice for future benefit, self-sufficiency, perseverance, aloneness, work, reliability, keeping commitments, doing it, hard facts of situation, forced releasing, subdued feeling, sublimation, patience and forbearance, deciding. Issues around coldness and unawareness of personal needs, depression, overcompensation either resisting or indulging in neediness, fear of loss or loneliness. Immense strength when approached openly.

★ **Moon-Chiron:** Supermothering, miraculous fulfilment of needs, facilitation of security, manifestation of deeper requirements, caring, knack for helping others/being helped, calming magical or healing touch, appropriate response, godsends, as thou sowest, so shall ye reap. Issues around subservience, overextending care for others and draining self of own needs.

★ **Moon-Uranus:** Independence, moving on, having to accept changes, instability, vulnerability, stirrings, changes of course, unsettling moments, electric atmospheres, going away, things different from what is wanted, release. Issues around reliability, avoidance of realities, attachment/independence, trust, getting in contact with needs, withholding and alienation.

★ **Moon-Neptune:** Flowingness, emptiness, music, subtle nuances, stillness, sensitivity, receptivity, uplift, insight, imagination/paranoia, strangeness, unearthly atmospheres. Issues around uncertainty, vagueness, self-forgetting, unconnectedness, unconsciousness.

★ **Moon-Pluto:** Encounter, insecurity, confrontation with truths, harshness, underlying 'stuff', unconscious needs, loaded atmospheres, toomuchness, honesty and emergence, clearouts. Trust issues, clinging-or-releasing, feeling wounded, big-dealing, manipulation or motherly domination.

★ ☿ *MERCURY.*

Mercury activates connective nerve pulses, the information exchanges which go on within our brains and nervous systems, between these and our senses and body parts, between our senses and hands, speech and hearing faculties and people and the world around us. Thus, when ☿ energy is flying, the systems are whirring, and contacts are being made, within and between people, between places and parts. In the sphere of thought, ideas are buzzing. The ☿ functions within us, when activated, are energised into alertness, readiness, and our brains are activated in gathering data, forming associations, processing experience, and converting these into ideas and words which can be stored in memory or shared with others through talk and writing, and nowadays, electronic media. When ☿ connects, journeys are straightforward, and A is linked to B.

★ **Mercury-Venus:** Affability, friendship, association, liking and being liked, communication of love/caring, verbalising feelings, sensitising thoughts. Evaluation, measuring up and weighing, aesthetic thought, creative expression or craft or design, Issues around chatter, relating for the sake of it, and unclear mixing of thought and feeling.

★ **Mercury-Mars:** Opinions and strong ideas, rhetoric, debate, argument, ideas vying against one another, verbalising wants; shooting, martial artistry, skill and accuracy, acting on ideas. Issues around competitiveness, interference, conflict-or-diplomacy, expression of anger and frustration, separative and divisive views.

★ **Mercury-Jupiter:** Intellect, abstract ideas, philosophy, advanced thought; considered judgements, opinions and conclusions, negotiations and money transactions, big ideas, designs, donations, generalisations, -ologies, knowledge, meetings, conferences. Issues around busy brains, over-interpretation of significances, ivory-towerism, intellectualism, addiction to constant movement.

★ **Mercury-Saturn:** Careful thinking, skepticism, caution, logicality, statistics, concentration, mental work, agendas, recipe-following, reservations, organisational thinking. Issues around blocks on thought faculties, depressive or negative thought, doubt, difficulty with words or speaking out, fear of relying on one's own ideas. Fear of astrological calculations!

★ **Mercury-Chiron:** Problem-solving, investigation, genius and mental gifts, ability to shift contexts, lateral thinking, appropriate solutions, connections meant to be made, 'chance' meetings, ideas whose time has come. Issues around bewilderment, mental subservience, attachment to logic, inability to understand the a-logicalities or magical realities of life, difficulties solving problems.

★ **Mercury-Uranus:** Excitement, thirst for 'buzzes', quick thinking, sudden changes of mind, ideologies, brightness. Issues around tension, scattered or wild thoughts, hyperstimulation, racing, projection of ideas on others. Fast talk, electricity in air, sci-fi, 100 answers at once.

★ **Mercury-Neptune:** Visionary and idealistic thought, poetry, free association, inspirations, psychic communications, fantasy, universal considerations. Issues around muddleheadedness, absentmindedness, difficulty speaking for self, unclear agreements, 'spacing out'.

★ **Mercury-Pluto:** Profound thought, research, un-

derlying messages, raw honesty, secrets breaking, truth, mental breakthroughs, powerful ideas and forceful words, persuasion and persuasions, deep connections. Issues around mental domination/violence, con-tricks, trusting others' utterances, manipulation, mental breakdowns, blurting, flare-ups and cover-ups.

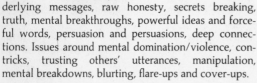

★ ♀ ***VENUS.***

Through ♀, the world softens and finds its unity, and we draw unto us things and people we like and love. All things are rounded and agreeable, inclusive and satisfying, and warmth abounds and enjoyment is had. Venusian rain and cold is still soft and caressing! Through ♀ we evaluate things, perceive music, colour, taste, feel, enjoyment, and we feel for others and the world, sensing our oneness with all. Through ♀ we also hold on, overlook ugly truths, ruminate on what's not right and lose consciousness over having and keeping.

★ **Venus-Mars:** Sexuality, push-pull in relationship, intense feeling and passion, demonstrative love, wanting and choosing, making love. Issues around love-hate, discomfort and demandingness in relationship, depravity, oversexuality, or, conversely, being out of touch with our bodies, even ascetic, conflicts between heart and genitals.

★ **Venus-Jupiter:** This is about wellbeing, chocolate, socialising, amicability, companionship, trustingness, faith in people, good times, caring and welfare, giving, prosperity. Issues around waste, decadence, attachment to wealth, obesity, good-lifing, ungenuine smiles and being used — nice-guy behaviour.

★ **Venus-Saturn:** Solitude, self-sufficiency, learning to feel, leanness, commitment to relationship, appreciation of tradition and old things, calmness. Issues around fear of feeling, inability to be close or make relationships last, coldness, isolationism, loneliness/clinging, emotional shutoffs, trust in love, closedness, perversion, poverty-consciousness.

★ **Venus-Chiron:** Knack for caring, learning relationships, empathy, social skills, 'chance' meetings, soul-links, knowingness, feminine power. Issues around fraught relationships and getting tied, victimhood to others' or own feelings, emotional space, attachment.

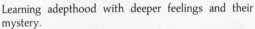

Learning adepthood with deeper feelings and their mystery.

★ **Venus-Uranus:** Independence, love-affairs, dilettantism, changeable feelings and relationships, need for heart stimulation, bounciness, attractiveness, valuing of freedom. Issues around fear of dependence, distrust, emotional consistency, getting close, sensuality without feeling, alienation, separativeness, avoidance of owning feelings.

★ **Venus-Neptune:** Ideals and romance, 'perfect' love, compassion (with-feeling), rose-tinted glasses, creative imagination, music and artistry. Issues around fear of personalised affection, unrealism in relationship, impracticality, impossible relationships, delusions, disappointment in love, offering or seeking (burdensome) caring, indefiniteness of feelings, emotional confusion, susceptibility to domination.

★ **Venus-Pluto:** Transformation in love, love-power, intensity, sensuality, total bliss-seeking, closeness, absorption in relationship. Issues around loss of selfhood, fear of punishment or laying oneself open,

fear of loss, power struggles in relationship, demandingness, oversexuality.

★ ♂ *MARS.*

Mars energy is about getting things going, getting what we want, asserting our own way, battling with life, engaging with the world, using our muscle and clout and making things work. Its root lies in sexuality and self-gratification, roaring life-energy which wants immediate results. But assertion involves tact, skill and direct dealings rather than force or competitiveness, otherwise rebounds are created which do not lead to the desired outcome. Go for it, intentionally but not wildly!

★ **Mars-Jupiter:** Assertion of power, making big things happen, overcoming resistance and inertia, pushingness, strength, athletic ability, achievement, affecting the world, outward expression. Issues around bombast, force, rivalry, insensitivity, excess, creating rebounds and dissention, expectation of success, overlooking details and small things.

★ **Mars-Saturn:** Capacity for hard work and perseverance,concentration of power, discipline and exertion, painstaking one-pointedness, skill, technique. Issues around repressed wants, fear of asserting self, sexual blockages, held-down anger, self-punishment, overstrain, self-denial, violence, conflicts between work and fun, difficulties with father or those above.

★ **Mars-Chiron:** Remarkable physical skills, ability to work miracles and get what is wanted, healings, hidden strength, engineering, warrior archetypes, ability to do right thing from many viewpoints. Issues around victimisation and force, exclusion, black magic, connivance, sexual domination.

★ **Mars-Uranus:** Freedom-fighting, independence, rebelliousness, impulse, eccentricity, mutation, suddenness, zap, striking out, striking. Issues around violence, projection, inconsistency, impatience, speed, difficulties with elders and authority, non-involvement, outsideness, distrust of men or strength.

★ **Mars-Neptune:** Elevation of will to universal service, transcendence of desire, idealised sexuality and masculinity, healing/channeling ability in action, 'will of the gods'. Issues around weakness, susceptibility, machoism, idealisation of sex, glamour and appearances, domination by others, inability to fend for self.

★ **Mars-Pluto:** Deep libidinous power, primal sexuality, taking on big challenges, hard work, total dedication, drive, relentless activity, high goals, self-control and ability to go against the odds. Issues around power battles, pain in sexual encounters, exploitation, brutality, hidden motivations, fear of power or total assertion.

★ ♃ *JUPITER.*

If we believe strongly in something, we create it as a reality — a reality within us, or, if we move ♃ power strongly enough, a reality in the world around. We pick up many of our beliefs in childhood and adolescence, and run them quite mechanically unless they are questioned. Self-validating, life-affirming thoughts are not as common now as they could be, and thus saturnine self-limiting beliefs often have the upper hand: yet the way through saturnine questions is pointed at by ♃ , for if we have faith and a positive solidity, then anything we wish for, if it is well conceived and worked for, can become reality. Jupiter helps us go out and take on the world, go in and develop our own personal inner world, and in time, unite the two. It brings benefit, growth, extension, consequence, power to create, knowledge and conviction.

★ **Jupiter-Saturn:** This is about getting organised, making commitments in order to progress, balancing optimism with caution, committees and structuring, planned growth, urge to 'make it' or make a mark on the world, and encourages a strong social awareness and sense of standing. Arouses issues around faith-as-escape or depression-as-self-undoing, or oscillation between them, treading sharp edges, risktaking, assuming positions of influence, and either self-restraint or courage. This combination engages gears.

★ **Jupiter-Chiron:** About being of service, consultation, finding or giving help, changing viewpoints, counsel/counselling, magical touch, ability to manifest apparently impossible new initiatives. Issues around being a victim of others' advice or pressures, non-understanding of unusualities, either unbelief in deeper currents or questions of how to work with them, intellectual uncertainty.

★ **Jupiter-Uranus:** About freedom and challenging authority or conformity, changeable fortunes, high-risk living, adventure, big schemes and leaps in the dark, eccentricity, 'I'll do it my way'. Issues around restriction\imprisonment, commitment, perseverance and consistency, difficulty settling into patterns.

★ **Jupiter-Neptune:** About idealism, visions, spiritual aspirations, dreams and speculations, high times, sense of inner freedom, working for the benefit of all beings. Vivid imaginal times. Issues around groundedness and practicality, precision, esoteric realism, spreading self too wide, omitting to look after own interests, making goals realisable, focusing on committed activity.

★ **Jupiter-Pluto:** Deep drives to succeed, overcome limitations, take on causes, challenge the known and regular, bring benefits to many, achieve for posterity, help. Issues around conflicts of power, excessive push, insensitivity, relentlessness or ruthlessness, overexertion, non-acceptance of the status quo, force.

★ ♄ *SATURN.*

Through ♄ things become grounded, specified, formed and made acceptable. It works through social consciousness and our sense of responsibility toward others and all. If we own the consequences of our acts, ♄ becomes a creative force, leading to inner freedom through commitment, but if we allow others (parents, authority figures, social pressures

and laws) to dictate to us through guilt and fear of implied threatened consequences, then ♄ becomes a force which deflects us from realisation of our purpose and we compromise ourselves to what is demanded of us. Saturn faces us with hard facts: if we run from them, it cuts us down. If we accept them, they become a positive learning experience and a way through. ♄ leads us to the Path, the turning in the deepest seat of consciousness which arises when we grasp that all the concerns of our life limit us, and that there is something greater and deeper to life. Thus saturn's blockages, fears, no-gos, guilt-complexes and self-obstructing beliefs can be transformed into a sense of substance, purpose, direction, identity and service.

★ **Saturn-Chiron:** Learning deep lessons from life situations, so as not to repeat mistakes, unconscious creation of learning experiences which both define limits and unveil ways through, under high pressure. Factual, functional questions, questioning of purposes, tight scrapes and fine lines, finding needles in haystacks.

★ **Saturn-Uranus:** Rebelliousness, changes of rules, questioning norms, reform-or-revolution? Sudden breaks and separations, or ability to stick with extremely trying circumstances, inside/outside acceptable norms. Issues around conventionality, perpetual dissatisfaction, needs for change, fear, social castigation, guilt for past assertions, or running away from realities and consequences of acts, dualism or schizoid behaviour.

★ **Saturn-Neptune:** Bringing ideals/visions into concrete form, discrimination between 'reality' and 'illusion', applied arts, skill in expressing dreams, sense of service to the whole. Issues around paranoia, fear of loss of self, inability to distinguish facts from imaginings, self-denial, sublimation, sense of unworthiness, separation of spirit from body, lack of resistance to disease or confrontation, transference of own illusions on to others, unclear boundaries around self, fear of insanity.

★ **Saturn-Pluto:** Tests of capacities to deal with

immense difficulty, shoulder burdens, suffer, accept restrictions, make it in the end, survive against odds, face up to raw truths and deep pain. Issues around self-punishment, withholding of own power, violence, inner darkness or hopelessness, total resistance to change or inner truth, fear of death or the abyss, fear of being called on to be totally present and succeed in life. Fear of social chaos.

All the planets below form aspects only occasionally, lasting sometimes years, and affecting history, the group psyche, and impersonal longterm developments or 'dispensations' from deeper origins.

★ ⚷ ***CHIRON.***

Through ⚷ we shift our standpoint, and thereby can perceive the way through often ridiculous situations, outwitting normality, finding solutions appropriate from multiple viewpoints. Chiron gives access to our magical selves, our ability to learn from life's symbolism and deeper meanings, and to act from our centre in the effecting of integrated personal and universal ends. Maverick qualities, skills, concrete ways of expressing our spirit and kinds of activities which access our spirit. Healing, bridging and resolution. Being in the right place at the right time. Or chronically missing the point of it all.

★ **Chiron-Uranus:** The bringing into the world of deep impulses for change and innovation, realisation of visions, invention, initiatives taken on transpersonal issues, unforeseen yet **in order** developments, idealistic movements offering appropriate solutions. Brings up issues of faith in the power of the unknown to resolve issues, difficulties in adjusting to changing times, rejection of anything new.

★ **Chiron-Neptune:** The channeling of insight and revelation, accessing of spiritual sources, spiritual healing, sense of the beyond, deep sense of service, 'will of the gods'. Issues around oversensitivity, self-defence, trust in inner truth, psychic discrimination and objectivity.

★ **Chiron-Pluto:** Capacity to jump over the abyss, make quantum leaps, navigate troubled waters in a poised, alert intuitive way, and face the lessons of the times, bring to pass what is long due. Issues around fear of the great unknown and the power of the moment, distrust of deeper urges or imperatives, resistance against the inevitable.

★ ♅ *URANUS.*

Uranus brings radical changes and shifts, new ideologies, mutations and innovations, breaks with the past, releasing of old hangups or restrictions, breakouts and individual initiatives toward a collective end. It works by impulse, flashes and spurts, often announcing itself through dissention, alienation, divergence, protest or revolt. It prefers to avoid confrontation with hard facts or practicalities, and either evades and bypasses resistance or inertia, or seeks to take them by storm. Uranus stirs things up and makes them wobble vulnerably. But it can also make deceptive habits of perpetually changing and staying on the move in order simply to remain, when all is said and done, the same! Habitual restlessness does not facilitate true change. Yet true change *begins* with uranian quickening, seeking and ideology.

★ **Uranus-Neptune:** Open inner channels, inherent sensing of the beyond, deep questioning or quest, illusion-breaking, revelation, change of levels of consciousness, new insights dawning. Issues around inner dissatisfaction and spiritual discomfort, perpetual searching, 'not this, not that', phobias.

★ **Uranus-Pluto:** New seeds of change, visionary outbreaks, rebirth on collective dream level, deep rumblings in group psyche, strong interventions from collective unconscious, or divine intervention. Issues around polarisation, schizophrenia, insanity, fear of the mysterious, repression of the new, resistance to change.

★ ♆ *NEPTUNE.*

Through ♆ higher consciousness percolates into us, sideways, mysteriously, through loosening up the old, melting it, sifting it and causing new states and awarenesses to enter in. It must be grounded to work through, otherwise the higher self cannot reach through to personality: otherwise it can take it over, possess people, cause them to lose track. While it allows the flow to move, it can land us up in a fog, and while it can attune us, its imaginal stimulation can also cause us to hang on to illusions, glamours and glosses over concrete issues. ♆ stimulates inner vision and the deep sources of spiritual, psychic and creative inspiration and inner contact. It opens up the vast unknown — and occasionally dunks us in it to open us up!

★ **Neptune-Pluto:** The destruction of illusions, rebirth of new visions and outlooks, cleaning of the slate, investigation of the mysterious or the infinite. Awareness of the Dream. Issues around the dark night of the soul, haunting by ghosts of the psyche, unsubstantiated fears, deep resignation or profound acceptance.

★ ♇ *PLUTO.*

Pluto drives through inevitable destruction and renewal, burning and crushing all that is no longer useful, yet vivifying all things through the freeing-

up of life-energy. It has a soulquaking transformative influence, and forces confrontation. It has deep libidinous power, stimulating unconscious urges for life or urges for death, whichever prevail, and breaking through blocks and resistances to life-energy. Yet, it challenges our fear of these things too, and can feed that fear to strengthen repression, reflecting in obsessive, self-destructive and fetishistic behaviour. Through resisting change we ultimately discover the true need for it — thus resistance, fascism, violence are a part of change, not a final blockage of it. Plutonic power and life-urges always win through.

Some examples

The above interplanetary relationships represent a hierarchy of different cyclical significances, largely related to the speeds of the planets involved. Any cycles or aspects formed by the moon to another planet is a short-lived affair, albeit significant, even on occasion crucial, in the moment. Cycles involving ☉, ☿, ♀, or ♂ brew energies which have significance on more of a week-by-week basis. ♃, ♄ and the outer planets raise bigger and deeper questions, however. None are more important than any other, for each level of cyclicity is relevant in its own context of reality: the atmosphere on the evening of Wednesday 25th April is relevant around that time, but loses significance from the longer memory-perspective of what has gone on during the course of a year or a decade. Conversely, a longterm perspective is relevant for providing a sense of overall context to our lives, but the application of it in its nittygritty details — catching a train, meeting people or dealing with an immediate crisis — requires an awareness of more immediate time-factors.

Not long ago I ran a series of two week-long groups in a house in the mountains. I planned to drive there on the Thursday, when there happened to be a ♂ ☌ ♃ in ♓. The fullmoon on the Tuesday preceding had been a very strong one, for ☉ in ♐ had been ☌ ♅, ☽ in ♊ had been ☌ ⚷, and the whole lot had been □ ed by this ♂ ☌ ♃. It had been an its-all-too-much fullmoon, but there was an underlying tone to it of seeking to forgive others' transgressions, to wipe the slate clean and look at things afresh, and to release, understand and let the flow of things go as they will. On that fullmoon I happened to ring one of the participants on the group to offer her a lift, for the journey was long. When we started out on the Thursday, it turned out that this was a very significant quirk of fate — here comes the ♂ ☌ ♃ in ♓ — for both she and I had a lot of releasing and forgiving to do, and both being in the same boat was helpful to both of us. The ♓ bit was that, while a ♂ ☌ ♃ is a go-for-it, strong-willed and usually outwardly-assertive kind of aspect, we were both electing to process our pent-up energies internally, by departing from the scene and journeying toward a place where a deeper releasing would be possible. Another quirk of fate, however, was that we stopped by a friend halfway on our journey, who, it turned out, seemed really *meant* to meet both me and my passenger, at that very moment: the three of us connected on a deeper, wordless level in a way which was encouraging and strengthening for all of us. In other words, the mysterious element of ♓ had modified the ♂ - ♃ energy, making it into a set of connections which had not then seemed important, but which, from another, wider perspective, was very significant.

We continued on our journey on the Friday, on the buildup to a ☿ ☌ ♄ in ♐ that evening. I deliberately put myself into a patient mode, which proved to be useful, for all the way along the winding roads of Wales we were manifesting tractors, slow trucks and dozy drivers in front of us and wind blowing against us, making the journey something of a test. Nevertheless we got there — but the conscious patience (a response both to ♂ ☌ ♃ in ♓ and to ☿ ☌ ♄ in ♐) was worth it, for we arrived tired but happy, unfrayed by potential frustrations. At the exact moment of the ☿ ☌ ♄, Jessica, my passenger, had me down on the floor while she was manipulating my back and cracking my bones — a very relieving bit of saturnine therapy!

The next day there was a ♐ ☿ □ ♃ ♓ at 6.45pm. All of the people coming for the group arrived within one hour after that! It's amazing how people fit in with astrological realities even if they do not know they are doing so! This double ☿ aspect was also activating an inaccurate ♓ ♃ □ ♄ ♐ (which itself was activating important factors in my own chart): the significance of this for me was that this event was the first manifestation of an entirely new chapter of work (in connection with the Oak Dragon Project), which involved a new stage of getting myself organised and making my work work better. The ☿ incursion into a longer-term ♃ - ♄ aspect marked a significant little stage in a bigger process. Interestingly, the Oak Dragon Project was born in the context of this ♃ □ ♄, which had been hanging around during most of 1986, and I found myself recollecting, on the evening of the ☿ □ ♃, that I had in fact returned to England six years before, from living abroad, on an almost-exact ♃ ☌ ♄. So here we have an example of how a shorter-term cycle (☿ - ♃ / ♄) interweaves with a longer-term one (♃ - ♄).

So the group went on. Late on the Sunday there was a ☿ □ ♂, when some honest truths in the group had to be faced, and one of the participants chose to go home because of difficulties he was encountering. Things brightened up in the evening of the Monday, however, in connection with a ♀ △ ♃, at which time everyone started mixing freely and in a friendly way, and the energy of the group lifted off. On the Thursday, there was a ☿ ☌ ♅, around which time I was *expecting* an outburst of genius and excited prattling amongst the group, but interestingly, this did not happen. What did happen, though, was that, internally, several of the participants came to conclusions about the questions they individually were working with — conclusions which, while not greatly exciting, were relieving to each of those individuals. On the Friday a combination of ☉ ∠ ♀ and ☿ ∠ ♇ forced everyone to face up to the fact (☿ ∠ ♇) that the group was ending, and that we all had to get used to the idea that we would be parting company (☉ ∠ ♀). Which duly took place the next day. On that day was a ☉ ☌ ♆ : I learned that in future I would time groups *not* to end on such an aspect, for it leaves everyone somewhat unfinished. Such an aspect, bringing up a generally spacey, indefinite atmosphere, is best for the middle of a group rather than its end. You live and learn. In fact, another group of people was to arrive that day, to start a new week-long session: in classic neptunian style, many of them were unable to come (despite prior arrangements) at that time — they all arrived two days later on a ♂ □ ♅, which brought enough zap and initiative and drive to get everyone there. Yet again, all of the people arriving got there within one hour after the aspect, which was at 5pm. Sometimes it's uncanny tracing these astrological movements of energy!

Experiencing it all

The trouble with giving potted descriptions of astrological concepts is that they can restrict possibilities for wider understanding through oversimplification. While these brief paragraphs will hopefully give you ways of tuning into tones of energy, their scope is not limited by what is stated. We can all experience the liberating and fulfilling sides of a planet one day, and then the restricting and unwholesome side the next, for our mode of consciousness makes the difference. Growth is a path of liberating energy, getting it to move naturally and easily through our being, yet, anachronistically, our increased awareness of the issues underlying our thoughts, words and deeds can make it feel as if our difficulties are increasing rather than working themselves out. This is in fact due to a growth of consciousness: hangups were there all the time, but unwittingly lived out.

Observe time as it moves, and you will gain a *feel* for the workings of the planets together. When, later, you involve yourself with transits to natal positions, you will have more material with which to gain a direct experience of what we are talking about, in your own life and through observing those around you. Piece together the jigsaw bit by bit. Don't give up: when you feel it is all getting laborious, try less hard, and let your deeper self lead you to what you need to find. When you feel at a loss, as if you will never fully understand astrology, you're on the edge of something: let it come. You have your own way of seeing things and working with astrology: let it speak.

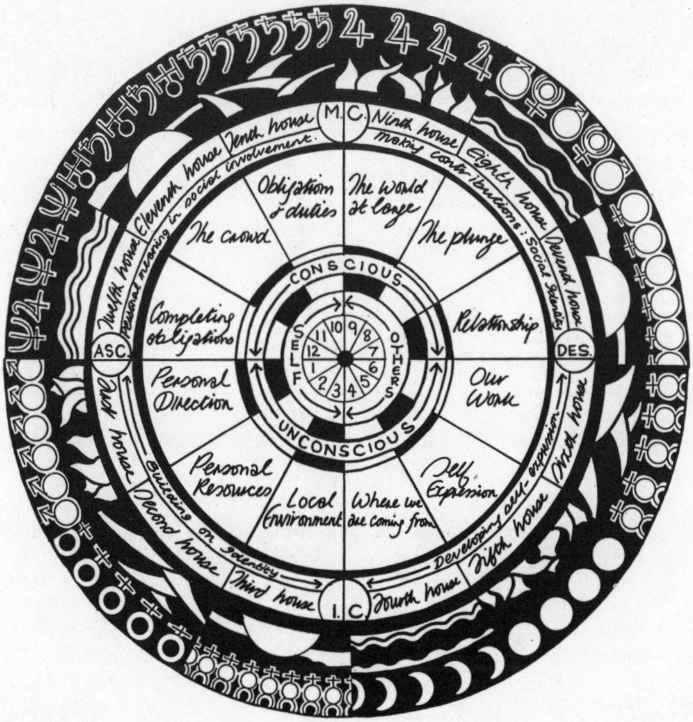

14 Planetary arrays

Here we shall look into the overall shapes of planetary arrays. Arrays give an overview of background, whole energy atmospheres at a given time, giving us ways of pulling together our understandings of astrological situations.

Planetary Arrays

At any moment, the planets as a whole form an array, a spread, which at various times can take on interesting patterns. The planets do not have to be in aspect: what we are looking at here is overall patterns, which can be discerned either through visualising the positions of the planets in your mind's eye, or by drawing them on a chart wheel, thereby building up a *whole* picture of *all* the planets, not just a couple of them. This helps in diagnosing the main message of the time. A whole range of different arrays are possible: below we shall run through the main options.

The general rule is that the more tightly packed a group of planets is, the more focused, specific, concentrated and subjectively-arising is the energy. The more widely-spread the array is, the more dispersed, varied, eclectic and objectivised is the energy. The question for tighter arrays is whether the subjective bias implies an imposition on the world, or is responsive to the world. The question for wide arrays is how to become free of victimhood and dominance of out-there considerations, to integrate personal expressive needs into overall environmental requirements.

Here, therefore, we shall look at a number of common patterns of array, which have certain typical characteristics. Since the planets can form any number of different patterns over time, it is necessary to see the patterns given here as models, which might not fit exactly, but which suggest how to understand the array you might be looking at.

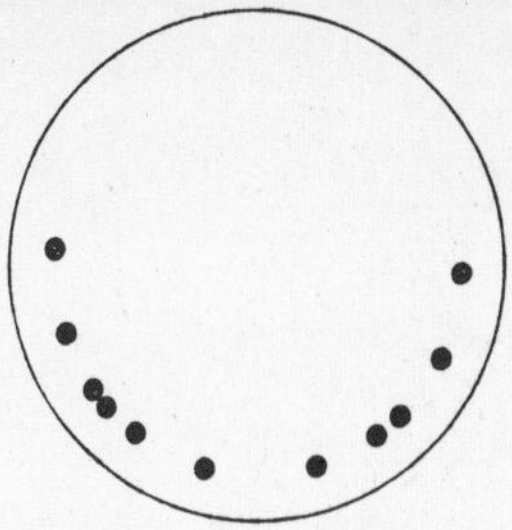

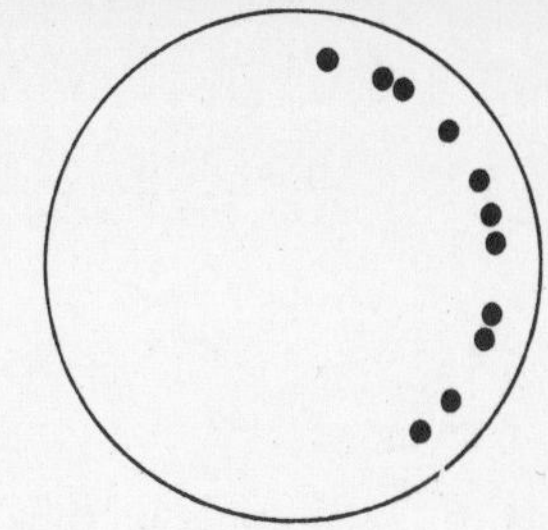

★ Hemispheric pattern (Bowl)

When all planets are arrayed within half of the zodiac, leaving the other half empty, time-energy and activity is highly focused in one particular area of life (symbolised by the full half), and the other area of life remains either unfulfilled, foreign territory or a vital aspect of reality which is being grossly omitted or overlooked. Any tight clusters within this bowl will focus issues even more. But the question is whether the issues connected with the signs in the empty half can be integrated. This configuration will counterbalance itself over time, for while all planets can be in one half of the zodiac at one time of the year, the moon and faster planets will move out of this, leaving the slower planets where they are, eventually forming a *seesaw* or similar array, bringing about a sharp contrast.

Interestingly, the discovery of ⚷ in 1977 changed many perceptions of planetary arrays — mainly because it appeared into human consciousness in ☍ to a bowl of planets then in the autumnal area of the zodiac, forming a 'bucket' out of a bowl. The last bowl formation of consequence to take place was around the autumns of 1945-48, when all planets lay between ♋ and ♐ (except when ☽ swung into the empty part of the zodiac to form a bucket). This was a time of searching for social significance, sparked off particularly by the ♃ - ⚷ - ♆ conjunction in ♎ in autumn 1945 — a configuration which brought peace and the dawning of the welfare state, the United Nations, the seeds of the European Community and the beginning of the post-war 'social democratic' heyday. At the time, the institutional-corporate emphasis, in the ascendancy until the 70s, was no doubt welcome after so many decades of disruption, but it led, by the 70s, to an excess of bureaucracy, rules and laws.

★ Bundle or Cluster pattern

In this formation all planets are tightly arrayed within 120°. This concentrates energy further than the Bowl, to the extent that the collective psyche can be single-minded, obsessed or imbalanced, so focused on a particular preoccupation that there is little objectivity or perspective (an absence of oppositions). This piles all the energy into particular issues, to the exclusion of anything which is regarded as peripheral or trivial. It certainly makes things come into being, converting potential into kinetic history, for this is a powerful concentration: but the question is what the purpose is, and whether the means are justified in their intensity.

Thus, it is wise to consciously widen awareness to overall issues, to see how the question at hand fits into the whole picture, and to not become exasperatingly hyper-focused. The signs opposite this array give contrasting insights into how this should be counterbalanced — otherwise there is the risk that such a situation will go off at a tangent, creating ripples and effects which later are regretted.

An example of the bundle at work was the mid-WW2 period, around autumn 1942, when all planets lay between the signs ♊ and ♍. As with the above example of a bowl formation, this array formed only in autumntime, when the faster-moving planets swung into the same zodiacal area as the slower-moving ones. A time of one-pointed, even fanatical fighting, with little thought about the wider consequences, and with all planets focused in the self-oriented summer signs. As soon as ♆, ⚷ and ♃ moved over the autumn equinox point into ♎, this narrowness of perspective eased off, and international cooperation grew.

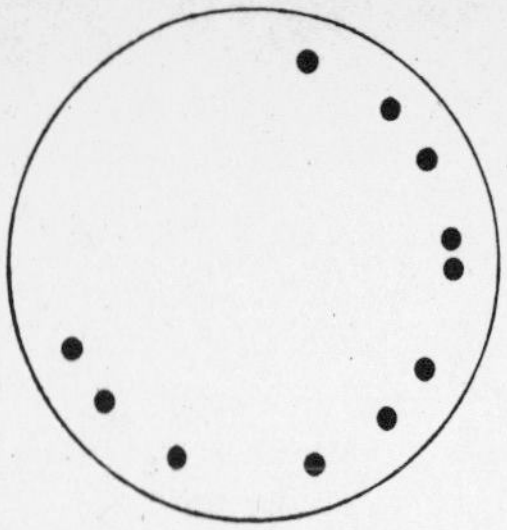

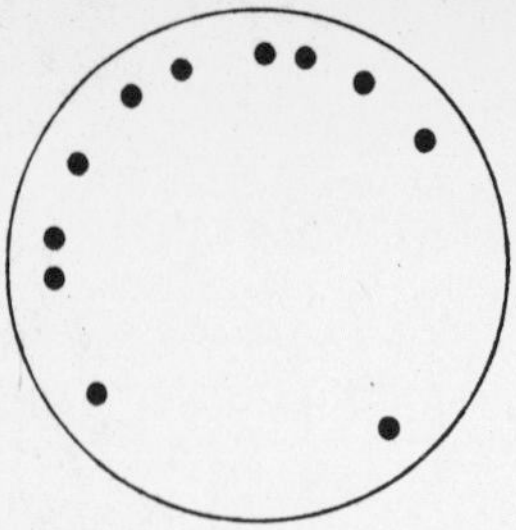

★ Locomotive or Open-angle pattern
Here, all planets occupy up to two-thirds of the zodiac, leaving a 120° gap empty. Here, energy is quite all-round in expression, but there is an extreme focusing on the empty one-third of the zodiac, as if it were a hole to be filled, an area of life which must be attended to: the centre of this empty half, and its sign, is particularly significant.

The empty part points to an area of life which must be fulfilled to make the array whole, and sometimes frenetic energy can or must be put into it to plug gaping holes or deal with important unattended details — especially when the moon moves through it, forming oppositions to other planets. In time in general, the empty part of a planetary array shows the missing link, the area which should be consciously focused upon in order to make the whole array work: this focusing does not happen naturally, however: it must be *intended*. This shows a hidden gift, the vital piece in the jigsaw, the weak link in the chain.

Autumn 1952 provides an example of an open-angle array: by this time, ♃ had crossed to ♉, and ⚷ was in the lead of the other slower planets in ♑, forming a gap between them. Another example is autumn 1966, when a gap appeared between ♄ - ⚷ in late ♓ and ♃ in late ♋. The former array focused energy on empty ♓ — need for deeper vision — and the latter focused on empty ♉ — need for ongoing, steady perseverance and groundedness.

★ Bucket or Wedge pattern
Here, all but one planet occupy up to half of the zodiac, but then one planet, a *singleton*, occupies the empty half. The singleton then becomes a *focal* planet: if this planet can be grasped and made use of, it focuses all of the other planets and turns the key to the whole energy-configuration. Often it can be the case that there is resistance, fear or hesitation to use this singleton, for the stakes can be high, and it often represents something in the meaning of the time which is quite radically different from the dominant tone of the array.

If or when there is an ☍ formed between this and a planet(s) in the full half, then this ☍ provides a link to dilemmas, and any flowing aspects such as a △ will ease up any conflict involved. Since there is a good chance the singleton will be retrograde (unless it is ☽, it becomes initially a mystery to crack, a factor which takes some grappling and wrestling, but which pays big dividends when mastered. The leader and trailer of the main body give clues as to how we can move forward (leader) and also work with the effects of our acts and choices (trailer).

In the early 1980s, especially in autumntime, bucket formations have formed with ⚷ as the handle, provoking some interesting opportunities to wreak miracles and outrageous resolutions to perceived problems in the world. This applies particularly to the rise of grass-roots movements, non-organised groups of people who were then beginning to play a large part in affecting overall attitudes, or who were seeding new solutions to large-scale world problems: here came the rise of feminism, the green and disarmament movements, Islamic fundamentalism, Polish Solidarinosz and third world local movements. In springtime, however, when faster planets moved to join ⚷, a seesaw configuration formed, featured strongly at fullmoons. In a bucket, power is generated by the main body of planets, but focused by the singleton, while in a seesaw, power is generated by both sides, and juxtaposed in apparent conflict. Chiron, in this case, made a subtle yet strongly magical contribution to world affairs as its debut into the world, summoning strength to become clearly effective when in ♊ from 1984, bringing about some major flips of perspective from that date onwards — dramatic psychological changes in the East-West dialogue moving the emphasis to the North-South dialogue being but one example.

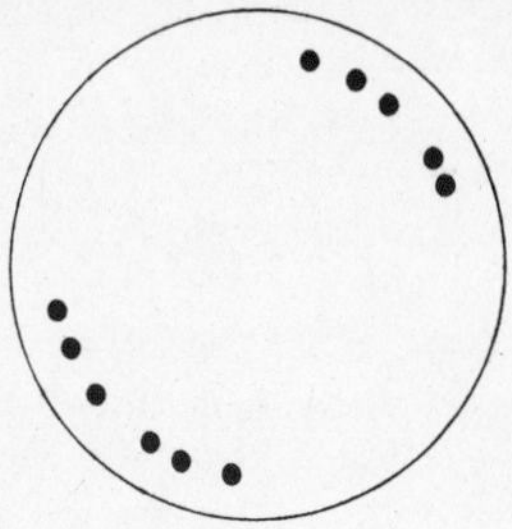

★ Seesaw pattern

Here there are two clear groups of planets, ideally in opposition to one another, with at least two signs on either side separating them, and no more than one sign empty in either group. This carries an amplified ☍ symbolism, just as the Cluster carries an amplified ☌ symbolism. In other words, life can resolve itself into two quite separate components, which tend to pull against one another and each demand dominance, while the task at hand is to recognise that this is the case, and that dualism has its polarising and negative consequences: it is necessary to consciously integrate the two if any significant progress is to be made. If this is not done, then longterm splits of consciousness can occur, reflected in society and social groups, and a cold or active war between them can ensue, at great cost.

If the configuration is splayed to one side, then there will still be two factors at work, but they do not necessarily conflict: instead they can subvert one another or simply consume energy until they are introduced to one another and consciously set to work with each other.

The results of this dualism can be varied, depending on the relative weighting of each side, and the planets involved. One can dominate the other, but be irked by guilt or subconscious sabotage; one can lead the other, but keep it subservient; both can oppose one another, leading to indecision and non-resolution; one can be consciously held as 'me' while the other is projected outwards and seen as 'others' acts towards me', without being owned; or both can be consciously recognised, and a balance is sought, through oscillating between extremes and then learning to take a middle path. If ☽ swings through this configuration, one side, then the other side will alternately be featured and brought into question. Crucial points come when ☽ forms a □ to both sides.

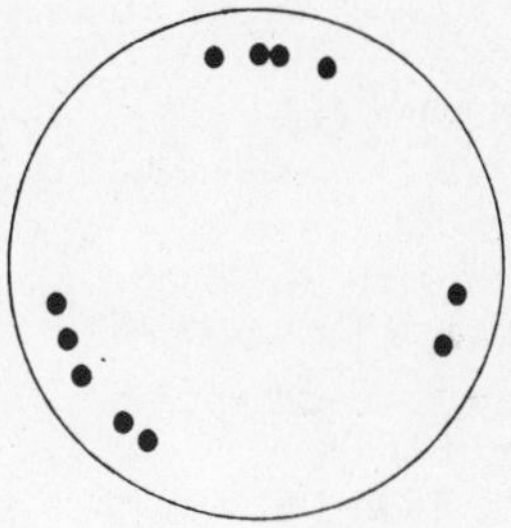

★ Tripod pattern

This pattern is formed when there are three groupings of planets, distinct from one another, and ideally forming trine links between each other. This can make for a time where there is considerable understanding and stability (depending on the symmetry of the pattern), a capacity to have energy left over for activities which have great creative or inventive potential. Or it can make for a time when we tend to squander our energy, or when there is a lack of drive. These times are relaxing, bridge-building times, fostering agreement and a smooth flow: growth and developments are furthered.

Whether this pattern flows well depends on its symmetry and the planets involved, and where they sit. If, for example, the pattern forms a roughly T-square configuration, then there are big hurdles to cross, pointed out by the empty gap, and much can be achieved if the opportunity is seized. If there is a preponderance of ⚼ aspects, then longterm aims and projects and historical perspectives become the issue. With a preponderance of △ aspects, life can become rather easy and decadent, and while there can be good fortune, there is a question here as to whether it is utilised to great avail.

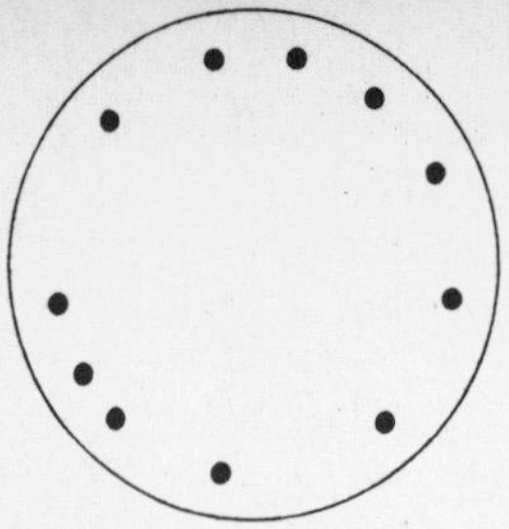

★ **Splash formation**

Here the planets are randomly arrayed with no particular outstanding patterns to them. Deducing what this implies depends on any dominant aspect-patterns in the array, which might pull out main themes. This formation suggests an all-roundness, a versatility or wide spread of issues, which might either be related but contrasting (if strong aspects are present) or unrelated and diffuse. A clear message or theme is not present, and life goes on. There are various assorted issues to work through rather than one or two 'biggies'.

A Splash is often the formation which is identified when no other formations can be found, making it a general-purpose pattern which can answer various calls. Thus it is not clearly a pattern in itself, rather a non-pattern. Look at the empty gaps in the splash, if there are any, for indications of areas of life which need attending to.

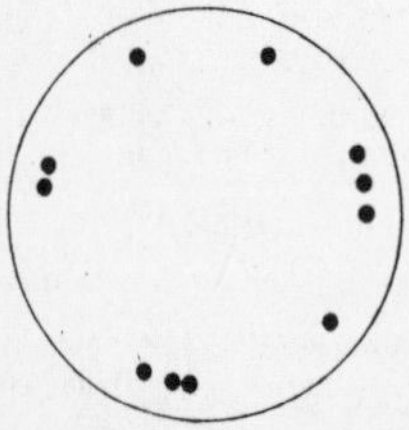

★ **Splay pattern**

This is not unlike a Splash, except that there are distinct clusters of conjuncting or close planets in it, which give it a coherence, and establish dominant themes and movements of energy. There will be certain areas of life which possess special meaning, indicated by the concentrations present. These areas of life take on a dominant flavour, and the planets involved can become critical, turning-point influences which can be decisive in an otherwise generalised field. Splays should be interpreted case by case.

★ **Star patterns**

Occasionally, the planets can form into a regular or symmetric pattern, highly inter-aspected, which resembles a star, or structure with 4, 5 or more points to it. Or they might not be clearly aspected, but form an array of planets which form some noticeable shape in relation to one another, containing a certain symmetry. The planets do not have to be aspected to each other though: they can simply form a pattern which stands out. It can be, for example, that while the planets do not form standard aspects to one another, they do form angles which repeat themselves throughout the array, or which form a symmetry: situations such as this indicate a uniqueness to the moment, a special magic which comes only once every now and then, with abnormal or incomprehensible features. How this will manifest precisely depends on the planets involved, signs and aspects — usually you will find *thematic* links however, where different astrological factors, unrelated to each other, point to a particular message which is coming through. Every power point in time is in some way *meant* to be, and carries a special dispensation.

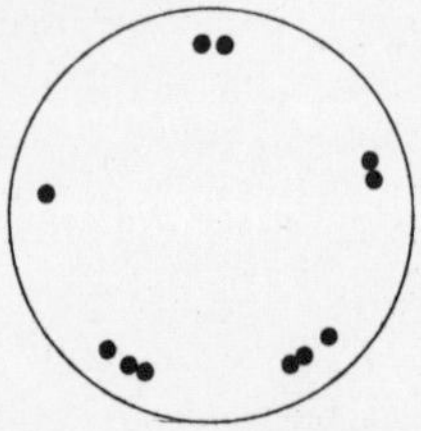

The arrays give us an insight into the overall atmosphere in a period of time. They don't tend to activate energy specifically, except through aspects forming within them between some of the planets involved. But they do give a period of time a certain flavour, and lend an overview of the whole current of time.

I cannot say that I am an expert in this particular field of astrology, and more examples need presenting from history. That's all in motion for my coming book on astrological cycles of history. Meanwhile, this chapter is offered as a starter, to give you an idea of the basic dynamics of arrays in action in time. I would appreciate hearing from you if you have done research in this area, to hear what your conclusions are!

15 The slower-moving planets and their capers

The slower planets move on their own time-spectrum, and outline energy-flows and high-points which affect years, decades and centuries. Here we shall look at how they work, providing the deeper background issues of history which the faster planets then take up and act out in the shorter-term.

World change

There are two main kinds of historical change: that which takes place within the realm of the known, and that which works within the realm of the unknown. The western cultures of the last millenia have had a strong tendency to overlay their own realities on the natural order of things, building civilisations which function in the realm of the known, excluding the unknown or containing it within manageable limits. At times of change, these limits are pushed out, and a new social-psychological hybrid, mutation or transformation comes about. Often these changes are initially resisted: today we live in a time when this is very much the case.

To create a civilisation which moves in accord with nature and wider global and universal dynamics, we need to incorporate the energy-impulses of the outer planets consciously into our culture. We need to adapt our hold on the known such that it responds to the unknown, and we need to take the fear out of our relationship with the unknown. This means opening the channels between the worlds of ♃ - ♄ and ⚷ - ♅ - ♆ - ♇ . This is the challenge of today. Individuals who are consciously growing are admitting the outermost planets into their lives: the challenge is now to make this a social phenomenon.

Revolutions and major social changes have usually been carried through in unconscious ways, omitting a sense of inner unity with the essential or divine energy-waves stimulating them. In reaction to the religious ethics of each *ancien regime* to be overthrown, humanistic movements (marxism, social democracy, maoism, capitalism etc) have, while opening possibilities for humans, also closed the doors between humanity and cosmos: thus lands where revolution has been at work have landed up with bureaucracies and new czars which have not provided the kind of change originally dreamed of (USA and USSR, India, China, plus many third world countries provide examples). Humans alone cannot transform the nature of life: we can do this in the context of channeling the wider cosmos and the natural flow into the realm of the known, for the intelligence inherent in the cosmic flow infinitely surpasses that within the political/humanistic ideologies and philosophies of people and society.

To bring about heaven on earth, we need to *allow* heaven into our lives, and in doing so, we shall be further guided in moving forward. This we could call the *goddess* approach. Today, for example, we need to prove that nuclear waste can be rendered harmless *psychically*, through penetrating the fundamental intelligence which gives nuclear products their radioactive properties: a seemingly ridiculous proposition when seen from within the realm of our stock of *known* possibilities. Yet this is probably the only solution available to us, and the problem has arisen to stimulate us to *do something* about it! Necessity is the mother of invention.

Discoveries

It is traditionally said in astrology that a planet is discovered when human consciousness is ready to take it. Thus ♅ was discovered in 1781 (13 March), ♆ was discovered in 1846 (23 September) and ♇ in 1930 (announced 13 March). These dates illustrate how furtively these planets work, for each of these periods of history marked a major turning-point: ♅ came as changes connected with the industrial revolution came into full force, manifesting in the French and American revolutions; ♆ came along just as Karl Marx was publishing the first marxist ideas, and as the first oriental and psychic impulses were coming through in western consciousness, both of these symbolising the positive effects of the new industrial order, by then becoming established; ♇ came at the time of the rise of dictatorship and modern globalism, the beginning of the modern electronic age.

In 1977 (10 October), ⚷ was discovered: since the full implications of a new consciousness can take decades to see, it will be a while before we understand the change it symbolises, yet any sensitive person can sense that since 1977, *something* has been different. Chiron is the link between the two worlds — the known and the unknown, *tonal* and *nagual*: the time is now coming for demonstrating this.

Evolution of consciousness

Here we are entering into a large-scale realm of astrology: the study of history and its movements. The danger with astro-historical analysis is that we can read significance into anything if we want to, to find proof for our theories. Acts of parliament, new monarchs, battles fought or specific events matter little here, except inasmuch as they might symbolise or catalyse very fundamental changes of orientation in history. Thus we have a challenge ahead of us: to rewrite history looking at the underlying trends running through time, and to rewrite it as a history of the *evolution of consciousness,* where events, heroes and world changes serve as an expression of these group-psychic changes. This is the history (or herstory) of all people, and of group psyche and humanity as one being, child of the planet Earth.

We are now in a time of immense (r)evolutionary changes of consciousness — changes which are greater than we currently realise — and our present time, far from being historically boring, is a valuable time for us to observe and be a part of. Not least because we as individuals each consciously or unconsciously channel the energies of the outer planets ourselves, and are moving into active rather than victimised relationship with them as we grow and transform ourselves. We are the creators of the future, and need to set a new precedent by consciously choosing how it is going to be, through our individual acts and choices, through our conscious participation in history-making: politicians, popes, generals, experts and managers can no longer do it for us. In our time, social intent, change-inducing contributions by individuals to society and organic structural changes, appropriate to each situation, locality and people are crucial issues: when ♅, ♆ and ♄ each enter ♒ in the 1990s, this will become highlighted.

Manifestation: jupiter and saturn

The outer planets ♅, ♆ and ♇ move in tune with cycles and waves of motion within the collective unconscious: their dynamics are represented to us by artists and dream-weavers, by figureheads of change, by social movements and issues which stir and wobble the status quo in so many ways. ♃ and ♄, however, work within the realm of the known, on a social level, through the social forms and institutions we create, through the agreements, norms and laws with which we work, through cycles of prosperity, politics and every department of society. In a transformative sense, these two can bring through deeper impulses in their relations with the outer planets, through the aspects they form to them.

Jupiter, on a 12 year cycle, regularly conjuncts the outer planets every 13-20 years, and encourages people to move *forward* into the area of life suggested by that outer planet and the sign it is in. For example, the entry of ♆ into ♑ in January 1984 brought with it an impulse to ground and realise the visions and spiritual experiences which 13 years of its sojourn in ♐ stimulated: seeds of a new 'religion' emerged in the 1970s, which now demands bringing into hard reality, normalising and integrating during neptune's passage through ♑. Hapwise, ♃ moved into ♑ *on exactly the same day* as ♆ (rare!), bringing a boost to this deep ethic, a surge of activity where many new ventures, businesses and openings were embarked upon, manifesting this deep impulse. From this time on, also, the perception that things are falling apart (♆ in ♑) took root in the collective psyche, giving rise to a 'let's do it now before it's too late' syndrome characterising our time.

♃ in this case brought the neptunian flavour into a more concrete form, which the ♄-♆ ☌ of 1989 must test, weed out and institutionalise: for some this is a test of our ability to ground our dreams and meet real-life challenges with them, and for others it will demand an acceptance that things *are* disintegrating more than foreseen, and that either definite reforms (constitutional, legal, structural) must be legislated, or that large scale chaos *could* ensue, despite any attempts to resist this. The ♄ ☌ ♅ in 1988 (also around the opening cusp of ♑, the winter solstice point) will show the way it has to go, and force the choices necessary, just as the ♄-♇ ☌ in late 1982 laid the cards on the table for many, forcing a choice either to open up to the truth of what is happening in the world, or to close down and pretend that everything is *perfectly normal*. Governments chose the latter stance, and for many individuals this became a squeezed-out turning-point.

The ♅ ☌ ♇ in ♍ of 1965-66 was grounded in a similar way by an ☍ from ♄ ☌ ⚷ in ♓: technological changes (♍) which then gave birth to the microchip and the full coming of the atomic age were counterbalanced by a grounded spiritual burst from the piscean planets. The seeds of the new dispensation, the emergence of a new vision and spiritual imperative which is still today working itself through, were grounded in definite, reachable forms — sex'n'drugs-'n'rock'n'roll, new diets and lifestyles — which ordinary people could relate to and use, as a gateway to further things. The 'permissive society' arose through neptune's passage through ♏, and the headiness of the time was supplemented by ♃ in ♊ in 1966.

The cycle of ♃'s relationship with ♄ is also worth watching. It is 20 years in length. Interestingly, they create a *mutational* cycle where, once every 60 years, they conjunct at roughly the same place in the zodiac. In addition, successive 20 year conjunctions occur in signs of one element, the element changing (on a *Great*

Mutation) every so often. ♃ conjuncts ♄ in ♑ in 1842, in ♍ in 1862, in ♉ in 1881, in ♑ in 1901, in ♍ in 1921, in ♉ in 1940, in ♑ in 1961, in *libra* in 1981, and in late ♉ in 2000. The recent ☌ in 1981 is a harbinger of future conjunctions in air signs in the 21st century.

This cycle is the cycle of organisations and institutions, socio-economic forms and current-affairs issues, money, engineering, tangible energy and resources, production and consumption, manifest cultural forms and norms, education and international relations. Note however that conjuctions mark beginnings, and in themselves represent watersheds: the action happens *throughout* the cycle, with interesting crunch-points at the □ s and ☍ s. Thus we have ☌ in 1961, □ in 65, ☍ in 1970, □ in 75-76, ☌ in 1981, □ in 86, ☍ in 89-90, □ in 1995 and a ☌ in 2000. Think about it. When one of these cyclical turningpoints involves an outer planet too — as was the case in 1986, with ⚷ interceding and forming a T-square — interesting developments can follow along to the end of the cycle.

Worth noting also are the seven year cycles connected with ♄ : it takes this time for a thought-form to become grounded in normal reality, for individuals. This is more connected with the motion of ♄ than its cycle with ♃ . The movement of each of these through the signs bring through strong movements in the social realm. It is particularly worth observing changes occurring around the times when ♃ and ♄ cross the quarter points and cross-quarter points in the zodiac.

Deeper stuff

There is a difference between a sign change (ingress) and a major aspect involving the outer planets. When there is a *sign-change*, there is a change of orientation in group awareness, in which old issues lapse, and new issues arise. What was important to people earlier moves on to new themes and underlying preoccupations, floating around in the collective psyche, often symptomised in the headlines of newspapers.

A recent change of this kind occurred in 1984, when ♇ entered ♏, ♆ entered ♑ and ⚷ entered ♊ (note the ✶ and two ⚻ s), and another occurred in 1956 when ♅ entered ♌ , ♆ entered ♏ and ♇ ♍. At these points in modern history, future possibilities percolated through to become current realities. Such synchronisms of outer-planet ingresses are not usual. They symbolise major shifts in the themes and archetypes which are active at any time in the collective psyche. If only we were more aware of this, and *consciously* participated in it!

When an important outer-planet *aspect* forms, there are *definite* dynamics which are set in motion in the group psyche, producing true transformations and breakthroughs (or breakdowns, depending on our collective choice). These are times when *dispensations* are filtered through from deep down (or high up!) which lay the seeds of immense changes, even if they take years or even millenia to emerge fully. To go a long way back, the last time ♅, ♆ and ♇ were engaged together in a *very* major mutual conjunction was 580**BC**, at the time of Buddha, Lao Tzu, and Pythagoras and Aristotle, and the height of the celtic culture in Britain: this could be regarded as the beginning of the end of the old magical/ feminine world, and the beginning of a new, objectivised consciousness, the foundation to our modern civilisation and whatever it itself is leading toward.

In 1395-6**AD** there was ♅ ☍ ♆ ☌ ♇, the end of the european medieval period, and the seed point for the ending of the power of religion, and the beginning of the power of materialism, as the dominant force for social change — at this time, exploration and imperialism had their roots, and the old ways of the pre-christian era took a nose dive during the witch-burnings and inquisitions of

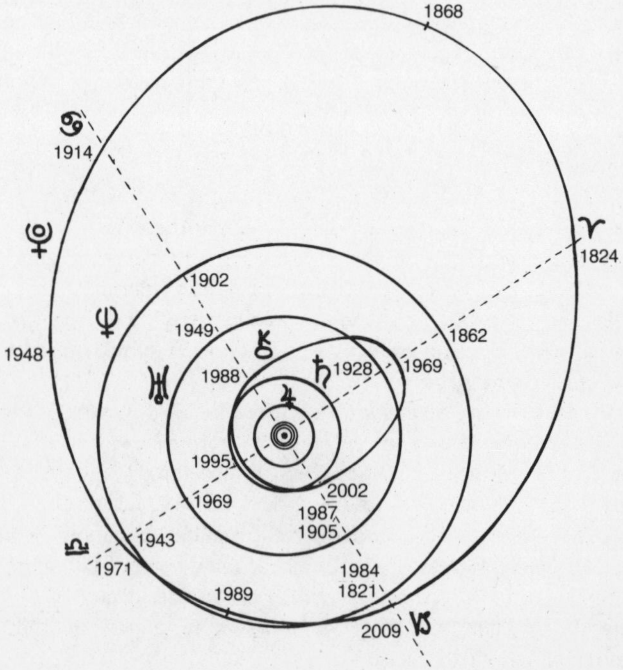

The orbits of the outer planets, roughly to scale

the time. A more current example of such major changes is the ♆ ☌ ♇ in ♊, ☍ ⚷ ☌ ♅ in ♐, from 1892 to 1907 (in history, a short period) about which, more later. Each of these changes represents a historical watershed of *immense* proportions.

Orbits

Uranus moves round the zodiac in 84 years, ♆ in 165 years and ♇ in 250 years. ♅ conjuncts ♆ every 171 years, ♆ conjuncts ♇ roughly every 490 years, and ♅ conjuncts ♇ anywhere between 100-200 years, variable because of ♇'s eccentric orbit. ⚷ is on a cycle of 51 years, eccentric to the extent that figures are difficult to give. ⚷ is closest to the sun (*perihelion*) when at 8♎ (1945 and 1995-6), furthest (*aphelion*) when at 8♈ (1920 and 1970), and ♇ is in perihelion at 12♏ (in 1988) and at aphelion at 12♉ (1865-6). ⚷ comes inside the orbit of ♄ at perihelion, and outside the orbit of ♅ at aphelion (note the symbolism — ⚷ acts as a link between conscious and depth-conscious living), and ♇ comes inside the orbit of ♆ at perihelion (1978-2000, closest 1988).

Pluto is a bringer of the *inevitable*, and manifests through destruction of the old and forced, even manic, emergence of the new. When ♇ was discovered, the good old days of nineteenth century expansion were killed, and the heavy extremes of the twentieth century came forth in economic depression, totalitarianism and major technological change. ♇ turns the pages of history, disastrously, rips us out of the past and thrusts us into the daunting future, because the seeds of it have already *unconsciously* been set up, and because the time has now come. Cracks become chasms, and the inevitable emerges. Unless some new planet is discovered, ♇ has the last word on historical change.

The outer planets through the signs

★ ⚷ *CHIRON*

Chiron is a bringer of resolution. When in any sign, ⚷ brings up paradoxes and issues in *definite* forms, which create a situation of great compromise and dilemma, seeking resolution. Often old solutions no longer work, and hiding the issue fails: an impasse develops where it seems there are hundreds of questions and no answers. Then, appearing seemingly out of the blue, usually from a grassroots level, a solution emerges, in a very challenging way, very appropriately and miraculously answering definite questions, and offering simple, basic yet big solutions. This can be difficult for society to handle, slow as it is to adapt: unfortunately we have a

The motions of ⚷ through the signs

♋ protectionism, identity, welfare, nationalism (1938-41); ♌ self-interest, dominion, self/national expression, leadership, heroes (1941-43); ♍ healing wounds, divisions, work on what has been spoiled, reorganisation, rebuilding (1943-4); ♎ international/interpersonal relations, mediation, agreement, treaty, subgroup interests (1944-5); ♏ calling on resources, pragmatism, execution of changes, facing realities, magical forces (1946-9); ♐ education, globalism, far horizons, law reform, social welfare and prosperity (1898-1902, 1949-51); ♑ structures, constitutions, getting down to things, stabilisation, sense, authorities (1902-4, 1951-4); ♒ social planning, new ideas, internationalism, invention, movements (1904-10, 1955-61); ♓ caring, relative realities, insights, spiritual impulses, madness, glamour, paradox (1910-18, 1961-8); ♈ self-discovery, chauvinism, agitation for change, self-interest lobbies, pioneering activities, forging ahead (1919-27, 1968-77); ♉ self-sufficiency, grounding, solid determined progress, technological emergence, pleasure, affluence (1927-34, 1976-83); ♊ perspective changes, ideas, communications, trade, bridging dualisms, shifts of allegiance (1934-38, 1984-88).

dangerous tendency to create wars, disasters and civil strife as ways of bringing these changes through — this we must change.

The arrival of chiron in 1977 happened at a time when grassroots solutions to current major questions in the world suddenly became obvious — even though the ideals and dreams had been around for some years, definite movements developed which offered real chances to break through on deadlocked situations: feminism, the green movement, the third world/local movements, alternative healing, self-help, community action and the peace movement, plus many local variants. ⚷ precipitates issues such that bridges must be built, linkages made, and activities initiated to make for *workable* transition into whatever new order is needed at the time.

Note the involvement of ⚷ in the ♅ ☍ ♇ (1898-1901) which marked a watershed not only of centuries, but in the beginning of transference of power from the British Empire to the modern American state, plus the Boer and Russo-Japanese wars, together with major rumblings in all old imperial nations such as China, Austria and Britain. ⚷ in ♒ was instrumental in both the near-revolutions of 1905 and the near major wars of 1955-6. It was involved also in the healing process around 1945, when ♆, ♃ and ⚷ conjuncted in ♎, in the happenings of the mid-sixties (⚷ ☌ ♄, in opposition to ♅ ☌ ♇), and in the line-up of 1988-93 (⚷ ☌ ♃ opposing a conjunction of ♄, ♅ and ♆).

Note also the yod formed by ⚷ to the three other outer planets in 1979-82, an important substratum to the changes of the late eighties, and an initial emergence in form of the seeds planted in the sixties. Owing to the acceleration of ⚷ when it is around ♎, it forms far more aspects, and is far more actively involved in historical developments than when it is around ♈.

★ ♅ *URANUS*

Uranus is a bringer of uplift. It reveals new avenues forward, and breaks us off from the past. Which can be shocking, yet it takes a load off the world by offering a new mutation or vector in the group psyche. New ideas and ideologies come forward, which bring radical, in-principle changes to history. Often these outbreaks do not last in form (for example, the French revolution blew itself out in a decade, and 1960s flower-power wilted), but plant seeds for a new order, based on new perspectives, innovations and total situations, suddenly different from before. ♅ conjures up new visions and possibilities, the forms of which might pass (like the Beatles) but the effects of which unfold for decades or more afterwards. ♅ is a true bringer of revolution, of overthrow of the old, in whatever manner is needed, so abruptly that established

The motions of ♅ through the signs

♅ in ♐ radical changes of perspective, new cosmologies, crises in international relations, leaky boundaries, legal and educational crises, new freedom movements (1898-1904, 1981-88); in ♑ governmental/structural/institutional instability, revolt or radical reform, cutting off from past history, precipitated grounding of visions (1904-12, 1988-95); in ♒ inventions, shattering ideas, independence, ideologies, opening of the new, sudden new developments with longterm implications (1912-19, 1995-2002); in ♓ awakening, chaos, intrusion of unknowns, omens of times to come, eruptions from the unconscious, escapism, spiritual impulses (1919-27, 2002-10); in ♈ new heroes, initiatives and mutations, militarism, competitiveness and ribaldry, daring steps (1927-34, 2010-2017); in ♉ making what has been started happen, building, excess, xenophobia, dogged resistance to influence, building up of the need for change (1934-41, 2017-2025); in ♊ new ideas, discoveries, alliances, shifts, contradictions, social mobility (1858-65, 1941-49); in ♋ security issues, welfare, changes in national interest, conservatism, preservation or disruption of order (1865-72, 1949-56); in ♌ self-determination, independence, rock'n'roll, struggles against domination, power issues, 'never had it so good' (1872-78, 1956-62); in ♍ technological innovation, financial disruption, dissent, extremism, protest, affluence, new political ideas (1878-84, 1962-69); in ♎ radical changes of relationship, detente, sudden reversals/oscillations, new arts, new values, issues around conventionality (1884-91, 1969-75); in ♏ encounters, revelations, therapy, business instability, march of progress, rising depression, alternatives, quests (1891-98, 1981-88).

ways cannot adapt, and simply have to yield.

Uranus moves around the zodiac at a regular pace, spending seven years in each sign, marking out a regular pulse of reorientation with regards to the different issues the zodiac symbolises. While ♅ brings through what land up being key positive changes, often from the upstarts and crazies of the world, the radicals, eccentrics and deviants, its passage through the signs can equally well demonstrate the different ways in which established systems *resist* change, repress movements and discourage innovation.

♅ marks out seven-year generations of people who each are stirred up and face or seek change in their own ways, according to the sign involved. It shows the *source of insecurity* in a generation, the area of life where earthquakes are happening and new cosmic intrusions are entering. ♅ opens up questions and will not let them rest.

♅ was involved (with ♄) in a strong ☍ to ♇ in 1901, and a ☌ in 1965-6 (☍ ♄). These represent fierce breakthroughs of consciousness (in mutable signs) and life-forms: humanity took to the air on the ☍, and reached the moon on the ☌. It last opposed ♆ in 1907-8, and conjuncts it in 1992, both times when in ♑, putting great pressure on all rigidities and structures, making life at the top very trying! Note the rise of Hitler when it entered ♈, the rise of the modern welfare state when it hit ♋, and the rise of the global village, Japan, Islam and the Third World from when it entered ♎. ♅ in ♑ heralds new and looser structures to deal efficiently with new realities, or a lapsing into rigid resistance to institutional change, with possible breakdown.

★ ♆ *NEPTUNE*

Neptune spends around 13 years in each sign, marking out distinctive periods in which life-as-dream manifests different fundamental beliefs and reality bubbles. ♆ reveals both the illusions which a generation can fall into, and its own particular way of elevating itself and reaching its peak of awareness.

♆ is a bringer of light, of new awareness — and new glamours. It dissolves old forms and makes them suddenly invalid and outdated, falling apart through inability to deal with new energy, through unworkability or irrelevance. All that is structured and fixed becomes questionable and hazy, and in the space created, new possibilities have the opportunity to grow, spontaneously, out of the dreams, fantasies or paranoias of the people. When ♆ was discovered, new cosmologies emerged (such as marxism, darwinism, theosophy, spiritualism) and the urban-industrial-imperial era was in full swing. That was over a century ago, and our realities

The motions of ♆ through the signs

♆ entered ♊ in 1888, in a time when new ideas were rampant, from scientific discoveries to early socialism, spiritualism and magical philosophies through to the dreams which stimulated air travel; it entered ♋ in 1901, and many realities which were known and established took a beating — it was no longer safe to hold on to the past, for present issues at home (the end of the extended family) and in nationhood (the arising of new political forces) were making the ways of the 19th Century outdated; something had to break, which it did when ♆ entered ♌ in 1914, and a heroic struggle for dominion and mastery broke out, which will properly end when it enters ♒ in 1998 — ♆ in ♌ gave birth to superheroes and superstars, film, modern commercialism and radio glamour, a glorification of personality and selfhood; ♆ moved into ♍ in 1930, a time of faith in science and industry, work, technology and economy, giving rise to Keynesianism, assembly lines and the atomic bomb, a triumph of materialism, which lost its drive yet found new context when ♆ entered ♎ in 1941-2; here the fortunes of WW2 changed, alliances formed and changed, and relationship (or lack of it) and coexistence became the issue, leading to the dissolution of the British Empire, the rise of the EEC and the ascendancy of power blocs around USA and USSR — projected fear of the 'enemy' thrived as a way of keeping changing social relations in check; the rise of the dream of the good life gave way to the plunge into the new which happened as ♆ entered ♏ in 1956, giving birth to the 'permissive society', drug-use, the 'Cold War', and the rampant energy of change blowing through the sixties, shuddering, deep, an unconscious questing for death and resurrection, with some honest truths put in for good measure — outer space was conquered and inner space was opened up; ♆ entered ♐ in 1970, opening up new perspectives, an outburst of religions and beliefs, a new internationalism through travel and media expansion, a belief in progress, science, expansion and wealth, despite strong signs that the opposite was going on underneath — knowledge and outlook have changed, experience has been learned from, and insight has dawned; in 1984 ♆ entered ♑, leading to a combination of tottery institutions and governments with growing undercurrents of revolt, change from beneath, glamours of power and authority being undermined by an insidious need to be very practical and apt in dealing with real questions current in the world; outcomes of the ♑ phase are yet to come, and the footing on which ♆ enters ♒ is as yet unknown — from 1998 it is likely however that significant reforms, new social vision, a new sense of hope and reconstruction will begin, tending toward a glorification of collective interests and a personal searching for significance in the vastness of the new situation, a global village and a new horizon. ♆ moves into ♓ 2013-2026, which might well provide a very meaningful, deep opportunity for generations now being born — or a void interlude, a tired emptiness and chaos after decades of projection of illusions. Whether the new age implies a new spiritual order of life on earth, or a sci-fi manifestation of a technological dream depends largely on us, and what we do with history.

The motions of ♇ through the signs

♇ entered ♊ in 1882, preceding ♆, forcing through a barrage of new ideas (eg creation vs evolution, christianity vs psychism), electrical technologies, giant steamships, the telegraph, and later the aeroplane. All was buzzing, and innovations were cropping up everywhere, not as yet creating wholesale changes, but laying the ground for the story of the 20th Century. Then in 1912, ♇ entered ♋, and the big plunge broke out, a

and perceptions have changed vastly since.

The present position of ♆ (in ♑) goes back to the aftermath of the Napoleonic Wars, and all the changes which they brought: the old order had collapsed, and new forms needed building to meet the new realities of the day. This was the beginning of the concept of democracy proper. Interestingly, the last ♅ ☌ ♆ was in 1821, in ♑. A similar situation befalls us now, where dramatic technological progress plus changes in consciousness and lifestyles are invalidating old forms of organisation, constitutions, law and order, social status and institutions (whether in the world or in the mind). The choice before us is whether we can make a transition into a fundamentally new way of organising our lives by flexible, appropriate reorganisation, or whether the structures of the world will resist change and provoke breakdown. We have the possibility of anything from a new dimension in world totalitarianism to anarchy: and the choice is ours, now. A middle path of radical reform and major institutional change is probably the wisest option — but we modern humans tend not to make historical changes through wisdom and foresight, only through imperative and crisis.

♆ was opposed by ♅ in 1907-9, a time of shattered dreams for some, and of new promise for others as revolutions failed and the Great War loomed under the blind eye of the old 19th Century order. ♆ figured strongly in both world wars, yet in the 1960s acted as the safety valve for the powerful oppositions of that time: a dream was fetched from the depths of the group psyche (♆ in ♏), which will be well manifest by the time ♆ is in mid-aquarius around 2004. ♆ figures strongly in the lineup in 1989-93, except at this time ♇ acts as the safety-valve — perhaps here we have an opportunity to be really honest with ourselves, and turn about to tackle the genuine problems the world faces?

★ ♇ *PLUTO*

Pluto's eccentric orbit makes it take on a variable role in history, at present strong, since it now moves at its fastest and is closest to the sun, in its home sign scorpio. It is in the same position now as it was at the birth of the urban-industrial system in the mid-18th Century. At that time, people were beginning to say goodbye to their villages and land, taking off for the cities and the New World, and the inevitable march of 'progress' was showing itself. Scientism as religion, new political philosophies, new technologies and the death of the old were symptomised by the romantic painters and writers of the time.

Now we find a squeeze-through into the post-industrial age, with forced unemployment, uprooting of tribes and refugees, fight-outs all over the world, and governments which blatantly ignore and conceal the truth of the situation characterising the time.

The world unconscious is rife with monsters and demons, sexual diseases and cancers threaten, the ghost of destruction hovers, and this is it, a time of breakthrough or breakdown, a testing time in which the consciousness and light of the new dispensation received in the sixties has to work itself through into a cruel world if we are to maintain peace, sanity and justice and reaffirm life on earth.

The ♆ - ♇ ☌ of 1890-1 and the ♅ ☍ ♇ of 1901 laid the tracks for the 20th Century, which became fulfilled at the ♅ ☌ ♇ of 1965-6. Something new started in the 60s: even though it has looked as if everything has been progressing *as normal* since then, our civilisation has been running only on momentum, and awaits a profound change. Since the 60s world climate has been changing, its crowdedness has become an accepted reality, and the essential oneness of the world and the human family has become visible. Life on earth can now be destroyed in a choice of ways, and yet nature is balancing this with an increased awareness and level of activity in ecology, human relations, psychology and spirituality. The West is slowly becoming the spiritual node of the world, and Oceania is becoming the industrial centre. Concepts and outlooks are transforming faster now than ever before, and we are approaching a probable quantum leap for humanity.

Options

This quantum leap is related to a cycle of evolution which moves far further than ♇ cycles, which themselves are like the second-hand on the clock of human history. But the timing of the smaller-scale, century-by-century changes which facilitate this evolution, this spiralling or exponential curve is marked by the major antics of the outer planets, focused into daily life by the inner planets and earth-moon itself. The clock ticks on. At every turn we are presented with choices: for the universe has it that we should be creatures of free will and creative potential.

Yet we have a mysterious way of ignoring our options, and avoiding the fundamental question: what are we alive for, and what sort of world are we actually seeking to create? World is a collective dream, yet until we realise it is so, it takes on a very concrete, hard, rough form. When we grasp that it all *is* a dream, the real reality begins, for we need to dream a garden, a world of fulfilment, freedom, creation, peace and enlightenment (of some sort or another, and we need to dream it collectively, without unquestioningly following the ideologies of advanced thinkers or social leaders.

The answers are simple. So simple that it seems we cannot address ourselves to them. But we are getting there: in the end there is nothing we can do other than create a heaven on earth, and

plunge into transformative war, totally new situations, depressions and slumps, insecurity and fear: the mother principle was being violently beaten, and people were being ripped out of their slumber by the shock of the modern age. Patriotism and controlled mob rule became common, security became a big issue, and all manner of sensitivities were trodden on. The nuclear family became the norm, and the nuclear bomb became a possibility, to be unleashed after ♇ entered ♌ in 1938-9. All hell broke loose when ♇ ingressed into ♌, and it is said that humanity went through two centuries-worth of consciousness-evolution in five years of war, through plain horror. Yet nature counterbalances everything: LSD, the awakener of the sixties, was discovered at the time of the first nuclear explosion, and a new generation of souls were born who have the opportunity to create and manifest a profound dream. The world rushed through changes, and was a very different place by 1956, when ♇ entered ♍. ♇ in ♍ brought new distinctions, gave birth to widespread computer use and the nuclear age, to the jumbo jet and Mick Jagger, to a new spirit of self-examination and introspection, and eventually to a vision of a new earth, which is still emerging. ♇ entered ♎ in 1971, when the Third World came of age, and previous imperial masters were rendered equal, when marriage shook severely, and relationship of all kinds was forced through a painful historical spasm — yet the libran tendency to enjoy life now and face the music later prevailed, and now ♇ has moved into ♏, from 1984-1995, and the consequences, nicely concealed to date, are breaking out in every field of life. ♇ in ♏ is the death of the old, the encounter with inevitable realities, the leak of secrets and the hard grating of the 'ruthless aspect of compassion' which the universe brings out to teach us of the path beyond. The new is fully emergent when ♇ enters ♒ (last in 1780, next around 2026), yet the seed for it is laid now: the historical cycle which began with the French and American Revolutions is now dying, and already we can talk in terms of the post-industrial age, even though we do not know what that is likely to imply.

we now stand in the learning process, at a possible graduation, wherein we are finding out how to create it.

16 Making history: the Twentieth Century

We could say that the 20th Century started around 1890 at the ♆ ☌ ♇ in ♊ (□ ♄) which took place then, staggered over 15 years with a ⚷ ☌ ♅ in ♐ in 1898 and ☍ aspects between all of them up to 1908. Let's look at this and other major historical power periods, for it is worth doing so in order to gain an insight into what we are entering into in 1989-93. What matters most in astrology is **the present,** ***but the past can give insights into how things actually happened before, and what we can learn from them, with regards to tackling our future options.***

The Industrial Revolution

This began when ♇ was last in ♏ in the 1740s. At the time, the prospect was, to many, horrendous, and the towns, canals and coal-mines opening up seemed to some to be the last degeneration of humanity into the Slough of Despond. Nowadays, we can afford to start thinking of this painful phase of history being the beginning of an urban-industrial phase out of which we now are moving, by means both technological and cultural-spiritual. Thus it finds new meaning, presenting us with a foundation for changes we only now are beginning to make in the fundamental nature of human life and reality.

When ♇ was in ♒, the French and American revolutions broke out, heralding the end of the old social, class and governmental order, the beginning not only of the republic and the concept (though not the practice) of democracy, but also so many other new laws, principles, norms, inventions, precedents and impulses which now are normal, but once were unheard of (for example, the metric measurement system). The machine age was upon us, together with all the experiential benefits and ills it brought.

When ♇ entered ♈, the steam engine emerged, powering new forms of production and travel, making all manner of new possibilities available: by the end of the century worldwide travel

Movements of ♅, ♆ and ♇ during the Nineteenth Century
For those of you interested in history, here is a brief look at the major antics of ♅, ♆ and ♇ in the nineteenth century. Form your own conclusions. We start at the end of the Napoleonic Wars, which were a watershed, the true birth of the modern state and the urban-industrial system we live in. Note the times when the planets cross the zodiacal quarter-points and cross-quarter points. Asterisks (*) indicate astrologically crucial years.

*1821 ♅ ☌ ♆ in ♑.
1823 ♇ enters ♈.
1829 ♅ in ♒ (home).
1832 ♅ mid-♒.
1834 ♆ in ♒; grand △ of ♃/♄ to ♅\♆, with a ♄ ☍ ♇ (kite).
1836 ♅ enters ♓.
1844 ♅ in ♈, and ♆ ✶ ♇.
1848 ♆ in ♓ (home).
*1850 ♅ ☌ ♇ in ♈.
1851 ♅ *and* ♇ enter ♉.
1858 ♅ enters ♊.
1862 ♆ enters ♈.
1865 ♅ enters ♋.
1868 ♇ mid-♉.
1872 ♅ in ♌.
1875 ♆ in ♉, ♅ mid-♌.
1878 ♅ enters ♍.
1880 ♅ △ ♆.
1881 ♆ mid-♉.
1883 ♇ enters ♊.
1884 ♅ enters ♍, ♅ △ ♇.
1888 ♆ in ♊.
**1890-1 ♆ ☌ ♇ in ♊, □ ♄.
1891 ♅ enters ♏.
1898 ♅ enters ♐.

Transits 1965~99

Two graphs for investigating longterm transits and changes sparked off by Jupiter, Saturn, Chiron, Uranus, Neptune and Pluto.

♋ Cancer ♌ Leo ♍ Virgo ♎ Libra ♏ Scorpio ♐ Sagittarius ♑ Capricorn ♒ Aquarius ♓ Pisces ♈ Aries ♉ Taurus ♊ Gemini

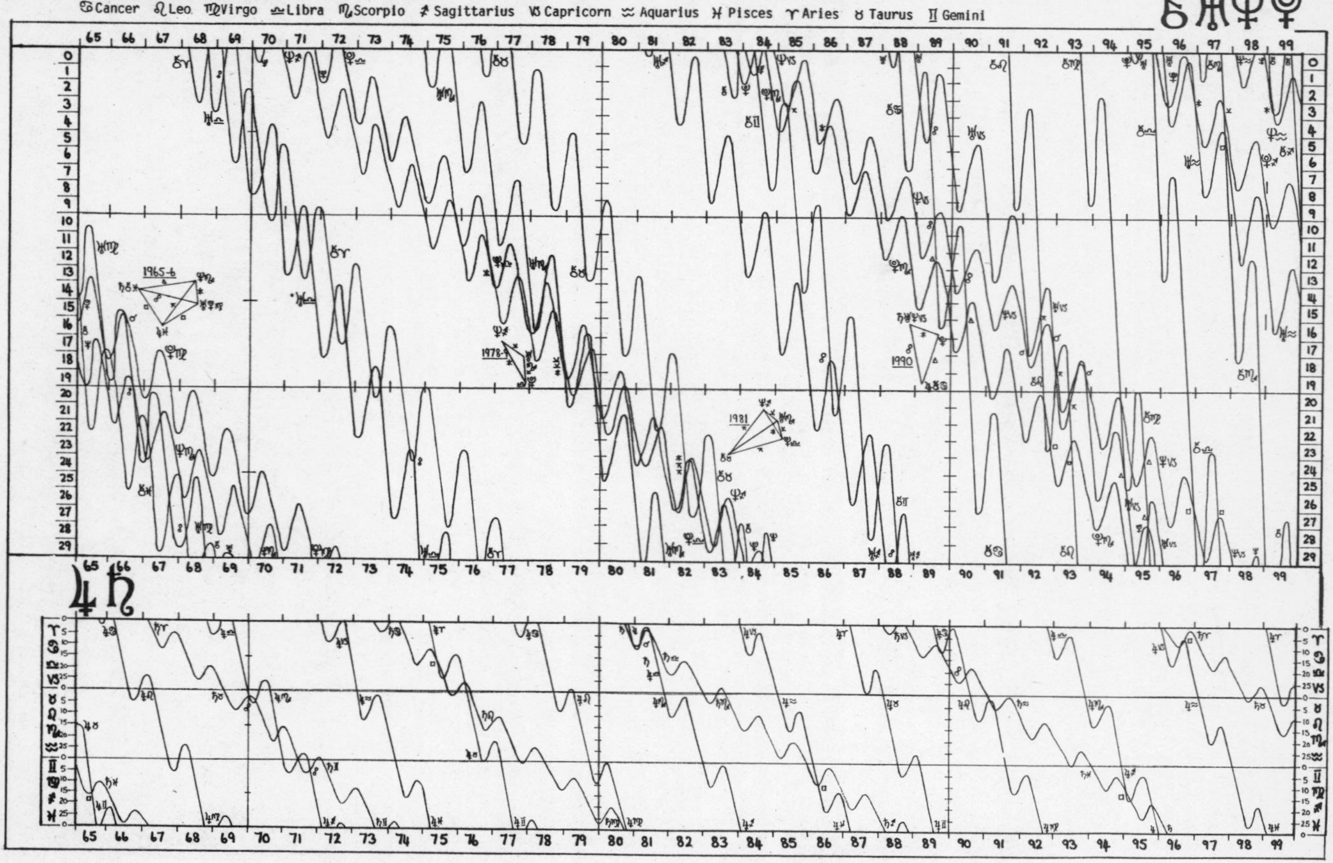

was well established, and the appurtenances of urban life, from cocoa to bank loans to widespread literacy, plus the new class system of capitalists, bourgeousie and workers were all normalised, as if they had always been so.

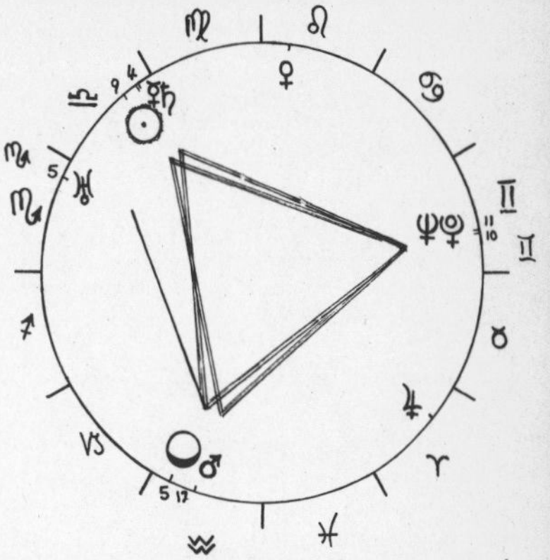

1st October 1892. Around the exact ♆ ☌ ♇, this chart shows how faster planets can enter into a longterm configuration to upstep its power. Note that astrologers of the time will not have known about ♇ or its position!

The last ♅ ☌ ♆ in ♑ in 1821 was very important as far as social structures went: the dawning industrial world, international trade, new ideas, new forms of imperialism, new laws and a fundamental infrastructural shift took place, facilitating new developments. This was a prime time for inventiveness and technological transformation — everything was shifting.

In 1850, there was ♅ ☌ ♇ in ♈ (the one following was in 1965-6 in ♍): this was the time of das Kapital, the Great Exhibition in London, the rise of Queen Victoria, the large-scale exploration of the American West by whites, of many scientific advances, and a transition into a world interconnected by trains and steamships. This was a time when the ideology of the industrial-urban world properly took off.

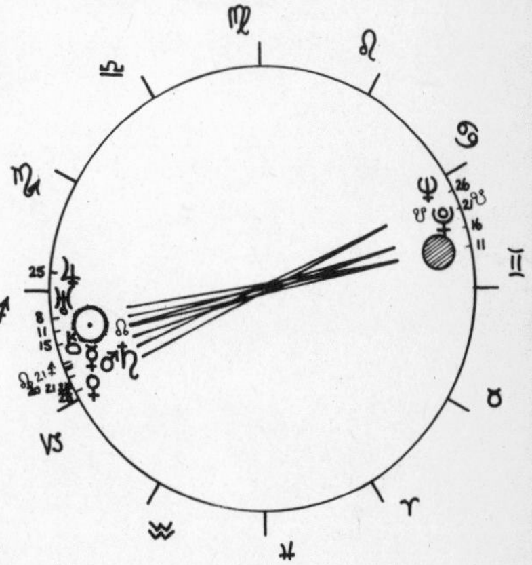

The lunar eclipse of 3rd December 1899. An exceptionally strong power point in time, highlighting the ♆ ☌ ♇ in ♊ and the ♄ ☌ ⚷ ☌ ♅ in ♐, both staggered over the 1890s, but strongly featured by the intervention here of the faster planets. This could be regarded as the chart for the 20th Century

Acceleration

But these astrological transitions were far outclassed by that which took place in the 1890s: this one is a historical turningpoint *par excellence*, the true beginning of the modern world, a global village in the making. This time saw the bringing into use of electricity, the invention of the aeroplane, of the beginnings of radio and telecommunications, of automation on a large scale — even in war, face-to-face fighting ended. The First World War was a *symptom* of this massive change, a trying out of new toys and a sweeping away of old ways, a "war to end all wars" (which it wasn't, for that was but the perspective of the time, seen from within the then-known range of perceived possibilities).

Each of these changes represent a change of consciousness too. They each present an opportunity for significant elevations of consciousness, and at each one, new religions, beliefs and ideologies get born: for example, in the 1890s, scientism found new strength, Freudianism opened new territory in understanding the psyche and Darwinism in understanding the natural world, East met West through Theosophy and all that it seeded, unionism and socialism became more widely embraced (yielding results in the following decades), and ideas went through a change profound and fundamental in effects. ♊ and ♐ were prominent, featured most strongly at the fullmoon of 3 December 1899 — though this was a 15 year long period involving several major outer-planet aspects.

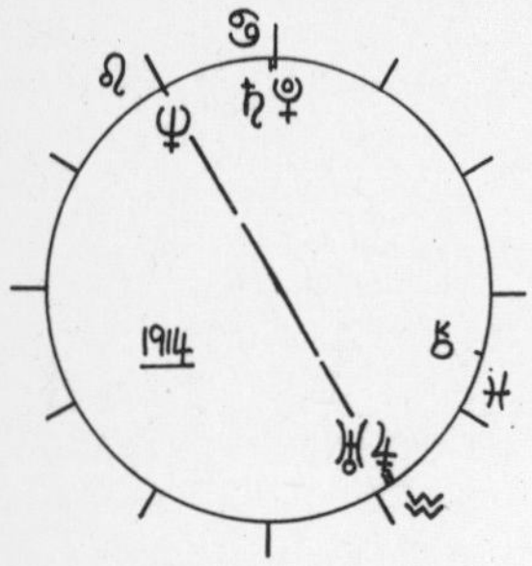

The outbreak of war in 1914 came in the aftermath of a ♅ ingress into ♒ in 1912, a ♅ ☍ ♆ in 1907-9 and a ♃ ☌ ♅ in early 1914. However the war was precipitated by ♇ entering ♋ in May 1914, ♆ entering ♌ in September, and a ♄ ☌ ♇ in October, near the summer solstice point, at 2 ♋.

At these turningpoints, seeds are planted. They can take time to surface into general consciousness — often the generation born in such a seed-time takes it upon itself to make such new seeds into mainstream movements, to take them from the fringes of society into mainstream. Thus the generation born in the 1890s were at their peak of power 40-60 years later, in the 1930s and 40s: the generation who brought out jazz, motor cars and family holidays for everyone, and the atomic bomb.

This configuration included all the four outer planets: a major, magnitude one line-up. Critical points in this staggered period of 15 years were brought about by interventions of faster-moving planets. For example, the solar eclipse of 6 June 1891 widely conjuncted the ♆ ☌ ♇ in ♊, and was in exact □ to a ♃ ☍ ♄ (♓ - ♍) — forming a powerful T-square. On the lunar eclipse of 3 December 1899, ☽, ♆ and ♇ were widely conjuncting in ♊, while ☉, ☿, ♀, ♂, ♄, ⚷ and ♅ opposed them from ♐, with ♃ close by in late ♏: this was within a moon of the turn of the century! This configuration drew a line between the 19th and 20th centuries, marking the beginning of the end of the British Empire, the large-scale movement of white Americans into the West (the dawn of the cowboy mythology) and of Russians into the East, the dawn of the theory of relativity, and a culmination of longterm evolutionary trends which had started in 580BC, in the Classical period. A new mega-phase of history started around 1899, which is to last centuries: the world was from this time opened up, explored and mapped, and global culture was beginning.

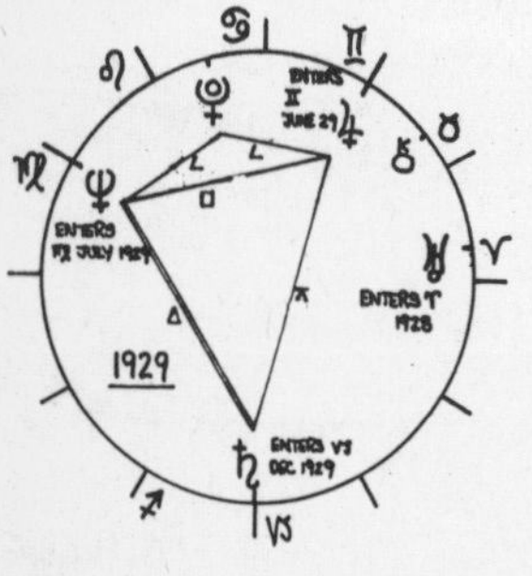

The Wall St crash, the cruxpoint of the Depression, took place in the context of four ingresses. Note the involvement of the earth signs, plus the position of ♇ in mid-♋: a confrontation with issues around security!

From the turn of the century until 1965, history went along on the tracks already established. There were some 'magnitude 2' aspects formed — notably in 1907, 1919, 1932-3, 1940-41, 1945, and 1953 — which are shown on the astrological calendar shown here, but few of them were earth-shattering in a way which is remembered for centuries. It sounds strange to pass off the lives of millions of humans like this, for this is a century of intense change and development, but here we are looking at critical turningpoints. With such an overview, the lives of individuals, nations and generations melt in significance: it's all a question of scale and sense of history-making.

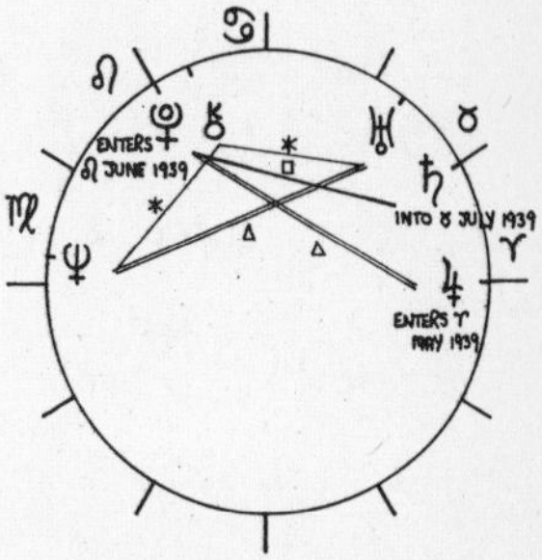

World War II broke out when ♇ entered ♌, with a little ingressional help from ♄ and ♃. ♆ entered ♎ in 1942, at the turning-point of the war. The first atomic detonation took place in 1940. Note the involvement of both ♄ and ♇ in 1914, 1939, 1956 and 1965, activating the human tendency to lapse into war – although by 1956 war became more localised (Suez-Hungary-Korea, and Vietnam on the 60s).

The Dream surfaces

Then came the mid-sixties. Nowadays it is fashionable to pass off these times as a wild holiday or an eccentric deviation from the norm, but this need to rationalise it away so is symptomatic of a time when something major really was happening. Here, the unknown impinged strongly on human consciousness, and new seeds were planted. The generation born at this time is an important one in history. It was also significant that the ♇ in ♌ generation, born 1939-56 was at this time growing into adulthood, ready to receive the dispensation: when that generation is at the peak of its power (1990-2020), its historical 'duty', is to swing the underlying tide of consciousness in the world, through creative expression and conviction and lifestyle. Those born in the 60s, with ♅ and ♇ in ♍, a more practical sign, are builders, cleaners of the world, technologists and potential founders of a new order: the ♇ in ♌ generation must clear the way for them. The 'generation gap' the latter grew into was an ideational/visionary watershed in history.

The configuration of 1965-6 is best symbolised by three symptoms, even though much more was going on: 1. the development of the microchip, bringing with it the material possibility to revolutionise our relations with the material world, even as far as the eventual ending of physical-mental labour and the work ethic as we know it — a small, quiet, intricate bit of technology which bears immense implications, very virgoid; 2. 'flower-power', a visionary explosion, mainly induced through use of LSD, but also surfacing in new politics and cultural waves, which, while seemingly impractical and impossible (at the time) to integrate into the social fabric, planted seeds which are potent and irresistible in the future — the germination of this seed took place at the yod formation in 1979, and made a first step into concrete realism at the ♅ ∠ ♇ (note the cyclical symbolism) in 1986; 3. the sexual revolution and 'permissive society' born out of ♆ in ♏, leading toward a probable end of the concept of marriage and family as we have known it for centuries — a tendency which is becoming more real while ♇ is in ♏ 1984-96. The sexual

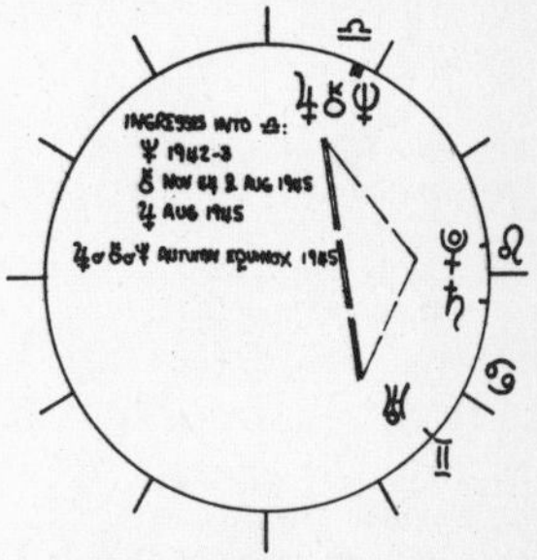

The making of peace. Alliances switched radically around 1945: ♎ and ♊ were strongly at work. ♃ / ⚷ △ ♅ in Nov/Dec 1945, ♃ □ ♄ in Dec 45, ♄ □ ⚷ in Jan 46. ♃ ☌ ⚷ ☌ ♆ took place at autumn equinox 1945

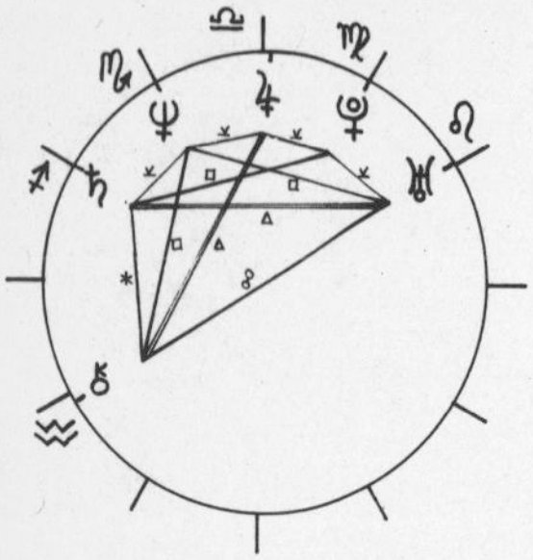

1956: the dawn of high-tech, and the beginning of many more new nuances than meet the eye. A cradle formation of ingressing planets, plus a T-square. Ingresses: ♅ into ♌ in June 1956, ♄ into ♐ *10th* October, ♆ into ♏ *19th* October, ♇ into ♍ *20th* October and ♃ into ♎ 13th December 1956

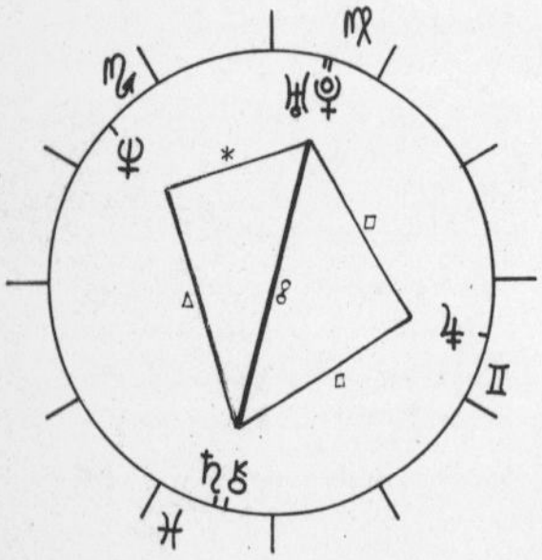

1965-6, the birth of a dream: alchemical spirituality, political awakening, the microchip, the breaking of rules, and cultural revolution. The planting of seeds of a new order yet to come. No ingresses: this is an energy-configuration. By 1967, ♃ was in ♌ and ♄ in ♈.

revolution was born in the sixties, and the consequences of it are being worked out while ♇ is in ♏, 1984-96. Other factors of note include the 'space race', the dawn of genetic engineering, large-scale planning, the rise of the guerilla and terrorist and the seeding of the new religious fundamentalism now prominent in the world.

Social polarisation characterises these major power periods in history, a division between those who seek or support change and those who resist it, in every department of life. In the 60s many issues surfaced, in education, international relations (the final end of the empires and the political rise of the third world), in war and peace, around nuclear power and weapons, around ecological issues ('Silent Spring'), music, intoxicants, in every field, even though the progress then made appeared to go backwards during the 70s: this is a sign that the changes implied are so great that they need time to filter through in ways that can be integrated. The salient question is, however, whether or not the institutions of society are willing to change themselves in accord with the time, and whether the psyches of all humans are prepared to open up: and this is what the events of the early 1990s are about.

The dawn of the post-industrial era

Although this has been brewing since the 60s, and was inherent in what has been building up since the beginning of the century, even since the beginning of human history, the post-industrial era moved from being a futuristic concept to a current dawning reality, when three outer planets changed signs in 1984 — ♇ into ♏, ♆ into ♑ and ⚷ into ♊. So did the 'new age', which transformed from being a dream of UFO visitations, New Jerusalems and avataric transformations into a harder reality which we ourselves must bring about through our own efforts, within and without.

What this ingress did was to serve notice on resolution of the issues of our time. Unknowing or lack of awareness is no longer an excuse for resisting world change: those who resist from 1984 onwards do so by burying their heads in the sand, consciously. Although it is unwise and dangerous to try to predict futures too closely, since such can affect our behaviour in working with them, it is clear that the coming ♑ - ♋ line-up, with ♇ in mid-scorpio in perihelion adding to it, is a parting of the waves in history, *possibly* the time when the old order gives way to the new, or begins doing so. There are many expectations prevalent amongst new-age believers that the change will be simple and miraculous (which in one sense it will be), but also there is an omission to look at the saturnine side of this transition: ♄ admonishes us to give time, effort, work, focus, sacrifice and very grounded approaches to bringing through change.

The strong ♑ and ♏ flavour of this change suggests that we have to look at nitty-gritties, things we would prefer in our ideals to skip over. We have to look at the *boring* aspects of life, and start major structural alterations in the house of humanity. These signs do not let us get away with anything. The old order will hang on until the time when the new order is ready and worked up for the change. While we need to allow the child in us to surface — to bring out the natural, human, sensitive, playful side of ourselves — the power cannot be placed in the hands of spiritual children: the change is more fundamental, more gradual, yet more thorough and momentous than we previously have understood.

A UFO visitation doesn't automatically make everything groovy on earth: *we* have to *make* things groovy, with our own hands, hearts, tongues, feet and brains. Anachronistically, this involves *receiving* the new order into being, rather than *creating* it. We have all the solutions available to us, both spiritually and technologically, or close at hand: but we yet have to generate the overall global will and capacity to apply them. Thus, the ♄, ♅ and ♆ conjunction in ♑ implies *structural* change. We can do this willingly and forward-sightedly, or we can do it by having to face up to the consequences of the breakdown of our old institutional ways. It could at worst be a large-scale shoot-out: at best, the 100th Monkey could do its work, and a new consciousness could take strong root in humanity, stimulating appropriate transformations in every area and niche of human life, from all angles — or at least, the beginnings of them.

The multiple conjunction in ♑ implies a major change in our institutions and laws, a radical expansion of our social-cultural limits. What will be affected are laws, money, legislative and executive institutions, traditions and all the stabilising structures of our society: the father archetype, even God Himself (as an image of the ultimate authority and paternity) is in for a shake-up. We are likely to see a fundamentally new strain of decision-makers and executives appear suddenly, as if by quirk of fate, and all of the established ways by which we organise things will prove to be inadequate for our current needs. The financial world is already showing large signs of shake-up (although the 'Big Bang' is yet to come), and governments, secret services, the Church, presidents and royals are all suffering (or benefiting from) major rumblings. The salient question, however, is whether institutions and structures can be loosened up sufficiently to be able to channel the new

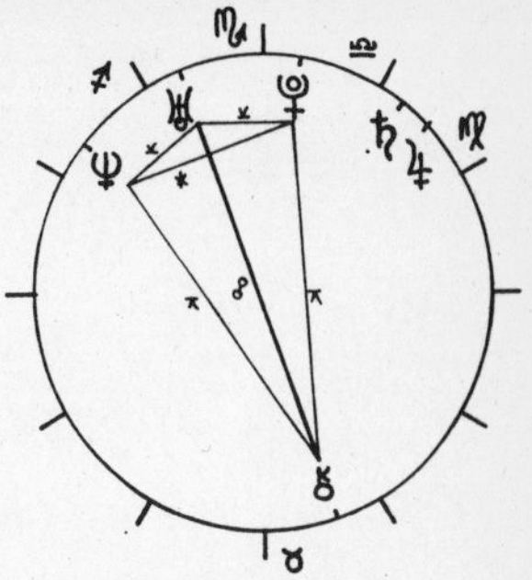

The 60s vision breaks into the open: a major yod involving all four outer planets. Note the ♃ ☌ ♄ in ♎ which took place in December 1980. There are also a ♄ □ ♆ and a ♄ △ ⚷ present

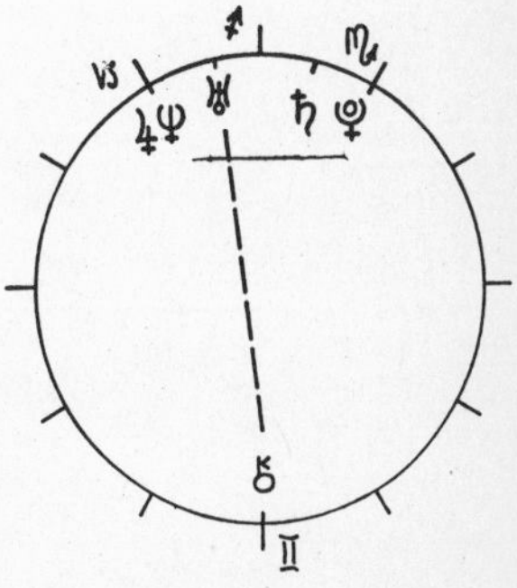

The need for honesty: the post-industrial age begins. ♃ ☌ ♆ on the winter solstice point in January 1984. The multiple ingress of ⚷, ♆ and ♇ into new signs brought a new flavour to the time, one of realism or encounter. This is the beginning of the buildup to the 1990s.

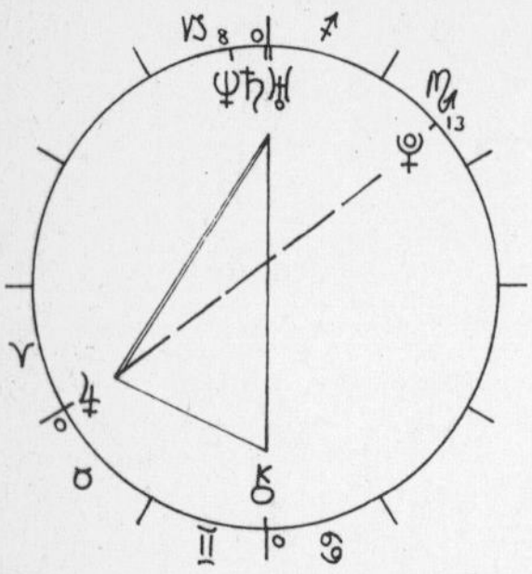

The beginning of a process: watch it happen. ♄ ☌ ♅ on the winter solstice point 14-16 February 1988. ♃ ☍ ♇ April 1988. The final ♄ ☌ ♅ comes in October 1988, followed by ♄ ☌ ♆ March 1989. ⚷ enters ♋ July ♄ ☌ ♆, ♃ ☍ ♄ and ♃ ☍ ♆ on 13-14 November 1988. Note the hotting up of the ♑ - ♋ lineup

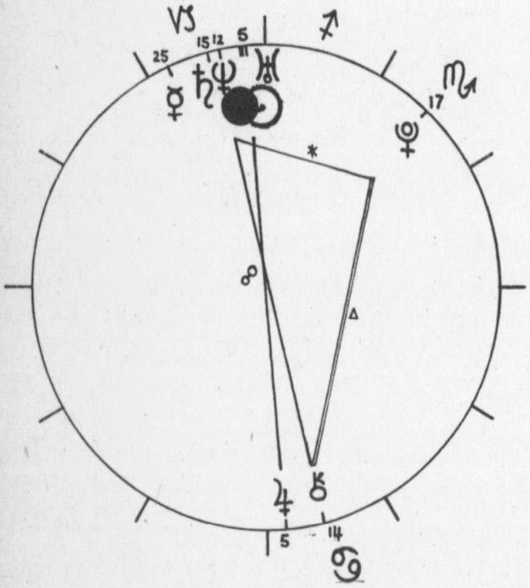

One of the peaks of the ♑ - ♋ process: newmoon on 28th December 1989

energies coming through humanity and history, or whether they have to be swept away because they are blocking it. What might prove to be the case is that, if key people in power use their position to *stimulate* rather than resist or slow change, their position as a positive force in human life might be reaffirmed: after all, institutional structures, by nature, are supposed to exist to serve the people, rather than have people serve them. Institutions exist to focus and channel interhuman agreement and coexistence: if they prevent it, social life-force must by nature break them apart.

Watch what happens when ♅ enters ♑ in 1988. ♆, which entered ♑ in 1984, has already been eating away at many areas of life previously considered safe and secure, but ♅ works more radically, and is by nature more diametrically opposed to ♑ian ways than ♆. The presence of both of them in this sign bodes well for ♑: it implies a complete and fundamental enlivening of the ♑ archetype, for structures can be *built* to be flexible, while still stabilising society. Or, they can be rigid, and overcome by self-created disruption and destruction. Saturnine viewpoints claim to be rational and sensible, but they actually have to stand the test of real life, like anything, and in the final analysis, *workability* is the key: 'rationality' has the danger of being the rationality of a self-protecting minority in power, losing its grip on reality.

The movement of ♇ to mid-♏ implies the most intense phase of the honesty process ♇ is forcing us through at present. The chips are down, and everyone knows what the deal is (or is turning the other way, deliberately). This is *encounter*, a wrenching from the past, a death of obsolete forms, to whatever degree lands up being necessary in order to teach us and clear the way for what comes next. Yet ♇ is in ✱ and △ to this great opposition of five slower planets, and thus acts as the source of *release* in the configuration. ♇ is here (astrologically, at least), the saving grace in the equation. What is now becoming an everyday occurrence of secrets exposed, 'insider trading' and corruption revealed, leaks, lies and jilted interpretations is a sign of ♇ at work: there comes a point where excuses will no longer hold.

Interesting also is the ♃ ☌ ⚷ in ♋ in 1989-90, offering a beneficient slant to the flavour of the time: an appropriate dose of caring and the urge and necessity to care, protect, nurture and promote welfare is what these planets suggest. This can also be somewhat xenophobic — in other words that I'll care for you if you do it *my* way — but here, with all its pros and cons, we see an upwelling of the mother principle in the group psyche of humanity, contraposed to the father-principle of ♑, which at this time will be going through a major shake-up and reassessment. Traditionally, ♋ represents the people, and ♑ represents the state and institutions. The main issue is around the latter, but the former is coming in in a positive mode, through ♃ and ⚷. There comes a point where rationalistic argument, institutional enquiries, constitutions and even armies will no longer be able to stand up against the basic feelings of ordinary people: true choices are made in the heart and guts, not in the head. ♋ is coming into its power, with some help from ♏: deeper sensitivities and plain simple human matters are focusing and likely to express themselves more forcefully than they have in recent decades.

A configuration such as this arises out of the world situation which is developing as it builds up: history has a continuity to it, even though leaps and jumps occur. ♆ has already moved into ♑, and at the time of writing, ♅ and ♄ are on their way to form a ☌ around the cusp of ♑ in 1988. An ongoing ♄ ☍ ⚷ goes on from March 1986 through to 1995 (while ⚷ is accelerating until it reaches ♎ in that year), which moves from ♐ - ♊ into the major configuration in 1989-90, and further to ♈ - ♎ by 95: this ongoing configuration, involving ♅ too, poses knotty paradoxes and obstructions, which by their nature, stimulate or force a focusing of energy on resolution of perceived problems through massive contextual shifts and overdue needs for concrete application of real, appropriate solutions by sincere and effective people. ♃ meanwhile steams through the springtime signs (an individualising, exploring and forward-moving development), to reach the summer solstice point by August 1989, joining ⚷. The configuration is building up.

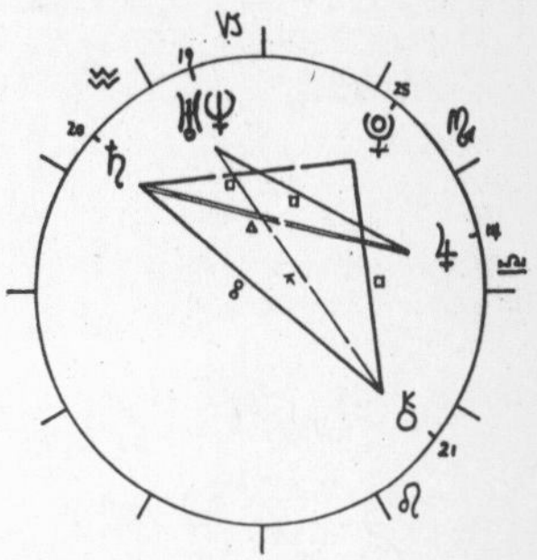

A jump into the unknown: as the ♅ ☌ ♆ becomes exact on 2nd February 1993 (Candlemas), other configurations come into the picture too: ♄ ☍ ⚷ (ongoing since 1986) on 8th February, ♄ □ ♇ 20th March (equinox), and ♃ □ ♅ / ♆ 16-17th September 1993. Be there!

At this time we should not underestimate what is at stake, or the implications it has. If we want world transformation we'll probably have to give up the sugar in our tea, and the tea as well! But what replaces these is far more valuable. Yet this transition, reaching its peak at the ♅ ☌ ♆ in 1992-3, is but a beginning. Possibly a beginning to a new order which itself lays the foundation for a greater new order which develops over future generations — possibly brought through for real by those born with ♇ in ♏ around the time of 2030-50. As with the dispensation of the 60s, this dispensation is likely to take some decades to work through into visible form and positive outcomes.

We are, however, privileged to be experiencing all the outer planets in their home signs in relatively quick succession: ♆ in ♓ in the early 21st Century, and ♅ to ♒ 1996-2003 and ♇ in ♏ now — it isn't often that these plus ♇ and ⚷ all visit their home signs within one human lifetime. The chances are, therefore, that change-energy will be running quite freely over coming decades. We must beware, however, of the impractical tendencies suggested in ♅ and ♆ both being in ♒ at the turn of the century/millennium: there is a danger that the energy-release from this, plus ♇ in ♐ lets off too much energy for integration into the concrete world — the chinese cultural revolution of the 60s demonstrated that liberating energies can become excessive. To every action there is an equal and opposite reaction: conservative action and radical reaction are the game at present, but what happens when the action becomes radical and the reaction becomes conservative?

The Aquarius-Leo Age

There are many misunderstandings about this. First of all, it is not clear *when* it begins — estimates ranging from 1550 to 2300. If we are astronomically diligent, the beginning of the age is yet to happen in the 23rd Century: thus all the excitement about the Aquarian Age is a very piscean phenomenon! There is, however, a chance that we could regard the whole 20th century as a watershed period between the ages: time will only tell. Believe what you want to believe — we have all done so for the duration of the Piscean Age.

Secondly, as with ingresses of planets into signs, the astrological ages, 2160 years long, represent major changes of theme and viewpoint on a global scale, in the human psyche as *one* psyche. While there is a spiritual dispensation at the beginning of each age, the cusp of a new age does not automatically imply a major global rise in consciousness of the kind which is expected by some new-agers. It simply implies a change of themes preoccupying humanity on a longterm scale. The visions of the next age are already seen, ranging from angelic, spiritual scenarios to the drones and mutants of science-fiction: what we create in future generations (our future lives) is very much our mass choice. The imaginal expectations concerning the aquarian age, generated over the last few decades, are very piscean, and it could be that the new age is a phenomenon of the end of the piscean age, not the beginning of the aquarian age. There have been many times in history when we have believed that we are on the edge of a new age.

Thirdly, since this cycle of 25,000 years is related to the gradual precession of the equinox points backwards through the stellar constellations, shifting the constellations away from the signs by one sign per 2160 years, one degree every 72 years, we need to look at *both* of the equinox points, not just one. Thus, since around the time of Christ (although the date of this cuspal change is also

The motions of ⚷, ♅, ♆ and ♇ in the Twentieth Century
The astrological calendar below includes ⚷, plus a few critical ♄ - ♃ involvements. Notice how ⚷ changes speed, fastest in ♎ and slowest in ♈, and how ♇ accelerates during the century, up to 1988. Years with an asterisk are astrologically very significant years.

*1898 ⚷ ☌ ♅ in ♐.
*1899 ⚷ in ♐ ☍ ♇ in ♊.
*1901-2 ♅ in ♐ ☍ ♇ in ♊; ♆ enters ♋, ⚷ enters ♑; ⚷ ☍ ♆.
1904 ♅ enters ♑.
1905 ⚷ enters ♒.
*1907-9 ♅ in ♑ ☍ ♆ / ♃ in ♋.
1908 ⚷ △ ♇, ♒ to ♊.
1910 ⚷ enters ♓.
*1912 ♅ enters ♒, ♇ enters ♋.
*1914 ♆ enters ♌.
1915-6 ♅ at mid-♒.
1918 ⚷ enters ♈.
1919 ♅ enters ♓; ⚷ in ♈ □ ♇ in ♋ and ⚷ △ ♆ in ♌.
1922 ♅ in ♓ △ ♇ in ♋; ♆ at mid-♌.
1926 ⚷ in ♉.
1927 ♅ into ♈.
1928-9 ♆ enters ♍.
1930 ♆ ∠ ♇, ⚷ mid-♉, ♇ discovered.
1931 ⚷ ⚹ ♇.
*1932-3 ♅ in ♈ □ ♇ in ♋.
1933-4 ⚷ into ♊.
1934-5 ♅ enters ♉.
1935 ⚷ in ♊ □ ♆ in ♍.
*1938 ♅ mid-♉; ♇ enters ♌; ⚷ enters ♋.

debatable), we have been experiencing a pisces-*virgo* age, and now we are moving into an aquarius-*leo* age. ♓ - ♍ is both about the power of beliefs, ♓, and the development of technology and material wealth (♍ is a harvest sign). This has been an age of cosmologies (♓) and systems (♍), which reached an interesting peak in the 1960s, when ♓ - ♍ were strongly featured by a major line-up.

The age of ♒-♌ is thus *both* about social solidarity, new social forms, rationality and collectivism (♒), to name a few themes, *and* about individualism and personal creativity and significance (+leo). In other words, we need to explore what are currently seen as the advantages of collective cooperation without losing the significance of the individual: the collective needs to serve the individual as much as the individual needs to serve the collective. This was an important principle which such aquarian dreams as socialism, or modern communal philosophies, have tended to miss out on: the individual gets forced into being but a cog in society. To participate wholeheartedly in a collective social adventure, an individual has to feel personal significance: social cohesion cannot be applied through rules, bureaucracies and ideologies, for it must come from the heart of every individual human, as a freely-inspired impulse without coercion.

Fourth, a confusion (♓) has arisen between the notion of a *new age*, and the notion of the *aquarius-leo* age. The notion of the new age is derived from the observation that humanity has reached a stage of *critical mass* in its evolution — a stage where the evolution of consciousness, together with the population explosion, technological changes and overkill, planetary issues and so many other areas of life have reached a globally crucial stage, which has never been reached before.

Everyone is involved now, and every species, even in the remotest corners of Earth. We now have the capacity to devastate everything. We are now reaching a point in population growth where something *has* to happen to prevent a historical lemming phenomenon. We are reaching into space, without exactly knowing what we want to do with that privilege. We are collectively reaching a major ♄ initiation, in which all of the experiences we have gathered through history (or many lives) are coalescing into a set of conclusions which are likely to bring a fundamental shift of consciousness and orientation — probably focusing more on inner worlds, having exhausted so many possibilities in our manipulation of the world around us.

Thus it is necessary to separate the 'new age' from the

*1940-1 ♅ / ♄ ⚹ ⚷ ⚹ ♆ △ ♅ / ♄.
*1941 ⚷ enters ♌; ⚷ ☌ ♇; ♅ enters ♊, ♆ enters ♎.
1942 ⚷ mid-♌.
1943 ♅ ⚹ ♇, ♊ to ♌; ⚷ enters ♍, ⚷ □ ♅.
*1945 ⚷ enters ♎; ♄ □ ♃, ☌ ⚷ ☌ ♆; ⚷ ⚹ ♇.
1946 ⚷ △ ♅; ⚷ enters ♏.
1947 ⚷ □ ♇.
1948 ♇ mid-♌; longterm ♆ ⚹ ♇ starts (until 1987).
1949 ♅ enters ♋, ⚷ enters ♐.
1950 ⚷ ⚹ ♆, ⚷ △ ♇.
1951 ⚷ enters ♑.
1952 ⚷ ☍ ♅ (on and off until 1989).
1953 ♅ □ ♆ □ ⚷ ☍ ♅.
1955 ⚷ enters ♒.
*1956 ♅ enters ♌, ♆ enters ♏, ♇ enters ♍.
1959 ♅ mid-♌.
1961-5 ⚷ in ♓ ☍ ♇ in ♍.
1962 ♅ enters ♍; ⚷ △ ♆, ♓ to ♏ 1963 ♆ mid-♏.
**1965-6 ♃ in ♊ □ ♅ ☌ ♇ in ♍, ☍ ♄ ☌ ⚷ in ♓ □ ♃; exact ⚷ ☍ ♅ 65-74.
1968-9 ⚷ enters ♈, ♅ enters ♎.
1970 ♆ enters ♐.
1971 ♇ enters ♎.
1973 ♅ ∠ ♆.
1975 ♅ enters ♏, ⚷ enters ♉.
1977 ⚷ discovered.
1978 ♅ mid-♏.
*1979 Yod: ⚷ ⚻ ♇, ♇ ⚺ ♅ ⚺ ♆, ♆ ⚻ ⚷, ⚷ ☍ ♅ (⚷ aspects inexact).
1981 ♅ in ♐.
1982 ⚷ exact ⚻ ♆ and ♇.
*1984 ♇ enters ♏, ♆ enters ♑, ⚷ enters ♊.

aquarius-leo age: these are most probably separate, albeit synchronous phenomena. The critical mass or planetary abyss we find ourselves on the edge of relates to the evolutionary curve of human history and its potential quantum change. There is nothing extra special about the ♓-♒ cusp to make it inherently what could be the biggest change-point in human history since the discovery of the use of fire or the beginning of agriculture. It just so happens that these two transitions are taking place at around the same time (give or take a century or so).

1986 ♅ ∠ ♇, ⚷ □ ♇, ⚷ ☍ ♅.
1988 ♅ enters ♑; ♄ ☌ ♅ and ☍ ⚷; ⚷ enters ♋; ♇ closest to ☉ (perihelion).
*1989 ♇ mid-♏; ⚷ ☍ ♆, △ ♇, (♆ ⚹ ♇); ♄ ☌ ♆ in ♑, ♄ ☍ ⚷ in ♋.
*1990 ♃ ☌ ⚷ in ♋, ♃ ☍ ♄, ♅ and ♆ in ♑; six planets in ♑, Feb 1990.
1991 ⚷ enters ♌.
**1992 ⚷ □ ♇; ♅ ☌ ♆ in ♑. 1993 ⚷ enters ♍.
1995 ♇ enters ♐, ⚷ enters ♎; ⚷ ⚹ ♇, ⚷ △ ♅ and ♆.
1996 ♅ enters ♒.
1997 ⚷ enters ♏; ⚷ □ ♆/♅.
1998 ♆ enters ♒.
1999 ⚷ enters ♐; ⚷ ⚹ ♆.

These are but the main features of the century. Not mentioned are major faster-moving configurations which crop up from time to time, such as the seven-planet ☌ in ♍ on the newmoon of 23 Aug 1968, or such things as a grand cross involving ☉ and ☿ in ♍, ☽ and ♅ in ♐, ♃ in ♓ and ⚷ in ♊ in Sept 86. Faster-moving configurations involving the outer planets are interesting in that, while short-lived, they can be *intense* moments in history, when important issues can arise and critical events can take place: keep your eye attuned for these, for they are crucial power points in time.

Quanta

Here come some beliefs of my own: with ♃ in ♓, ♐ rising and four planets in the ninth house, I live on them. They have been formulated over two decades of personal growth, and you might or might not agree with them, but I share them with you, for, to me, they form the main point of this book!

Our planet is going into labour, and we as the most intelligent and conscious physical beings on her are, whether we like it or not, being handed stewardship of a planet and ecosphere which we ourselves have mishap — an ecosphere which we must actively bring into a new balance, since we have so fundamentally disrupted the old natural balances. Any aware person sees this, and sees at least some of the implications of it in that microsphere of life each of us knows and works with.

This quantum leap, still future tense but increasingly becoming present tense, is an evolutionary factor which is not directly connected with the dawning of the ♒-♌ age, although they are in some way synchronous. It could equally happen at any other time. But it seems that we as a race are ready to make this change, from being *products* of a planet to being *co-creators* in the universe, through our own divine wisdom. For we have manifested a situation where, if we do not make the change into a mode of global consciousness where we can end such things as war, exploitation and institutionalised insanity, we shall quite clearly end everything. God will not save us unless we save ourselves! We have set up a conundrum which is immense, and which cannot be resolved by the normal means at our disposal: logic, negotiation, money, technology, prayer, revolution, sex or *anything* we have done before are no longer working for us in the way we would perhaps wish.

This planetary initiation is a turning in the deepest seat of consciousness. Within race-memory we have stored up enough experiences of different ways of going about life that we have now,

I believe, exhausted what is possible within our current paradigm of consciousness. It is rather similar to what is happening on an individual level for many people, each in their own way, in the world today. Precipitated by a major crunch, many people are coming to the point where there seems to be no way forward within the framework they have created to live in — breakdown of marriage and security are, in the industrial world, one of the biggest causes of this realisation. When a person reaches this point of total compromise and paradox, a tunnel-experience ensues, in which soul-factors are dug up in desperation, and an eventual breakthrough comes, whenever that person realises that they need to go through a change of consciousness. This deep turning happens only once, fundamentally, for further such experiences tend to be reaffirmations of this turning.

Since you are reading a book such as this, you will presumably have gone through some such turning, at some stage of your life (or are in it!), and thus you will have personal experience of it. You have made the turning in advance of the mainstream of humanity, and are a pioneer on the new frontier. The human race as a whole is on the edge of such a turning: a lot of energy is about to be released. How can there be loneliness when there is a human family to belong to? How can there be unemployment when there is so much to be getting on with to make the human world an acceptable, even rewarding, place to live in?

What came to me during 1986 (helped by camping out under radiation from Chernobyl!) is that we have already changed the face of our planet to a degree where it is no longer possible to change things *back* to acceptable levels of balance. We have caused mutation, mass psychological changes, extinction of species, changes in the composition of air and oceans and soil, and a human rootlessness no longer bound by local community traditions, to the extent that nature and humanity have forgotten what things were like before. We can only change *forward,* and if this means that old species and scenarios die, and new ones arise to take their place, then this must be so. The genetic pool of humanity is radically changing, and the ecosphere too: nature and human nature are so fundamentally imbalanced in the old sense of balance, that we must create an entirely new balance. As with a gardener in an artificial garden environment with its own human-creates balances — dependent on the creative intervention of the gardener — we must evolve a vision of what kind of world we are seeking to create, and then take it upon ourselves to create it and sustain it dynamically. We are no longer being watched over and protected from mishap by our gods, the fairies or any other force: we have to consult our own conscience and sensibilities, make our own deeper decisions, and do it. Nature responds to the phosphate or caesium we dump in the sea, develops new ways of working with it, and goes about doing so: we thus have to consciously *choose* what inputs we make into our ecosphere (and psychosphere), to allow nature to respond in ways which are life-enhancing, both for us and for all the other species we are unwittingly taking responsibility for. Similar things must go on in the world of humans: decision-makers need to look further ahead at the new psycho-social facts which we create whenever laws are made or inventions are marketed. As many people as possible need to be brought into the decision-making process, and social constitutions need evolving such that a true social feedback system really works, effectively, as appropriate to each group, tribe and nation, and the world as a whole.

Crisis

Hence the arrival of ⚷ into consciousness. ⚷ offers us opportunities to create miracles: to work with the known world in ways derived from deep down, from the unknown. ⚷ arrived synchronously with the growth of grass-roots movements of a new order. And the riddle we must solve in every detail and corner of the world as we experience it is soluble only through miraculous means, through a concentration of energy and intent, of hope, faith and heart-energy which is so intense and so open to possibilities that a way through is found. This means crises: crises of the kind we are starting to grow used to now, personal and social and global.

In a crisis, *everything* comes to a crunch. It all becomes too much to handle. It's all too complex and fraught, and no one understands what is going on any more. We are forced to accept that we are out of control. We are faced with death. It feels like eternity, as if it is never going to end. Yet in this space, there is hope: for a new mode of consciousness dawns when the old one breaks down. People are capable of superhuman feats and absolute instant wisdom when there is a total crisis going on — war stories demonstrate this. Another element of totally alert, totally capable awareness comes into play.

When catharsis breaks loose, it seems like hell, but the calm and the light are very close: this can be seen in any therapy room, any decent argument which clears the air. Catharsis is deep-level processing of blocked energy, in the heart, gut and root-centre, and sometimes in the soul. Mind is suspended. Inner conflagration generates heat and pain, and a molecular reaction takes place, fundamentally reprogramming things within. At the end, peace and rest, healing and enlightenment. That is, *if* the person catharting is willing and ready to break through and get to the other side. This is our choice. As a race.

After doing therapy and experiencing catharsis myself, I found a great faith dawning within me, concerning the future: it is indeed possible to go through very fundamental change when one is burned throughout by the fire of pain. And in terms of time, it is fast — even though the buildup of energy can take a long time, and even though it can take a lot of energy reaching the point where one is *willing* to work things out.

The choice lies with us. It lies in our responses, individually and collectively, to the waves of shock arising annually in our time are critical in forming future potentials. And it lies in our willingness and capacity to *create* global catharsis in a creative way, to precipitate change by choice. It's rather like stopping smoking: it's a matter of choosing to go through a temporary crisis in the knowledge that the long-term end is fruitful, healthy and positive. And the most major blockage to progress seems to be the question of *trust*: in ourselves and our capacities, and in others and the human race. Love and trust, as Jesus taught at the beginning of the ♓ - ♍ age, is the way through. We all need to come to this conclusion, not because someone said so, but because we, individually, *know* that it works and has no substitute or half-measures or conditions.

Working history

We are not just passive recipients of history. We have been so, but can no longer afford to do this. Astrology is not just a way of passively understanding what is *happening to us*: it is a means of moving into the stream of time and energy through *conscious experiencing* and *active expression*. Hence the emphasis in this book on experiencing things for yourself. It follows that from this, since we can begin to identify the forces at work in change, we can also work with these forces.

In other words, when we say ♇ is in ♏, we need to *do* something about it. This is about honesty, facing up to things, being prepared to look at things we wish to avoid, and being prepared to *go through it*. When individuals like you and me go through personal transformations, we are contributing to the group psyche, swinging the energy just a little bit each time. There comes a point where individual changes become infectious, where the energy reaches a crossover point from moving uphill to moving downhill on momentum: this is the 100th Monkey effect.

In astrology, we can consciously *work* the energies we can identify. We can do it through meditations and imagings, through self-transformation of our basic way of being (such that it percolates out through our dealings to others), through spiritually invoking the powers of change we can identify, and through working in the world, in whatever area of life we are best working in, to channel what we experience through to others — or to *allow* this flow to take place by taking our egos out of the way.

Astrologers of old were not only counsellors and time-tellers: they were magical workers, who engaged with the forces they could identify, and who worked them consciously. The nexus of this is the raising and purification of consciousness, and thereby changes naturally arise as a result. This implies working to remove blockages to the flow (a fundamental principle in healing), working to further and enhance the movement of the flow, working to develop skills such that the divine spark can be manifested through our actions of thought, word and deed, and working to clarify our awareness, such that we can stay on the flow.

Astrologers of the present day have a similar role — and this is why it is vital for any practicing astrologer to be going through personal growth — for the astrology alone does not transform us or the world. The spirit which lies behind astrology, and within us is the essence of this role, and the astrology is a framework to manifest this spirit — as one of many paths of growth.

This implies a major revolution in astrology — which is but one department of the whole of reality which is itself going through great changes. I shall leave you with this thought, for each of us needs to bring about this possibility in our own way, in whatever activities best express our essential spirit, in the locality and domain where we function best. And our inner self is the guide. We do not need to think too much about the future — we need merely to be aware that it is there — for it is in the immediately-present moment where the core of this work lies. And it starts now. It is time to stop holding back. There is great and growing support for forward steps on the evolutionary path, and fear and reservation are becoming increasingly difficult to support.

Future generations will look back at this phase of history in the way we look back at the past — fascinated, but wondering how on earth we got ourselves into this mess. Yet knowing that it was a stage on a path toward something else. We now have the capacity to *create history* more than we ever have done, and the future is ours. When the creative potential, the capacity for work, innovation and progress in humanity is unleashed, all things will be possible to deal with. The tide can be turned, at least in terms of basics, in our lifetimes and that of our children. The future is an open door.

Between 1995-8, ♇ enters ♐, and ♅ and ♆ enter ♒: this is another one of those multiple ingresses, and it promises a new breeze. A probable turn for the positive, a step forward. New issues will arise, and our capacity to work together in this world will be explored one step further. The truth-encounter of ♏ and ♑ will be over, and a wide-open field of possibility is likely to be revealed. What specifically those possibilities are is difficult to say, for we are in a phase of quantum leaping, into which entirely new factors are entering — factors we are not even aware of right now (in the 1980s). We have the possibility of a whole new set of options with which to work responsibly, sanely and consciously, or we have the possibility of a global party, which might be fun at the time, but leaves a trail of devastation and hangovers behind it, as parties do. It must be remembered that ♒ is a meeting point for uranian *and* saturnine energies, and that ♐ is the prelude to ♑. ♐ and ♒ both plant seeds for germination in ♈, in the long term: we need to be far-sighted and wise at the turn of the millennium, not escapist and wild!

When a major power period or point in time is approaching, it is impossible to see beyond it, for so many unknowns come into the equation. So we just have to work with what we've got. But there are astrological grounds for hope, in the short-term future. Let's stay alive and grow to see it.

17 About astrological charts

An astrological chart is a cut made into time, a frozen still-shot of a particular moment. It is a way of getting an exact and close look at the nature of the time at any moment, and the way in which this energy will manifest in real-life issues at the place for which this chart is calculated. Here we are going to look briefly at charts without looking at how to calculate or draw them.

What an astrological chart shows

A chart is a map which shows how the earth and heavens stood in relation to each other at the time for which the chart is calculated. It shows the twelve signs of the zodiac, and the exact positions of the planets, wherever they stand in the zodiac at the time in question. It shows the aspects between the planets and also the orientation of zodiac and planets to the earth at the moment in question. A chart is calculated reckoning in the position of a person or observer on the surface of planet earth — for at any one time, a person in Idaho will be experiencing day while a person in Kiev will be experiencing night, and while the planetary positions and aspects will be the same for both people, the orientation of their own places on earth to it all will be different.

Thus, in the calculation of a chart, we work from the basic data of the exact place on the earth's surface — expressed in terms of earth longitude (east-west) and latitude (north-south) — and the (preferably) exact time and date of the moment in question. For human births, this time is that of the taking of the first breath, the first independent act an incarnating being makes on its own behalf. For the beginnings of ventures, activities or events, we take the moment when the event in question definitely took shape or was acknowledged outwardly to have begun: for example, a meeting starts when silence is called for the meeting truly to begin; a house-occupation starts when the occupants enter the door with the intention of staying there from that day on; an event starts when the first definite sign of its 'eventness' is acknowledged to have taken place; for a journey we use the time when we leave from the front door or make our first step. The buying of a house, the decision to do something or the purchase of the ticket for the journey is a preparation for 'birth', not birth itself, and is equivalent to conception of a child or stages of pregnancy.

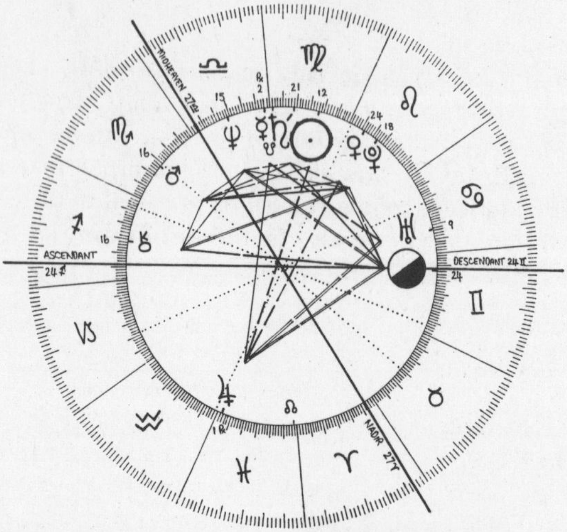

The chart here shows what what happening astrologically at the time of the author's birth: the time I chose to *come in on*. The wheel on which it is drawn is marked off in one-degree segments and signs, and the signs and planets are drawn in. The horizontal line across the chart represents the visible *horizon*, drawn as if we were standing at the place of birth, looking due south: above this line is the visible sky, and below the line is the area of the heavens obscured by the earth (which we stand on). The other line crossing the chart is the *meridian*, which is a line going from due south, directly upwards until it hits the ecliptic and directly downwards through the centre of the earth. The way this chart is drawn, however, this verticality doesn't show: an astrological chart does not set out to be astronomically accurate, but rather to be astrologically useful. Its data, however, is astronomically accurate.

In this example chart, all of the planets except for one are above the horizon — although ☽ is crossing it, setting at the time of birth. The planet below the horizon, ♃, is called a 'singleton', and plays a key role in the overall array of the planets, in that it forms the 'handle' to a 'bucket' shape chart. Notice also that the position of the sun in a chart shows the time of day: in this case, ☉ had moved past the midheaven, and was moving towards setting, still high in the sky in the mid-afternoon (2.45pm **GMT**).

In this and any chart, we therefore show four main factors:
★ the planets and their positions,
★ the zodiac and its orientation,
★ the aspects between the planets (the lines in the middle part of the chart) and
★ the twelve houses (comprising the four main angles, and then the cusps or dividing lines between houses, which are drawn in this chart between the inner and the outer edge of the chart wheel.

The Houses

When looking at time and change, we could well include looking at the houses, but tend not to, because they change so fast: only when focusing on a particular time, and doing a chart for it, do the houses really become important. The four angles and the houses show earth's orientation to the heavens, and earth rotates on its axis once a day, meaning that, on average, the sign on the ascendant changes once every two hours. The angles and houses, in an astrological chart, show a different level of reality to the planets and signs and aspects. The latter show the nature of the *energy* available at the time, and the way it affects the psyche. The houses show the way in which this energy manifests itself in concrete, earthly *life-situations*, and the way in which life-situations can feed back to the psyche and prompt it to go through internal processes.

Below is a brief look at the houses, to give you a help in identifying them at work: when you get along to doing transits, it is well worth looking at planetary transits through houses.

★ **Ascendant and House I**: personal direction and intentions, ways of externalising one's nature, presentation of persona or our outer face, personal priorities — what's in our own interest;
★ **II**: personal resources and custodianship-ownership of them, skills, business on our own account, our own ground, our attachments and relations with the land or anything we would possess;
★ **III**: our local environment and community, sources of support, neighbours, kith and kin, soul-siblings, grasp of how things tick, communication, intelligent relations with our local world;
★ **Nadir and IV**: where we are coming from, sources of security, fundamental feelings of okayness/agitation in ourselves, home or territory, knowns, private world, experience of mother archetype,

being-in-ourselves, defined in our own way or by habit;

★ **V**: self-expression, creation, procreation, coming out of ourselves, games, stances, gambles, projection of self, love affairs;

★ **VI**: our work, ways of facing up to things, adjustment to what is wanted/demanded, self-correction, illness and healing, making a contribution, serving, helping, learning how to do things, technique, listening.

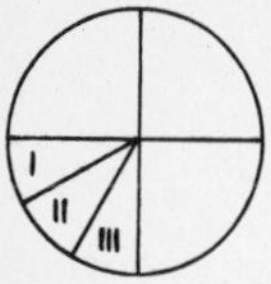

★ **Descendant and VII**: one-to-one relationship, finding the balance between self and other, partnership, what others make us aware of in ourselves (our shadow), agreements, other-awareness, them;

★ **VIII**: the plunge, making relationships *do* something, engagement, shared resources, social capital, business, taking risks, commitment, hidden truths and underlying realities, doing it;

★ **IX**: the world at large, our understanding of things, law and custom, overall philosophy of life, higher education, gathered experience, social self-extension, social worth.

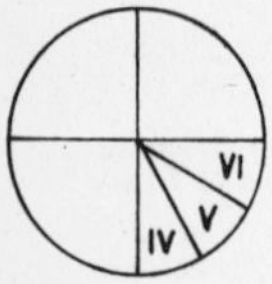

★ **Midheaven and X**: obligations and duties, social role and standing, acknowledgement from others, own role in the social contract, taking responsibility, being seen, fitting in, the father archetype, rules, authorities, maturity;

★ **XI**: the crowd, involvement in the collective, we-awareness, social trust and concern, belonging, groups and movements, tribe;

★ **XII**: completions, social accountability, restrictions which must be accepted, hidden agendas, deeper meanings, inner truths, the universal, collective pressures, service, self-sacrifice, seeking after a new self.

The presence of planets in any house shows an emphasis on the issues of that house and the area of life that the planets and the psyche express themselves through, and through which areas we learn. The sign on the opening cusp (boundary) shows the manner in which we approach and tend to deal with the issues of that house, personally. Widely extended houses show areas of life which require greater attention than narrower houses. *Intercepted signs,* which sit within an extended house without crossing a house cusp, show areas which require special attention, because they have within them inherent contradictions to do with the contrast between the sign on the opening cusp, and the intercepted sign.

Astrological charts

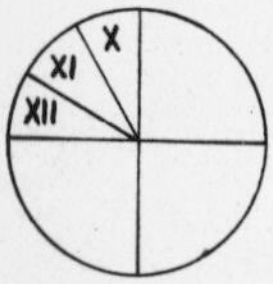

★ Birth charts

The most common use of astrological charts is the chart we can calculate for the moment of a person's birth. Through this we can identify, with appropriate skills, the potentials which that person has for picking up certain specific kinds of programming or conditioning, and the potentials s/he has for realising their true nature by freeing them up. Actually, a chart shows a totally neutral assessment of a person's nature, as if they were enlightened and already working their energy openly and without limitations: but since most of us are working at partial capacity in our beingness and doingness, charts have become most used, in the modern psychological world we live in, as a way of diagnosing difficulties, and of pointing to ways by which these can be resolved. The work of an astrological counsellor is to relate a person's perceived problems to the technicalities in the birth chart, and to catalyse a perspective-change, such that, hopefully, the client goes away feeling as if those problems either are surmountable or aren't there at all, or that they were misidentified.

★ Events charts

One way of studying the nature of time and the way it manifests is to look into *events charts*. Any event which interests you can be used: all you need is the time, date and place when it happened or started happening or first came to general attention. Thus, if you are driving along and, suddenly, a car crash takes place in front of you, you can do a chart for that moment, to see what was going on. Or if something major takes place in the news, try to find the time it took place, and do a chart for it (taking into account the place where it happened). Or if an event is planned for the future, you can do a chart to see what the likely energy is which is available. Or if you are looking at the past, you can do charts for events, and then trace what happened afterwards (for example, by looking at transits), in order to learn some astrology from this, and to see into the fundamental energy-issues which were behind the event. The possibilities are endless.

With event charts it is also possible to take the birth charts of major figures involved in the events (if possible), and to compare these with the event chart to see how decisive individuals were being personally affected by the time and the event, either as causative or recipient agents: thus, it can be possible to look at the charts of the people in that car crash, or at the charts of the leaders of two countries who are engaging in war or conciliation. It is possible also to take the exact time of, say, a fullmoon (from Raphael), and to calculate a chart for that, in order to get a closer look at the meaning of the time, or the possible outcomes which may arise, short- or long-term, from what you were experiencing at that fullmoon.

You can run off a chart for anything you are interested in, and build up a collection of charts as part of a research project. It doesn't matter how much you know about astrology: some people learn astrology by doing it this way! For example, if you are interested in, say, the astrology of gardening, you can plant your seeds at the times you feel best, then work out charts for these different times, then watch the plants growing, and retrospectively re-examine the charts: you might well find that common factors run through them or that the most successful plants were planted when the moon was in certain signs, or when certain aspects were happening. Only by experimenting, *playing* with astrology, can we really find inroads into a living understanding of it.

★ Horary and electional charts

These subjects can fill a book in themselves. A mention will suffice here, to point out another use of charts. It is possible to use charts *oracularly*. Which means that you can do a chart for the exact time a question pops up to be answered, or for the time a person comes to you with a question. Horary astrology is a complex field, which rests on the notion that the arising or the asking of a question is itself a significant event which plays a part in the unfoldment of the situation which the querent is interested in. If this interests you, then you should follow it up.

Electional astrology, a lengthy form of dowsing, involves casting charts for different possible times on which to do important things, and using one's skills to assess which the best time is: our criteria are important here. Thus, when planning dates for the camps and events I run, I do a juggling act between my ephemeris and the calendar, seeking to find dates to start them which fit best in terms both of astrological time and in terms of weekends, public holidays and social factors: it has all been a very interesting experience, with some great successes and some questionable outcomes from which I've learned!

Void of Course Moon

One interesting astrological feature here, of immediate applicability to anyone interested in the astrology of time, is the *Void of Course Moon*. The moon is void between the time when it forms its last major aspect (☌, ⚹, □, △, ☍) to any other planet, and its ingress into the next sign. This can be minutes or hours: if any planets are situated late in a sign at the moment in question, it will be shorter, if there are none in latter degreerol. We are faced with death. It feels like eternity, as if it is never going to end. Yet in this space, there is hope: for and that's that. Also, in general, it is inauspicious and often difficult to start off any new venture, big or small, when ☽ is void: you will find that there is no energy to support it, or that it takes just as long to complete the venture as it would have done if you had waited until ☽ entered a new sign. It's well worth keeping an eye on lunar voids.

Transits

In this book we have been looking at time in general, from a transpersonal viewpoint. We have been looking into the possibilities available for gaining direct experience of what astrology talks about. What follows this chapter is one on *Transits*, which brings in the individual element: in other words, use of transits shows the way in which *you* are personally affected by the movements of time. Time is like a transpersonal subtle energy-environment within which we live. Yet we ourselves, as individuals, are a universe unto ourselves, interacting with this environment. The subtle energy-environment actually comes inside us, and moves through us. But each of us is equipped with human energy-processing circuits and machinery which uses this energy in different ways, making of it what we can, while we can.

Which means that there can be 100 people celebrating a fullmoon together, yet that fullmoon energy (and the overall energy-web which it is temporarily focusing) is experienced differently by each person. One person might have the fullmoon activating their natal ☉ □ ♅, another might have it forming a transiting kite formation to a ♀ △ ♂ in their chart, another will have it straddling the fifth/eleventh houses, while another might have little that is really significant happening. The first will experience this as a challenging fullmoon bringing up core-questions and deep personal dilemmas-to-breakthroughs, the second might experience an outbreak of need for intimacy and loving, the third might experience a clash between their own personal interests, and those of the other 99 people as a group, and the fourth might be happily watching all this and thinking that they're missing out on something! Either way, it's the same fullmoon, powerful for all — although exceptionally powerful for some — and each person is processing the available energy, consciously or unconsciously, in their own way.

The idea behind transits is this. When we are born, take breath into our lungs and make our first noises, we are starting on a journey, on our own — joining other people following theirs. Apart from dying, birth is the most significant and momentous act of our lives, in which every ounce of our powers are engaged and no holds are barred: it's life-and-death. Enlightenments and fundamental rebirth experiences can make us feel like a new person, but we are still essentially the same person, occupying the same body: the difference is that we have opened up our channels, become more *ourself*, and we feel born anew. It can be relevant to calculate a chart for this moment too — if an exact time can be found! — but such a rebirthing does not replace our birth as the most important moment we ever experienced in this life.

Birth is so timeless, so total, and we are so vulnerable. What's going on at this moment is vital: it has more power to affect us than any other experience in life. We choose to get born at a particular time, and this time is accurately described by a birth chart. It is a slice out of time, frozen like an action-replay, for closer examination. Yet the planets keep moving on! Each at their own speed, they move on through the zodiac, and then form aspects to the places where they were at the moment of our birth. These are called *transits*.

Transits then become a way of understanding how our own personal lives are unfolding, and how time-energy is affecting us, offering us possibilities and options as we move through life. They can mark personal crises, leaps forward, times for carrying on, times of transition, times of normality, heady and hearty times, big times and little times. By observing transits, and consciously opening ourselves to the fullness of what we are experiencing, we can learn a lot. Observing the planets in motion gives insights into the nature of time, and observing these motions in relation to our charts gives insights into the way that we ourselves are working with time, in our own microcosmic selves.

If you find that you have T♆ △ N♃ (T = transiting, N = natal), it doesn't matter whether you know what that's going to do or not. Simply rest assured that it is going to offer you *options*, and that it is going to *energise* you in some way. Watch. Watch the months leading up to the transit, the time of its exaction, and the time following it. In your moments of clarity, step outside the process and look at it: for *that* is what T♆ △ N♃ is doing for you, and your responses to that situation are what you are doing with it. It can certainly be helpful looking at the odd book, or consulting someone else to help you get a fix on what you're looking at, but remember to use your own life as the laboratory and the experiment: don't replace your living experience with the opinions or prognostications a book or expert might offer.

Getting an astrological chart

In this book we are not going through chart calculations or chart drawing. To work with transits, it *is* necessary to have your own chart, but there are ways and means of getting one without too much trouble.

Whether or not it is right to learn the calculations is your choice, depending on how easily you can master it, and whether it is timely for you to do so. If you have difficulties with calculations, then the best thing to do is to leave the question until you *so much* want to learn calculations that you overcome your difficulties! The calculations are not actually very difficult: they require one or two evenings of concentration and application of logic to master the first chart, then practice with about ten charts over time, to iron out loopholes, errors and questions which might arise. It is good to get someone who knows to work through it with you, to make things simpler. But nowadays, if you don't want to do calculations, it is perfectly easy to get a computer to crunch the numbers and cough you up the data, which you then can draw out. Or get a friend to do the number-crunching. It is well worth drawing out your own chart however, for the action of drawing out each detail draws your attention to it, and helps you get insights into the whole chart while you are doing it. Drawing a chart in your own style increases its power.

Once you know how to work with charts, infinite avenues open up before you. It is good to have a special folder or file in which to collect charts of people you are involved with or who catch your interest. You can use them as 'subjects' in your learning of astrology.

You will find that your perception of charts changes over time, as you come to understand new things about astrology and life, and sometimes a feature of a chart which you hadn't ever seen before pops out at you and reveals a whole new slant. For some reason, it took me 12 years to see that I had ♃ opposing the midpoint between my ☉ and ♀ — partly it was because I had used narrow orbs on aspects, and thus discounted the inaccurate ☉ ☍ ♃ and ♀ ☍ ♃ aspects present, and partly it was because I was not ready to *see* this until a certain time of my life! Major breakthroughs in your understanding of astrology always take place in connection with breakthroughs in your life.

Astrological charts are power-objects. Even if you do not understand your chart, the very possession of one can start you off on a journey of self-discovery, of becoming yourself, which is a process of great value in itself. Life is not a thing, it is a process. Even though we fix ourselves on to goals and aspirations which each appear to be *the* final answer to all our problems, the essence of life is really about *process*. Getting there, to the end of the road, is of lesser consequence than the *travelling* of that road, for goals change as we go along, and the nowness of our life is spent travelling, not arriving. For in arriving, we must set out again!

It is not important to seek fully to understand the meaning of a chart. Its meaning will change, deepen and extend as life goes on. A chart is an inroad into yourself, a horo-scope by which to *see*. It has empowering qualities. It represents who we are in the cosmic design.

Bringing our own astrological charts into an examination of the nature of time and change shows how the universal process of unfoldment of astrological energy affects us as individuals. In other words, the astrological configurations we have been studying in this book — which apply to humanity as a whole — all play different games with our individual charts, highlighting peaks and troughs of energy of an individual nature. The next two chapters, on transits, show how we can go about working on more of an individual basis. They have been left until the end of the book to underline the essence of overall change itself — we astrologers are so self-preoccupied that we head for personal matters and our own charts almost to the exclusion of a wider approach. Please excuse my setting this personal element at the end: it is for a good purpose! Having looked at the next two chapters, however, you might be in a position to see the main drift of this book in a different light: how 'I' as an individual fit into the overall grand cosmic scheme of things. For we are on the edge of a vast collective realisation that we are one humanity, one being, and each of us as an individual plays a part in this wholeness.

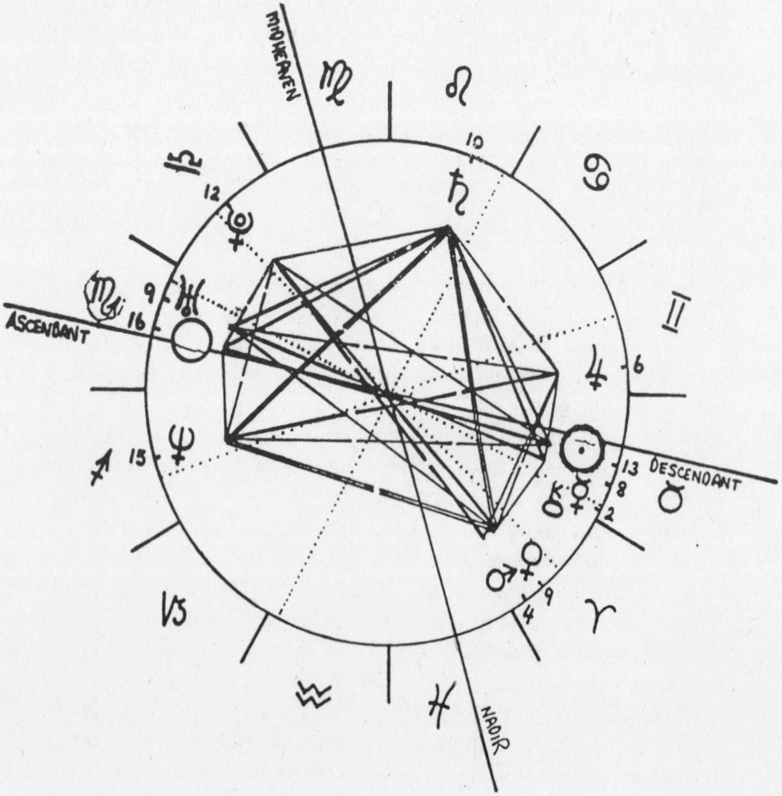

An astrological chart. This shows the signs in relation to the four angles, the positions of the planets and the angles, or aspects, between them. A full explanation follows in chapter 17. The meridian (midheaven-nadir) is here shown leaning as a graphic ploy in chart-drawing rather than an astronomically-correct representation. The chart is for Kuanyin (my daughter), born 8.45pm on 3 May 1977 in Stockholm, Sweden. She's a fullmooner.

18 Self as river: about transits

We have looked at the way time and change move, so far. Here we are going to look at the way that change moves through us, personally. As soon as we are born, the planets keep on moving, and enter into relationship with the planets and places in our charts, indicating the way that temporal energy-weather particularly affects us. Transits show our personal time-links with the universe.

So what?

I learned astrology by doing transits. Disappointed with social sciences and university I moved to the mountains of Wales with an astrology book (Dane Rudhyar's *Astrology of Personality*), Raphael's Ephemeris and a friend, with an astrological chart and a load of questions the then-available books and courses weren't answering. For many moons we sat there, in front of the fire, of a quiet evening, working out and observing our transits, and discussing them and what they felt like, what they seemed to be doing, and all of the things going on inside us — for we had newly discovered inner growth — and gradually, the workings and implications of astrology and life started falling into place.

Being a maniac for details, I observed even the transits formed by ☽, and being in a contemplative phase at the time, I took it all in assiduously. Having decided that I would seek to uncover an astrology which would talk to *me* and apply to my own life, rather than to intellectually elegant schemata, it took years, seven, in fact, to search it out, and get clear enough inside myself how to share this with others — my retrograde ☿ and ♃ were taking their time to brew their own concoction.

If you devote yourself to examining transits and the general movements of the planets, using your own personal life and experiences as the raw material for your researches, you will find that something very deep goes on in your understanding of astrology and life, just as I found. There is something very close-to-home about transits: *transits are about you.* They are a way past books (such as this one!) and a way into direct experience, living wisdom rather than stored knowledge. If you find yourself memorising words and concepts, try to switch to simply observing, feeling, cogitating, chatting with others: books are here but to stimulate your own thinking, not to replace it. There is no hurry to understand things: a few things understood well can be far more productive than many things partially grasped.

Basic principles of transits

The motions of the planets in the heavens perpetually affect our birth charts. If you look in your ephemeris, each of the planets currently in motion will be found to be sitting in a particular house in your chart, and some of them will be forming aspects to your natal planets, some of these applying, some separating, others exact. If there are multiple aspect structures in your chart, then several planets can be activated by a transit, all at roughly the same time — and if there are two or three transiting planets affecting such a structure, then there's a *whammy* going on. Transits show how the cosmos affects us personally, and the way our lives go through changes, and the options we are offered at each turn.

Here we shall look at some of the basic factors you should take into account when working and playing with transits.

★ Orbs

There is a certain range of influence where we can say that a transit is either working or not working. While orbs are not rigid things with strict boundaries (neither are rainbows), we can safely say the following: ★ orbs formed by ☉ and ☽ to natal positions are wider than those formed by slower-moving planets; ★ ☌ and ☍ aspects have widest orbs, and lesser aspects (such as ⚺, ∠, ⚻) have the narrowest orbs; ★ natal ☉ and ☽ have the widest orbs, but also you can widen out orbs of other natal planets if two or more of them in the chart are involved in a structure which is being activated; ★ planets crossing the four angles are strongly involved with them when within 10° of them; ★ houses tend to start having an effect about 5° before the cusp, when looking at transits, and are already at peak strength at the opening cusp; ★ the norms set in the symbol list at the front of the book hold for transits as well as aspects in a chart.

★ Applying and separating transits

There is a pattern to the formation of aspects which is quite observable if you test it on slower-moving transits. Transits apply, become exact, and then separate, and there is quite a different feeling to each.

You can sometimes feel the undercurrents of a transit brewing as soon as the transit*ing* planet enters the same sign as the transit*ed* planet, (even if there are still 20° to go, in the case of a ☌ or ☍). The issues around that transit (especially in the case of a challenging aspect) can start bubbling under before the orb is reached — if you double the orb that could be expected for a certain transit, and examine your experience, you will probably find that the underlying components of the experience are making themselves felt quite early on in the application of the transit. But the real issues, surfacing in more concrete form — either distinct questions and processes or events — become apparent when the transiting planet is applying to around 3° from the transited one. In other words, we often find ourselves becoming aware of something, of a need for change, and going through apprehensions, unclarities, wrangles and resistances towards the issue.

Something interesting takes place here. For our tendency is to resist change in various ways, and to block an accreting energy-configuration: we tend either to want things not to change, or to wish for them to change in specified ways, thereby blocking what *is* forming. We are offered a choice. ★ We can release resistance around that 3° threshold (in which case we are free to use the energy of the transit creatively, when it is exact); ★ we can release it on exaction of the transit (for the pressure of energy or events heats our wires to the extent that we *get* the message and allow change); ★ we can hold on through this, suffer consequences and learn what we need to learn in retrospect (in which case the energy of the transit has been taken up breaking a resistance rather than moving forward — although this itself is a forward step) or ★ we can resist all the way through, and use the transit to reinforce our hold on things, in fear of breaking new territory of the psyche (as a result of which we generate greater or further problems which sooner or later come into view — for example the coronary attack which resulted from years of repressed anger, or the miscarriage which results from previous rigid fears of getting pregnant).

Even in the latter case, we must acknowledge that if we or another have a need to resist things (for example, an obsession with smoking), we are *needing* to do so *in order to exhaust our need*, and to learn the consequences of what we are doing — which, even if it takes lifetimes to learn, is well learned when experientially done. But the more we can do to free up this energy, the more fruitful, meaningful and happy we can become.

Transit work thus becomes awareness work. It's not so much a question of anticipating certain kinds of issues which are expected to come up when one planet transits a natal one, as of always being prepared to learn what life is teaching us from the very message of its experiences, using the symbology and attuning capacities which astrology has to guide us intuitively on our way. We have choice.

Getting into the swing of it, we can use our awareness of transits to get clear on the issues as they arise, or even before, thereby making each major transit-wave into a reaffirmation of life, and a forward step. Momentum builds up after a while, such that 'difficult' transits become welcome: something to really get to grips with!

This is true especially as the transit is approaching exaction, in its last 2-3° of applying. Here, if we are either awake to the message, or at least prepared to hear it, we are choosing to allow the universe *through* our being, and thereby to use the time fruitfully. Rather than be a victim of circumstance, which this would seem to be, we would actually be *using* the circumstances to allow our true self (which is always in tune with the universe) to come through and guide us through whatever the situation is — and turn it into something much more than a mere situation.

The exact transit itself is a transition into a new state. This can be fundamental and challenging (☌ , □ , ☍), or developmental and flowing (⚹ or △), a subjective frame of mind, and/or an objective situation. If we have allowed the new state to take shape, it becomes a present fact rather than a future possibility at the exact transit. If we have blocked the change, then either something breaks, to awaken us to what we are doing, or our blockage is hardened, capable of surviving further, until some later test.

As the transit begins to separate, the effects of this change demonstrate themselves, and things fall into place and become increasingly normalised or integrated. Inner changes move into outer form, the dust of the flurry settles, and things become more easygoing. Details work out, and outcomes are clearly seen, and present themselves to be worked or dealt with, or enjoyed.

This process is not so marked with faster transits, because their stages are not so defined as slower ones might be — although even a lunar transit (for example T ☽ ☌ N ♄) can distinctly show itself in a state of mind and a predicament which lasts for between a few hours and a day (depending on the aspect), and goes through a series of changes on the way. But if you observe the onset, climax and aftermath of a slower transit, you will find these stages coming up markedly.

A classic pattern to a challenging transit might go: ★ rumblings and hints, ★ anticipations, fears, consternation, ★ resistance, ★ confrontation and let-go, ★ revelation and discovery, ★ climax and motion, ★ assimilation, ★ normalisation, ★ moving on. Experiences differ according to the transits, to your state of being and evolution, but you will find that you get into the *feel* of transits, and can recognise symptoms in yourself. Thereby you can consciously make life into a series of learning processes, accepted and made good use of.

★ Tides

Transits can certainly become a *process*. Slower planets, but also occasionally faster planets (apart from ☉ and ☽), have a habit of forming three-stage transits (even sometimes five-stage, in the case of ♆ and ♇): a direct, a retrograde and a second direct transit. In this case a larger process ensues. The approach to the first transit involves a weeding out and leaving the old behind: we get 'news' of what we need to do or learn or open to. At the first transit an in-between state is entered in which the old is left, but the new is still potential. Everything moves on for a while, until the transiting planet turns retrograde. At the retrograde transit it can feel as if things are literally going backwards, yet deep down there can be a resolving and focusing of intent which marks the *core* of the change. After a period of testing, the transiting planet turns direct again. At the final transit, the new state is entered into, and the past is past and the future now present. Thereafter, we consolidate the change and move on.

★ Cyclical sequence

Don't forget that transits represent *stages* of all sorts of cycles. If T ♃ is □ N ♂, then it will be either a waxing or a waning square, a stage in a longterm cycle which has a continuity and theme to it, however long it is. In the case of the whole cycle of relationship between T ♃ and N ♂, this cycle is 12 years. Thus it can be illuminating to check back at what happened at previous stages of the cycle, or in previous cycles, and you will find demonstrations from your own life of how your chart and you tick.

It can also be of some value to look forward in time, with the notion of sensing future waves of energy which further activate the ongoing story of the cycle — although to seek to foresee what will take place is a diversion from the real point of life. There is one rule in life I have always found to be reliable, which is that *the Unknown prevails.* Yet the Unknown is sniffable, openly intuitable, if we approach it in a non-neurotic way, without anxiety for our own self-preservation. Life loves us, especially when we love life.

★ Durations of transits

The duration of different transits thus varies according to the planet transiting. Lunar transits can be discernable mainly for 3-12 hours, although if a fullmoon is going to hit our ☉, it is possible to sense this impending transit even days before. Solar transits last 2 days to one week, depending on what aspects they involve; ☿, ♀ or ♂ transits can last 2-14 days, occasionally more, depending on the aspects involved and the speed of these planets at the time — the faster the planet, the shorter and more zappy the transit. The effects, preludes and implications of transits spread over a wider period than the actual perceptible energy-flow connected with them.

♃ and ♄ transits can last from weeks to 3 months, or up to a year if there is a 3-step pass involved. ⚷ transits depend largely on its speed (increasing until 1994), ranging in length between ♃ and ♅

transit durations. ♅, ♆ and ♇ transits each can dominate our lives for just under a year, owing to their 3-step transiting patterns: the implications of these transits, if critical ones, can stretch out over a period of three years either way of the transit, although they will be mainly perceptible one year either side. A major transit such as T♆ or T♇ ☌ N☉ or N☽ can be seen from a distance to last up to ten years either side of exaction, if underlying unconscious groundswell is taken into account.

★ Multiple transits

Quite often it is the case that slower transits by outer planets over a year are featured and punctuated by faster transits of ☽, ☉ or inner planets over days, accentuating underlying issues. If, for example, Fred has N☉ 10♉ and T♇ is at 4♏ applying to a strong ☍ to take place in 2 years' time, the underlying issues surrounding this might well get featured, focused and tasted when T♃ in ♒ forms a □ to natal ☉, and this series of experiences will be further highlighted by a whacky fullmoon on, say, the 7♉/♏ axis. Fred might experience quite a lot of inner wobbling at this fullmoon, which gets partially resolved when ♃ forms its □, but which awaits full and fundamental resolution at the later T♇ ☍ N☉. Fred could be said to be attacking his natal solar issues in stages and deepening layers — the issues are getting bigger and more fundamental as he goes along.

Or perhaps our friend Joan might have T♆ △ N♀, into which a T☉ ☌ N♀ in △ aspect to T♆ marches, to form a temporary grand trine: if the love in her is able to flow, this might be a happy and flowery experience, but if it cannot, then it could be disappointing, desolate or empty for her. She is being offered an opportunity to give and receive love without conditions, and trees could teach her as much about that as humans.

All sorts of interesting patterns can emerge over time. We can have what technically are quite separate transits taking place simultaneously, building together into a total situation, which might well have one underlying message or sequence. Occasionally, a new dimension of a chart can reveal itself, because even though a strong relationship between two or more planets in a chart might be absent, a person can have chosen to be born at a time which would create a chart wherein, at age 37, that person encounters five major transits involving these in the space of 1-2 years, changing everything in sight! In other words, in choosing our time of birth, we are also, by way of a by-product, electing to experience transits in a particular and unique way, which will characterise our life immensely.

The main types of transits

There is a whole range of different kinds of transits, influencing us in different ways. They enter into our lives through different levels of psyche and reality: largely, something which is coming through from a very deep place, which has a potentially fundamental effect on our being, has to come through *slowly* in order for us to be able to deal with the full implications of it. On the other hand, life is made up of quick successions of faster transits, which characterise our daily lives and all their panegyrations. Slow, root-level transits never take place in isolation: a T ♆ ☍ ☉ takes nine months to go through its climax, and builds up over a period of at least three years, unravelling its effects over a further three years afterwards, but the specific forms in which these basic issues are raised and tested in our lives will be precipitated by faster transits getting caught up in the major configuration. Thus, while we shall separate out different kinds of transits below, they interlock like big and small cogs in the building up of the sumtotal of our experience.

★ Fundamental lifecycle transits

These affect all of us, at roughly similar times in life. They start in very early life, when there can be cases of an outer planet retrograding *back* over its natal position, and then again, direct — this happens only in the first year. Then comes T ♅ ⚺ N ♅ at 7, T ♅ ⚹ N ♅ at 14, T ♅ □ N ♅ at 21, T ♆ ⚺ N ♆ at 13, T ♆ ⚹ N ♆ at 26, T ♇ ⚹ N ♇ at varying ages, currently 25-32, T ♅ △ N ♅ around 28, T ♅ ⚻ N ♅ at 35, then the mid-life change, a combination of T ♅ ☍ N ♅, T ♆ □ N ♆ and T ♇ □ N ♇ around age 38-43 (although the ♇ aspect is becoming earlier in the next two decades, owing to its eccentric movement), and so on. These affect the evolution of our inner awareness, and the contacts we have between soul and personality. ⚷ transits to itself can vary, according to the speed of ⚷ at birth and in subsequent years: one born with ⚷ in ♋ will experience T ⚷ □ ⚷ around age 7, while one with ⚷ in ♒ will encounter it at age 27-ish — nevertheless, we all go through the same ⚷ cycle, even though its mileposts will vary.

★ Structural lifecycle transits

These involve ♃ and ♄. ♃ forms quartile aspects (☌ , □ , ☍ , □) to natal ♃ every 3 years, and ♄ forms them every 7 years to N ♄. ♃ *returns* (T ♃ ☌ N ♃) take place around ages 12, 24, 36, 48, 60, 72 and 84, and ♄ returns (T ♄ ☌ N ♄) around 28, 56 and 84. The ☍ s are also important as climaxes to these cycles. These transits bring up issues around how we organise the forms of our lives, life's work, social position, finances, ventures, commitments and sense of selfhood.

★ Psycho-spiritual transits

These are transits by outer planets to other outer planets, which can take place at various times. There are generational similarities here, though — for example, many nowadays experience a T ♇ ☌ N ♆ around age 26-8, or a T ♆ ☍ N ♅ around age 35-40. The timings of these are more of an individual matter, though. These transits do not directly affect life-issues and mundane questions, but do affect our innermost psyches, and what is going on in the unconscious. People who are tuned into their dreams, inner dynamics, psychic selves or creative inspiration will experience these awarely, while others might experience perhaps uncomfortable feelings deep down which have no explanation or obvious relation to life circumstances. They open up channels within. ⚷ transits to natal outer planets often precipitate paranormal experiences of quite a tangible kind, ranging from UFO experiences to concrete spiritual quests or meetings to therapeutic or healing experiences.

★ Major transformative transits
These involve major transits by outer planets to major points in the chart, such as ☉, ☽, ♄ or any any *focal* planets in the chart. A T♆ or T♇ ☌ or ☍ N☉ or N☽ is definitely one of the biggest crunches a person can encounter in life, usually precipitating such a major change that life after it can be radically different from life before it. It seems as if *everything* is coming up and being forced through change: this is a major life-initiation with no qualms. ⚷ and ♅ ☌ or ☍ aspects are only just marginally less drastic transits, and still very major steps to be made. □, △ and ⚹ aspects by outer planets to major chart points are also big ones, provoking root-level changes which mark major breakthroughs and watersheds. All these transits have the effect of connecting us with important inner strands from other lives, expressing an urge from our soul to come out into the open and do its work through personality — which sometimes can be an initially-threatening experience for our little egos! Other times it can be a welcome liberation.

★ Transformative transits
These are still very major ones, but they affect *facets* of our lives rather than core and root questions. These aspects involve ⚷, ♅, ♆ and ♇ aspects to natal angles, ☿, ♀, ♂ and ♃. An outer planet major aspect to N♀, for example, can have a deeply stirring effect on our capacity to love and be loved, and has the capacity to rock any loving relationship and force a choice to re-enliven it or end it. One to N♃ can make for a tremendous leap of faith, a new outreach of self to world, an investment of energy in a fundamentally new venture, a change of values, even a religious or cosmological awakening — but still, while it can feel as if everything is at stake when such a transit is afoot, in fact, we are working on one part of our being.

★ Transformative house transits
When one of the outer planets moves into a new house in the chart, and spends some time in it (years to decades), the area of life symbolised by the house will be fundamentally affected, and re-evaluations, new modes of acting, lessons to be learned and changes

of approach will be precipitated. ♇ in IX will provoke big changes of outlook, possibly through travelling, education, inner quests or shocks which change our ways of seeing things. ♅ in IV will disrupt all our relations with security-sources, home territory and sense of personal selfhood. ⚷ in VII will bring into our lives people and relationships which reflect our shadow to us, either causing us trouble or, if we are prepared to face our shadow, giving us situations and companions which facilitate our discovery of what we unconsciously project on others. Outer planets crossing any of the four angles stimulate important changes in our activity and situation in the world, a shift of themes.

★ Major structural transits

When ♄ or ♃ form aspects to natal planets and positions, we take a step in formulating our social and worldly identity more clearly, developing our work, career and standing, organising our lives and playing the roulette-wheel of life in concrete terms. If you have a T♄ ☌ N☽ it is essential to accept events and tendencies taking place, and to acknowledge that you alone have created them — in this case, financial, health, domestic difficulties, sense of failure, depression or deprivation — for through doing this you will see what the issues are, and through resolving to open up areas where you might habitually say No to receiving the support and security you need, you will be able to make a decisive change for the better. If you have a T♃ □ ♄ it is very favourable to face up to things, make new or further commitments to what you know you have to do, and get on with it, for the tide is in your favour — but if you wait for or blame others, delay or evade the issue, circumstances will tend to come down on you and force things. These transits pass quicker than transformative ones, sometimes in one, sometimes in three steps, but they have a big effect on life-directions and longterm plans and purposes, activity, roles, work and prosperity. Transits of ♃ and ♄ through houses features these houses strongly: ♃ will favour growth and expansion in the area of life shown by the house, and ♄ will force confrontation of fears and blocks in that area, consolidation and decided overcoming of obstacles, within or without. Major steps are made when either of these planets crosses one of the four angles.

★ Mercury, venus and mars transits

These are faster, and last days or a week or two, depending on the transit and the speed of the planet — occasionally, if a retrograde period is involved, this can become a longer process. Lesser aspects can sometimes be difficult to perceive, in the effects they have on our lives, but major aspects are very distinguishable. These transits affect our states of being quite strongly, but they pass quickly, and while sometimes bringing up specific instances in which something must be resolved, fundamental changes depend on the involvement of outer planets, either by transit or in the chart (for example, if you have a T ♂ ☌ N ♇, a power-struggle could ensue, or anger can emerge, lasting a few days, but having no longer term effect unless underpinned by a deeper transit, or unless you are consciously digging up ♇ issues; or if you have a ☿ ☍ ♃, your mind could be buzzing, or it might be auspicious to make a journey or connect up with someone or something offering the promise of something good, but this will not have a drastically major effect unless there is something deeper going on which this transit latches into. Keep your eyes on house transits of these planets too.

★ Solar transits

These happen regularly once a year. In fact, if you look at your aspect table, you are looking at a programmed sequence of aspects which the sun passes through annually (together with each other planet in its own period of orbit). It is well worth studying these yearly patterns, for you will be able to develop a feel for the kinds of experiences you gather through the year. You can look into cycles of unfoldment involving, say, T☉ to N ♂, which start at the ☌ and climax at the ☍. When ☉ is ☌ a natal planet, you are in your own territory, and things work your way, while when it is ☍ that planet, your way comes in question, and it is worth looking at others' ways of moving that planet's energy. The regularity of solar transits makes them very useful for tuning in to the *feeling* behind your natal planets and positions. Note also that solar transits through houses and over angles can be very revealing, for they feature that house or angle in a yearly personal cycle which repeats itself, such that, if you wish, you can look over the past several years and examine the way you have, for example, tackled your twelfth house, together with the different kinds of feelings and experiences you have picked up in relation to it.

★ Lunar transits

These are rapid, lasting hours, or at most one day. Even then, you can go through various changes of mood in relation to the issues at stake: for example, a T ☽ ☌ N ♄ might, while applying, take you through feelings of difficulty, lack or incapacity, when in fact, when it is separating, it becomes clear that you needed this experience to precipitate a change of mind, which then brought about a happy development, such as a pleasant evening with friends, a cheque through the post or the dawning of a goodly feeling inside which heals your hurts. Major moonphases are well worth watching: if a new or full moon falls in □ to your ♂ it might be well to exercise great patience, to let people know what you want but avoid going over the top by biting their heads off! If a halfmoon falls on your ascendant, it's time to *do* something for your own benefit, to choose to follow your own instincts and quit waiting around for the blessings or support of others.

★ Transits of planets to themselves

The cycle of relationship of a transiting planet to itself in your chart reveals much as to how your natal planet works, and moves through its phases and facets. T ♀ △ N ♀ will give you an alright feeling to life, with everything flowing smoothly and effortlessly, while T ♀ □ N ♀ will precipitate a feeling of, perhaps, temporary dryness of heart, clinginess, resentment, or a need to do something to improve a friendship or intimate bond. When you have a T ♂ ⚹ N ♂ things might go your way, but you might encounter rivalry or envy when you have T ♂ ☍ N ♂ — yet it is still *your* ♂ which is in operation and manifesting these circumstances. The solar return (birthday) is a coming-together of selfhood, giving an opportunity for an overview of the year and your general progress, while the solar ☍ can bring much into question about your way of being, with some necessary adjustments.

Do it

It can take some time to grasp the ins and outs of transits — in fact it takes years, if not lifetimes! But you can start now, and you will gain valuable insights from the first moment. Observation is what counts! Transit work gives us an opportunity to see into the way in which we set up outer circumstances unconsciously — a revelation as to the way world acts as a mirror to ourselves — and a chance to find out how much we blame our circumstances on other things and other people. The buck stops here: if the world is to be healed of its ills, we ourselves need to cease putting negativity into it. We don't have to eat others' negativity, but we do need to acknowledge and work with our own. For we are the people who benefit.

Transit work is an ongoing work for the rest of our lives. By being aware of what is happening astrologically, we gain a direct, conscious experience — we can come into contact with the real nature of the ♂ or ♓ in ourselves without having to recourse to others' definitions or descriptions. We can understand astrology and ourselves on our own terms, in our own way, and discover how there are both benefits and problems arising out of the way we move our energy, for there are at least two sides to everything! For there is no right and no wrong: there are only outcomes.

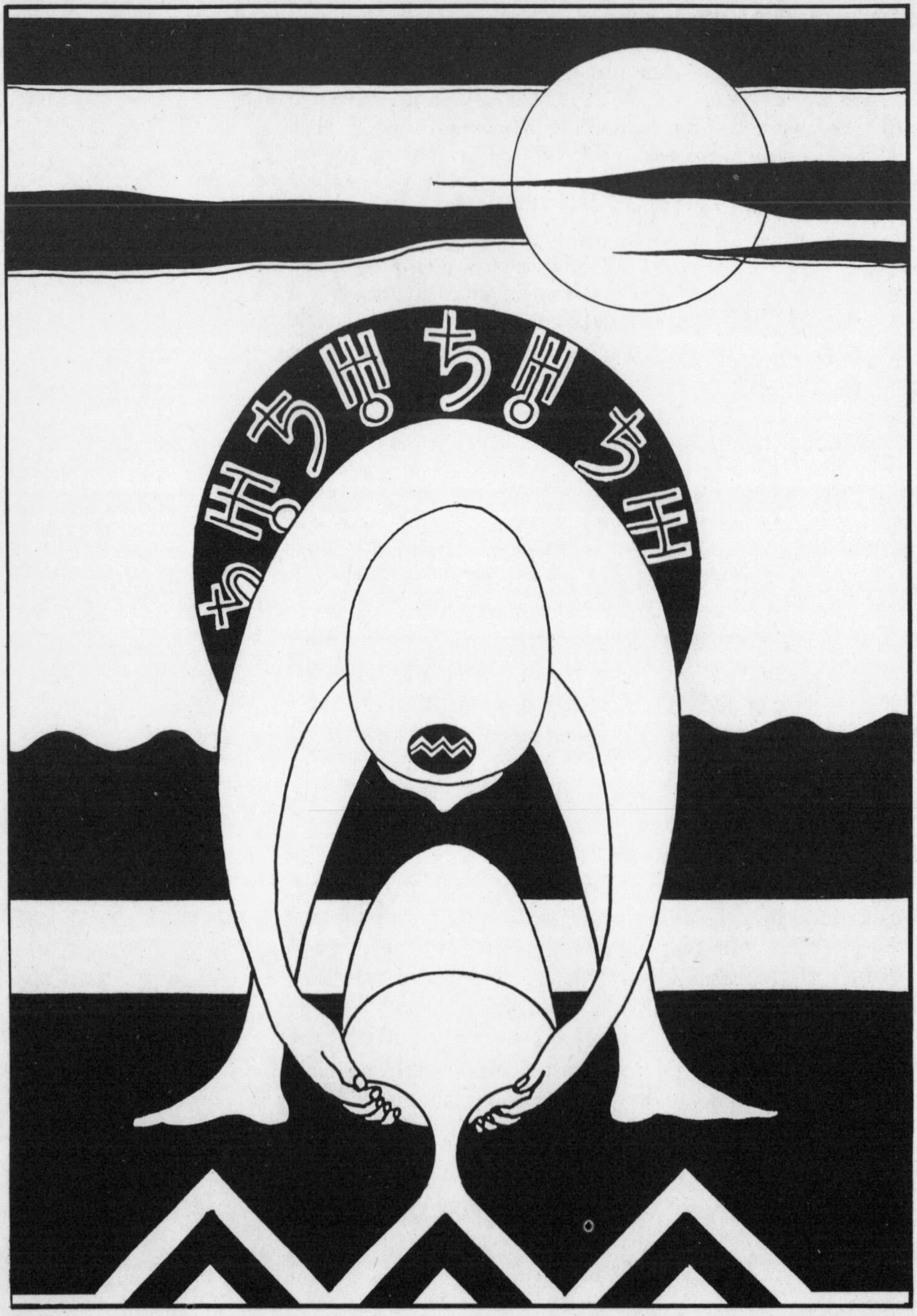

19 Working with transits

Here we are looking at the actual techniques with which to work with transits. Choose what you want to do, and give it a try.

Doing Transits — options

The principle of transits is that you can look at the ephemeris to find out where the planets stand now (or at chosen times past or future), and then compare these positions with your birth chart. Two major factors are important: the aspect(s) any transiting planet might make to one or more of the planets in your chart (and any two or more planets in aspect in the chart are thus likely to be transited at the same time, or in close succession), and the houses in the chart which any transiting planet might be moving through.

The simplest way to do this is to simply keep an eye on the ephemeris, and keep a mental note of your chart, and work out transits taking place as you go along. If your ♃ is at 12 ♉, and transiting ♃ (T ♃) happens to be moving through 12 ♋, then a little mental juggling will tell you that a ⚹ aspect is going on. *Hmmm, I wonder what that means?* The thing to do is watch, and to develop a mode of consciousness whereby you can perceive what is special — for you — in your life at the time. Understanding that a transit is going on can help you tune into the issues afoot in your life, and it can point to how your ♃ actually works in your life as you live it, *and* it can help you understand what that T ♃ is up to in itself, *and* it can help you take hold of your life and use your opportunities well. You don't even have to have a clear vision of what a ♃ ⚹ ♃ does: to know that it is taking place is well enough to be getting on with.

There are some interesting techniques for working with transits: wallcharts, diaries and graphs are all really good to make, and reveal a lot in the process, and are very useful once done.

First, however, we need to look at some preliminary considerations which might help you clarify what you are seeking and how to get it. In astrology it is dead easy to drown in an overload of data and concepts, so here are some choices.

★ Check with yourself whether you would prefer to look into shorter-term, daily-life, or into longer-term transits — they are not mutually exclusive, but they involve different techniques, and it is good to focus on one of these first. Graphs are better for long-term, and transit diaries for short-term work.

★ How much detail do you want to go into? It is good to put limitations around how much you tackle at any one period, for otherwise you will catch astrological indigestion, a common ailment. In other words, sort out with yourself how many positions you want to examine in your chart, and how many aspects you want to use when looking at transits. You can change what you look into over time, but it is best at first to limit the number of items you look into, to avoid confusion. Therefore, in your transit work, try starting out by observing:

★ lunar ☌ and ☍ aspects to planets, lunar nodes and the four angles, plus, optionally, movements through houses;

★ the places where the four quarter phases of the moon fall in your chart by house or by transiting aspect — a combined soli-lunar effect;

★ major aspects (☌ , ∗ , □ , △ , ☍) formed by ☉ , ☿ , ♀ and ♂ to natal planets, (but leave out such transits as ∗ , □ and △ to the four angles or the nodes, in order not to complicate things);

★ major, or even, if you wish, lesser aspects (such as ⚺ , ∠ , ⚼ and ⚻) formed by slower-moving planets to natal planets (though here again it can be well to avoid lesser aspects in transits to angles or nodes), plus ingresses of slower planets into houses. This will give you well enough to get on with — although you will no doubt find extra items of interest on the way.

★ How much energy do you want to put in? It can be of very great benefit to create a personal transit diary, and to work with it over time, keeping notes each day, even over a period of years — but this works only if you realistically have the will and opportunity to do it. Alternatively, it is possible to put in a couple of evenings' work to create a year-long transit list to stick on the wall, so that you have something to check periodically, and much less time and energy will be used — but also you will get less benefit!

Choose one of the options below to start with, and see how you go with transits. You will find that this is one of the most valuable things you ever did with astrology. Give it some time.

	♋	♌	♍	♎	♏	♐	♑	♒	♓	♈	♉	♊		
0		⚼♆			∠♆			∠♆			⚼♆		0	
1	⚼☽			∠☽			∠☽			⚼☽			1	
2	⚹⚷	□⚷	△⚷	⚻⚷	☍⚷	⚻⚷	△⚷	□⚷	⚹⚷	⚺⚷	☌⚷	⚺⚷	2	⚷ 2♉09
3													3	
4	□♂ IX	△♂	⚻♂	☍♂	⚻♂	△♂	□♂ III	⚹♂	⚺♂	☌♂	⚺♂	⚹♂	4	♂ 4♈44
5													5	
6	⚺♃	⚹♃	□♃	△♃ XI	⚻♃	☍♃	⚻♃	△♃	□♃	⚹♃ V	⚺♃	☌♃	6	♃ 6♊23
7													7	
8	⚹☿	□☿	△☿	⚻☿	☍☿	⚻☿ II	△☿	□☿	⚹☿	⚺☿	☌☿	⚺☿ VIII	8	☿ 8♉13
9	□♀△♅	△♀□♅	⚻♀⚹♅	☍♀⚺♅	⚻♀☌♅	△♀⚺♅	□♀⚹♅	⚹♀□♅	⚺♀△♅	☌♀⚻♅	⚺♀☍♅	⚹♀⚻♅	9	♀ 9♈01 ♅ 9♍36
10	⚺♄	☌♄	⚺♄	⚹♄	□♄	△♄	⚻♄	☍♄	⚻♄	△♄	□♄	⚹♄	10	♄ 10♌24
11													11	
12	□♇	⚹♇	⚺♇	☌♇	⚺♇	⚹♇	□♇	△♇	⚻♇	☍♇	⚻♇	△♇	12	♇ 12♎00
13	⚹☉	□☉	△☉	⚻☉	☍☉	⚻☉	△☉	□☉	⚹☉	⚺☉	☌☉	⚺☉	13	☉ 13♉13
14													14	
15	⚻♆	△♆	□♆	⚹♆	⚺♆	☌♆	⚺♆	⚹♆	□♆	△♆	⚻♆	☍♆	15	♆ 15♐53
16	△☽	□☽	⚹☽ ☌MC	⚺☽	☌☽ ☌ASC	⚺☽	⚹☽	□☽	△☽ ☌IC	⚻☽	☍☽ ☌DESC	⚻☽	16	☽ 16♍49
17			⚼⚷			⚼⚷			∠⚷			∠⚷	17	
18													18	
19		⚼♂			⚼♂			∠♂			∠♂		19	
20													20	
21	∠♃			⚼♃			⚼♃			∠♃			21	
22													22	
23			⚼☿			⚼☿			∠☿			∠☿	23	
24		⚼♀	∠♅		⚼♀	∠♅		∠♀	⚼♅		∠♀	⚼♅	24	
25			∠♄			⚼♄			⚼♄			∠♄	25	
26													26	
27		∠♇		XII	∠♇			⚼♇		VI	⚼♇		27	
28			⚼☉			⚼☉			∠☉			∠☉	28	
29													29	

Tools of the trade

★ Wallcharts

A simple yet effective way of following transits is to devote some time to artistically drawing your chart to stick up on the wall (on a soft board which will take pins), and then to get some mapping pins (the ones you can write on) on which planetary symbols are marked. Then you can keep track of the movements and patterns of the planets in relation to your natal planets and positions. One person I met painted a chart mandala on metal, then using magnets for planets. Any number of variations are possible.

★ Transit Diaries and Personal Ephemerides

These involve a bit more work, but have great rewards. There are two stages, the first of which sets up a tool for use in the working out of the second, (and which is useful in all subsequent transit or progression work, without need for further changes). Stage one is to make a special *Aspect Table.*

How to make an Aspect Table. Give yourself at least one evening for this. You need a piece of paper, ruler, pencil and pens, and your chart. This table does not show transits itself, but we use it for finding transits. It needs 12 columns and 30 rows, and the columns are marked with the signs of the zodiac, while the rows are marked with the degrees of each sign, numbered 0-29. Draw this now. Thus we have a table with 360 spaces, one for each degree of the zodiac. This will become a sort of index to your chart and all potential transit aspects to natal positions.

Next step. Take the positions of the planets in your chart, and write them down, on the left or the right of the table, on the appropriate rows, in degrees and minutes: for example, if your ☉ is at 18 ♓ 26, then find the 18° row, and write down ☉ 18 ♓ 26 (see diagram). Do this with all the planets.

Then, take any planet, and move along its row until you reach the column corresponding to the sign position of the planet in question — in this case, we find the ♓ column on the 18° row. When you have found the right space, write in it the ☌ symbol, plus the planetary symbol (don't fill all the space, for you might have to fit 2-3 other aspects in there eventually). What we have done, therefore, is fill a space which shows us that when a transiting planet moves through ♓, it will conjunct the sun when it reaches 18 ♓. Do the same thing with all of the planets in your chart.

In fact, when a transiting planet hits 18° of *any* sign, it will form an aspect of some kind to the sun. Thus, what we are going to do now is write in all these potential aspects. Take one planet, and write along the row the following sequence of aspects, plus the planetary symbol in question, both leftward and rightward from the ☌ space: ⚺, ✱, □, △, ⚻, ☍, ⚻, △, □, ✱, ⚺. You should by now have filled that row with aspects to the planet in question. If you have written them in correctly, you should have a complete cycle of aspects occupying the row in question. To the left of the ☌ point are the waning aspects (in which the aspect cycle is moving to a close), and to the right are the waxing aspects (opening up the cycle). Carry out this operation for all of the planets.

You will probably find some interesting patterns emerging. In the example diagram, the person concerned (my daughter, Kuan Yin) experiences a tight sequence of four transiting aspects whenever any transiting planet passes through 8-10° of any sign — if a planet hits 8-10 ♏, it will ☍ ☿, ⚻ ♀, ☌ ♅ and □ ♄ (and you can rest assured that when ♇ hits this point in 1987, big changes are likely for her! I would imagine it to imply a major extension of her world-view, and an honesty process [♇ ☍ ☿ and ☌ ♅] and a major choice of life-priorities [♇ □ ♄], probably involving me, her father!)

This table can carry more information too — and it is up to you to choose what you're interested in looking into with transits. Next, we shall insert ∠ and ⚼ aspects for all the natal planets — a bit more complex, for they involve 45° and 135° angles. Take one planet: if it is in the first half of a sign (0-14°), then count 15 spaces down its column, and if it is in the second half of a sign (15-29°), then count up 15 spaces. If you have counted down, then move one column to the right from the space you have found, and write in the ∠ symbol, plus that of the planet. If you have counted up, then move two columns to the right from the space you have found, and mark in the ∠ and planet symbols. If you run a check, you will see that there are 45° between the ∠ position and the ☌ position. Thus, a planet at 18 ♓ will have a ∠ at 3 ♉, and a planet at 5 ♐ will have a ∠ at 20 ♑. Then, in either case, move ★ leftwards along the row the ∠ is

An example of a page in a Personal Ephemeris: Kuanyin in March 1988.

	Slower transits	Faster transits	Lunar transits	Planetary movements	Comments
TUE 1	♇✶♅. ♃ ENTERS [VI].				
WED 2		♂⊼♃ PM ☿✶♆ LATE		☽♍ 13.00	
THU 3		☉✶☉ AFT.	[☽☌MC] LATE.	☉△♀ 07.00. FULLMOON 16.00 13♍.	Productive fullmoon.
FRI 4		♀ ENTERS [VI] ☿□☽ AM.			
SAT 5		♂△☿ PM.	☽☍♂ NOON. [☽XI] PM. ☽☍♀ LATE.	☽♎ 1.30	
SUN 6		♂□♀ NIGHT ☉□♆ AM.	☽☌♀ EARLY.	♀♉ 10.00. ♀☌♃ 17.00.	
MON 7		♂✶♅ EVENING. ☉△☽ AM. [☉☌IC]	[☽XII] NOON. ☽☍⚷ LATE	☽♏ 12.30 ♀△♅ 15.00. ♂☌♆ 18.00.	
TUE 8		♂⊼♄ EVENING ♀☌⚷ EVE ☉∠⚷ NOON.	☽☍☿ EARLY ☽☌♅ EARLY. ☽☌☽ LATE. ☽☍☉ EVE.	♃♉ 15.45. ♀△♄ 11.00	Watch what happens today.
WED 9			[☽☌ASC] EARLY	☽♐ 21.00	
THU 10			☽☍♃ NOON. [☽II] AFT.		
FRI 11		♂□♀ AM	☽☌♆ EARLY. WANING	WANING HALFMOON 11.00. 21♐	
SAT 12	♄∠☽ AM. ♃⚼♆ PM. ⚷∠☿ AM.	♂△☉ AM	[☽III] NOON	☽♑ 2.30. ♃△♅ 12.00.	Note major slow transits!
SUN 13		☉∠☿ NOON. ♀☌☿ EVE			
MON 14			☽☍♄ LATE.	☽♒ 05.00	
TUE 15		☉⚼♅ EARLY AM. ♀☍♅ AM. ♀□♄ EVE.			
WED 16		☉⚼♄ EARLY AM.		☿♓ 10.00. ☽♓ 06.00.	
THU 17		♂⊻♆ AM	[☽☌IC] LATE AM.		
FRI 18	♃☌⚷ PM.	♂✶☽ NOON ♀☌☉ AFT. ☿✶⚷ AM. / ☉∠☉ NOON	☽☌♂ EVE. [☽V EVE] ☽☌♀ LATE	☽♈ 06.00. ♃△♄ 11.00. ♀☍♀ 19.00. / NEWMOON 02.00. 27♓	Could be an interesting newmoon.
SAT 19			☽☍♀ EARLY		
SUN 20			[☽VI] EARLY. ☽☌⚷ EVE. ☽☌☿ LATE	☉♈ EQUINOX 9.40. ☽♉ 7.00.	
MON 21		☿□♃ AM. ♀☍☽ [☽☌DESC] EVE.	☽☍♅ EARLY. ☽☌☉ NOON. ☽☍☽ EVE [☽☌DESC]	☉□♅ 21.00.	Watch venus.
TUE 22		☿✶☿ AFT. ☉⊻⚷ EVE.		☽♊ 11.20. ☉□♄ 17.00.	
WED 23		☿△♅ NOON. ☉⚼☽ AM.	☽☌♃ EARLY. [☽VIII] EARLY. ☽☍♆ LATE.		
THU 24				☽♋ 19.30. ☿△♂ 17.00	
FRI 25		♂⚼♃ AM. ☿✶☉ EVE. ☉☌♂ AM.	[☽IX] EARLY	WAXING HALFMOON 05.00 5♋	
SAT 26		☉✶♃ EVE. [☉ ENTERS V]			
SUN 27		☿□♆ EVE.		☽♌ 7.00.	
MON 28		[☿☌IC]. ♀∠♀ EVE. ☿△☽ EARLY.	☽☌♄ EARLY.		
TUE 29		☉☌♀ AM		☽♍ 20.00.	
WED 30	♃⊻♂ AM	☉△♄ LATE.		☉□♆ 21.00.	
THU 31	♀℞⊻♀ (♆⊼♄)		[☽☌MC] EARLY		

in by three columns, and mark in another ∠ symbol (there should be a gap of two empty spaces between the two ∠ s). To find the ⚼ aspects, count along the row three more columns in either direction, and fill in the space, three more again, and you have found the two ⚼ aspects. All four aspects should be on the same row, spaced with two-column gaps. Now you can do this with every planet.

Then, insert into your table the house cusps and four angles, in the appropriate degree spaces. If you want to, mark in also the □ aspects to each of the four angles too.

It is possible to mark in minor aspects, midpoints, nodes or any sensitive points or details which you are interested in. You could even utilise different colours, and insert the details for another person on the same table, if you want to study their transits in connection with yours (with their consent: astrological privacy is important!).

You now have a special aspect table, which lasts for life, which you can use in the working out of both transits and progressions. You might well have noticed that you have found some interesting revelations into your chart even before using it! Keep this table with your chart, for when you dip into your ephemeris to check your transits, you can use this table to simplify things.

In the next stage, you can use either a normal diary (or better still, a 5-year diary), or you can make a notebook into a personal transit ephemeris. Or, alternatively, you can draw out a large sheet with, say, three months' transits on it, and space for notes. You can design the project exactly as you feel best, or evolve it along the way.

★ A Transit Diary

It's all a matter of working through your ephemeris, using your aspect table, and noting down in your diary all the transits which take place over a period. If you have the time (1-2 evenings), you can work out a year's transits. It is good to use different colours for different kinds of transits when you enter them, so that you can later get an instant view of the significance of transits: mark ☽, ☉, ☿ / ♀ / ♂, ♃ / ♄, ⚷ / ♅ / ♆ / ♇ separately, for their transits are of a different order to each other. It can be best to start with the slower-moving transits, and also to mark in advance warnings of their approach in preceding weeks or months — since their buildups are as important as their climaxes. When you get along to faster transits, especially of ☽, you might see what is meant by information-overload! Make sure you feature solar transits, for these are most edifying to observe, and stick to but the main lunar transits.

It can be beneficial, if you are so motivated, to write in some of the major general astrological phenomena as well, from the ephemeris, such as main moonphases and major interplanetary aspects. It is good to estimate rough times of transit exaction as well. Then, over time, keep rough notes as to what went on for you each day, so that you have something to go on when you later retrospectively examine your transits and experiences. Keeping a journal is in itself a valuable occupation, but when this is linked up to astrological research, it takes on far more meaning.

★ A personal transit ephemeris

Get yourself a good notebook, and start a section with your chart in it, notes, others' charts or whatever. Then mark out a double pages for either each month or each week. Write the dates down the side, with appropriate spacing, and then draw five columns to cover the two-page spread. They represent: ★ longterm transits by the slower planets; ★ faster transits by ☉, ☿, ♀ and ♂; ★ lunar transits; ★ general planetary interaspects, ingresses, lunar phases and stations, and ★ comments and observations. Try to estimate the timings of transits, by referring to the exact positions of your natal planets, and estimating their exaction from the ephemeris.

Play around with the possibilities, for there are many! It is worth expending some energy on doing this personal ephemeris for a whole year. Once you have done the spadework, the benefits can be many: doing the spadework alone will spark off many illuminations. In this ephemeris you have a ready reference book to carry round with you, in order to keep a check on what is going on for you as time goes on.

★ A Transit Wallsheet

Use a largish piece of paper, select the time periodyou want to cover and devise a way of fitting it on the paper, then use the five-column pattern as above. If you want to do a sheet for a year, leave out some of the more detailed information such as lunar transits or the lesser aspects formed by faster planets. Otherwise, do a sheet for a monthly or three-monthly period, and put it up on the toilet wall, or by your desk or bed, for regular reference.

★ Transit Graphs

Graphs have great advantages, in that they demand less work, and give a good overview of the duration of transits and their waves through time. They give a sense of buildup and follow-on with transits, a feeling of process. Transit graphs are available at astrological bookstores, through the author (c/o the publisher) or through Chiron, Bowlish Villa, Shepton Mallet, Somerset, UK).

The example here is of a blank transit graph for five years. Along the horizontal axis is the timescale, in this case months and years. Along the vertical axis lie the degrees of all signs. Thus although the paths of the planets on this graph intersect each other at points in time, only sometimes will this intersection show a conjunction: the intersection can denote any of the aspects which are functions of 30° — ⚺ , ✶ , □ , △ , ⚻ and ☍ . The sign in which any planet is moving is marked alongside its path, and major aspects between them are marked at intersections. Note how the wavy lines illustrate the direct and retrograde motions of the planets.

To insert your own transits on a graph like this, you need to mark down the positions of the planets in your chart (here on the left-hand column), and then draw straight lines across the graph at the correct degree-positions down the graph, estimating, within each degree, the position on the line which will correspond to the exact minutes position. A planet at 15°30′ will have its line in the middle of the 15° space, while one around 15°50′ will have it towards the lower boundary.

When you have drawn in the lines for all the planets, you need to work along each line in turn, identifying all the aspects shown at the places where the wavy and straight-drawn lines intersect. Some of these intersections will show major aspects, others lesser ones, and it is worth picking out the major ones. It is also useful to mark outer-planet aspects in a different colour from, in this case, ♃ / ♄ transits. You need to choose how much detail you want on the graph, by electing, for example, to mark in only ☌ , □ and ☍ aspects, or these plus ✶ and △ aspects. It can be worth marking in the four angles as well, and planetary transits over them. When done, stick it up on the wall for reference.

There are graphs available to cover each year, and all the planetary movements therein, or to give an overview of a long time-period such as that shown here for 1965-2000. You can draw your own graphs if so inclined, plotting them from ephemeris readings. Some graphs are available which feature special aspect families such as octiles (∠ , □ , ⚼), quintiles or septiles as well. The possibilities are many.

★ Transits by computer

Of course, a computer can cough up your transits for you, and save a lot of time, but there are two disadvantages: often you can receive a printout with a vast amount of data on it, the main elements of which must be picked out with a pen, in order to guard against drowning in irrelevancies, and also the act of manually working out transits takes you through the process of considering them and noticing patterns. It is possible, of course, to let a computer do the slave-work, and then to copy out the main elements manually on to a wallsheet, into a diary or a notebook.

A scan over your whole life

It is well worth looking back over your life, right back to the beginning if you feel for it. There are a few different things to look for. If you plot the years of your life down the side of a large sheet of paper, you can then work your way through the ephemeris to find out *all* the major transits of your life. The best ones to look for are outer planet major aspects to planets, plus outer planet transits of the four angles. If you are unsure of your exact birth time, you can in fact carefully 'rectify' your chart and birth time by checking to see whether major transits of the outer planets plus ♄ coincided with major changes in your life (moving house, leaving school, getting married, taking a big step), and if there is no coincidence of transits with events, then you can juggle your four angles around a bit to get a tighter fit: usually you will get several verifications of the new birth time if you have found the correct one with this method.

You can also check the dates of the most important ♃ and ♄ transits: major aspects to natal ♃ and ♄, to natal ☉ and ☽ and to the four angles. Look also for multiple transits — two or more transiting planets aspecting one planet in your chart — or transits to natal configurations. If there are some inaccuracies in the timing of multiple transits or the positions of configurations, then look on the periods of time involved as times of process, when different elements of the same basic issue were brought out over a period of time.

Some interesting patterns emerge. For example, at the same time as I left school, ♅ and ♇ were both conjuncting one another on top of my natal ☉: I changed radically, and it took several years for me to find what my new identity really was. That major transit laid the foundations for what seems to be the course of my life: my inner growth began then. But interestingly, 17-18 years later, I had T♅ □ N☉, plus T♇ ∠ N☉ close to each other. Looking back at what started when I was younger, I could see that the later transit, separated by a goodly number of years, was part of the same development: at the first I began awakening, and at the second I began expressing some of the results of that awakening in a definite and public way. As far as my soul is concerned, a couple of decades make small odds: and in terms of what such major transits mean, thank goodness they come only once every so often! It is well worth looking for similar patterns yourself.

Write down the transits which interest you on this sheet of paper, and then work through the events of your life. See if you can penetrate into memories which give you a taste of how it really felt then, and of what the transits did for you, and what you did with them. This is a chance to gain an overview of your life, to give you a perspective which might help you on your way into the future.

A friend for life

Once you have grasped how to do transits, you might well find that they stick with you through your life, as a way of keeping tuned to its underlying thread. New turns appear on the road, and new lessons arise which you never thought you would come to. The unfoldment is fascinating. And gradually you build up a stock of associations and memories which act as a reservoir of perspective: this is more for the enrichment of the present than the glorification of the past. We rework our past as we go through life, and the different periods we go through, seen from a transit perspective, take on different perspectives. An excellent muse!

20 Time and motion studies

On the very day I write this chapter, transiting uranus is forming an exact trine to the pluto (in VIII) in my chart. Uranus is transiting through my XIIth, approaching the ascendant. I went over to some woods in the sunshine and looked at spiders' webs dancing in the puffs of breeze, and lay on a wonderful oak tree with a leaning trunk. I let my energy out, let the tree take it, and absorbed the energy of the tree through the front of my abdomen, hugging the trunk.

It was immensely restful. The tree didn't care about all my screw-ups. Suddenly I felt that the life-changes I had been finding some difficulty in accepting were totally alright. It was OK to go with it, and my underlying anticipation concerning the immensity of these changes and my capacity to work them melted away.

I'm rattling on to you about this to give an example: if this book is of any use, my hope is that it encourages you to get into the living feel of all this buffoonery that astrology is. We need to make it personal, eat it. Like everything, astrology is an illusion, a transitory fart in the voidness, but for us now, in terms of the collective illusion we have all chosen to live in, it's a very useful means of getting clear on what on earth is really going on around here.

No astrologer, no matter how brilliant, interested, impassioned or successful, can really tell you neat answers about how it all works or what will happen to you when, say, ♆ is sextiling your natal ☉, or ♃ is conjuncting your descendant. Sure, we can try, but the insights and expressions an astrologer may receive on behalf of a client in no way replace the direct and full experiencing of the energy in question, by the client, in real-life terms. An astrologer can only really help us make sense of our present, help us get hold of the issues and themes and energies at work. Even though I may be considered to be a 'good' astrologer, I certainly do not understand the full implications of what ♅ is doing to me when it trines my natal ♇. And thanks be for that! I can get some inroads into the question, and attune somewhat to energy frequencies involved, but the clarity and all-knowingness often projected on me as an astrologer is not there. Not to the degree many people expect.

Astrology does, however, give me the language to be able to get a precise tuning on the kinds of energies at work for me at any moment. Not that I will come out of it with a pat answer about what the outcomes will be — this is neither the point of astrology as a tool of consciousness, nor of life, as an educational gift of the universe. Neither is astrology meant to give us a nice comforting mental understanding of what's befalling us, because this would be a removal of creative potential and the essential richness of life. Astrology isn't a way of by-passing life or avoiding its experiences — or, particularly, as many would have it, receiving the 'good' experiences and avoiding the 'bad' ones. *Every single event of our lives is good if we make of it a conscious learning experience.*

A few days ago, I went to London to sort out some things, and visited a close friend in jail, who is likely, according to expectation, to be spending some 7-10 years there. When the inmates were trooped out behind the partitions, to meet all their visitors, there he was, *totally* occupying his space, shining with a light which I had not witnessed amongst any of the 'free' people I had met in the previous few days, in city or country. He shone with the light of *acceptance*: he was totally acknowledging his fate, accepting that it was his own doings which had transported him there (although there's no way you or I would regard him as inherently a criminal!), accepting that the ruling which was to be made over him was going to be right, in some way, even if he knew not how.

T ♇ is coming up to conjuncting his natal ☉ ☌ ♆, and T ♄ is currently □ to his N ♇. You might guess that he was inside for drugs. My present to him was a book on mindfulness meditation: I had T ♅ △ N ♇, and I was in a position to meet him with his T ♄ □ N ♇ and give him a meditation book! (Sometimes this astrology business is very freaky, the interconnections it reveals!) Yet he, in his apparent misfortune and subjection, was demonstrating to me that he was making his experience into something wonderful, positive and enlightening: he was demonstrating that his body could be beleaguered, but his soul was free as a bird.

I knew from that moment that somehow he wouldn't be in for

long. Even though rationality has it that he's due for *seven years*, I knew that he was *learning* too fast to need it. We manifest every single life experience in order to learn from it all, and once we have exhausted the need for the experience, we unmanifest it. Sometimes there are mysterious reasons why we should have certain kinds of experience (for example, King Wen was imprisoned for 30 years, because the universe *really* wanted him to commit his knowledge of I Ching to paper, for the benefit of people living far beyond his time) and it helps to be open to them, but they always have an immensely positive feeling to them, even if, objectively, we might be in dire straits.

If, however, we *get it*, and go with whatever life is intimating us to do or sort out, situations change, either in our disposition to them, or in circumstance, or usually both. It doesn't *feel* right that my friend should be kept inside for so long — intuitively I sense one year or so, and astrologically I sense that the T ♇ ☌ ☉ is the crucial factor (his ☉ is at 8 ♏). But then, this might be wishful thinking, so I must put this thought on the 'possible reality' shelf and see what happens, with best wishes for my friend's growth and happiness.

When this book is two years old, check me out and see if my friend is still behind bars. If my feelings are proven incorrect, then I'll have to be honest with you and admit that my perception of the whole situation was too simplistic, and that I made pronouncements prematurely (a common failing in astrologers and soothsayers). It certainly does not point to the invalidity of astrology: it points to my invalidity as a practitioner!

Which just goes to show that, if we are honest with ourselves, we must concede that it is not entirely possible, or even desirable, to foresee the future. Just as well, too: if we could, we would be shutting the Great Unknown out, and we would thereby lose something very meaningful and life-full. I manifested seven years living in Sweden (an extremely organised, rational country) to find out how a whole society can structure its known universe to try and fend off the Unknown (the experience got me at the root of my ♄ in ♍, and taught me to leave gaps in my ego-world for the spirit and the magic of the Unknown to work through me).

In Sweden is a national-scale example of how we humans can believe we've got it all taped and sewn up, figured out and fixed up — no criticism of the nation is implied here, for every nation has its drawbacks and national mistakes. In the 70s, although there were obviously problems left to sort out, the nation had reached a peak of development and stability. Yet, within a few years, there were foreign submarines (symbolising dark elements lurking in the unconscious) espying its defences, rainshowers of radiation from Chernobyl falling on its clean lands and people, and, worst, infidel foreigners (presumably, although to date the answer remains unsolved — yet more of the Unknown!) came along and shot one of the guarantors and creators of this stable security, the State Minister himself (Olof Palme — one of the few spiritual adepts to be in a position of political power). Swedes as a nation have manifested for themselves a learning that you cannot consciously create an entirely safe reality: just when you're not looking, the unknown will get you, and open up an entirely new set of possibilities! Every nation has its own story, and every individual too: Sweden merely serves as an example of a human trait. Without these disruptive *divine interventions* life would not only be very boring, but also it probably wouldn't *work*, for it's a miracle that we got here in the first place!

So, poor old Mike (say I, from my limited perception which chooses to make 'freedom' better than 'imprisonment'), he might be two months *or* a decade inside, and I as an astrologer have no true way of saying, with 100% reliability (to the extent that I would be willing to stake *everything* on it), what is to befall him. But I *can* use my astrological and life experience to get an inkling of what he is inwardly experiencing out of all this. I can use astrology as a way of giving these strange circumstances a cosmic context: I can see, from the above-mentioned transits, that there is *something major* afoot for Mike, and that his inner guardians are lovingly taking him through an initiation which will force a cleansing (already visibly accepted) and an emergence of something deeply new (yet probably ancient too). It is something which will bear fruit in the fullness of time, but which *could* be expected to be showing itself clearly by the time the T♇ ☌ N☉ ♆ is over.

In fact, deducing from what I know of him, he will probably be clear about the essence of his learning by the time the *first* transit is exact: conscious people can *bring on* a transit and its lessons *as the transit is applying*, such that when the transit is *really* at work, exact, our energies are loose, we aren't holding on, and we're allowing the forces that are working through our deeper being to guide us along the directions we really need to follow — *even if we do not know why*. That's the rub — to do what feels right even if you don't know why.

Similarly, with my own T♅ △ N♇ I am aware that my best strategy to celebrate this energy-condition is to come to this place and talk to an oak tree. And the oak tree, after cooling me out, told me to get out my portable computer in the garden, under the sun (ridiculous, isn't it?) and write out the energy going through me at this moment. So you, dear reader, are experiencing a little blast of my ♇ in the eighth, trined by ♅, bless you, and my deeper self is telling me to rewrite this chapter. Why, I'm not sure, but I'm doing it anyway.

Levels of Time

Actually, this concluding chapter was *originally* a neat diatribe on how all the planets have their own time-spectrums and realities, which interweave on an energy level, entering and departing from our lives in intricate fashions... I was feeling a bit dissatisfied with the original chapter, because, although it was probably sufficiently titillating for me to be able to get away with it, it lacked the *ooomph* that my conception of a concluding chapter seemed to require.

What's really on my chest is this: what's the best way to encourage you to get into living and working with astrology to the degree where you breathe it and use it in the very working of your life? I decided that all I can do is point to some of my own experiences, and hope you'll get what I'm on about. Astrology is *not* just a neat way of explaining things, giving things contexts or understanding. It does serve these purposes, but the true usage of it goes back to what the ancients were doing with their knowledge: they were using their astrology as a way of identifying how to work with energy alchemically, magically. In order, first, to facilitate the flow of the universe, and second, to fit their own lives into this flow such that their own fortunes might be in some way furthered. This is no less than shamanic energy-work, work which involves a total dedication of our beingness — and this work is of such vital importance today. There is no way we are going to save the world from destruction by carrying on in our own little ways as we have been: we need a fundamental change. We need all manner of tools to aid us, and a living, breathing astrology is one such tool.

We have manifested a situation of *potential* holocaust, chaos and collapse in the world in order to face ourselves with the consequences of our own personal and collective acts and omissions. We are manifesting threat because we will not change by using our wisdom and insight. We have to have our arms twisted. We need to feel ourselves to be, collectively, in such a hopeless mess, with such dire consequences, that we *really get the message* about what we are doing here, and about what we can do to fulfil our being here. *It's really going to hurt.* It must. We're on the edge of becoming a new humanity, and we came here to be here for it, to do it. Like (re)birth, it demands labour. And it leads through amazing doorways.

The situation is so critical that we need to use *every means at our disposal* to come through to a state of being where we can allow our rites of passage, as a human race on a globe, to take place. This means opening up. It means being aware — in whatever way is best for each and every one of us. If astrology is a valid path of awareness for you, then *use it*. Apply it.

Levels of time. We tend to addict ourselves to a solar perception of time, and an *out-there*-oriented mode of consciousness. Our society reinforces this through 'education', technology, the nine o'clock news, the bank manager, and *facts* (questionable little things that they are). I hope that by the time you've got to chapter 20, you've taken heed of chapter 2, and started tuning in to *lunar* time, and its own realities. Have you noted yet, in your own life, that ☿, ♀ and ♂ also operate on their own time-spectra, interjecting into our lives in recognisable times and ways? These layers of time interweave through our consciousness, but we spend a lot of our energy being unconscious of this. It is possible to *feel* directly what part of your being, of your body, is resonating at any moment — where you're *coming from*. And it's possible to use astrology in a way which points out the remarkable patterns, tides and flows of these tapestry-weaving energies.

♃ and ♄ interject each in their own ways too: they have longer-term perspectives, and occasionally, we squeeze our attention and energy into working with these, toward the longterm ends which we perceive in our lives. These energies concern our capacities to invest energy in certain directions which we perceive will be purposeful and fruitful, and to reap from life the gleanings which help us better ourselves in future.

All of the energy-cycles are at work all the time, but there is a threshold of consciousness wherein one or a few energies pop out as temporarily dominant, activating particular subpersonalities in our being, preoccupying us specifically. When you're driving hard through life, it's ♂ energy, when you're feeling appreciative or close to another, it's ♀ energy, and when you're getting down to those tedious but important chores you've been leaving, it's ♄ energy. Recognising this, we can choose to move *with* life, use the energy available to help us.

But the time-levels which really interest me are those interjected by the outer planets. Weirdness creeps in when ⚷, ♅, ♆ and ♇

are talking — unusualities, abnormalities, breaks with the past, unknowns. Usually, these will interject when we're not looking, when we don't want them to, just at the times when we think we've got it sussed and made. Often we'll resist, and try to maintain and shore up our normal *known* realities. But it doesn't work. Sooner or later, we find it doesn't matter a sod about what we want, hope for, feel we deserve or fear: another reality intercedes which opens us up to something beyond.

It is precisely these things beyond our comprehension, which are the stuff that quantum leaps are made of. And it is a quantum leap which will both get us through our own personal dilemmas, and get us all through the global dilemmas we have created for ourselves. Nothing less will do. We've tried all the other ways, and even dictators, emperors and supreme soviets have not been able to stop the tide when it is flowing.

Yet all is not lost, for it is only our *known* universe we have exhausted of answers: the Unknown is yet to come. It starts right now, and happens right here, in real, tangible terms. Despite its unknowability, the unknown is possible to befriend. It is possible to recognise the experiential symptoms of the unknown when it is calling us.

We can do so by using the astrological language to look at our pasts, and at our present moments, thereby to become familiar with the way it all works in our own lives. It is possible to go out of a starlit night and talk, alone, with the universe, the powers that be, the 'management', the flow: it is possible to receive all of the information, guidance, directives and tips we need if we can but open ourselves up to what life is saying. This communication comes through our inner feelings and our *seeing* of significance in events around us. It is possible to allow our soul to guide our personality, to speak with God directly — our ephemerides and astrological tools are a way of tuning into what is necessary in order to do so. We ourselves are the mediums of the divine voice, the actors on the stage of the Great Director (although, if the brahmins are to be believed, all this life stuff, and the universe, and everything, are what happens when Brahma falls asleep!)

In other words, I, Palden, have woven this web of astrological illusion for you, in order, quite simply, to share with you that if you pay attention to your inner self (and astrology is one way of doing so) and live and work with it, you will discover gems and jewels of truth, in your own experience, in ways which are applicable for you and versed in your own language. These gems are far greater than what I can allude to in a book: they're found by doing it, using it, even, for a while, drowning in it. And if you do so, you'll find that things start working out. And you'll feel a new dimension of happiness dawning, in very real terms.

I cannot say that I am a master of this kind of activity, and cannot say that I am ultimately happy — far from it! But I can say that I've managed to make some very significant changes in my livingness since I started out in life, and that I'm feeling the different for it, and feel motivated to share this with you. In my higher moments I'm clear as a bell, and in my moods and struggles, I'm like a lost soul in the Slough of Despond. But there's a quality of consciousness which is being generated through all this craziness, which has the capacity to work miracles and render joy out of sorrow and sight out of blindness. It comes through. And I'm after more!

You've tasted it yourself. The breakthroughs, the despair, the contentment and the hunger, the togetherness and aloneness — whatever it is that you experience in your own life — they're all part of this magical brew we call life, and they're all there, passing states of being, to allude to what does not pass. The planets go their ways, and always have, and time and things come and go: but there is something left behind, which we call consciousness, which sees and experiences all. We learn from our souls. We learn most when it hurts most, when it shakes and quakes and rumbles, when there's nothing left to hang on to. Is this kind of experience going on for you now? Increasingly, for me, it is becoming an ongoing process. And I'm the happier for it: I'm happy to be consciously choosing it, rather than having it thrust upon me. Although it was thrust upon me in the beginning — until I realised that it wasn't others imposing their *stuff* on me, but it was the unconscious part of me manifesting them to represent parts of myself to my conscious self!

When you've learned what you feel is enough astrology, chuck away your ephemerides and books, and you'll find it really starts working. It's possible to know what's going on without these props, but we need them in order to get us to a stage where we know we know. Let astrology course through your veins, live it, and drop it — and by then you'll feel alright. And you'll be manifesting a world which is alright too, for everyone.

As I write this very sentence, a friend walks down the garden with her washing, singing quietly to herself in the sunshine. The geese are getting all steamed up, and advancing on her, hooting. She mutters to them and walks straight through their gaggle, and they hoot after her — they regard her as a threat even though she's the one that feeds them. She's still humming to herself.

It's a funny thing, life, isn't it?

If I understand the flow of my life and the Unknown correctly, the book which is to follow this one is about *Working with History* — re-creating the past, and consciously creating the future. Stay tuned to this station. Or come to the Oak Dragon Living Astrology Camps we have each year!

Astrological symbols

Use these tables for regular reference until you have absorbed the symbols as an oft-used alphabet.

The signs of the zodiac

The Zodiac = 360°. Each sign = 30°. 1° = 60′.

Sign	symbol	element	mode	gender	dignity	detriment	exaltation	fall	strong	house
Capricorn	♑	earth	cardinal	yin	♄ [♅]	☽	♂	♃	☿ ♀	X
Aquarius	♒	air	fixing	yang	♄ ♅	☉	☿		♀	XI
Pisces	♓	water	mutable	yin	♃ ♆	☿	♀		♂ ⚷ ☽	XII
Aries	♈	fire	cardinal	yang	♂ [♇]	♀	☉	♄	♃	I
Taurus	♉	earth	fixing	yin	♀ [♇]	♂	☽		☿ ♄	II
Gemini	♊	air	mutable	yang	☿ [♆]	♃			♀ ♄	III
Cancer	♋	water	cardinal	yin	☽ [♅]	♄	♃	♂		IV
Leo	♌	fire	fixing	yang	☉ [♅]	♄		☿	♂ ♃	V
Virgo	♍	earth	mutable	yin	☿ [♆]	♃		♀	♄ ⚷	VI
Libra	♎	air	cardinal	yang	♀ [♇]	♂	♄	☉	☿ ⚷	VII
Scorpio	♏	water	fixing	yin	♂ ♇	♀		☽	♃	VIII
Sagittarius	♐	fire	mutable	yang	♃ [♆]	☿			☉ ⚷ ♂	IX

The outer planet co-rulers in [parentheses] are my own system, worthy of contemplation, but generally not used by astrologers. Chiron connections are *suggested* only: it is too soon after its discovery to make definitive statements about its rulership patterns. *Strong* planets are not in general use either. Explanations for these delineations are to be found in the text of the book.

The planets

Planet	symbol	home\ dignity	detriment	exaltation	fall	orb (°)	period	home houses
Sun	☉	♌	♒	♈	♎	7-15	1 year	V
Moon	☽	♋	♑	♉	♏	7-15	27-28 days	IV
Mercury	☿	♊ ♍	♐ ♓	♒	♌	3-7	+/- 1 year	III VI
Venus	♀	♉ ♎	♏ ♈	♓	♍	3-7	+/- 1 year	II VII
Mars	♂	♈ ♏	♎ ♉	♑	♋	3-7	2 years	I VIII
Jupiter	♃	♓ ♐	♍ ♊	♋	♑	2-5	12 years	XII IX
Saturn	♄	♒ ♑	♌ ♋	♎	♈	2-5	28 years	XI X
Chiron	⚷	♎? ♐? ♍? ♓?				2-4	51 years	
Uranus	♅	♒	♌			2-4	84 years	XI
Neptune	♆	♓	♍			2-4	165 years	XII
Pluto	♇	♏	♉			2-4	250 years	VIII

Sign-connections for chiron are debateable. ♅, ♆ and ♇ do not follow the same rulership patterns as the inner planets. **Orbs**: an orb is the rough area around a planet where it has a noticeable influece when in aspect with another planet – the two values given here are tighter and looser values, which you can use with your own judgement, according to how you find orbs to work. A planet is in **detriment** in the sign(s) opposite its **home**, and in **fall** in the sign opposite its **exaltation**. A **period** is the time it takes for a planet to make one round of the zodiac.

Aspects

Aspect	symbol	angle (°)	signs apart	divisor	orb
Conjunction	☌	0	0	1/1	5-15
Opposition	☍	180	6	1/2	5-15
Square	□	90	3	1/4	4-8
Trine	△	120	4	1/3	4-8
Sextile	∗	60	2	1/6	3-6
Semisquare	∠	45	1.5	1/8	2-4
Sesquiquadrate	⚼	135	4.5	3/8	2-4
Semisextile	⚺	30	1	1/12	2-3
Quincunx (inconjunct)	⚻	150	5	5/12	2-4
Quintile	✯	72 144		1/5 2/5	1-2
Septile	✡	51°25′ 102°50′ 154°15′		1/7 2/7 3/7	1-2
Novile	△̣	40 80 (120) 160		1/9 2/9 (3/9) 4/9	1-2

The lowest group in this table are the main **minor aspects**, which are not used in this book, but are included for reference in case you should wish to research them. Orbs used with aspects can be tightened or loosened according to the planets involved – they can also be loosened if there is a larger configuration of three or more planets going on.

Houses are always marked using roman numerals, I-XII.

R = retrograde (backwards), **D** = direct (forwards), **S** = stationary (standing still), **St.t.R** = stationary turning retrograde, and **St.t.D** = stationary turning direct.

Syntax.

When writing down two planets in aspect in astrologese, write the faster planet doing the aspecting first, then the aspect, then the slower planet being aspected – for example ☽ △ ☉, ☉ ⚻ ♂, ☉ □ ♃, ♂ ∠ ♃, ♃ ☍ ♅.

T = transiting, N = natal (in the birth chart) – thus T♃ ⚼ +N♀, always putting the transiting planet first, regardless of its speed.

When writing a planet in a sign, it is usual to write either ♀ ♒ or ♀ in ♒. When it is moving into a sign, write ♂ into ♈ or ♂ enters ♈. When involving houses too, it is usual to write ☉ ♊ in IV. When two planets are aspecting another one, you can write either ☿ ☌ ♀ ∗ ♆, or ☿ / ♀ ∗ ♆. When a few planets are in a configuration, you can write ☉ ∠ ♃ ∠ ♆ △ ⚷ △ ☉ (a kite), as long as it is clear what is meant – otherwise add a little diagram to clarify.

Glossary

American Ephemeris, the: a detailed and accurate ephemeris covering 100 years per volume, recommended for general astrological work, available either for noon or midnight GMT.

Angles, the Four: four points in an astrological chart marked by the *ascendant, descendant, midheaven (zenith) and nadir*. See *horizon* and *meridian*.

Aphelion: the time and point where a planet is furthest from the sun; see also *perihelion*.

Apogee: the point or time when moon is furthest from the earth.

Aquarian Age: one of the twelve great ages, each lasting 2160 years, brought about by the *precession of the equinoxes*; properly known as the Aquarius-Leo Age; we are entering this age sometime around now or in the future — the date is debatable — and are leaving the Pisces-Virgo Age, which has prevailed since around the time of Christ.

Array: a general spread of planets in the heavens or a chart which forms an overall shape, without having to involve aspects or configurations; examples are hemispheric/bowl array, bundle/cluster, locomotive/open-angle, bucket/wedge, seesaw, tripod, splash, splay and star.

Ascendant: the point on the eastern horizon, on the left of a chart, where the zodiac, sun, moon and planets rise; opening cusp of the first house, the place of persona and personal aspiration.

Aspectarian: a list of aspects formed between planets in a given time period, with their times — for example the Complete Aspectarian in the back of *Raphael's Ephemeris*.

Aspects: angles of relationship between two moving planets; stages in a synodic cycle at which recognisable developments, transitions or crises can occur, found by subdividing the zodiac by divisors such as 2, 3, 4, 6, 8, 12. Minor aspects are finer angles found by dividing the zodiac by 5, 7, or 9.

Aspects: fundamental: ☌ and ☍ ; **challenging:** □ , ∠ and ⚼ ; **flowing:** △ and ⚹ ; **incidental:** ⚺ and ⚻ ; **applying:** approaching exaction, into aspect; **separating:** moving out of aspect; **retrograde:** an aspect formed by either one or two planets in retrograde motion.

Astrology: the study of the motions of the planets and rotation of earth in relation to them and the zodiac, for the purpose of eliciting meaning and significance from them, as indicators of fundamental energy-permutations on earth, in our lives; the study of subjective time; the mother of all sciences; a path to awareness and a brilliant way of whiling away the hours!

Astronomy: the objective study of the heavens and their physical mechanics through observation.

Birth, moment of: the valid moment of birth of a person or animal is its first breath, while for a venture or event it is the first moment it can definitely be said to have started as a real event, usually physically (such as moving into a house, convening a meeting, getting into the car for a journey).

Cardinal signs: see *modes*.

Chiron: a small planet (not an asteroid) which orbits eccentrically between the orbits of ♄ and ♅ , on a cycle of 51 years, discovered in 1977; it works through the knower within us, through lessons learned, and with a miraculous touch, if we are open to it.

Configuration: a structure of aspects between three or more planets, linking them together as a whole circuit.

Constellations: star patterns to which symbolisms and identities have been given; those on the ecliptic own the same names as the signs, but are moving apart from the signs at the rate of one sign every 2160 years (see *precession*); the constellations are not used in astrology generally — the confusion of names for constellations and signs is regrettable.

Cradle: usually, three consecutive ⚹ aspects plus one ☍ in a bowl-like structure; can be a string of 3-4 consecutive aspects of the same type, plus a wide aspect such as ☍ , ⚼ or △ .

Crisis: an intense situation where things come to a

climax or crunch, characterised by a slowing of time, feelings of extreme difficulty and obstruction, irresolvable problems and an inevitable giving up of previous expectations or ways of seeing things — a possibility for a breakthrough or a new start.

Cross-quarters: the four midpoints between the quarter points of the year (*solstices* and *equinoxes*, at or around 15° of the four *fixing* signs; **Beltane** in early May, 15♉, **Lammas** in early August, 15♌, **Samhain/Hallowe'en**, early November, 15♏ and **Candlemas/Imbolc**, early February, 15♒; at these points the seasons go through definite cyclical changes; these are points of energy-manifestation, and were marked by the ancient British and others as fire festivals, to mark stages in the annual cycle of life-force; the **cross-quarter points** are the four points at 15° of the fixing signs, which the planets cross each at their own times.

Cusp: the boundary of either a sign or a house.

Cycles: diurnal: the cycle of day/night; **sidereal:** the motion of the moon or any planet around the zodiac; **synodic:** the cycle of aspects between any two moving planets; **lunation:** the synodic cycle between sun and moon, creating moon's phases; **metonic:** the 18.6 year retrograde cycle of the moon's *nodes* around the zodiac.

Descendant: the point on the western horizon, on the right of a chart, where zodiac, sun, moon and planets set; opening cusp of the seventh house, the place of relationship.

Detriment: a planet is in detriment in a sign opposite its home sign(s), and its energy is in some way hampered by the quality of that sign, while still being strong; see also *rulership, exaltation, fall.*

Direct motion: forward motion of a planet through the zodiac; see *retrograde* and *station.*

Eccentric planetary orbits: the orbits of ☿, ⚷ and ♇, which are elliptical and inclined to the *ecliptic* — while all planets are on slightly eccentric orbits, all apart from these named orbit on roughly circular, regular ecliptic orbits, for our purposes.

Eclipses: a partial or total cutting off of the light of the sun (at newmoon) by moon passing in front of it, or of the moon (at fullmoon) by earth's shadow passing over the moon; these are mega-transitions; they can occur only when a new or full moon is close to the lunar *nodes*; they tend to happen in twos or threes around the time of this closeness, at opposite times of the year, varying through the *metonic cycle*; the ancients paid great heed to these and their symbolism and stillness.

Ecliptic: the plane of the solar system; as seen from earth, the path of the sun through the heavens — most of the planets orbit within a few degrees of the ecliptic.

Electional charts: charts cast in order to help in the making of choices and the selection of auspicious times for planned activities.

Elements, the four: fire, earth, air and water, characterising different energies and attentions which work through the zodiac signs; there are three signs of each element, in trine formation, each of which represents one of the *modes.*

Energy-weather: subjective atmospheres, nuances, energy-conditions, which can be sensed in life, and described astrologically.

Ephemeris: a book of tables showing the motions of the planets, plus other useful data, usually for either noon or midnight GMT each day; the sourcebook of the modern astrologer.

Ephemeris, noon or midnight: as long as you are clear as to which you are using, neither is better; if you are better using the 24-hour clock, use a midnight, and if better using am/pm, use a noon ephemeris; calculations of charts, and estimates of timings must be adjusted when using either.

Equator: 1. terrestrial: 0° latitude, an imaginary great circle around the planet which is perpendicular to the poles of earth's rotation; 2. celestial: earth's equator projected out into space, used largely by astronomers, inclined at 23° from the *ecliptic.*

Equinoxes: spring (0♈) and autumn (0♎), the midpoints between the *solstices*; the days when sunrise to sunset are equal through day and night; times of energy-transition.

Events charts: charts drawn up for events, in order to examine them closely, timed for their happening or beginning.

Exaltation: each planet is exalted in one sign, where its energy is refined and elevated to a qualitatively perfected level; see also *rulerships, fall, detriment.*

Fall: a planet is in fall in the sign opposite its exaltation — here its energy is qualitatively ob structed and comes over problematically; see also *rulerships, detriment, exaltation.*

Fixing (fixed) signs: see *modes.*

Focal planet: a planet which, by dint of its position, sometimes also rulership patterns, tends to focus the energy of a chart or array.

Genders, yang and yin: the male and female forces, respectively; these alternate sign to sign through the sequence of the zodiac (*fire* and *air* signs are yang, *earth* and *water* signs yin), and hemicyclically (summer is yang, winter yin).

Grand aspects: major and rare aspect structures where a string of planets encircles the zodiac with a string of the same aspect — for example, the *grand trine, grand cross,* grand sextile or grand octile.

Grand Cross: at least four planets in mutual □ aspect to one another, with two ☍ s across the cross; a very powerful and challenging *configuration.*

Grand Trine: three planets forming a triangle of △ aspects; a powerful and harmonious *configuration.*

Group psyche: collective consciousness, aware and unconscious, and its various states at any moment or time; the transpersonal.

Halley's Comet: a prominent regular comet, well-known, which lives mostly out beyond ♇, but plummets into the solar system to swing closely to the sun once every 76 years (last in 1910 and 1985-6); it introduces new, unforeseen energy and issues and turns of events into the concrete sphere of life, usually of small form but big significance.

Hemicycles: half-cycles of lunar or planetary motion; these can be waxing/waning, beginning and ending at ☌ and ☍, or objective/subjective, beginning and ending at the two □ aspects.

Home signs: see *rulerships.*

Horary charts: charts cast oracularly in order to answer questions; the time of the asking of the question is used, and special rules apply.

Horizon: the *ascendant-descendant* line, horizontally drawn across a chart, above which is the visible sky, below which is the area of the sky hidden by earth; see *meridian.*

Houses, tables of: a book of tables used in calculating the *houses* in a chart — a basic astrological tool.

Houses, the Twelve: a twelvefold subdivision of the earth's sky (six houses above and six below the *horizon*), found by subdividing the quadrants between the *four angles* into three. There are different systems of calculation of houses: the one used in this book is the Koch or Birthplace system.

Indigestion, astrological: what happens when you study too much astrology — the best remedy is to talk to trees, climb mountains, shower in cold water or drop the lot for a while.

Individualisation: a process whereby people explore their own individuality and define their own realities, toward individual ends; the process at work in the zodiacal hemicycle beginning at ♑ and ending at ♊, and in the waxing hemicycle of any planetary relationship; see also *wholisation.*

Ingresses: the entries of planets into new signs, crossing over their *cusps;* usually these indicate a change of themes, and a fresh breeze, and a choice.

Intercepted signs: signs which can crop up in a chart which do not cross any house cusp, always in pairs, opposite one another; more common in temperate and polar latitudes, or when one of the solsticial signs is rising.

Issues: charged ideas, feeling-tones, associations, around which we preoccupy ourselves, restricting openness of responses to life, triggering trains of reactions when certain questions or associations come up.

Kite: a *grand trine* with an ☍ from one of the planets to another, which forms two ✶ aspects to the remaining planets.

Latitude: terrestrial: N-S coordinates of position on the earth's surface; ecliptic: position above or below the ecliptic — for most planets only a few degrees.

Lights, the: generic term for the sun and moon, to distinguish them from the planets.

Longitude: terrestrial: E-W coordinates of position on earth's surface; ecliptic: position along the ecliptic, measured in degrees and minutes of signs; see *latitude.*

Meridian: the *zenith-nadir* line, roughly vertical in a chart, running through the centre of earth from the point where the zodiac culminates in the sky to a point beneath the earth.

Midheaven: the point sun reaches in the sky at midday; a point where a line moving up from due south meets the ecliptic; top of the *meridian;* opening cusp of the tenth house, the point of social identity.

Modes, the three: the three phases of each season; modes of operation of the zodiac signs; the **cardinal** signs initiate and set the tone for the season (♈, ♋, ♎ and ♑), the *fixing* or *fixed* signs carry through the purpose of the season (♉, ♌, ♏ and ♒), and the *mutable* signs conclude and assimilate the season (♊, ♍, ♐ and ♓).

Mutable signs: see *modes*.

Midpoint: the degree half way between any two planets, where it can be said that the combined energy of those planets is strongest, regardless of whether they are in aspect; some astrologers use many midpoints, but others do not; they can be useful when two planets are 15-45° apart, for sometimes it will be found that their midpoint forms a strong aspect to another planet, where neither would individually be in aspect — this gives extra underlying meaning to a chart or situation.

Mutational cycles: a mutation is a ☌ of ♃ and ♄; successive conjunctions tend to fall in signs of the same element, but when there is a change, there is a Great Mutation.

Nadir: the bottom end of the *meridian*, a line projected downwards through the centre of the earth from the midheaven; the point sun reaches at midnight; opening cusp of the fourth house, the place of personal identity.

Nodes, lunar: the points where the moon's plane of orbit round earth intersect earth's plane of orbit round the sun (the ecliptic); these are at opposite sides of the zodiac; at the north node, moon is climbing above the ecliptic, at the south it is falling below it; the nodes move retrograde through the zodiac in 18.6 years (a generation); also called Dragon's Head (N) and Tail (S); when a new or full moon occurs close to the nodes, there will be an eclipse.

Occultation: an eclipse by the moon of a planet or star.

Octile: one of the aspects of the 45° family, mainly ⚼ and ∠, but also including ☌, □ and ☍.

Octile Triangle: greater: ⚼ □ ⚼; **lesser:** ∠ □ ∠; **octile kite:** ⚼ ∠ ∠ ⚼, with an ☍ on the long axis and a □ on the short axis; **octile rectangle:** ⚼ ∠ ⚼ ∠, with two ☍ s crossing it.

Orb: an area around a planet or aspect wherein it may be said that the aspect is operative; orbs can be defined closely or widely, and do not have fixed or definite cut-off points.

Perigee: the point or time when moon is nearest earth.

Perihelion: the time and point where a planet is closest to the sun; see also *aphelion*.

Precession of Equinoxes: a 25,000 year cycle of motion in the earth's axis of rotation, caused by gravitational pulls from sun and moon, causing the *equinox points* to move westwards through the constellations at the rate of one degree every 72 years, one sign every 2160 years — at present, they are 25° from the start of the cycle. See *Ages*.

Planets: functional: ☿, ♀ and ♂; **social/identity-forming:** ♃ and ♄; **transformative:** ⚷, ♅, ♆ and ♇; **existential:** ☉ and ☽.

Power points in time: times when there is a more intense or poignant energy-configuration at work than usual, where it is possible to make greater than usual leaps of consciousness or to attain subtle states; when slower-moving planets are involved, we can have **power periods** which can last several years and affect history on a longterm basis; exceptional energy-weather.

Psyche: the whole of our consciousness, including awareness, thoughts, feelings, all modes of consciousness, imagination, perception and sense of self.

Quarter phases of the moon: newmoon, waxing halfmoon (first quarter), fullmoon and waning halfmoon (third quarter).

Quarter-points: the opening cusps of the *cardinal* signs; the *solstice* and *equinox* points.

Raphael's Ephemeris: a somewhat archaic but very useful noon ephemeris, packed with data, easily portable, covering each year in a separate volume.

Rectangle or mystic rectangle: △ ✶ △ ✶, with two ☍ s crossing it; can be formed by octiles too.

Retrograde motion of planets: the apparent temporary backward movement of the planets (not sun or moon) through the zodiac, caused by our being on a moving observation platform — the planet itself does not truly change direction.

Rising and setting points of mainly sun and moon, but also planets and stars, on the local horizon were used by the ancients both for observation of their motions, and for ceremonial and energy-working purposes; when sun or any planet on the ecliptic is in a summer sign it rises NE (in the northern hemisphere), when in a winter sign it rises SE, and when in an equinoctial sign it rises E; moon can oscillate up to 5° N or S in *latitude* of the ecliptic; the ancients built alignments of stones or markers to various rising and setting points.

Rulerships of signs: Each planet is at home in, or rules, two signs, and sun and moon each are at home in one, while the outer planets each co-rule a sign with other planets; rulerships qualify the character of each sign, and show which signs best embody different planetary energies; in its home sign, a planet is strong and typified. See *detriment, fall, exaltation.*

Singleton: the sole planet in the empty hemisphere of the zodiac in a bucket *configuration,* also called the 'handle' — this becomes a strongly *focal* planet.

Solstices: winter (0♑) and summer (0♋), in which the sun is lowest or highest in the northern hemisphere sky; the shortest and longest days of the year; the gateways to the timeless or to the power of life.

Stations: times and zodiac places where any of the planets is stationary, turning either from *direct* to *retrograde* (St.t.R), or from *retrograde* to *direct* (St.t.D); these are times when it is possible to feel a planet's energy clearly.

Stellium: a multiple conjunction with at least three planets involved.

Summer Times/Daylight Saving Times: many countries change their clocks by ordinance for parts of the year, usually by one hour, ostensibly to lengthen the evenings for recreation; each country has its own dates, although there is beginning to be standardisation in all states of USA and in the countries of EEC. Details are found in D. D. Chase's Timezones books, or in the ACS World Atlas or American Atlas; dates of the current British Summer Time are found on the opening page of *Raphael's Ephemeris.*

Time: 1. clock time: accurately measurable objective time, based on the diurnal cycle of 24 hours; 2. subjective time: inner experiential time, which can stretch and contract with changing energy-weather or states of consciousness.

Time zones: each country is in a timezone, which is measured in hours east or west of Greenwich, so that all clocks in that zone are coordinated; in astrological calculations and ephemeris consultations, account should be made if you are in another zone than Greenwich (GMT or UT), since all ephemerides are calculated for GMT. See also *Summer Times.*

Transits: motions of the planets in the heavens in relation to planets, cusps or points in an astrological chart; a useful technique for understanding personal changes.

Trapezium: a four-sided aspect structure with two sides parallel and the other two sides the same aspect.

T-square: a □ ☍ □ aspect structure.

Unconscious: that part of our psyche which talks in urges, imaginal symbols, knowings, irrational fears, of which we are unaware or partially aware; distinguished in this book from the conscious (what we tell ourselves is going on), the subconscious (what we could be aware of quite easily, were we more awake) and the superconscious (our sense of spirit, our centre or visionary capacities; the unconscious can also be seen as personal and/or transpersonal/collective in its content and experiencing.

Void-of-course: when the moon has gone through its last major aspect (☌, ⚹, □, △, ☍) to other planets before leaving a sign it is void — it is best not to start new activities until it has ingressed into the next sign; this can be used with other planets as well.

Wholisation: a process whereby individuals find their belongingness in society and the world at large, fitting in to what is asked of them; the process at work in the zodiacal hemicycle beginning at ♋ and ending in ♐; see also *individualisation.*

Yang: see *genders.*

Yin: see *genders.*

Yod: a ⚻ ⚹ ⚻ aspect triangle; this can be upstepped with an ☍ from its apex to the midpoint on the ⚹, bringing in two ⚺ aspects.

Zenith: see *midheaven.*

Zodiac: the twelvefold subdivision of the ecliptic, anchored in the *quarter-points* which mark the extremes (solstices) and midpoints (equinoxes) of earth's cycle of polar axial tilting to the sun, or seasonal cycle.

Index